MW01628628

# GENDER AND POWER IN THE JAPANESE VISUAL FIELD

# GENDER AND POWER IN THE JAPANESE VISUAL FIELD

EDITED BY

JOSHUA S. MOSTOW | NORMAN BRYSON | MARIBETH GRAYBILL

UNIVERSITY OF HAWAI'I PRESS | HONOLULU

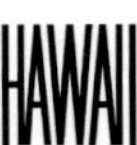

Publication of this book has been assisted by grants from the Kajiyama Publications Fund for Japanese History, Culture, and Literature at the University of Hawai'i and the School of Hawaiian, Asian, and Pacific Studies, University of Hawai'i.


Printed in the United States of America
08 07 06 05 04 03 6 5 4 3 2 1

**Library of Congress Cataloging-in-Publication Data**
Gender and power in the Japanese visual field / edited by Joshua S. Mostow, Norman Bryson, and Maribeth Graybill.
p. cm.
Includes bibliographical references and index.
ISBN 0-8248-2572-1 (alk. paper)
1. Feminism and the arts—Japan. 2. Gender identity in art. 3. Women in art. 4. Arts, Japanese. I. Mostow, Joshua S. II. Bryson, Norman. III. Graybill, Maribeth.
NX180.F4 G44 2003
700'.452042'0952—dc21 2002152312

University of Hawai'i Press books are printed on acid-free paper and meet the guidelines for permanence and durability of the Council on Library Resources.

Designed by April Leidig-Higgins

Printed by Thomson-Shore, Inc.

Dedicated to the
memory of
Chino Kaori
(1952–2001)
scholar, teacher, friend

*se wo sekeba*
*fuchi to narite mo*
*yodomikeri*
*wakare wo tomuru*
*shigarami zo naki*

# CONTENTS

# ILLUSTRATIONS

## COLOR PLATES



*Color plates follow page 200*

## FIGURES

# ACKNOWLEDGMENTS

Chino Kaori's "Gender in Japanese Art" first appeared in English translation in the journal *Aesthetics*, no. 7 (March 1996), published by the Japanese Society for Aesthetics. Ikeda Shinobu's "The Image of Women in Battle Scenes: 'Sexually' Imprinted Bodies" first appeared in Japanese as "Kassen-e no naka no josei-zō: 'sei' o insareta shintai," in Itō Seiko and Kōno Nobuko, eds., *Onna to otoko no kūkan: Nihon josei-shi saikō*, vol. 2: *Onna to otoko no tanjō: kodai kara chūsei e* (Tokyo: Fujiwara Shoten, 1996). David Pollack's "Marketing Desire: Advertising and Sexuality in Edo Literature, Drama, and Art" appeared in an earlier version in Sumie Jones, ed., *Imaging Reading Eros: Proceedings for the Conference, Sexuality and Edo Culture, 1750–1850 (Indiana University, Bloomington, August 17–20, 1995)* (Bloomington: The East Asian Studies Center, 1996). A Japanese version of Kim Hyeshin's "The Image of Women in National Art Exhibitions during the Korean Colonial Period" appeared in Kumakura Takaaki and Chino Kaori, eds., *Onna? Nihon? Bi? Aratana jendā hihyō ni mukete* (Tokyo: Keiō Gijuku Daigaku Shuppankai, 1999).

# GENDER AND POWER IN THE JAPANESE VISUAL FIELD

CHAPTER ONE

JOSHUA S. MOSTOW

# Introduction

*Gender and Power in the Japanese Visual Field* represents the results of a group research project that critically examines the representations of gender and sexuality in Japanese visual cultures. We include not only examinations of representations from Japan's medieval, early modern, and modern periods, but also interventions in the study and re-presentation of such visual artifacts in contemporary scholarship. In other words, essays in this volume not only reexamine artifacts from the past, but also examine the historiography that surround the objects, that is, their reception history. In all cases, our concern is how the cultural constructions of gender and sexuality serve the purposes of power, especially as it is organized under state and interstate regimes.

## Feminist Art History Outside Japan

Feminist art history is a relatively new development both within Japan and without. In North America its inception is often dated to the publication of Linda Nochlin's 1971 essay "Why Have There Been No Great Women Artists?"[1] It took about a decade before critical mass had been generated to publish *Feminism and Art History: Questioning the Litany*, edited by Norma Broude and Mary D. Garrard, and advertised as "the first collection of feminist art historical essays to appear in the United States." That volume contained seventeen essays "arranged chronologically and cover[ing] every major period from the ancient Egyptian to the present."[2] A decade later the same editors published a second volume, *The Expanding Discourse: Feminism and Art History* (1992). As they note in their preface, this second time their "task was entirely different [from that in the 1982 volume]. We were confronted by a rich harvest of scholarship in art history, nourished by new theoretical and critical perspectives and by the new interdisciplinary fields of 'women's studies' and 'gender studies.' The problem now was what to select from that wealth of publications that might best represent its abundance, diversity, and main conceptual threads." Despite this call for "diversity" and the very title of the volume, however, the editors decided at the beginning of their work "to limit the scope of this volume to the period from the Renaissance to the present."[3]

In their first volume the essays on Egypt and Crete fulfilled an important theoretical function. In their introduction, subtitled "Feminism and Art History," Broude and Garrard claimed that knowledge of "Goddess worshipping culture[s]" created a "new historical perspective [that] has permitted for the first time a clear vision of the controlling part that sexual attitudes and assumptions have played both in the creation and naming of 'Art' and in the writing of art history."

> Just as Renaissance humanists were able to define the "Dark" or Middle Ages for the first time as a separate transitional age, bounded at either end by differing cultures, and could therefore understand it as a distinct period with cultural characteristics that were unique to it rather than universal, so feminist have named as "patriarchal" that period of more than five thousand years which reaches down to the present, and which began with the gradual replacement of a long-standing Goddess-worshipping culture by patrilineal and God-worshipping civilizations.[4]

In other words, the authors seem to be suggesting that it is owing to some new knowledge of the existence of prepatriarchal cultures that feminist scholars have been able to contemplate the possibility of postpatriarchal perspectives. While this version of events does not reflect the development or the theoretical underpinnings of feminist art history or feminist critical thinking as a whole, it did at least affirm the necessity of including ancient and Near Eastern art in the discussion. In the 1992 volume, however, the editors have restricted, rather than "expanded," the focus and range of the collection, and not one of the twenty-nine essays addresses non-European or ancient art. To paraphrase the Chinese art historian Craig Clunas: a historian of Asia cannot but be baffled by the powerful assumption throughout much of these volumes that there is no need to take into consideration any place other than certain parts of northwestern Europe or northeastern America in order to explain what is supposedly distinctive about them.[5] If these places are not seen as distinctive, then the exclusive focus on the modern West can only be interpreted as cultural myopia at best and cultural imperialism at worst.

In their 1982 introduction Broude and Garrard noted that "the most basic and, to date, the most visible" result of the influence of feminism on art history had been "the rediscovery and reevaluation of women artists."[6] At the same time, however, they claimed that their book was not "about women artists." Nonetheless, five of the seventeen essays do concern themselves with women artists. The biographical approach was also the starting point for the entry of feminist criticism into the field of Asian art history as practiced in North America. In 1988 two exhibitions devoted to Asian female artists were mounted: *Japanese Women Artists, 1600–1900*, curated by Patricia Fister for the Spencer Museum of Art at the University of Kansas; and *Views from Jade Terrace: Chinese Women Artists, 1300–1912*, organized by James Robinson, Ellen Lang, and Marsha Weidner at the Indianapolis Museum of Art. Catalogs were published for each show, and in 1990 a complementary collection of essays appeared: *Flowering in the Shadows: Women in the History of Chinese and Japanese Painting*, edited by Weidner.

## Gender and Art History in Japan

What of the situation in Japan itself? While the art historian Richard Barnhart observes that "the inevitable trend of [the Chinese] patriarchal tradition has been to obliterate the origins of [women's] essential contributions" to the development of art,[7] Weidner herself notes that "the majority of famous women of Japan's past are well regarded, usually for their political or literary roles."[8] Nonetheless, with one important exception, the role of women in Japanese art was not a topic of much interest to Japanese art historians before the 1980s.

This important exception is the tradition of research on the term *"onna-e"* (literally, "women-pictures"), a word that appears in documents from Japan's Heian period (794–1185). The expression seemed to function as some sort of contrast or in relationship to *"otoko-e,"* that is, "men-pictures," and these binary terms encouraged Japanese scholars to hypothesize two distinct pictorial styles, modes, or repertoires intended for viewers of different genders and/or designed or executed by those of different genders. The words seem to have become a topic of interest in twentieth-century scholarship for the first time in 1933, in an article by the male scholar Tanaka Ichimatsu.[9] However, the first sustained research on this topic was conducted by Shirahata Yoshi, who published articles on it in 1943 and 1958.[10] The first date is significant, as it was chiefly because of the Second World War that women such as Shirahata were able to take up positions in the national museums that had been left vacant by men who had gone off to fight. This historical fact is a reminder that—both in Japan and outside it—the rise of feminist art history has been largely initiated by the presence of an increasing number of female scholars in the field.

In the immediate postwar period there was a decline in the number of women involved in Japanese art history in the context of museums and universities. It was instead a man, Akiyama Terukazu, who published the most exhaustive studies on the topic of *onna-e*, now defined as one of the two fundamental modes of *yamato-e*, or "Japanese painting." It is perhaps no accident that Akiyama's most important students were also women or that many of the contributors to this volume studied with either Akiyama, his students, or both.

Work on *onna-e* proceeded along largely formalist lines, in accordance with the entrenched emphasis on style in the field of Japanese art history. Then, in 1976, came the completion of the first dissertation in English on *onna-e,* Louisa McDonald Read's *The Masculine and Feminine Modes of Heian Secular Painting and Their Relationship to Chinese Painting—A Redefinition of Yamato-e,* and the Japanese translation of Linda Nochlin's "Why Have There Been No Great Women Artists?" It would take another fifteen years before these two vectors would merge.

This convergence was preceded by both more translation and the application of feminist concerns to Western art by Japanese art historians. A little less than ten years after the translation of Nochlin, Western art historian Wakakuwa Midori published *Lives of Female Painters (Josei gaka retsuden),*[11] a book of biographies of female artists in European and American history. In 1990 Hagiwara Hiroko published *The Tempest in This Breast: English Black Women Artists Speak (Kono mune no arashi: Eikoku burakku josei āchisuto wa kataru).*[12] But the watershed year appears to have been 1992, when translations of such works as Joan W. Scott's *Gender and the Politics of History,*[13] and Rozsika Parker and Griselda Pollock's *Old Mistresses: Women, Art, and Ideology,*[14] were appearing along with original essays such as Suzuki Tokiko's "Feminist Art History" ("Feminisuto no bijutsushi"),[15] and Chino Kaori's "Toward Rethinking of Japanese Art" ("Nihon bijutsu o kangae-naosu tame ni").[16]

The present volume was not simply born out of a desire to bring together a number of writings in Japanese feminist art history now that a critical mass of writings has been achieved. Rather, the creation of this volume had a specific motivation, which may explain some of the focal points and emphases in the collection as a whole.

The original impetus for this volume came during the 1994 Kyoto Conference on Japanese Studies, or "Kyōto Kaigi," as it was called in Japanese. This three-day international conference was held to mark the tenth anniversary of the International Research Center for Japanese Studies, or Nichibunken. The program included sessions during all three days of the conference on *shunga*, or early modern Japanese erotica.[17] These back-to-back panels were the first culmination of a multiyear project conducted jointly by Haga Tōru of Nichibunken, and Sumie Jones of Indiana University. Before the Kyōto Kaigi, members of the research team had met at the British Museum, Gakushūin University, and elsewhere.[18] This research project was part of the "*shunga* boom" of the 1990s. This boom was in turn related to a larger "Edo boom" that started in the 1980s,[19] and to the emergence of a kind of photograph with the curious name "hair nude" *(hea nūdo)*.

## Pushing the Censorship Envelope

Pornography is rarely debated in Japan in terms of freedom of speech. The rules seem generally understood between the police and the publishers, with the latter slowly and usually cautiously chipping away at restrictions, a process tolerated by the police until some "line" is crossed, whereupon one publisher is arrested, his goods confiscated, the remaining publishers back down, and the process of gradual erosion is resumed—a kind of pornographic Sisyphean struggle. Well into the 1980s depictions of genitals were either covered with a white box or erased. However, an anticensorship battle was also being fought on the photographic front. For many years the photography sections of Japanese bookstores have been dominated by large glossy albums of nude young women. Here too the no-pubic-hair rule applied. This ban was finally defeated in 1991 by Shinoyama Kishin and the photos that came to be called "hair nudes," allowing the public exposure of pubic hair for the first time since the Second World War.[20]

The victory against visual censorship created a bonanza for Japanese publishers. Now every *shunga* that had ever been published could be republished in unexpurgated form. In fact, reproduction of *shunga* took over the field in the 1990s, reducing analysis or explanation to almost nil. By the late 1990s the *ukiyo-e* section of any major Japanese bookstore was 80 percent filled with *shunga*.

The academic art history community was entirely supportive of this development, as scholars of *ukiyo-e* had long been frustrated in their attempt to discuss the oeuvre of important artists, such as Utamaro, whose artistic production included a large percentage of pornography.[21] The *Complete Ukiyo-e Shunga (Ukiyo-e shunga meihin shūsei)* series has testimonials from a number of scholars, such as the Tokyo University art historian Tsuji Nobuo. In fact, even Japan's best-known feminist, Ueno Chizuko, applauded the publication: "Unless one sees *shunga*, one cannot understand the charm of its expressive richness. One can only rejoice over the announcement that the barbarian age that smeared them with black is at last over. With this the research of Japan's early modern and modern sexuality will no doubt at last become real." There is a decided whiff of xenophobia in Ueno's phrasing, which leaves little doubt that the "barbarian age" *(yaban-na jidai)* was that of Victorian morality, brought by the Black Ships of the American Commodore Perry. Indeed, the Japanese scholar Haga Tōru looks to *shunga* as the record of the erotic paradise that was Japan before foreign intervention. As Andrew Gerstle notes, Haga tries "to extrapolate abstract norms of sexual life among the Edo populace" from *shunga*.[22]

Such was the context for the Kyōto Kaigi in 1994. What was presented, by and large, was a combination of standard Japanese "celebratory" art history and pornographic explicitness. Paper after paper extolled the virtues of both *shunga* and early modern Japanese culture as evidenced by *shunga*. With one notable exception, no panelist even mentioned the subject of rape or thought to consider Edo-period *shunga* in the context of pornographic production in modern Japan. The approach, in other words, was entirely uncritical. It is this approach to *shunga* that the editors of the present volume sought to contest.

The writings in this volume are critical interventions in the standard art historical discourse on Japan both in Japan and in the Anglo-European tradition. In Japan, the art of the early modern period has over the last decade been offered by various art historians as accurate records of an age now past and as keys to a realm of sexual and aesthetic pleasure untainted by the foreign, religiously inspired pathologies of the nineteenth century. In response to such scholarship, two of the early chapters of the present collection (Pollack and Mostow) examine the ideological foundations of the erotic art of early modern Japan, both heterosexual and homosexual. Pollack situates such visual production in the larger frame of commodity advertising, while Mostow examines the misogynistic structure that underlies the discourse of male-male eroticism in seventeenth-century Edo (modern-day Tokyo).

Since the conception of this volume, Tim Screech has published the first critical study of *shunga* in any language, *Sex and the Floating World: Erotic Images in Japan, 1700–1820*.[23] Screech's study is a strong attack on the formalist approach to *shunga* favored by many *ukiyo-e* specialists in Japan. Japanese *ukiyo-e* researchers tend to concentrate on connoisseurship and style, ignoring the actual subject matter of the images. Screech insists that *shunga* was first and foremost an aid in masturbation, and he suggests that this was true not only of *shunga* but of other *ukiyo-e*, such as *bijinga* (pictures of beautiful young people), as well. As a polemical focus, this argument is long overdue, but it also risks being reductive: clearly there was more happening in *shunga* than simple arousal.[24] But the question of *shunga*'s position in the larger economy of *ukiyo-e* and the whole market economy of Edo is well taken and is pursued by David Pollack in the present volume. Pollack persuasively argues that *shunga* must be seen as one commodity among many, and one must recognize how it was intersected by other commodities, in the fashion of modern "product placement." More important, Pollack demonstrates the high level achieved in Japan's urban centers in the very commodification of desire by the eighteenth century, a ubiquitous marketing that paid little respect to any putative distinction between what might be seen as "high" and "low" art. The careful display of the economic base of Japanese early modern popular culture works successfully against the aestheticization of *ukiyo-e* or Japanese women so promoted by mainstream art historians in Japan.

The appropriation of early modern Japanese culture for the promotion of a particular political agenda is not limited to the Japanese themselves. Early modern Japanese homoerotic practices, known as *nanshoku* (male-male sex), have been labeled "gay" by some scholars and publishers in North America, asserting an equivalence between the widely accepted practice of male-male sex in Tokugawa-period Japan with practices found in the late twentieth century.[25] This understanding of Tokugawa sexual practices is criticized in the chapter by Joshua Mostow. Using one self-proclaimed *nanshoku* text and extrapolating from it the "grammar of desire" as represented in late-seventeenth-century Edo, Mostow postulates not two but at least four distinct genders to account for all the various rules of combination both promoted and prohibited by the text visually and verbally. The resulting structure has little in common with that of sexuality as conceived in late-twentieth-century North America, and it is difficult to describe any of the participants as "gay." The recognition of a more complex sex-gender system in turn helps us break out of binary constructions—a result that can then be applied to other overdetermined binaries, such as "Orient/Occident," "modern/premodern," or "Japan/world."

The present volume, however, has developed far beyond its original critique of *shunga* celebration. It soon became apparent that focusing exclusively on *shunga* created its own kind of cultural and intellectual *sakoku*, or isolationism. The editors decided that we needed to consider *shunga* in the context of other visual representations of women and in a period broader than just the Tokugawa period. With this fact in mind, we have included a range of essays that give some idea of the state of gender-oriented Japanese art historical research at the present time. We believe that what has resulted is the first volume devoted exclusively to feminist art history on Japan to be published in English.

This volume is not simply a Japanese "Broude and Garrard," for a simple comparison of the rise in feminist-inspired art historical studies within Japan to those outside is almost entirely inadequate, as it does not take into account the "feminizing" effects of Euro-American imperialism on Japan's emergence as a modern nation-state or the concomitant role of the concept of Japan as an "aesthetic nation," a concept embraced by thinkers on both sides of the Pacific. The present volume starts with what may be seen as the inception point of the critical examination of this discourse, that is, the consideration of "Japanese art" within the context not only of gender but as interpellated by colonialism, imperialism, and nationalism. Chino Kaori was, until her untimely death at the end of 2001, Japan's foremost feminist historian of Japanese art. Her essay "Gender in Japanese Art" has challenged Japanese art historians' conception of themselves and their enterprise, while at the same time showing the essentially gendered nature of power in Japanese cultural self-definition throughout Japan's history. Chino's piece demonstrates that, in the quasi-colonial context in which Japan has often found itself, the "feminine," as appropriated by male elites, fulfills an important function in the masking of power. The present essay was originally presented at the Eastern Regional Conference of the Art History Association of Japan (Bijutsushi Gakkai) in 1993. It is a measure of the novelty of the approach within mainstream art historical practice that the author was first required to explain to her audience the very concept of "gender." This essay, then, was originally written with a very specific audience in mind—one quite different from any that is likely to read it in English translation. It seems appropriate to clarify here a few points that may be subject to misinterpretation.

Some of the assumptions Chino is contesting are presented at the beginning of her essay. They include the belief that critical theory has no relevance to the study of Japanese art; that a purely aesthetic approach, unrelated to political issues of either the present or the past, is the only valid enterprise for an art historian; and that Japanese art is the physical expression of a transhistorical, unchanging ethnic Japanese identity. Chino suggests in contrast an art history that recognizes the political use of art both in the past when a given work was produced as well as in the present when that work is interpreted. This approach means considering Japan not in isolation but in comparison with other countries and cultures. While in the present essay Chino confines herself largely to a contrast between Japan and "the West"—an approach that is easily confused with Japanese exceptionalism, or *Nihonjin-ron*—in fact, as is apparent in a later article, "Japanese Art History and Feminism" ("Nihon bijutsushi to feminizumu"),[26] she is calling for consideration of Japan within an Asian context. On one hand, this means viewing Japan's premodern culture as sharing characteristics with other cultures that found themselves on the margins of the Chinese cultural sphere. On the other hand, and more controversial, is her insistence on seeing Japan's modern self-definition as intimately connected to its attempted subjugation of its Asian neighbors. Here again, in contrast to the predominantly aesthetic and stylistic approach of her colleagues—one analogous to the "pure literature," or *jun-bungaku*, approach in the literary realm—Chino argues for a Japanese art history that will examine the political and ideological program behind modern canonization.

Within this discussion, Chino asserts no essential Japanese nature. In contrast to the theory of cultural change offered by the literary critic Katō Shūichi,[27] Chino does not believe in an unchanging Japanese cultural core that endures and then transforms successive waves of foreign influence. Instead, it is the core itself that changes—the very definition of "Japanese"—as each previously "foreign" element is absorbed and displaced into the interior by a subsequent importation. Her distinction between the "public" *(kō [ōyake])* and the "private" *(shi [watakushi])*, then, is not one of the "true," or the "personal," in contrast to the "false" or "official," but rather, like the so-called private chambers of the shogun, simply a distinction between two culturally constructed and mutually dependent spaces. Put in other terms, *honne*, or so-called true intent, is simply one more kind of *tatemae*, or "front," but one that bears the function of "being the truth."

The theoretical concept around which all these arguments are woven is the familiar one of the distinction between biologically determined sex and culturally defined gender. While aware of the work of Judith Butler and other scholars who problematize such a distinction, Chino makes a strategic choice, since she can rely on her audience's acceptance of certain periods of Japanese art, especially the Heian period, as "feminine" (an interpretation that can be traced back to the Nativist scholar Motoori Norinaga [1730–1801] but was institutionalized in the Meiji period),[28] despite the obvious fact that power was largely in the hands of men. By exploiting this apparent contradiction, the author argues for the usefulness of a theoretical approach that draws a distinction between sex and gender, and at the same time demonstrates the utility of contemporary critical theory in a field where it has rarely been applied. By arguing that Japanese men in positions of power at some historical moments chose to define themselves as "feminine," Chino reintroduces the whole issue of choice, that is, purpose and design, which leads inevitably back to a consideration of the political and ideological messages of art and its interpretation. Ultimately, the theoretical flaw inherent in viewing "sex" as prediscursive and in contrast to a culturally constructed "gender" is analogous to that between a transhistorical Japanese identity and foreign "influence."

## Representations of Women: Medieval and Modern

Moving to Japan's early feudal period (1185–1333), Ikeda Shinobu explores the pornography of representation in Japan's earliest surviving painting of a battle scene. This chapter is especially important for introducing the issue of class, which is less explicitly treated in Mostow's chapter. The formalist tradition in Japanese art history (and perhaps its situating of itself in contrast to the dominance of Marxist historiography in most Japanese history departments) has made the application of the concept of class to the analysis of visual works almost as infrequent as the application of the concept of gender. This tendency may be influenced by the housing of most art historians in Japan in departments of philosophy—art history being thought of as a discipline related to aesthetics—rather than in fine arts or history departments. (A concomitant result of its cohabitation with the universalizing discourse of aesthetics has been the search for uniqueness in a distinctive Japanese "aesthetic consciousness," or *bi-ishiki.*)

Ikeda makes the surprising discovery that, within the image of what has long been thought of as one of Japan's most famous painted battle scenes, in fact very little fighting is actually happening. More important, in contrast to a mere three male victims, the scene shows the bodies of over twenty women being crushed or trampled to death. By carefully comparing the painted image to all the surviving textual versions of this event, Ikeda is able to demonstrate that the painting is not a simple illustration of a prior written text but has its own message, independent of any preexisting account. Understanding this message allows Ikeda to hypothesize the patron or ultimate recipient of the painting through the message he wished to receive. Ikeda cogently demonstrates how women, as women, are made to function as a contrast to the barbarous, hypermasculine warriors who are responsible for their deaths. This neat pairing allows the warriors' real antagonist, the males of the aristocracy, to absent themselves and remain ideologically invisible.

Ikeda's linking of the images of women under duress to pornographic gratification may seem something of a jump to some readers, especially her reading (following that of Kasuya Makoto) of *rokudō-e,* which depict the stages of decomposition of a woman's corpse, as pornography. Yet this is a reading well attested in at least contemporary Japanese culture, as evidenced by the prize-winning story "Maggot" ("Uji") by Fujisawa Shū and its accompanying illustration (Figure 1.1).[29]

The remaining chapters in the collection take account of the even more complicated context of modern Japan. Norman Bryson explores the introduction of Western painting methods to Japan in the late nineteenth century and the central role of the image of women in the transition to modernity. Bryson explores how women function as a crucial object of the gaze—and desire—of both Western and Japanese men, serving as a quasi-available sexual object that allows each side "to assimilate the other through the milieu of sexuality." "The circulation of women," Bryson writes, "accompanied and stimulated the general traffic of goods and ideas that made up the larger context of modernization." In other words, commodification and advertising are no longer simply domestic concerns, as examined by David Pollack, but bearers of the very process of modernization. Japanese men attain modern subjectivity by sharing with their European and American counterparts the same objects of desire. These objects were not just women on the dance floor of diplomatic balls, but also the representation of women in the media of oil painting, newly introduced to Japan and called *yōga*, or "Western painting." Bryson shows how portraits of European women by Japanese male painters demonstrated their intimacy with European culture as a whole. More important, Bryson shows how Japanese artists such as Kuroda Seiki (1866–1924) were able to step into the masculinist construct of "bohemian life": "Japanese artists joined ranks with European artists over the subordinated figure of woman." As Bryson stresses, however, this mode of vision is not simply a matter of voyeurism or "the male gaze"—it also involved a process of cultural assimilation that seemed an essential element of Japan's modernization.

Reimposing the supposed binarism that existed between *onna-e* and *otoko-e*, twentieth-century Japanese painters have created a distinction between Western-derived oil painting, or *yōga*, and a putatively national tradition, labeled *nihonga*, or "Japanese painting." Doris Croissant in her chapter explores how Tsuchida Bakusen (1887–1936), one of the recognized masters of *nihonga* in the early twentieth century, positioned his production to serve as a national response to Western painting. In particular, Croissant explores Bakusen's appropriation of the "primitive" and his recycling of *ukiyo-e* imagery. While the former is well known

**FIGURE 1.1.** Yamamoto Takato, illustration for "Uji" (Maggot) by Fujisawa Shū. From *Shōsetsu shinchō*, vol. 52, no. 5 (1995): 62.

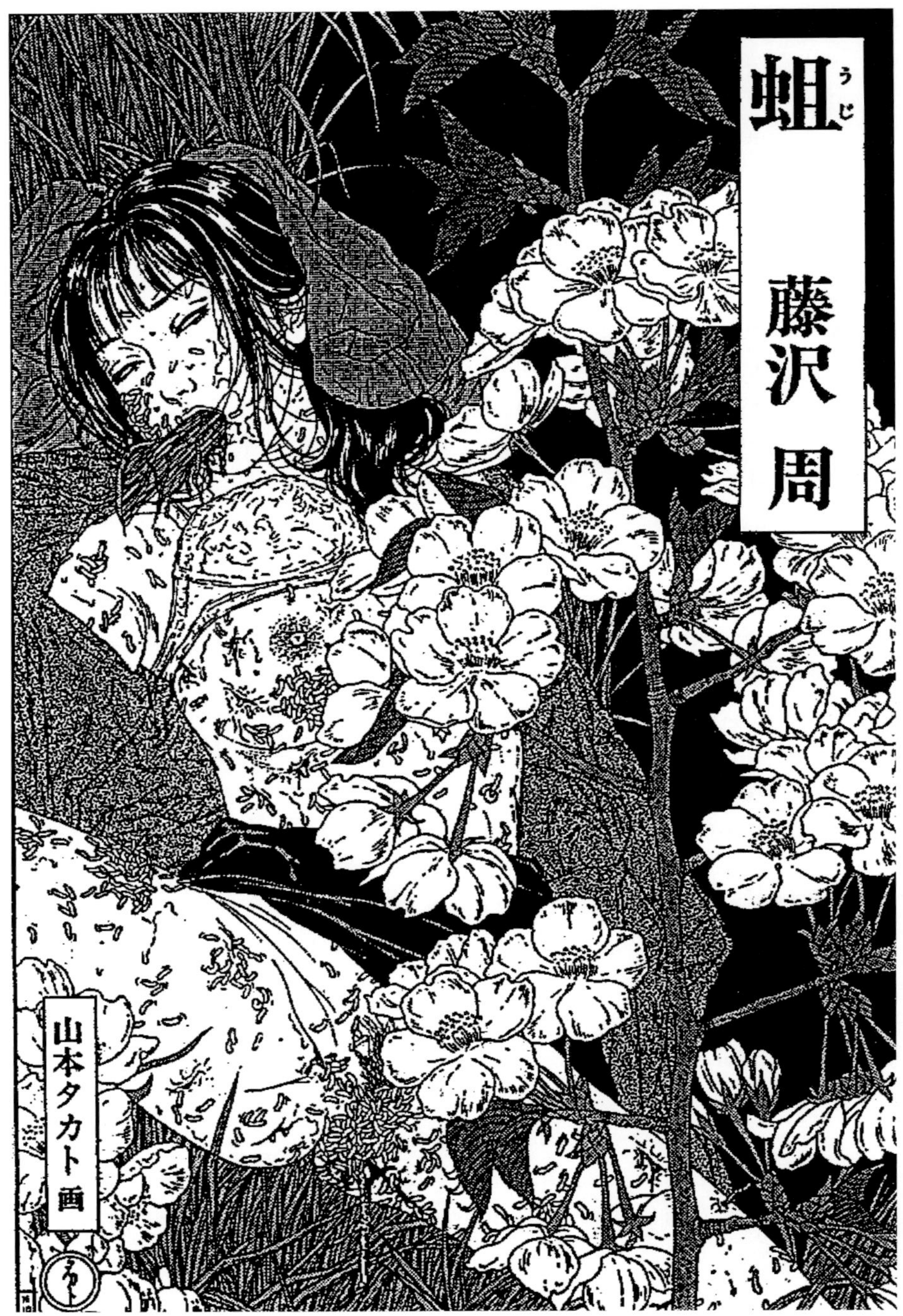

and much commented on by previous art historians, Bakusen's reliance on the eminently urban and even decadent vocabulary of Edo's floating world has been elided, if not suppressed. Yet, most obviously, the world of *nihonga* becomes a world peopled almost exclusively by women, who serve as the repositories of a national and "traditional" beauty, while their men compete in the modern West, in a move anticipated by Kuroda Seiki and the early *yōga* painters, as described by Bryson. Nonetheless, this near exclusive focus on women is an essentially self-feminizing move, not unlike some of the aspects discussed earlier by Chino Kaori.

In contrast to the robust or bucolic depictions of the rural and the "premodern" set in the Japanese countryside, Kim Hyeshin shows how these kinds of images were adapted to the representation of Japan's colonial conquest, Korea. Kim notes a preponderance of images of women in the works exhibited at *Sŏnjŏn,* the annual state-sponsored juried exhibition created under Japanese supervision. Landscape images tend toward the lonely and impoverished, reflecting the so-called Stagnation Theory of Korean development, which authorized Japanese seizure of an "undeveloped" land. While within the Japanese domestic sphere artists represented women either as a kind of internal primitive or as the repository of premodern culture, both the "primitive" and "tradition" took on a decidedly different valence when encouraged in Korean artists depicting their colonized homeland. Kim's chapter highlights Japan's role as a colonizer but also the situation of countries such as Korea, whose "modernity" came to them as a handmaid of imperialism. Japan's "Cultural Rule" policy makes explicit the political and ideological uses of art by the state—an operation that seems obscured on the domestic front, where artistic production is often glossed by the romantic myths of creative genius, as seen, for example, in 2002 in the major retrospective of the painter Yokoyama Taikan (1868–1958) at the Tokyo National Museum.

## Gender Discourse in Contemporary Japanese Visual Regimes

The final section of the collection engages contemporary visual representations of Japan. Within the discipline of Japanese art history, cinema is rarely considered as part of the same visual field as painting. Even within painting, there is a near total divide between the "modern" *(kindai)* and the "contemporary" *(genzai).* In this volume we challenge this compartmentalization.

Chigusa Kimura-Steven analyzes the figure of the woman in both Abe Kōbō's novel *Woman in the Dunes (Suna no onna)* and the film of the same title by director

Teshigawara Hiroshi. Using largely psychoanalytical theory—which has been strongly resisted by Japanese critics themselves—Kimura-Steven provides an illuminating reading of Abe's work, exposing the phallogocentrism of its plot. She then relates this plot to the interest of several artists, including Abe, in Surrealism and draws compelling analogies between the Europe of the Surrealism era and Japan during its postwar economic boom to explain the misogynistic tendency to be found in the art of both. This chapter is important not only for bringing cinema into the discussion but for linking Japanese art to an international context and such international artistic movements as Surrealism.

Gunhild Borggreen examines the very problematization of gender issues in the Japanese art world today and shows how a concept of "feminine-style art" has been created by the critics, despite strong stylistic commonalities in the art produced by both women and men. Borggreen reviews the art of the period to discover whether some peculiarly feminine style is evident. This examination leads in turn to a reflection on how stereotypical images of women and femininity are both imposed on and manipulated by female artists. Like Kimura-Steven, Borggreen situates the new promotion of female artists in the economic environment of the day. Likewise, "modern" *(kindai)* art and "contemporary" *(gendai)* art are hardly ever discussed in the same context or by the same people—the former being the province of "scholars" and the latter, that of "critics." Here again, it is our intention to challenge these categories—these exclusions—which serve an ideological function. Contemporary art in Japan often highlights and critiques the country's consumer society. Allowing such work to occupy the same space as "art" makes many scholars uncomfortable. And by insisting on the historical uniqueness of *shunga,* some scholars feel justified in discussing it without reference to modern pornography.

Finally, Sharalyn Orbaugh in her chapter argues that the "hybridity" of contemporary popular culture undoes many closely held identifications. Orbaugh shows how *anime* (animated films) and *manga* (comic books) are generically hybrid, moving from one medium to another; culturally hybrid, in that the distinction between what is inside and outside of "Japan" or "Japanese" is increasingly blurred; and, most significantly, sexually hybrid, allowing and encouraging cross-gender identification (or, as Orbaugh calls it, "cognitive transvestism") at the same time that the category "feminine" or "female" is simultaneously exaggerated and negated. The *shōjo*, or "girl," remains partly a liminal figure but has also been reified into a distinct gender. Yet while permeable gender boundaries would seem to represent an advance over compulsory heterosexuality, Orbaugh's conclusion resembles the situation described by Chino at the beginning of the volume: hypersexualized cyborg female bodies allow the male appropriation of certain "feminine" subject positions, in the process "reinscrib[ing] sex/gender ideologies [and] obviating any promise of resistance or social transformation."

In short, this volume examines issues of heterosexuality and homosexuality, pornography, modernization, colonialism, and nationalism, all in relation to the issue of gender and in the context of Asia and the postcolonial world. *Gender and Power in the Japanese Visual Field* refuses to be confined by standard periodization: it represents a forceful rejection of those periodizing schemes that would isolate Japan's early modern period (1600–1868) from its later emergence as a modern nation-state, and one of the issues that receives particular attention is the reception history of various artifacts through the nineteenth and twentieth centuries. The authors have approached their subjects through a range of different disciplines and specializations within the fields of art and literary history. The volume does not pretend to treat all visual genres or all time periods of Japanese culture, and there is no desire to be either comprehensive or doctrinaire. It will be apparent, for instance, that the concept of "gender" as used by Chino and by Mostow is not the same. We hope that the result not only will be of use to specialists in Japanese, or Asian, cultural studies, but that the collection will go some way toward demonstrating to those outside our fields the importance of considering histories beyond Europe or North America. For Asia and the non-European continue to be the mirror through which "the West" (mis)recognizes itself, in true Lacanian fashion. We hope that this volume will encourage many to question the eurocentric litany as well.

As the preparation of the manuscript of this volume reached its final stages, Chino Kaori died of heart failure on New Year's Eve 2001. All three of the editors were close friends of Kaori and are greatly indebted to the scholarly and personal support she gave us over the years. *Gender and Power* was to be the first in what we foresaw as a series of publications applying feminist and postcolonial theory to Japanese art. It is tragic that while such work will go on, Professor Chino will not be an active part of it. We dedicate this volume to her memory.

CHAPTER TWO

CHINO KAORI

# Gender in Japanese Art

This essay aims to apply the modern critical concept of "gender" to Japanese art. Accordingly, unlike in most studies in our field, I will be reporting no newly discovered works of art or historical documents. My intention is to take a new look at the very discipline and history of Japanese art history and to offer a new interpretation. I expect that some will object to my approach, arguing that modern Western critical concepts are either meaningless or inappropriate tools for analyzing something as ancient as Japanese art. Others may find the idea of applying to art an a priori concept fundamentally wrong. No doubt not a few Japanese scholars of Japanese art history will have these doubts and criticisms. Let me begin, therefore, with a review of the state of modern art history, incorporating my own experiences. I will define what I mean by "gender," and then from a broad consideration of several aspects of the Heian period (794–1185) within the history of Japanese art, I would like to suggest a new interpretation of Japanese art history through gender theory.

## The Modern Historiography of Art and Japanese Art History

The major trend in contemporary research in Japanese art history has been the detailed analysis and evaluation of one particular object in itself, or investigating the chronological relationship or relationships of influence between a number of objects. The name of the artist and the date the object was produced are carefully deduced, and, if the artist is known, the works are appended to his career and arranged accordingly, and research proceeds in terms of the interpretation of stylistic change. However, works of art are products of their own time and social conditions. In practicing art history, one should not be limited to studying only subject matter and style, a limitation that tends to divorce art from its historical, social, and political contexts. When studying a work of art, it is important to place it in its sociohistorical context.

However, sociohistorical contexts are not "objectively" revealed to the researcher. On the contrary, contexts change their contours in accordance with the researcher's interests. History cannot be reconstructed objectively. Art history does not exist in a vacuum, or in an "objective" or "universal" sterile state that places the work or scholar equidistant from all things and ideas. Consciously or unconsciously a researcher's individual and personal viewpoint conditions her or his methods of study.

I began to think this way during my stay in the United States in the autumn of 1992. While I was on the East Coast I had the opportunity to meet and to exchange ideas with many art historians. It was as if a fog had lifted and the narrow boundaries of Japanese art history were dissolved for me. For many art historians in North America, the issues I mentioned above emerge in the process of articulating their own ethnic or national identity in ways that question the existing assumptions of the art history discipline. These scholars in fact seem to be groping toward a new form of art historiography. From the standpoint of "gender, race, and class," these art historians see the traditional "universal" and "objective" art historical discourses as a set of values clearly based on those of "white, middle-class men." The assumptions of traditional art historical practice put others in an inferior position. It seems only natural that these art historians would have a difficult time accepting such a situation. Insofar as art history continues to be based on conventional evaluations of worth, the art that appeals to groups with different cultural norms outside the mainstream will never be the focus of "universal" art history. Such art will be completely ignored or treated at best as "special art," "marginal art," or "ethnic art." Art that is not mainstream will be allocated only a few pages in art history books or exhibited in the back corners of museums. Until the myth of "universal" art history is demolished, there will be no art for historians who study nonmainstream arts. I realized that I was no exception: as long as Japanese art history continues to be tied to the conventional value system, it will always be marginalized and exist on the periphery of the Western art "nucleus."

There are those who will say that Japanese art historians working in Japan can continue to study Japanese art and ignore the appraisals of foreign countries, that it is possible for those who appreciate Japanese art to continue to study Japanese art history without paying attention to world trends. However, the reason these Japanese art historians in Japan think they can afford to stay so unperturbed is only because Japan has become, owing to its economic power, one of the world's "centers." Such power seems to assure them that Japan's cultural identity can be preserved. Outside Japan, there are still art historians, especially in the Third World, who know that unless they assert their own identity in studying their art, they will culturally cease to exist. The same can be said about marginalized art within Japan, the arts of the Ainu, natives in the north, and of the Okinawans in the south. The art of these two groups has been marginalized by the centralization of "standard" "Japanese art history." Once Japanese art historians understand what previous Japanese art history discourse has marginalized, that is, subjugated as the "Other," our field of vision can come to encompass the relationship between Japan and Asia since the Meiji era (1868–1912). I will return to this point below.

It is time to open our eyes to the present state of the world, move with the trends both inside and outside Japan, and begin to experiment to create a new discourse for Japanese art history. In place of the previous "universal" and monolithic art history, we need to construct a new pluralistic art history. Even for Japanese art historians who study Japanese art, this methodological problem of identity is a very important issue.

If one considers the issues raised above, there is no argument against using modern critical concepts to explain Japanese art history. The conventional way of doing art history, that is, starting from the object, is still legitimate; however, in choosing artifacts as the subject of study, we ought to be aware of the problems involved in the valorization of the artifacts through the very process of selection for study (that is, canonization). When we study the span of Japanese art, we should be cognizant of the hidden value system that we have inherited from the West. There are many Japanese historians of Japanese art who think that this is of no concern to them, but they are simply unaware that they are transmitting their predecessors' theories and methods without realizing it. The art historical method of "explaining stylistic development," which has been widely accepted by Japanese art historians, is based on the work *Principles of Art History* (published 1915) by Heinrich Wöllflin (1864–1945). Japanese art history is a kind of composite discipline derived from Edo-period (1600–1868) connoisseurship *(mekiki)* and late-nineteenth- to early-twentieth-century Western art history methodology. And it is those essentially nineteenth-century methodologies that are now being called into question.

While some of my Japanese audience may concede that it is appropriate to apply contemporary methods back in time, so to speak, fewer would accept the assertion that works of art from the past are not only powerful in their own time but continue to exert an influence in our time as well. Yet we Japanese art historians cannot dismiss the social role the arts of the past have played and still play. The interpretations of works of art from the past that we continue to write in conjunction with reproductions in multivolume histories of art, or on television, computer, or disk media, mutually reinforce and are reinforced by those visual images as they are disseminated in society. The power that visual images exert on the viewer is strong in and of itself, but when combined with texts that explain the images, the effect becomes even stronger. The authority ("power"/*kenryoku*)[1] to manipulate words and images, and thereby move society, is not unrelated to the work of art history. Our work, regardless of the subject of study, whether it be ancient or medieval art, is already implicated in current political and social movements. This is also one of the reasons why art history, including Japanese art history, cannot be divorced from contemporary theories and concepts.

## The Concept of "Gender"

In order to write about the concept of "gender" *(jendā),* it is first necessary to define the concept of "sex" *(sekkusu)*. Sex is the division of "male" and "female" by "the differentiation of the male and female bodies in terms of their respective genitalia." Conversely, "gender" is here defined as "social/historical functions/categories established over and above those sexed bodies." Gender can be divided into "masculine" and "feminine." However, "masculinity" and "femininity" are not necessarily tied to the biological classification of sex, and the relationship between male and "masculine" and female and "feminine" is not fixed. In other words, it is not always the male who possesses "masculinity," and it is not always the female who possesses "femininity." The concept of gender can also change in accordance with time and place. While there are many ways of interpreting the concept of gender, here I have adopted the stance that all males and all females simultaneously possess both "masculinity" and "femininity." While both sexes have both genders, in the majority of cases, because of social and historical conditions and pressures, self-regulation has kept males confined to the "masculine" gender and females confined to the "feminine." In this essay, my use of the words "male" and "female" indicates a physiological division, without any of the associate attributes of "manliness" to the male or "effeminacy" to the female (the gendered substantives will be referred to as "man" and "woman"). Of course, there are some people who have hermaphroditic bodies, but speaking generally, the physiological sense of "male" and "female" should be fairly clear.

The problem of assigning meaning to the concepts here expressed as "masculinity" and "femininity," or "man" and "woman," is rather more complex. Until recently, the words "masculine" and "feminine" have often been thought to reflect values or standards of superiority and inferiority. More than is the case in Japanese, this tendency is particularly clear in English and European contexts. Just like the Japanese word *"memeshii"* (effeminate), the English word "feminine" seems to have negative connotations. There is, however, a recent movement that treats the issue of femininity from a different standpoint, a kind of paradigm shift that questions previous value systems. I hope that this essay too contributes to the reconsideration of the traditional concepts of "masculinity" and "femininity." In order to examine fully their meanings in context, I will use wherever possible the terms "masculine" and "feminine," which have played a significant role in constructing conventional ideas. But in other cases I will use alternative words that may be similar yet present positive and affirmative values in regard to the "feminine." Such terms are meant to serve as a positive, affirming rereading of "femininity," a word that is often assigned an inferior valence. In short, "masculinity" and "femininity" are to be placed on either end of a conceptual axis of affirmative and positive values.

From this standpoint, the two concepts connote different, but equally positive, meanings. "Masculinity" signifies "big, great, strong, grand (monumental), permanent, public, unified, fierce, aggressive." "Femininity" signifies "small, delicate, soft, modest, ephemeral, private, diverse, calm, harmonious." I must note that the list of positive and affirmative values for the feminine is drawn from a Japanese context—for instance, in English, the very words "small, delicate, soft," as used in traditional art history, seem to have a derogatory connotation.

I consider the concept of the paired genders of "masculinity" and "femininity" as just one of many tools for the analysis of the diverse arts of each of the world's periods and regions, and do not mean to imply that I think this concept the sole, absolute, or "universal" method. Further, I do not intend a dualism that in a single stroke divides all the arts of East and West, ancient and modern. "Masculinity" and "femininity" as used here are two tendencies joined in the middle, not mutually exclusive characteristics. The use of this pair of concepts here is an attempt to establish one axis in the complex field of Japanese art that is so difficult to verbalize. I believe that, compared to any previous framework, the axis of gender is especially effective for understanding the history and state of Japanese art. I will come back to the issue of the effectiveness of this axis and reexamine the meaning of the terms "masculinity" and "femininity."

## The Search for Identity in the Heian Period: The Double Binary Structure of "Kara" and "Yamato"

Before applying the gender axis to Japanese art history, I would like to place Japanese art within the context of East Asia, with particular focus on the art of the Heian period, which was so important for defining all subsequent Japanese art.

The Heian period began at a time when the powerful Tang dynasty had passed its peak and was in decline. The decline and defeat of the Tang dynasty in 907 meant, for Japan and other Chinese cultural satellites, the loss of a political and cultural "center." Various ethnic groups on the continent struggled for independence. Subsequent dynasties rose and fell. Each "non-Tang" dynasty strove to create its own identity. In the early ninth century, appreciation of Tang culture began to wane in Japan, and the Heian period cultivated a sense of identity that was a "self that is not Tang," or, more properly, a "self that is not 'Kara.' "[2]

The *kana* Japanese syllabaries, particularly the establishment of *hiragana*, are an example of this trend. However, unlike the Qidan or Xixia alphabets, in the case of Japanese *hiragana*, the "characters of Kara" were not abandoned, and Chinese ideographs were maintained as Chinese ideographs while at the same time Japan created a separate "not-Kara-but-our-own-characters" in the form of simplified, cursive versions of the original Chinese characters. In other words, this writing did not represent the creation of a self through the complete denial of Kara but rather imagined the coexistence of the Kara Other and the indigenous Self, each having a different existence and value. That Chinese characters and *hiragana* had different functions and uses is well known: Chinese characters were used in writing public documents, Chinese poems, Buddhist sutras, and official diaries; *hiragana* was used in composing Japanese poetry, fictional tales, and private diaries. The fact that Chinese characters were called *mana* (literally, "true names") in contrast to *kana* (literally, "temporary names") suggests an awareness of "public" *(kō [ōyake])* versus "private" *(shi [watakushi])*. Such things as Chinese characters *(kanji)* and Chinese poetry *(kanshi)* represent the world of the "Han" (in Japanese, *kan*) and "Kara"; such things as *hiragana* and *waka* (*yamato uta*, or "songs of Yamato") represent the world of the "self that is not Kara but Yamato."[3]

The apportionment of roles between "Kara" and "Yamato" is strikingly obvious in the wall and screen paintings of the Heian period. The Heian period division between *kara-e*, or "Chinese painting," and *yamato-e*, or "Japanese painting," was based on the distinction between the subjects depicted (in other words, Chinese subject matter or Japanese subject matter). Throughout the Heian period, *kara-e* and *yamato-e* coexisted, and as Akiyama Terukazu pointed out some time ago, *kara-e* was intimately tied to the "official lives" of the aristocracy. Whether *kara-e* or *yamato-e*, the general function of screens and wall paintings was to provide a visual expression of the character of the space that opened up in front of the painting. Take, for example, the case of the *kara-e* screens depicting the *Thirty-Two Chinese Sages and Saints*, which were installed for official ceremonies on the north wall of the central chamber of the Shishinden Hall of the imperial palace compound. The paintings were undoubtedly used to heighten the majesty of the ceremony that took place before them. In contrast to the official Shishinden Hall, the Seiryōden Hall was reserved for activities pursuant to "private and daily life." Even in this hall, however, "public" and "private" divisions were clearly defined by the sliding-door paintings. That is, the five paintings on the west wall of the emperor's living quarters (called the *"hi-no-omashi"*) were based on Chinese subject matter. On the reverse side of the same doors, which decorated the rooms of the ladies-in-waiting, the paintings depicted Japanese subjects. Similarly, the sliding doors called the *Konmei-chi no shōji* and the *Ara-umi no shōji* on the East Veranda (the *hiro-bisashi*) also depicted both Chinese and Japanese themes. On the sides facing the south, the panels depicted the Chinese subjects of *Konmei Pond* and *Figures with Long Arms and Legs*, while on the sides facing the north the panels depicted the Japanese themes of *Hawking in Sagano* and *Wicker Fish Traps in Uji*.[4] Frequently these screens included inscriptions that were written on small decorative squares of paper *(shikishi)* and pasted on the screens. Although there were exceptions, as a rule excerpts of Chinese texts were attached to *kara-e* paintings, while Japanese poems *(waka)* were inscribed on *yamato-e* paintings.

In short, the screen paintings of the Heian period, like the culture of the period in general, were based on a double-layered structure of "Kara" and "Yamato." However, when I use the term "Kara" or "Tang" (Japanese, "Tō"), this does not denote the actual Tang empire that existed across the sea. It is important to recognize that "Kara" means "'Kara' within Yamato," which has its antithesis in the concept of "'Yamato' within Yamato." In other words, these terms signify the "function" of "Kara" or "Yamato" within a new "Japanese" culture. Taken together, "Kara" and "Yamato" created a unified "Japanese" culture for the first time. Because "Kara" and "Yamato" were two aspects of Heian cultural identity, the Enthronement Ceremony *(daijō-e)* involved preparing two screens, one encompassing Chinese pictorial subjects and one encompassing Japanese ones. The ceremony visually instantiated the emperor's total control over Japan, that is, over the two realms of the binary structure, the "'Kara' within Yamato" and the "'Yamato' within Yamato."

Outside this double-layered structure there existed the actual Tang China. In art, an example of the difference is that between ink paintings *(suiboku-ga)* imported from China and those made in Japan. Yet the geographically real Tang seemed to exist not so much as a historical entity but as a function or category. This is apparent in the Japanese insistence on using the appellation "Kara" (Tang) in reference to paintings *(kara-e)* and things *(kara-mono)* imported from the continent even after the fall of the Tang dynasty. Even the countries on the Korean Peninsula were recognized as "Kara." The "Kara" outside Japan—while wrapped up in complex feelings about "the true 'Tang' across the sea, the great 'Tang'" and persisting in the Japanese consciousness like a kind of persecution complex—was a phantom "Kara" (or, rather, a phantom "great foreign country").

One can think of the identity that the people of the Heian period were groping toward in the face of the fall of the Tang empire as having finally been established through the kind of complicated double-layered binary structure explained above. (Since I am using "Kara/Tang" and "Yamato" as functional-notional categories and not to refer to actual places, I will hereafter dispense with putting the terms in quotation marks). This complex structure was like a safety valve that allowed for the acceptance of the Tang's advanced art and literature into the Yamato context. With a prepared place for the acceptance of the Tang-within-Yamato, there was no threat to the art from more ancient times, the Yamato-within-Yamato. Japan could take in and adopt only what it liked and wanted of the newly arrived art of foreign countries. No matter how enthusiastically new arts were taken in, the Japanese identity was never at stake, since the Yamato-within-Yamato and the Kara-within-Yamato were designed to coexist. Then, as the newly adopted arts were assimilated, they became gradually equated with the previous, existing arts, and they then shifted to the category of Yamato-within-Yamato, which allowed room for yet another absorption of newly arrived art in the space known as Kara-within-Yamato. Because this arrangement effectively renews itself as it absorbs arts and cultures from without, the category of Yamato-within-Yamato undergoes constant change and stubbornly survives. The reason old styles in Japanese art history are not rejected but live on can be found in this double-layered binary structure, which has continued to work effectively.

This double-layered binary structure can be represented in a graphic for easier understanding. (See Figure 2.1. Note, however, that the "a" and "b" within this figure are not two clearly separated divisions but rather two tendencies at opposite ends of a spectrum. This means that "B" is a continuum that has within it the spectrum with the two poles "a" and "b"). "A" is Kara, "B" is Yamato, "a" is Kara-within-Yamato, and "b" is Yamato-within-Yamato. The binary pairs "A/B" and "a/b" both indicate a distinction between "public/private" and "outer/inner" *(omote/ura)*. The identity that the Japanese chose for themselves as Yamato, while maintaining a consciousness of the great Kara, had the function of being "private" and "inner." The people of the Heian period (who were in direct contact with Tang culture) effected a self-definition, that is, an identity for themselves, that was not "public," not "outer," not "pretense," but the most intimate, deeply familiar and comfortable, Japan-within-Japan.

## Japanese Art History as Seen through Gender Theory

Further fascinating aspects of this issue of cultural self-definition can be discovered. For example, the double-layered binary structure that arose in the Heian period is also clearly reflected in the fact that Chinese characters *(kanji),* which were used for writing public, official documents, were called "men's hand" *(otoko-de)* (Figure 2.2); while *hiragana*, which was used for writing private, unofficial documents, was called "women's hand" *(onna-de)* (Figure 2.3). Even though the terms were "men's hand" and "women's hand," when writing Japanese poetry both men and women used the so-called women's hand, so it is clear that the distinction was not a biological one. In principle, "men's hand" was used only by men, and women were supposed to feign ignorance of it—to be able to read Chinese was considered "unfeminine." Except when copying Buddhist scriptures—an activity outside quotidian secular structures—women did not use the "men's hand." In contrast, men could avail themselves of either hand—a kind of cultural ambidexterity. In the same way, while the actual kinds of works referred to are unclear, it is reasonable to conclude that the terms *"otoko-e,"* or "men's pictures," and *"onna-e,"* or "women's pictures," seen in Heian-period documents, were not biologically based but functional-notional. In other words, perhaps surprisingly, in the Heian period the terms "man" *(otoko)* and "woman" *(onna)* were used in much

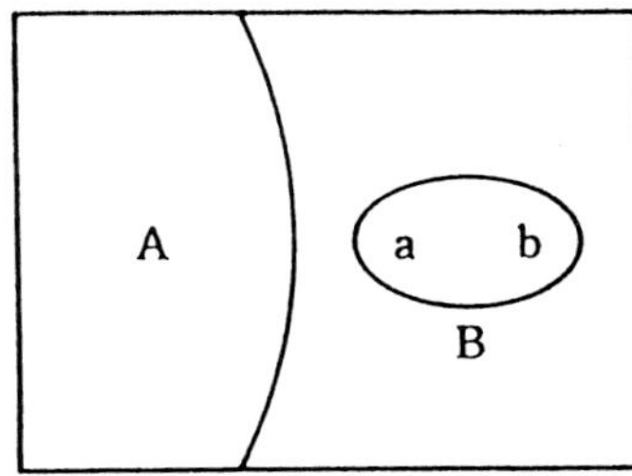


**FIGURE 2.1.** Graph of the dual binary structure

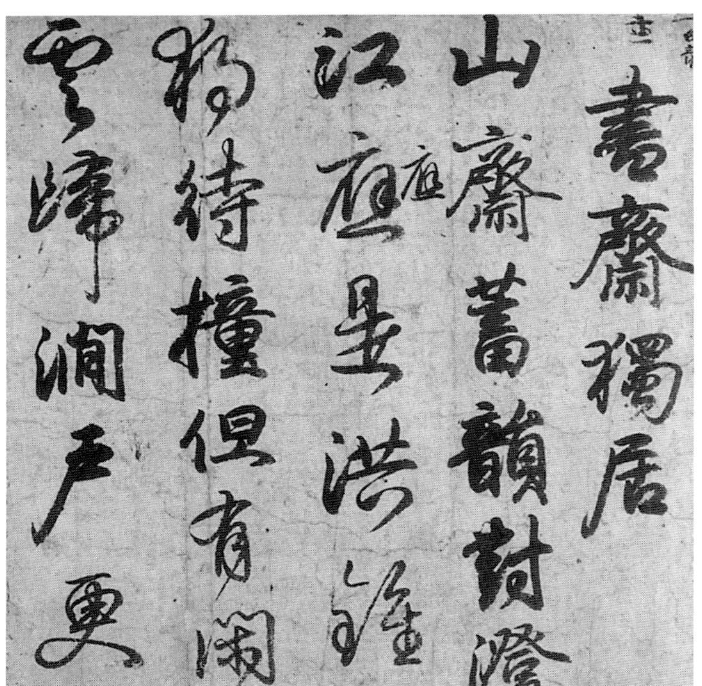

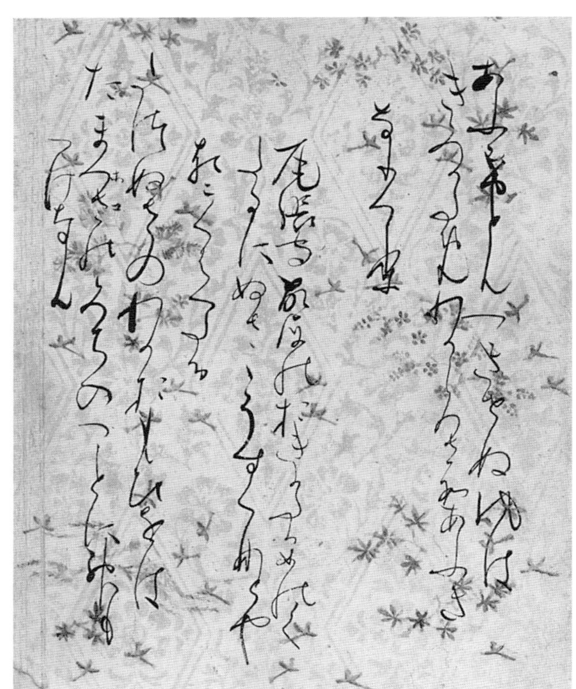

**FIGURE 2.2.** *(Left)* Ono no Michikaze (894–967), draft of *Poems for a Folding Screen (Byōbu dodai),* detail, dated 928 according to the colophon. 22.4 × 316.6 cm, ink on paper. Imperial Household Agency.

**FIGURE 2.3.** *(Right) Poems of the Thirty-Six Poetic Immortals: Collected Poems of Ki no Tsurayuki (Sanjūrokunin shū Ishiyama-gire: Ki no Tsurayuki shū),* first half of the twelfth century. 20.1 × 15.9 cm, ink on decorated paper. Eugene Fuller Memorial Collection 51.210, Seattle Art Museum.

the same sense as the modern concepts "masculinity" *(dansei-sei)* and "femininity" *(josei-sei).*

In fact, various aspects of the Heian period can be easily explained through a gendered reading. For example, the *Tosa Diary* (*Tosa nikki,* ca. 935), written by Ki no Tsurayuki (868–945), is not written in Chinese characters, even though Tsurayuki was a male. The first sentence of the diary reads: "I mean to see whether a woman, too, can keep one of those things called a 'diary' that they say men keep." By assuming the role of a woman writer, Tsurayuki composed the diary in Japanese, rather than Chinese. Tsurayuki, a "man," could only express the private, the "nonofficial" (in contrast to what would be contained in his official report), within the "feminine." Writing in Japanese must have seemed more natural than writing in Chinese, a language that was fundamentally foreign to the Japanese. For men of the Heian period, "masculinity" must have been a somewhat wearisome identity.

"Men," negotiating the distinction between the "masculine" and the "feminine," were therefore able to distinguish skillfully between the "public" and the "private." Men could move through the "masculine" and "feminine" realms at will, while women, except for special occasions, were confined to the "feminine" realm. This appears to be the composition of society at the time. Notice, however, that for the Japanese people of the period, their identity as Japanese was located not in the "masculine" but in the "feminine." Heian-period men sought their identity in the "feminine," clearly demonstrating the distinction between sex and gender.

Look again at the figure of the double-layered binary structure above, this time from the standpoint of gender. In this case, "A" is masculine, "B" is feminine, "a" is the masculine-within-the-feminine, and "b" is the feminine-within-the-feminine. If the concepts of Kara and Yamato are added into the construct, then the total structure of signification becomes Kara = public = masculine and Yamato = private = feminine. The signification of "a," the Kara-within-Yamato or the masculine-within-the-feminine, is quite subtle. When "a" is in relationship to "A," it pairs with "b" to form "B," which is then Yamato = feminine (in contrast to the masculine Kara). Conversely, when "a" is paired with "b" inside of "B," it takes on the contrastive function of "A" and signifies the Kara-within-Yamato = masculine. This must have been an extremely complex and difficult position, and those who were placed in it were the "men" of Japan. Japanese men, confined to the interstices of "a," must have experienced a very ambivalent "masculinity." The Heian man must have been haunted by the fear that there was a real Kara/masculinity across the sea and that he was a counterfeit and hence could not help but doubt his own masculinity. Surely this phantom Kara, all the more powerful because of its illusory nature, posed a threat to the Japanese men of the Heian period, in a way not dissimilar to that experienced by women who live constantly threatened to some extent by the more powerful men beside them. In this way, the anxiety and ambivalence of Japanese men's gender, the deep psychological wound that had its foundation in opposition to the "masculinity" of Kara, that is, the "great foreign country," was first inflicted in the Heian period.

When one looks at later periods using this concept of "femininity," which the people of the Heian period chose themselves as their identity, I believe the situation of Japanese art and culture becomes easier to understand. Below, while taking up a number of works of art as examples, I will examine the aspect of their "masculinity" and "femininity" or, more properly, their masculinity-within-femininity and femininity-within-femininity, based on their mode of expression, that is, style.

The defining characteristic of many late-Heian-period works of art is what I

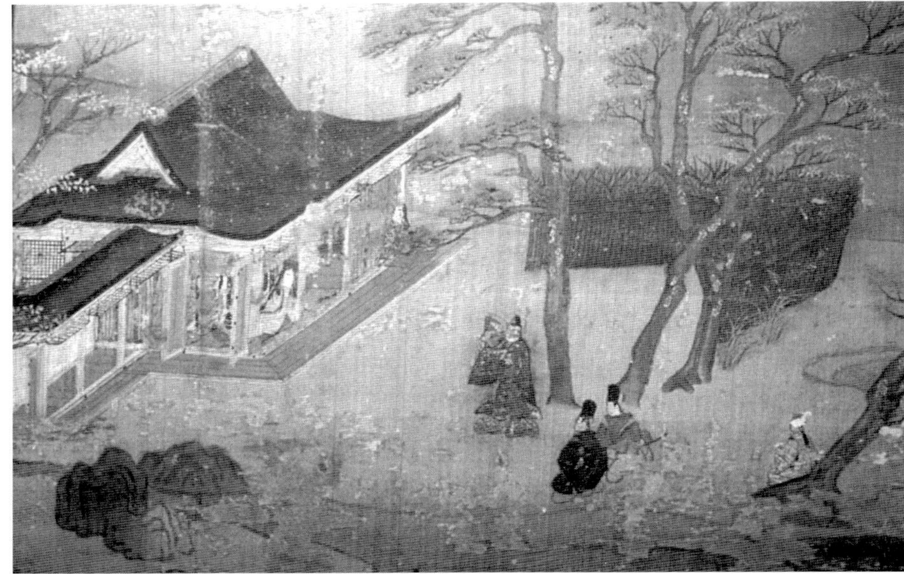

FIGURE 2.4. *Jingoji Landscape Screen (Jingoji senzui byōbu),* detail: *Courtier Dancing with Fan,* end of the twelfth to beginning of the thirteenth century. Each panel 110.8 × 37.5 cm, colors on silk. Jingoji Temple, Kyoto.

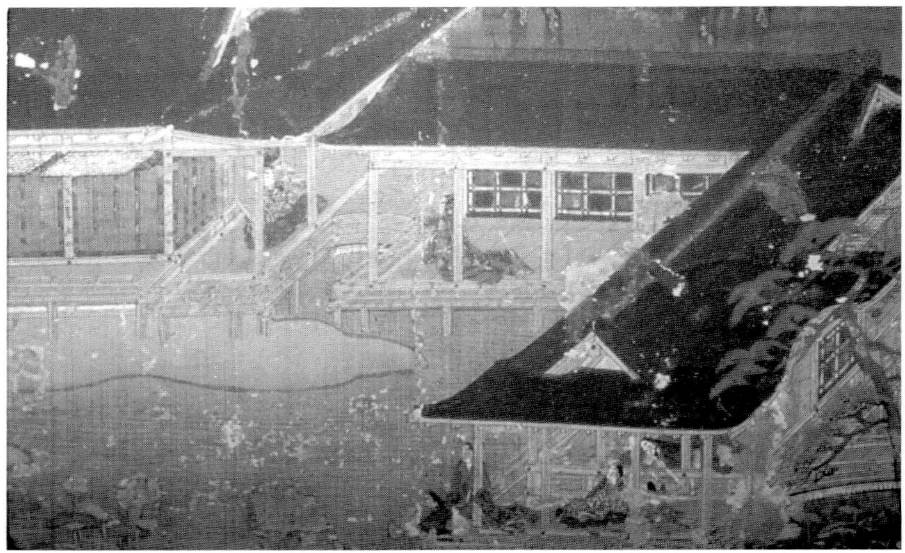

FIGURE 2.5. *Jingoji Landscape Screen,* detail: *Man and Woman Conversing over a Bridge, a Woman Gathering Lotuses.*

have previously defined as "feminine," in other words, "small, delicate, and gentle." These characteristics, although differing from genre to genre, are apparent in such famous works as the decorated paper used in the *Poems of the Thirty-Six Poets (Sanjūrokkasen)* (see Figure 2.3), the narrative pictorialization of the *Tale of Genji Illustrated Scrolls (Genji monogatari emaki),* or the *Thousand-Armed Seated Kannon (Senju Kannon zazō)* of Bujōji Temple and need no explanation. Here, rather, I would like to take up the *Jingoji Landscape Screen (Jingoji senzui byōbu)* (Plate 1 and Figures 2.4–2.5) and try to specify its expressive or stylistic characteristics.

The painting is composed as if made up of multiple vignettes scattered about, with no discernible central scene. The individual scenes are difficult to make out from a distance, and the overall impression is one of randomness. Close up, however, we find delicately depicted human figures, animals, and plants, set out as natural scenery that is gentle, calm, and redolent with a sense of the season. Each individual scene or vignette is small and modest, and separated by small hills and banks so as not to interfere with the other scenes, thus allowing each a coexistence within the sphere of the picture plane. The brushstrokes of the hills and fields that form the stage for each individual scene are unfailingly soft, as if we can see the traces of where the brush gently stroked the silk canvas. There are no dominant, overpowering motifs in the painting; neither are there strong and aggressive brushstrokes. Indeed, the *Jingoji Landscape Screen* is not just "small, delicate, and gentle," but it also has features that might be labeled "not unitary but plural *(igen-teki de wa naku tagen-teki),* not agitated but quiet *(hageshiku naku odayaka),* and not discordant but harmonious *(kōgeki-teki de wa naku chōwa-teki).*" And we cannot disregard the fact that the form of expression itself requires a particular way of viewing that absorbs the viewer into the painting's world, calling the viewer closer to the picture plane, to look and become familiar with the work by adding her or his own thoughts to those of the people depicted in the screen. In other words, a "not public but private" form of appreciation or reception is premised and woven into the very form of expression.

This example illustrates the characteristics of "femininity" in a work of art. Works that employ "femininity" in this way were produced even after the Kamakura period (1185–1333). Numerous examples can be found among paintings of stories and legends; illuminated scrolls of Japanese poetry; and paintings on small lacquer utensil boxes, writing boxes, and any number of "metropolitan" *(miyako-fū)* or "courtly" *(miyabi)* artifacts that embodied the aristocratic culture of Kyoto in contrast to warrior culture. Moreover, even in the Edo period (1600–1868), works that give a feeling of refined lightness can be called examples of this tradition. When we look at these works from the viewpoint of "femininity" gained from consideration of the various Heian works mentioned above, we see that they all display the same tendency. Not only are they "small, delicate, and gentle," but they also show a tendency to assimilate or indirectly quote the art and literature inherited since the Heian period. This connection was never overtly stated but was concealed within refined stylizations so that it could be enjoyed intellectually by a small group of cognoscenti. At the same time, their taste added to and modified the way in which details were executed. In other words, the "femininity" in Japanese art, in addition to the previously noted characteristics, also reveals characteristics of "courtliness, refinement, and elegance" *(miyabi, senren, jōhin)*. Thus, people in positions of power, even if they came from warrior backgrounds, to the extent that circumstances permitted, admired and sought to possess these "feminine" arts.

The pattern of desire, pursuit, and possession of such objects is repeated throughout Japanese history. Normally one would assume that aggressive warriors would prefer the "masculine" arts such as the sculptures of Unkei (1151–1223) and the dynamic sliding-door and wall paintings of Kano Eitoku (1543–1590) (Figure 2.6). Certainly such "powerful and grand" art found its patrons among such powerful warlords at Oda Nobunaga (1534–1582) and Toyotomi Hideyoshi (1536–1598). Hideyoshi's rash invasion of Korea and his taste for bold art can both be seen as reflections of his "masculinity." However, after the battles were over, artistic trends, which had been replete with "masculinity," began little by little to be overwhelmed by the "feminine." In the twelfth century, Unkei's style of sculpture was unseated by the much softer and refined style of his son Tankei (1173–1256). And in the Edo period, Eitoku's large-scale screen doors, with their monumental motifs and dynamic brushwork, gave way to Kano Tan'yū's (1602–1674) light and refined style of painting (Figure 2.7). Large-scale sculpture, such as the Great Buddha of Tōdaiji Temple in Nara, was never to be revived after its first appearance in the eighth century. The detailed designs and techniques originally found in such large-scale works either were absorbed into the other styles of Japanese art or faded away. Indeed, there was almost never a time in Japan when things that were "large, powerful, and monumental" were continuously preferred and held as the highest value. In fact, there was a tendency to denigrate these things as "grandiose, barbarian, and vulgar." The "feminine" —the small, delicate, and gentle—selectively absorbed elements of the contemporary "masculine" and survived as the predominant value. Compared to Western art history, where it is the "masculine" that ordinarily occupies the position of power, this tendency toward the "feminine" is very different. As I will discuss later, there are many countries and regions in the world that have had a "feminine" identity thrust upon them from the outside, but Japan was not actually invaded during the Heian period, and the "feminine" was not forced on it from without. Nonetheless, the people of Japan (who were still trying, in some sense, to stand above the Other) chose for themselves the "feminine" and supported

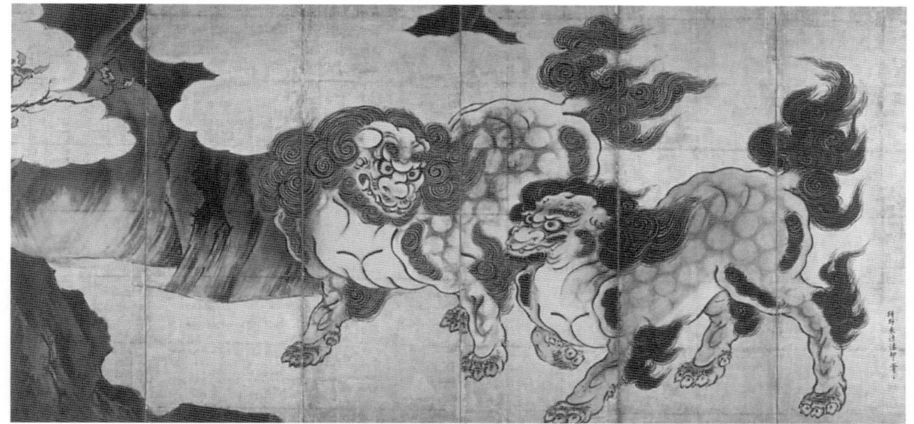

**FIGURE 2.6.** Kano Eitoku (1543–1590), *Chinese Lions Screen (Karajishi-zu byōbu)*. Six-fold screen, 223.3 × 453.2 cm, colors and gold leaf on paper. Imperial Household Agency.

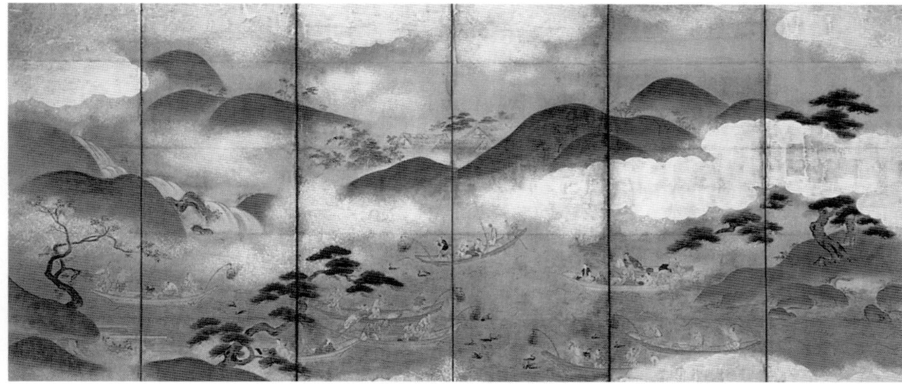

**FIGURE 2.7.** Kano Tan'yū (1602–1674), *Cormorant Fishers (Ukai-zu byōbu)*. One of a pair of six-fold screens, each screen 164.8 × 364.0 cm, colors and gold leaf on paper. Okura Culture Foundation, Tokyo.

the development of arts imbued with the "feminine." A comparison with other countries or regions that possess a similar history of art will help clarify this characteristic of Japanese art. Understanding the art of such countries as Thailand, Cambodia, Indonesia—and even England during certain periods—areas all of which sought their identity while peripheral to an imposing "center," will no doubt become a topic for research among Japanese art historians in the future.

However, for the present, I return to a consideration of Japan from within. Not grand, not powerful, not aggressive, the "feminine" has continued to be the ruling value system within Japan. Yet once this "feminine" became the value system of those in control, even it, which was defined as gentle and harmonious, had an ingeniously oppressive function. It was oppressive when those who could not understand what was "courtly, refined, and elegant" were labeled "barbarian and vulgar country bumpkins." This transformation occurred entirely within

Japan, according to the logic of the oppression of the "marginal" by the "central." According to the Western philosophical tradition, "culture" is "masculine" and "nature" is "feminine," but in Japan the formulation is strikingly reversed. "Culture," that is, "courtliness," is "feminine"; while "nature," that is, "barbarity," is "masculine." The "feminine" is the value system of the ruling class, reigning over the "masculine." This formulation is probably also intimately related to the conditions that preserved and sustained the emperor system. In any event, again the sex of those in power can be distinguished from their cultural gender.

"Femininity," as the culturally and artistically dominant mode before the Meiji period, does not at all mean "female" but rather the "feminine" embodied by "men," which is also what the emperor signifies as a system. Gender theory is an effective means of understanding Japanese art, because, more than anything else, it is capable of distinguishing sex from gender in such a complicated situation. A group of Japanese men surrounding the emperor skillfully manipulated the "masculinity" of the military "men" by means of the value accorded to "courtliness" *(miyabi),* or the "feminine," and thus controlled Japan culturally. Precisely because it was a culture that put value on the "feminine," the social pressure to keep "women" confined to the interior worked all the more strongly. Many beautiful artworks from the past are filled with "femininity," and that very beauty may be one of the reasons these works ended up having the function of binding the "women" of Japan so firmly within the "feminine."

The concept of the "masculinity" of Kara must certainly have evoked the feeling of a "great foreign country." How, then, was it possible for it to be relegated to the "periphery"? This "twist" is characteristic of the Japanese double-layered binary structure. The twist originated in the Heian period, when the identification of the self, Yamato, was allied with the "feminine," in contrast to the "masculinity" of Kara. Japan's obsession with the "great foreign country" was grafted onto the inferiority complex of Japanese "men." Their complex resulted in a rejection of and contempt for all "foreign countries." This, then, is the reason that Japan's "femininity" can encompass both "grandeur" and "barbarity." Recalling the diagram above, when Japan ("B") faces "A," it manifests "marginality" by way of harmonious and peaceful cohabitation with the "central A." But within "B," "b" behaves as the "center" that controls, suppresses, and marginalizes "a." This was the fundamental structure of the Japanese value system up until the modern era.

However, in the modern period the conditions surrounding Japan changed significantly. I would like to conclude by sketching them briefly. First, there was a change in discourse concerning the conditions of Japanese art. During the Meiji period, Japanese leaders who had studied in the West aggressively sought to valorize "masculinity." Emperor Meiji himself favored "masculinity," or perhaps one should say that the men in control of the government carefully guided the emperor's actions in order to promote a masculine image of the ruler, with modern Western-style military uniforms and the like. Seen from a "masculine" value system, Japanese works of art, filled with "feminine" signs, were seen as shameful, cowardly, or literally "effeminate." It is the misfortune of Japanese art historical research in the modern period that an art historical vocabulary that positively and actively valorized the conditions of Japanese art, centered on the feminine, did not exist in Western art historical discourse. This being the case, for Japanese scholars of traditional Western art history as well as those who studied Chinese art history, the "inferior position" of Japanese art was tacitly understood as given. Indeed, having studied Western art historical discourse and not having questioned its valorization of the masculine, we scholars of Japanese art history, too, find ourselves in the same circumstances, that is, assuming the inferiority of the very works we study.

However, the gravest situation of the modern era arose when Japan assumed a "masculine" identity and attempted to subjugate various countries in Asia, imprisoning them in a "feminine" role in relation to Japan's "masculine" role. This is the second, and most fundamental, problem surrounding modern Japanese art. The brutal policies inflicted on China, Korea, and other Asian countries were supported by Japan's "masculine" identity. In countries that had the feminine role forced on them, for example, Korea, a delicate, graceful art began to be produced after 1910 (see Chapter 8). Such a trend is attributable to Japanese "masculinity" strongly restraining the art of Korea. Discarding the "femininity" that constituted their own identity since the Heian period, the Japanese sought to imitate the "West," in place of Kara, and to assume the opposite gender role of the "masculine." This period, when Japan aggressively turned toward the invasion of various Asian countries, is Japan's modern period—it is also its present period. When I think about Japanese art of this period, I am rendered speechless, with great pain in my heart.

While art is a beautiful fruit, born from historical, social, and political conditions, it is at the same time a frightening instrument that comes actively to form social and political trends. Art is, itself, an extremely political "discourse." Even when thinking about Japanese art history from the perspective of gender theory, we cannot ignore this aspect of art. Because, as I stated in the beginning, we all, undeniably, live deeply implicated in the political conditions of the present.

## Conclusion

Above I have examined the situation of Japanese art using the concept of gender. Since I have used "masculinity" and "femininity" as complementary concepts, each with its own positive and affirmative value—rather than as in the Western philosophical tradition, where the masculine is posited as superior and the feminine inferior—the overall results of my argument may seem somewhat strange. Nonetheless, this aberration better than anything else describes the situation of Japanese art. In the definition of gender that I gave at the beginning of this essay, I did not link "femininity" to "marginality and subjugation" and "masculinity" to "centrality and domination" but rather considered them separately. This strategy too was designed to highlight the discrepancy with Western traditional thought. When we apply to these concepts the double-layered binary structure explained above, we can understand their complex interpenetration, and when we then look at Japanese art, aspects that were previously difficult to explain become clearly arranged and visible. Applying a combination of the axis of gender with the axis of "central/peripheral" or "domination/subjugation" in the analysis of Japanese art is, I believe, extremely effective.

Yet, no one, absolute, "universal" art history exists. It is always possible to reexamine the state of Japanese art and its history from a viewpoint distinct from what has preceded. It is important that we not be afraid of new ways of thinking or new hypotheses, that we not neglect a constant reexamination and rethinking, and that we always attempt to continue our analyses from a plurality of angles. The new interpretation of Japanese art history through gender theory proposed here is just one example of such an attempt.

CHAPTER THREE

IKEDA SHINOBU

# The Image of Women in Battle Scenes: "Sexually" Imprinted Bodies

A broad overview of the paintings created in Japan's ancient and medieval periods confirms the great variety in the modeling of the human figures in these paintings. In previous Japanese art historical studies, these differences have been explained as changes in expressive form, or style, that followed the passage of time or as expressive conventions suited to the subject of the painting.

Further examination of these paintings, however, leads to the surprising discovery of the remarkable difference in the gaze turned on the "feminine" images and the "masculine" images. Needless to say, a difference in the representation of men and women is not simply an objective view of the biological differences between males and females. It is worthwhile to reconsider how gender—that set of social assumptions related to sex—gives rise to this difference in representation.[1] The "body" expressed visually supersedes the individual characteristics of "sex" and is nothing more than a depiction of a socially formed "gender" enmeshed in various elements of political, religious, and economic realities. In other words, the depicted "body" reflects a society's unique set of gender relationships, and it reproduces those relationships in the discourse known as visual art.

Here, I will discuss a scene from a handscroll created in the Kamakura period (1185–1333), *Night Attack on the Sanjō Palace (Sanjō-den yo-uchi no maki)* from the *Illustrated Scrolls of the Tales of the Heiji Era (Heiji monogatari emaki)*.[2] I begin with an analysis of the depiction of "sexuality" as it is expressed in the "women's" "bodies" that appear in this painting. I will also consider the depiction of the "males," before turning the discussion to the question of the gaze to which these representations of men and women are subjected, ending with a consideration of the social standing of the commissioner or recipient of this work. Although the scroll is an example of a work that depicts the war and violence that is fundamental to the existence of humankind in all periods and all regions, if we reexamine the *Night Attack on the Sanjō Palace* from the standpoint of gender, we may be able to form some idea of what the person (or persons) who commissioned or received this scroll thought about women, and themselves.

## The Pictures and Text of the *Night Attack on the Sanjō Palace*

The *Illustrated Scrolls of the Tales of the Heiji Era* were created around the middle of the thirteenth century and are famous as the oldest Japanese example of battle scenes in a handscroll format. The *Night Attack on the Sanjō Palace* scroll, in the collections of the Boston Museum of Fine Arts, is well known for its depiction of a fierce battle scene that spreads beneath the towering flames of the burning palace (Plate 2). In the first year of the Heiji era (1159) during the late Heian period (794–1185), military forces led by Minamoto no Yoshitomo watched for Taira no Kiyomori's departure from the capital and immediately launched a surprise attack on the Sanjō Palace, home of Retired Emperor Go-Shirakawa. This attack began what is known as the Heiji Disturbance, or Heiji no Ran.

I focus my discussion on the scene of the battle itself, that is, the interior of the Sanjō Palace and the area around its gate. In the long pictorial format, a crowd of rebel warriors is shown grouped together in the midst of their raid. Warriors on horseback are advancing to the left, running through the scene of battle. The force of the surprise attack is effectively conveyed through this visual composition.

As for how the victims of the attack, the palace forces of the retired emperor, are depicted, not a single male of the palace forces is shown going out to meet the attack.[3] Only three casualties are shown: a figure seen tumbling down into a garden, pursued by a soldier holding a halberd (Figure 3.1); a figure who is being beheaded by a surrounding group of soldiers (Figure 3.2); and a figure who has collapsed next to the palace wall after being run through with a long sword (Figure 3.3). All are lower-level courtiers in court dress, their court hats lost and their topknots in disarray. These images have been drawn from a visual vocabulary that appears repeatedly throughout a variety of picture scrolls and are shown here in effective combination. For example, the detail seen in Figure 3.2, where one soldier holds the victim down from behind while another beheads him, is seen in other battle handscrolls, such as the *Picture Scroll of the Former Nine Years War (Zen-kunen kassen emaki)* and the *Illustrated Scrolls of the Mongol Invasion (Mōko shūrai emaki).* Indeed, this pose is so frequently seen that it can almost be considered a necessary element for a battle scroll. This kind of image might be said to

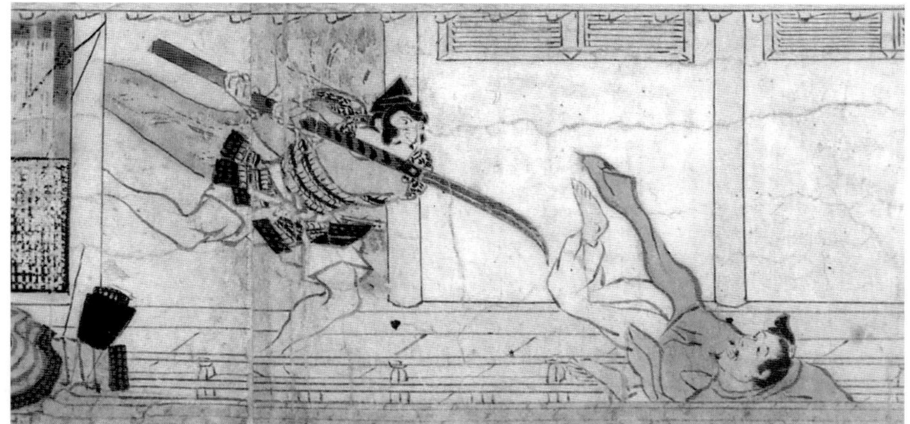

FIGURE 3.1. *Night Attack on the Sanjō Palace* from the *Illustrated Scrolls of the Tales of the Heiji Era (Heiji monogatari emaki),* detail: a man tumbling into a garden. Museum of Fine Arts, Boston.

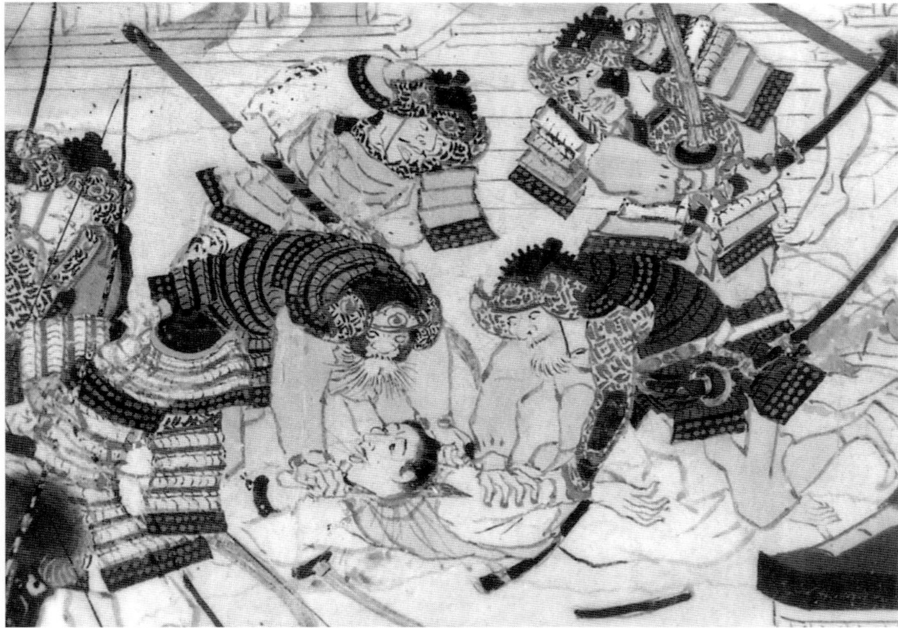

FIGURE 3.2. *Night Attack on the Sanjō Palace,* detail: a man being beheaded.

symbolize the violence of the soldiers and the fierceness of the battle. Similarly, a battle scroll is not complete without its image of women scattering as they flee in panic from the scene of the battle. The women of the court in each of the buildings of the Sanjō Palace compound, for example, the women fleeing into the garden from the interior of the building (Figure 3.4) or the barefoot women who have run outside the gate (Figure 3.5), are figural types, like those of the men being dispatched, and are frequently seen in later battle handscrolls.

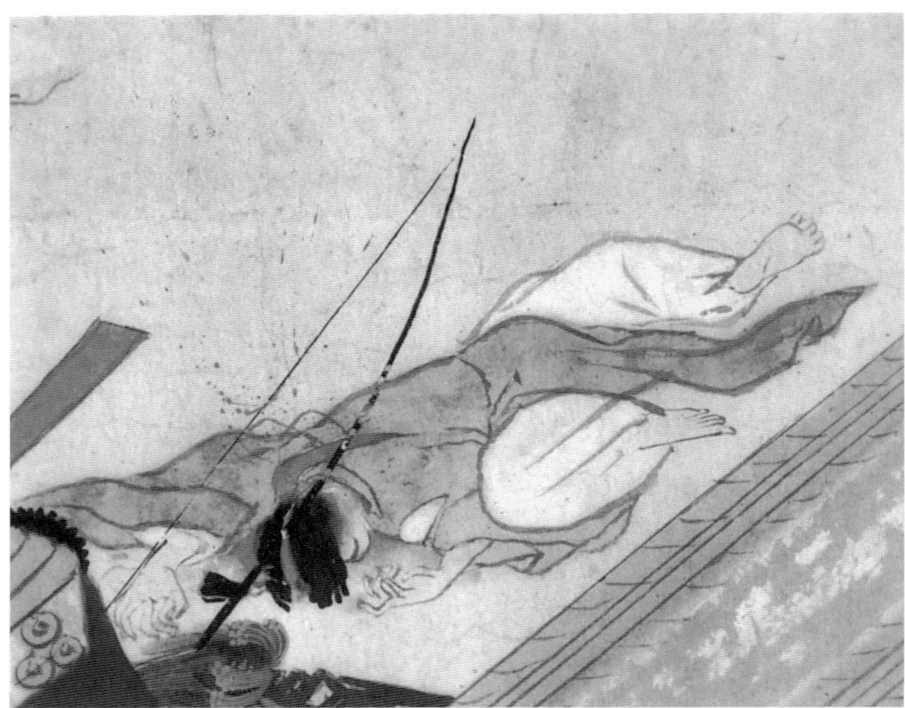

**FIGURE 3.3.** *Night Attack on the Sanjō Palace,* detail: a man collapsed next to the palace wall.

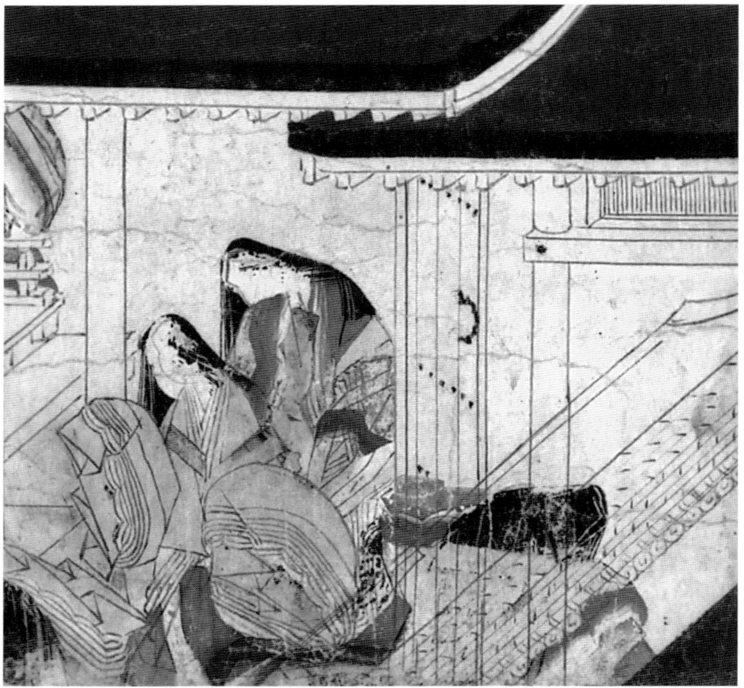

**FIGURE 3.4.** *Night Attack on the Sanjō Palace,* detail: women fleeing into the garden.

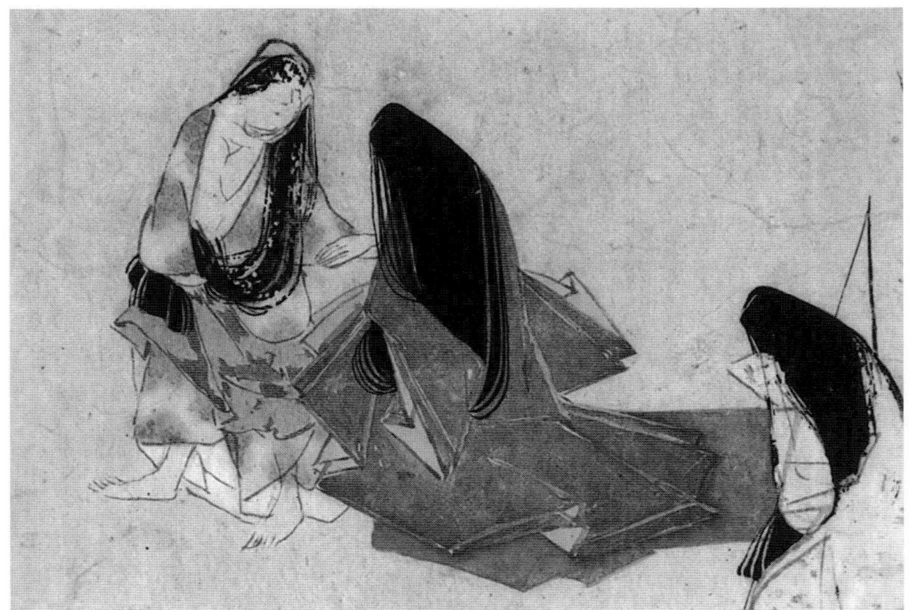

FIGURE 3.5. *Night Attack on the Sanjō Palace,* detail: women fleeing outside the palace gate.

And yet, the number of court women depicted in this scene is quite high. While three male victims are shown, twenty women are depicted. And the figures who seem to have fallen one on top of the other into the well in the garden or those who have died beneath the falling pillars of the burning palace (Figure 3.6) are figural images whose type cannot be found in other scrolls. Whoever views this scene, of bare legs peeking out between disarrayed hems, bared breasts, and stacks of collapsed women is struck by the forms of these wretched women. I believe that there is a reason for the depiction of this large number of court women as victims. First, I would like to consider the special characteristics of this painting through a comparison of the pictorial image, its accompanying text, and the texts of other versions of the tale.

The text accompanying this handscroll reads in part: "In the palace, the soldiers attacked from the four directions, setting fires, slaughtering those who fled, and cutting them down. Those who thought to save themselves fell in great numbers into the well. The upper- and lower-rank ladies-in-waiting and the girls of the apartments all cried out as they ran and fell. They were trampled by horses; they were trampled by people." It indicates that all the people within the Sanjō Palace were victims of the violence and that a number of these people fell into the well in their attempt to escape the fires. The only specific part of the text that refers to the female victims is "all cried out as they ran and fell."

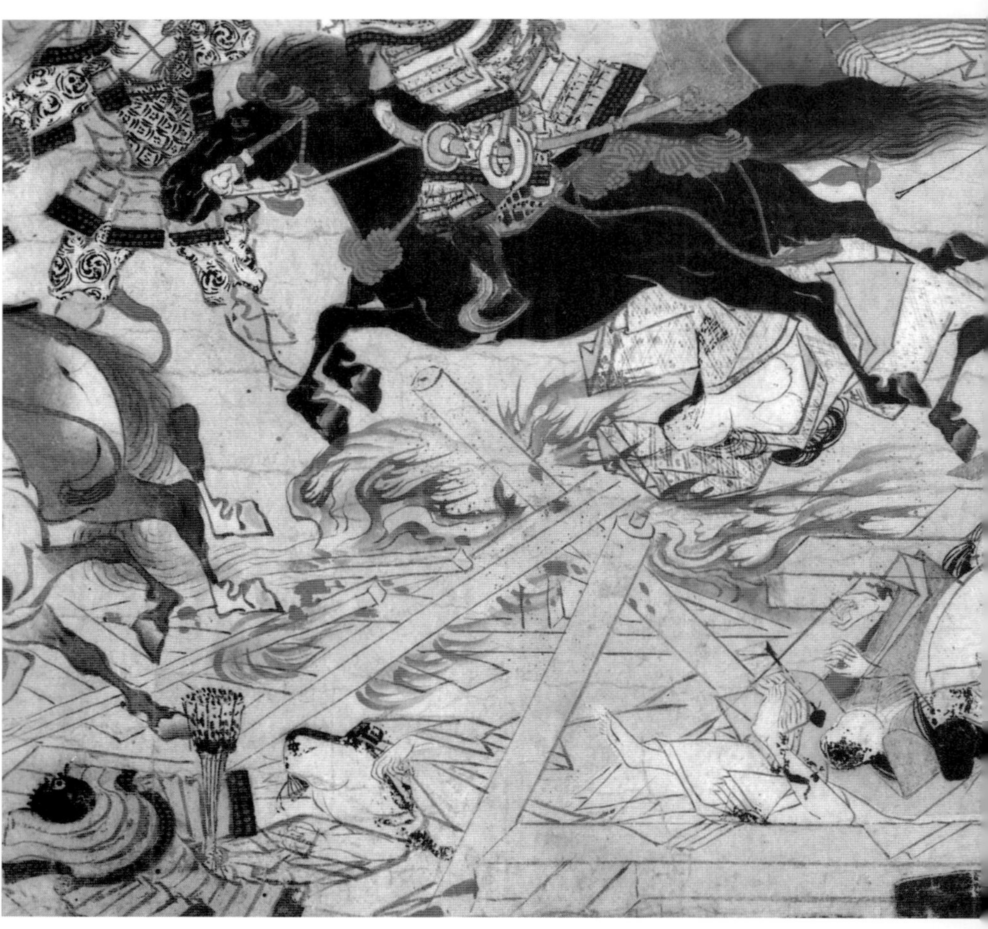

FIGURE 3.6. *Night Attack on the Sanjō Palace,* detail: women falling into a well and dying beneath the falling pillars of the burning palace.

Of the many and complicated textual lineages of *The Tales of the Heiji Era*, the so-called *kotaibon-kei*, or "old version" textual line, has long been recognized to have significant similarities to the *Heiji Illustrated Scrolls* text. Included in this lineage is the Yōmei Bunko-bon.[4] This version notes that members of the high aristocracy were among those who lost their lives in the battle: "Court nobles, high-ranking courtiers, the palace ladies-in-waiting . . . all were shot with arrows or cut down with swords." Further, in the same text: "Harried by arrows, distressed by the fire, they jumped into the well. Those below were not helped by the water, those above were buried in the layers and layers of ash and half-burnt pillars—none was saved." Thus the motifs in the painting and the related passages in the Yōmei Bunko-bon version are in agreement on the matters of the well and the burning, collapsing buildings. However, as in the case of the text ac-

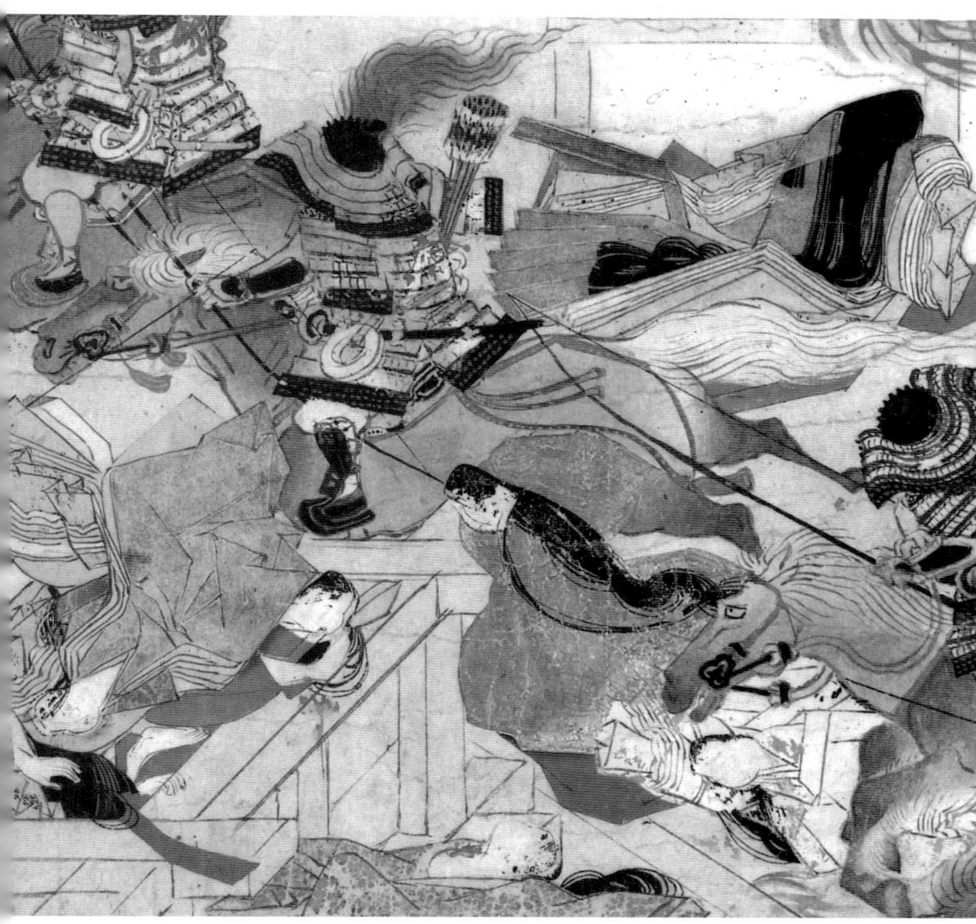

companying the handscroll, these written versions do not limit their discussion to only the female victims. And yet, the painting shows only ladies of the court losing their lives in the well or prostrate under the fallen and burning pillars.

In other words, a comparison of the text accompanying the handscroll as well as that of the Yōmei Bunko-bon with the scene depicted in the handscroll clearly reveals the handscroll painting's emphasis on women as victims.[5] In the past it has been thought that the scenes in a handscroll painting were simply pictorializations of the accompanying text, and there have been attempts to analyze the relationship between the two elements. There is indeed a close relationship between the text and the painting, and the text, like the painting, was edited in accordance with the desires of the commissioner of the work. Yet it is normal that discrepancies would arise between the two versions, as seen here. There are also instances where the image is conceived from and quotes from a different context than that of the accompanying text. One cannot overlook the fact that the image itself opens memory circuits and transmits messages, separate from the written text.

Further, it goes without saying that the battle scene depicted in the handscroll is not a direct reflection of the historical incident known as the Night Attack on the Sanjō Palace. The painting was created a considerable amount of time after the event and is a fabrication constructed from selected motifs that a particular person or persons wanted to see or wanted to show. In other words, the painting is a single discursive statement based on a visual reconstruction. What is noteworthy is that in this scene the painter focuses on the ladies of the court in his depiction of the victims of the Sanjō Palace battle.

## "Sexually" Imprinted Female Bodies

I now turn to the depiction of the "bodies" of the women in the scene of *Night Attack on the Sanjō Palace*. A number of the women are depicted lying down with their breasts exposed. Some are seen with just one breast visible, others are shown with two full breasts naked, and in both instances, the outlines have been clearly drawn on their white skin. These outlines are specific enough to indicate the protuberance of their nipples (Figure 3.7). Even when covered with clothing,

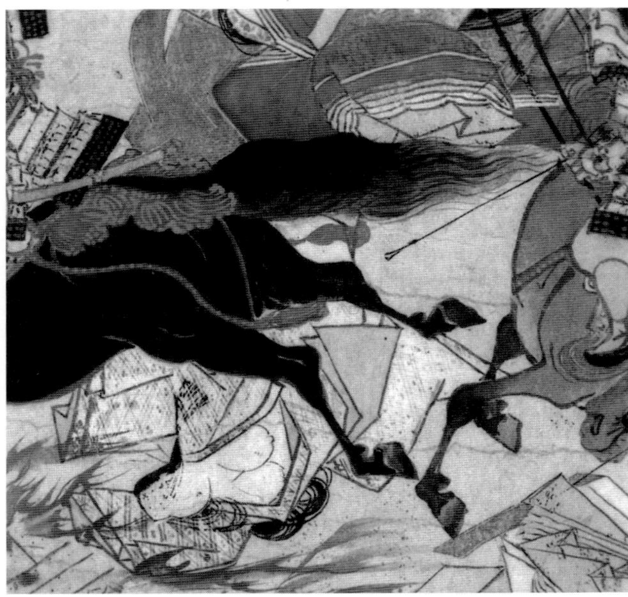

FIGURE 3.7. *(Left) Night Attack on the Sanjō Palace,* detail: a woman with her breasts exposed and nipples delineated.

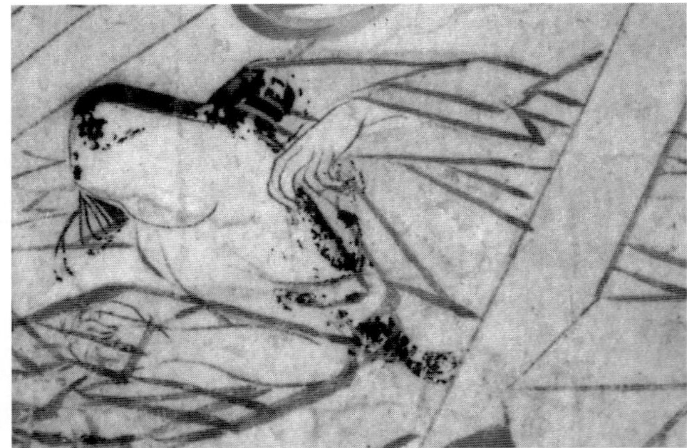

FIGURE 3.8. *(Right) Night Attack on the Sanjō Palace,* detail: a woman with her breasts partly shown.

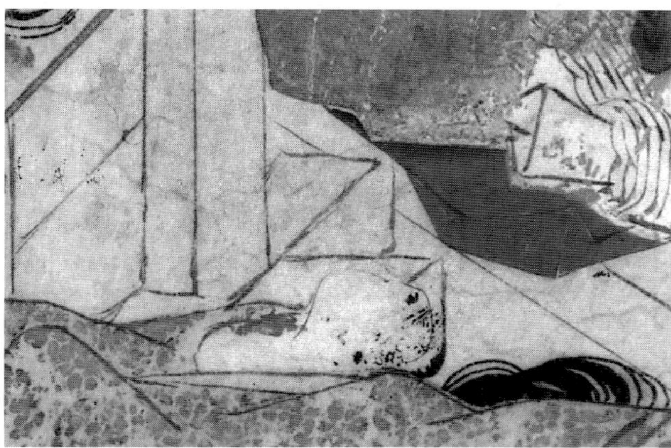

FIGURE 3.9. *Night Attack on the Sanjō Palace,* detail: another woman with her breasts partly shown.

some of the women are nonetheless shown with the swelling of their breasts clearly visible (Figures 3.8–3.9). We cannot overlook the fact that the women's bodies are shown in this manner, imprinted with the "sexual" characteristic of full breasts. Further, the women are shown lying down, wounded, and unable to resist attack. Might we not suggest that these female bodies, with the emphasis placed on their sexuality, are a form of pornography conveying sexual pleasure to male viewers? Further, the sexualized bodies of these women are shown violated by the rough barbarity of the Other—the warriors—in images not unlike those of rape. In other words, here the depiction of the sexualized bodies of women has been used in two contexts. First, the bodies provide sexual pleasure to their male viewers; second, they emphasize the impression of the Other, the barbarity of the warriors.[6]

Let us reconsider the context in which these female images were created. The "sexually" imprinted female body is not limited to battle paintings. Kasuya Makoto has shown that it was also depicted in such Buddhist didactic paintings as the *Picture of the Realm of Human Existence (Nindō fujōsō-zu)* in the Shōjū Raigōji Temple version of the *Six Realms of Rebirth* paintings *(rokudō-e)*.[7] As Kasuya indicates, female corpses were depicted as erotic images in accord with the desiring male gaze. In battle picture scrolls, as in Buddhist paintings, female bodies were depicted with their "sexuality" bared and emphasized. Images of full breasts shown in such detail that their nipples are visible, a white breast seen peeking out from luxurious clothing that has slipped from a single shoulder, upper bodies framed in flowing black hair—the images in both types of works share these formal characteristics, although the works differ in terms of subject and compositional format.

Further, the "female body" is seen in partial sections—whether the black hair or white breasts mentioned above, or the glimpse of a leg peeking out from disarrayed hems—and we can imagine that this too has been done to create an object of sexual pleasure for the gaze of the male viewer. The women depicted as victims in this manner were thus represented for the gaze of a commissioner or viewer of the work who viewed women as an objectified Other. A similar representational strategy of sexualized "female bodies" is found in literary texts. Hitomi Tonomura has noted her discovery of "the description of the dismembered female body" in the *Konjaku monogatari shū* (Tales of times now past) (late Heian period). We can apply Tonomura's discovery of "a discourse-wide shift of the female body from that of unified subject to fragmentary object" to the images of the women in *Night Attack on the Sanjō Palace* (albeit here they are generally represented as full bodies but dissected by their clothing).[8]

Next, let us reconfirm that the women of *Night Attack on the Sanjō Palace* were used to imprint visually and emphasize the barbarity of the warriors. An examination of the painting technique used in the features of the women being trampled reveals that they were drawn in the *tsukuri-e* technique of coloring in ink-limned drawings. This technique involves first drawing in an underlayer of ink lines, which are then covered with a thick layer of white pigment. Finally, the eyes and nose are redrawn on top of the white layer. In the handscroll's present state, the majority of the women's faces have had their white layer flake away, and thus these faces reveal part of the underdrawn ink lines. These facial features are drawn in the *hiki-me kagi-bana,* or "slit eye, hook nose," technique and can be said to express no individual characteristics. The fact that women's faces do not express any emotion might also be considered an effective way of turning the viewer's appreciation to their "sexualized bodies." I would also like to draw attention to the women's summary expressions, which contrast with the coarse expression of the warriors, further emphasizing the latter. Examination reveals that the features of the warriors were not created in the *tsukuri-e* method. The warriors and commoners shown in this handscroll, and indeed the lower- and middle-ranked courtiers as well, are depicted with a thin wash of color on top of which the lines of the eyes and noses have been drawn directly.[9] Further, in this handscroll the warriors' faces, even more so than the commoners', are shown with thick lips and big noses and eyes, further emphasizing them as barbarian or vulgar.

## Female Bodies and the Elimination of "Class" Differentiation

In the pictorial handscroll tradition during Japan's ancient and medieval periods, there was a practice of visually differentiating the class affiliation of the human figures. During the Heian period the aristocratic class, who ordered and appreciated these paintings, insisted on the conventions of the facial depiction technique known as *hiki-me kagi-bana* as a method of concealing the individuality of members of their own class. Conversely, the exaggeration of the eyes and noses of commoners and warriors intentionally represented their vulgarity. For example, the *Picture Scroll of the Story of Ban Dainagon (Ban Dainagon emaki)* is a representative example of the narrative tale handscrolls created around the retired emperor Go-Shirakawa during the latter half of the twelfth century. In this work, the faces of the police *(hōmen)* (Figure 3.10) have been depicted with a caricature-like sense of the grotesque, expressing their position under the cool, condescending gaze of the aristocracy. This depiction is in line with that of the warriors in the *Tales of the Heiji Era* scroll (Figure 3.2). The wife of the imperial archives menial *(shutsunō)* in the *Ban Dainagon* scroll (Figure 3.11) is shown with thin, wavy hair pulled back from her ears, bushy eyebrows, dotted pupils, and a small nose, thus conscientiously breaking every one of the conventions for the depiction of an aristocratic woman. In the genre pictures of the Heian period, both men and women of the nonaristocratic classes were depicted with complete thoroughness, thus setting them apart as Other. In the representative example of imperial court narrative painting scrolls, the *Genji monogatari* scrolls (twelfth century), such lower-class individuals as servants, and particularly older people, were depicted with extremely prominent cheek bones and protruding noses, and were thus differentiated through exaggeration. Conversely, among upper-class men and women, not just in regard to their "slit-eye and hook-nose" faces, but also in their postures and the perspective from which they are viewed, there is very little gender differentiation, and the gaze that interpellates them is largely symmetrical.[10]

In various works of the Kamakura period, however, we can discern a move toward an asymmetrical relationship between the gaze turned on men and that turned on women. I have discussed this issue in detail elsewhere.[11] In the male images shown in the *Illustrated Scrolls of the Tales of the Heiji Era,* there is a conscious differentiation of facial depiction, reflecting differences in class and position that follow the tradition established in the Heian period. Conversely, in the same handscroll, only the images of women reflect a common emphasis on the

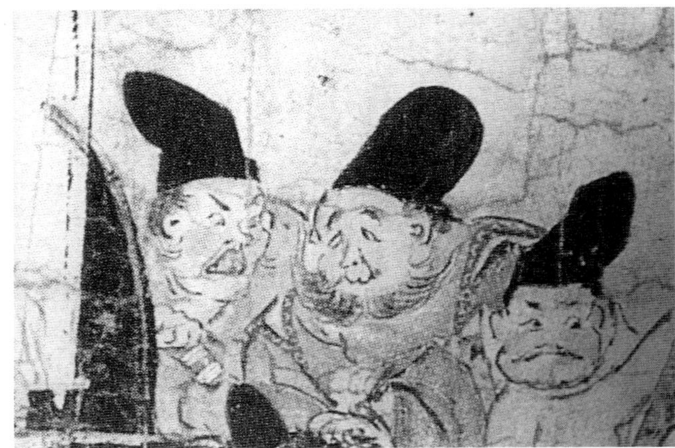

FIGURE 3.10. *Picture Scroll of the Story of Ban Dainagon (Ban Dainagon emaki),* detail: the faces of the police *(hōmen).* Idemitsu Art Gallery, Tokyo.

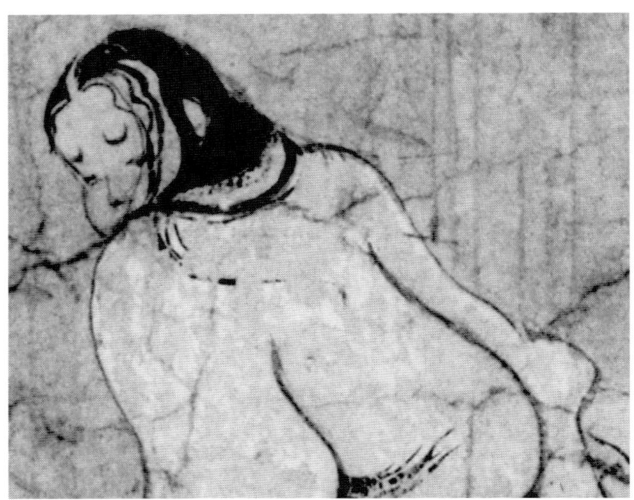

FIGURE 3.11. *Picture Scroll of the Story of Ban Dainagon,* detail: the wife of the imperial archives menial *(shutsunō).* Idemitsu Art Gallery, Tokyo.

special parts of the sexually imprinted female body (namely, the breasts and black hair discussed above), and there is a trend toward erasing all individual differentiation. A close examination of the women who are the victims of the attack will reveal that, in keeping with convention, even though we call them all "the ladies of the palace of the retired emperor," there is a mixture of those dressed in the multilayered clothing of the upper ranks and those of the lower ranks wearing *ko-uchigi.* And yet the emphasis is not placed on these class differences; rather, it rests on the depiction of the sexualized female body. The female has been limited to the body, with her status and position nullified; in sum, the female has been forcibly made "sexual."

## The Commissioner of the Handscroll

Let me summarize the depiction of men in the battle scene at Sanjō Palace. First, upper-rank male aristocrats have been removed from the ranks of the wounded or dead in the scroll's battle scene. Second, the special characteristics of the faces of the warriors emphasize their barbarity. I believe that these two aspects are intimately related to the position of the commissioner or viewer of the handscroll.

Although I have already published my views on this issue,[12] I would like to touch on them here. To state my conclusion first, the images of warriors depicted in this work were represented in accordance with the gaze of the upper ranks of the aristocracy, including the emperor, of the mid–thirteenth century and thus portrayed as existing only to serve the authority of the retired emperor and the aristocracy. The troop of men seen in the handscroll with their standardized, beautifully wrought armor—this superbly controlled corps of warriors—reappears throughout the scroll in a variety of formations, because they are a depiction of "those who serve" (the original meaning of the term "samurai") aristocratic society. The clustering of warriors as a troop in the middle of the composition can be considered a means of distancing the viewer from the actual existence of such warriors. Moreover, it seems that this manner of depiction is closely related to the gaze of someone who considers the warriors as something Other from himself. In the final analysis, in the gaze of the aristocracy, they are warriors-who-serve, and it is hard to find a sense of commonality between the implied point of view of the audience of this scroll and the warriors depicted in it. As previously noted, the facial expression of the warriors also indicates the gaze of the aristocracy looking down on the warriors, as if from another world. The images of warriors depicted here reflect the aristocracy's view of warriors, and they are thus warriors formed by the gaze of these aristocrats. I believe that this handscroll was an attempt to control visually the battle and the warriors who brought it about. The military class usurped political power in the thirteenth century, and their political strength was growing during this period. The aristocracy was thus wary of the growing influence of this military class. Consequently, what is depicted in the handscroll is not the warriors themselves but rather an ideal form of warrior that reflects the desires of the aristocracy.

If the commissioner of the handscroll was an upper-rank male aristocrat, we can propose that he would emphatically oppose any representation of himself as a victim of battle or even as mixed up in its confusion. There are only three men depicted among the casualties of the Sanjō forces, and they are not the uppermost "court nobles [and] high-ranking courtiers" mentioned in the Yōmei Bunko-bon text. Rather they are lower-class courtiers dressed in hunting robes *(kariginu)* and shown with high cheekbones and "lower-class" eyes and noses.

Thus, returning to the group of court ladies depicted as the victims in the *Night Attack on the Sanjō Palace* scroll, their sexualized bodies were undoubtedly seen and enjoyed by the viewers of this handscroll from two angles: first, they provided sexual pleasure for the men who viewed them; second, they helped emphasize the barbarity and Otherness of the warriors. In other words, they represent the entwining of two different power relationships: one is the gender relationship between male and female; the other is the class relationship between aristocrat and warrior. In this scene, the warriors' atrocity is visited without mercy on the bodies of the women. That image shows the construction of power by means of the gaze of the commissioner of the work, who stands outside of the work and its predations.

## Conclusion

The sexualized bodies of the women portrayed in the *Illustrated Scrolls of the Tales of the Heiji Era,* separate from the context of the narrative that takes as its subject the historical event known as the Heiji Disturbance, were, I have argued, provided for the viewing pleasure of the intended audience of the scrolls. The commissioner of the *Night Attack on the Sanjō Palace* handscroll has skillfully removed himself from the battle, locating himself in a safe place, to gaze upon the women and the warriors from afar and above. A careful analysis of the composition and expression of the figures represented and displayed in the scene reveals the commissioner's and the viewer's gaze on the Other.

Even today, from which perspective we view this handscroll, "women" are depicted and discussed in all manner of discourses. When faced with movies, photographs, images, and other such visual media, we must repeatedly seize the opportunity to pose the questions: "Who does this woman turn toward? Why is this woman shown naked?" And while the majority of Japanese alive today have never directly experienced war, through visual imagery war has become something that they too view as if from afar and on high. In the same manner as the battle scrolls created in the Kamakura period, the images we create today are mirrors reflecting our gaze on the Other, a gaze that lies within our hearts.

CHAPTER FOUR

JOSHUA S. MOSTOW

# The Gender of *Wakashu* and the Grammar of Desire

Over the last decade *shunga* (literally, "spring pictures"), which might be translated as "premodern Japanese pornography," has been promoted by certain Japanese scholars as an essential component of a transhistorical Japanese cultural identity.[1] Roughly the same period has seen the increasing acceptance of male homosexuality in Japanese media.[2] These two trends find a point of contact in the discussions of premodern Japanese "homosexuality," a discussion that involves scholars both in Japan and outside it, publishing in both Japanese and English. There are many groups with differing agendas involved in this discussion. Yet all approach the topic of Tokugawa-period gender and sexuality through the framework of modern, "Western" sexuality.

One of the first problems with the contemporary presentation of Tokugawa-period *nanshoku* (literally, "man-color," that is, sexual passion for males) is its translation as "homosexuality." This problem is not unique to the Japanese context and has even been discussed in terms of nineteenth-century England. Eve Kosofsky Sedgwick, for example, criticizes those who would read Oscar Wilde's pederasty as twentieth-century homosexuality: whereas the latter stresses "sameness" (homo)—same sex, same age, same power—Wilde, like most of his nineteenth-century countrymen, envisioned male same-sex relations as basically asymmetrical and between an older man and a younger man.[3]

This criticism was voiced by many reviewers of Stephen D. Miller's *Partings at Dawn: An Anthology of Japanese Gay Literature*, which included writing from the twelfth through twentieth centuries.[4] The same weakness vitiates the self-proclaimed "first" history of Tokugawa "homosexuality," Gary Leupp's *Male Colors: The Construction of Homosexuality in Tokugawa Japan*.[5]

## Gender/Sexuality Systems

I start with what might be called a late-twentieth-century, North American, white, liberal, bourgeois and heterocentric, pre-Foucauldian Creed of the trinity of sex, gender, and sexuality:

> We believe in two biological sexes, male and female. We may also recognize a biological third sex, such as hermaphroditic. We believe gender is socially constructed but nonetheless imagine only two possibilities, masculine and feminine, by which all sexualities are made. We believe in three possible sexualities, which proceedeth from sexual difference and gender, and which are understood to be innate: heterosexual, homosexual, and bisexual. People *are* one or the other. We believe that the most correct sexual relationships are equitable, that is, between individuals of roughly the same age and socioeconomic power. In fact, we criminalize what are labeled as pedophilia, and statutory rape, on one hand, and any sexual relationship based on power imbalance—labeled prostitution and sexual harassment—on the other. We believe that all relationships, regardless of sexual orientation, should be monogamous (and "forever and ever, amen").

Here, I would like to consider gender along more or less grammatical lines, that is, in terms of rules of combination. The *American Heritage Dictionary* defines gender as "a set of two or more categories, such as masculine, feminine, and neuter, into which words are divided according to sex, animation, psychological associations, or some other characteristics, and *that determine agreement with or selection of modifiers,* referents, or grammatical forms" (emphasis added).[6] The *Shōgakukan Random House English-Japanese Dictionary* makes things even clearer for my purposes: "[Grammar] *Sei:* Chiefly, the classificatory pattern of nouns as seen in their inflection, *it has no relation with biological sei (sex);* the number differs, based on each language, but there are many that have the three of masculine, feminine, and neuter, or the two of masculine and feminine" (emphasis added).[7] In other words, put very loosely, I want to consider gender in terms of the rules for object choice—who can select whom, who "agrees" with whom, or, bluntly (if agrammatically), who can conjugate with whom. In Japanese, grammatical agreement is called *"koō,"* which suggests a kind of Althusserian "interpellation," which is precisely my interest here. Such an approach is basically in line with those developed from the work of the feminist anthropologist Gayle Rubin,[8] such as the approach of Julia Epstein and Kristina Straub, who define sex/gender systems as "historically and culturally specific arrogations of the human body for ideological purposes. In sex/gender systems, physiology, anatomy, and body codes (clothing, cosmetics, behaviors, miens, affective and object choices) are taken over by institutions that use bodily difference to define and coerce gender identity."[9] Needless to say, historically the most common purpose of such definition and coercion is social control by male elites.

The "common-sense" credo above would indicate a paradigm something like that shown in Chart 1. The solid lines between arrowheads indicate the relationships most sanctioned by society, while dotted lines indicate those relationships understood to be possible, but to which some stigma adheres, with dashes indicating some stigma and dots even more. Thus, we look more positively on relationships where the partners are of similar age than those between youths and adults. This is not symmetrical, and our society presently looks upon relations between an older man and a younger woman with less comment than those between an older woman and a younger man. We are also more tolerant, I believe, of same-sex relations between relative equals than such relations where there is a large age difference. In fact, over-large discrepancies in power tend to be labeled presently as "sexual harassment," while too-large age differences are associated with pedophilia. To be complete the diagram should also include bisexuals of both genders and age levels. Regardless, this diagram, with its strong horizontal arrows, shows that our "common-sense" ideas stress the "homo" aspects of these relationships—the *sameness* of age and power; that is, like some latter-day gay readers of Wilde, we put a premium on the "sameness" of sex partners, their "equality," and attempt to deny or suppress the erotic attraction inherent in unequal power relations.

**CHART 1.** The "Common-Sense" Gender/Sexuality System

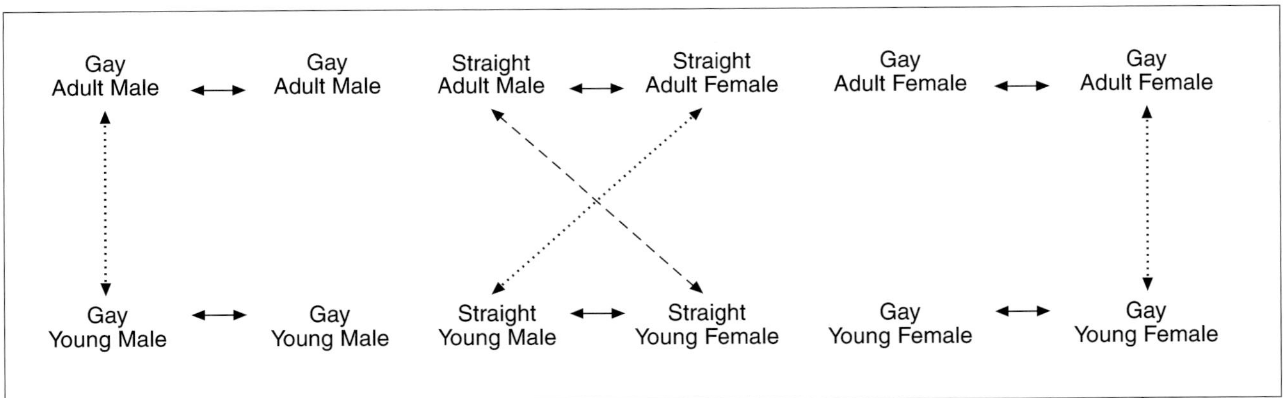

CHART 2. Seventeenth-Century Japanese Gender/Sexuality System

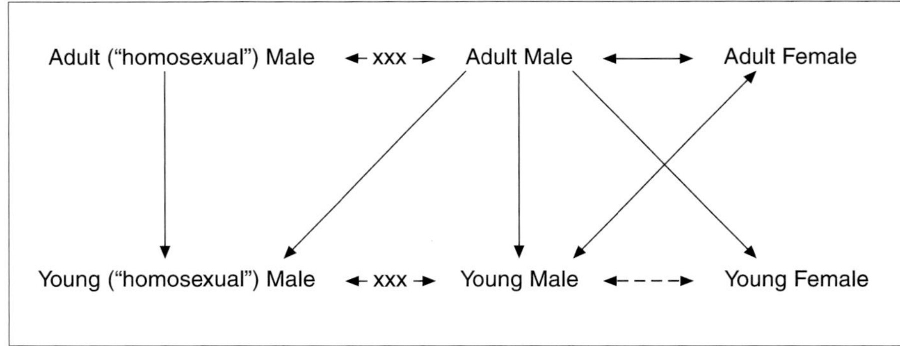


The gender/sexuality paradigm in early-seventeenth-century Edo, however, was very different, as I shall attempt to demonstrate. To give my conclusions first, I present the paradigm in Chart 2. Note that equitable relationships in the homosexual realm are largely absent; moreover the linchpin of the whole system is the structural denial of the possibility of female homoeroticism. Desire, too, is much less bilateral than in Chart 1, with a clearer distinction between the desiring subject and the object of desire (as indicated by the direction of the arrowheads). Finally, note that there is little need to identify individuals as "homosexual" or "heterosexual/bisexual"—only "pansexual" males (though, in fact, proscribed from other adult men and children of either sex), exclusively homosexual males, and exclusively heterosexual females are understood to exist.

### *The Perfumed Pillow of Youngman-Play*

I offer Chart 2 only provisionally; I want to extrapolate the gender/sexuality system that seems to underlie one specific text. The *Wakashu-asobi kyara no makura*, or *Aloeswood Incense Pillow of Youngman-Play*, is an anonymous "picture-book" *(ehon)* of twenty-four pages, in the *ōhon* format. It was published in Edo in Enpō 3 (1675) by Urokogataya, and its pictures are firmly attributed to the early *ukiyo-e* artist Hishikawa Moronobu.[10] The date of publication puts the appearance of this work one year before the completion of *Iwatsutsuji*, a collection of homoerotically interpreted poetry compiled by Kitamura Kigin in Kyoto;[11] three years before Fujimoto Kizan's *Shikidō ōkagami* (Great mirror of the way of eros);[12] and a full twelve years before Ihara Saikaku's *Nanshoku ōkagami*.[13] Only one copy seems to remain in existence, a rare survivor from the Tenna fire of 1682. In fact, this book may be the earliest extant example of homoerotic *ukiyo-e.* Moreover, the *Wakashu-asobi* provides an important example of a self-proclaimed early *shudō* text, which has recently been translated as "homosexual."

The first sentence of the preface seems to announce that the book is designed for followers of the "Way of Youngmen," or *shudō:* "Like the saké lover when he sees the announcement of the new year's vintage, when the man who has a taste for youngmen sees some forelock, his heart is stirred." An imaginary lineage of this Way from India and China is described in lines that will be echoed at the close of Saikaku's *Nanshoku ōkagami:* "In India it is called 'the Way of the Child' *(jidō);* in China it has been named . . . 'the flower of the rear garden' *(kōteika).* In our country, it is said that Kōbō Daishi of Kōya, from Kishū, promoted this Way in order to establish pure monks and deigned to call it 'the Way of Youths' (*shudō*)." The term *"wakashu,"* the author relates, is generally defined as a male from the ages of eleven to twenty-two or twenty-three (in Japanese count). Yet he goes on to note that at Kōya there are *wakashu* sixty years old and at Nachi there are *wakashu* as old as eighty. The definition of *wakashu,* he says, does not rely on age.[14] For his own part, the author defines it as a "love" or "attachment" *(renbo)* that he describes in hyperbolic terms:

> When the feelings are deep, and no distinction is made between rich and poor, and one treasures loyalty and has a tender heart; when one draws blood from one's arm [to seal a pledge], pierces one's thighs, rips off one's nails, is branded by an iron, goes against the will of one's master, is disowned by one's parents, one makes one's way through distant fields, spreads the dew on a grass pillow for oneself alone, makes a pillow of the rocks in the rugged mountains, and a mattress of moss—one is bitter against the morning bird and resents the ringing of the dawn bell—this is surely true love *(shinjitsu no renbo).*

*Shudō,* then, would seem to be defined by the degree—the absoluteness—of its practitioners' affections, rather than by the age or gender of their significant others. As such, a relationship with a *wakashu* is declared to be more intimate than that between parent and child, or between brothers; and the author explains that the practice of following one's master in death (*oi-bara*) "also had its beginnings in this Way." He concludes his preface in the guise of a proselytizing tract, with the words (no doubt a pun): "All should enter here, enter here!" *(moppara kono mon ni iri-tamafubeshi, iri-tamafubeshi).* Is this really a missionary tract, or is the author "preaching to the converted"—and, if the latter, is their faith really a kind of sexual monotheism, that is, exclusively "homosexual," or *onna-girai* ("women-hating"), and, if so, in what sense?

The devotion supposedly distinctive to this Way is demonstrated in the first scene of the picture-book (Figure 4.1). Surprisingly, the first exemplar is not from the warrior class, as is seen in the *The Great Mirror of Male Love*,[15] but is rather a *yarō*, or male prostitute:

> Although everyone says that there is nothing as flighty *(midzu-kusaki)* as a male actor, that is not so. Even among those such as pages *(koshō),* who polish the Way of Youngmen, many have not truly realized sincerity. A certain man *(aru mono)* had a relationship *(nengoro)* with a male entertainer and, finding him especially lovable, was visited by him in deepest secrecy so that no one knew. The years passed, and their relationship continued. Truly this was a laudable sincerity on the entertainer's part.

The tone here seems to be tongue-in-cheek, indeed, almost sarcastic, as seen, for instance, in the honorifics applied to the *yarō* (*kayohareshi*, an honorific passive). The overly polite phraseology matches the hyperbole of the introduction. Yet, the lauded virtue of this Way seems to be largely undercut by the very next scene (Figure 4.2), which presents a man with two *wakashu*. In other words, the "devotion" of the Way of Youngmen seems to be unilateral, that is, the *wakashu* should be devoted, but the man (*mono*, perhaps best understood as "subject") need not be.

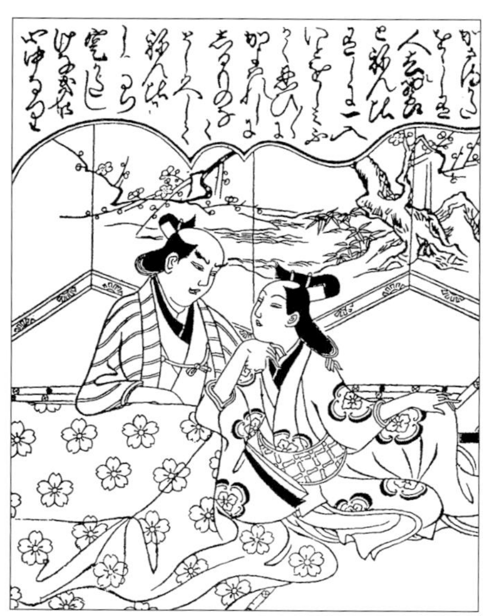

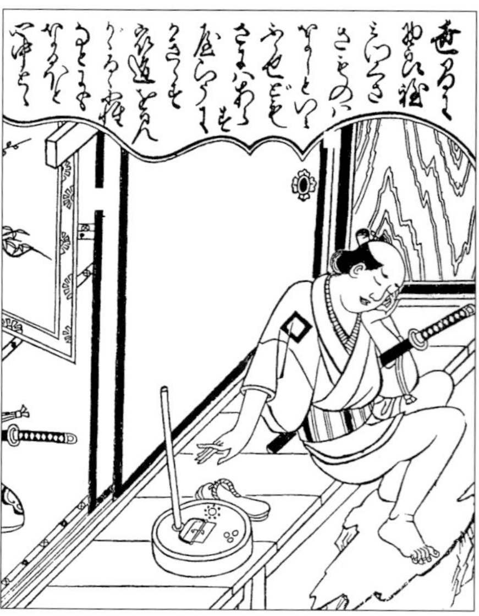

**FIGURE 4.1.** *Wakashu-asobi kyara no makura* (Aloeswood incense pillow of youngman-play), scene 1, illustrations attributed to Hishikawa Moronobu. Anonymous *ehon*, 24 pages, *ōhon* format. Edo: Urokogataya, Enpō 3 (1675). At the International Research Center for Japanese Studies Library.

Yet, this scene of a man's divided affections is immediately followed by betrayal clearly condemned (Figure 4.3):

> A certain insincere man *(fushinjū naru mono)* had a relationship with a certain youngman. Although the man's devotion was weak, the youngman could not, it seems, bring himself to end the affair, and things continued this way, until one time, he suddenly visited, and when he looked, the man was doing it with another youngman. The first youngman sat on the veranda, and when he listened, they sounded like they were having intercourse. He thought again and again that he need not verify it. Truly, with that kind of man, one gets angry with even the chance encounter of an evening. You should make a close inspection when having an affair.

The exhortatory phrasing of the text might even be understood to be addressed to *wakashu*, rather than men. Yet the picture is presumably designed for the viewer's pleasure rather than for condemnation. The phrasing also suggests that if the man were not insincere to begin with, the youngman might be able to overlook a one-night stand. Again, this kind of forbearance is clearly not reciprocal, as seen in the next scene (Figure 4.4):

> A certain man had an affair with a youngman, when one time he visited unexpectedly, and when he looked, the youngman was pledging his love to the

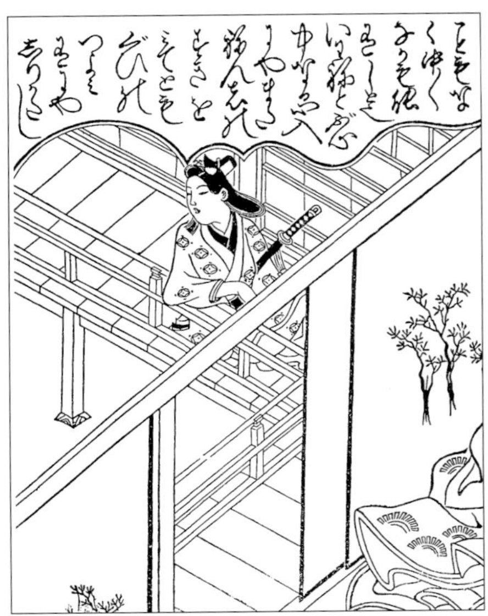

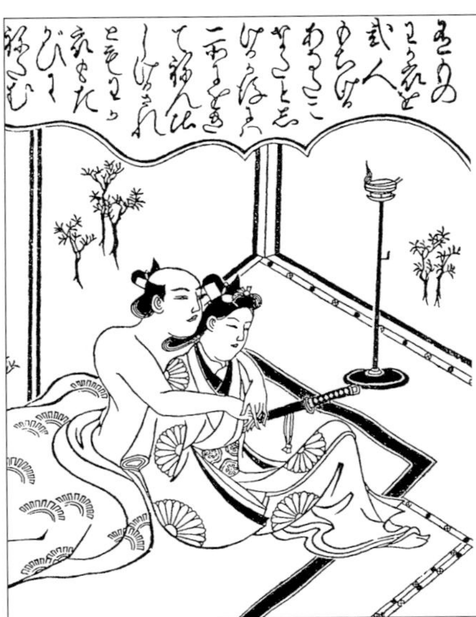

FIGURE 4.2. *Wakashu-asobi*, scene 2

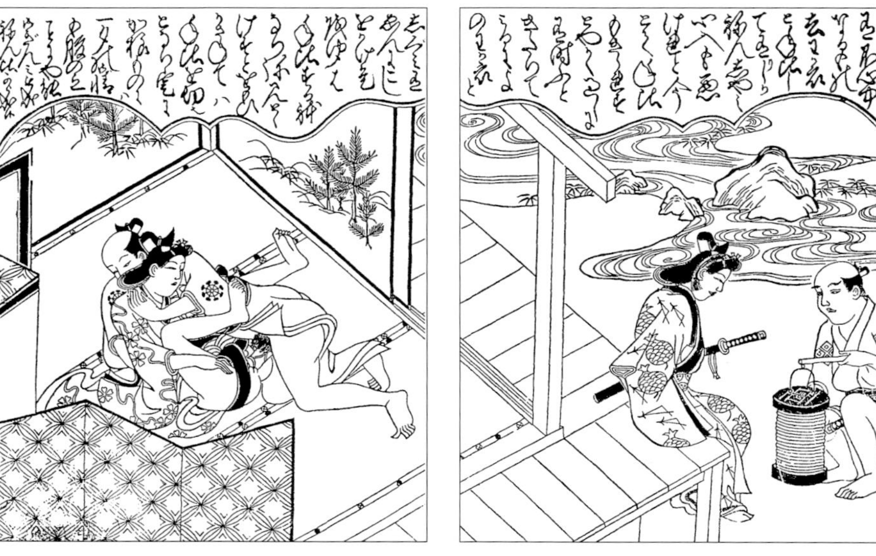

FIGURE 4.3. *Wakashu-asobi*, scene 3

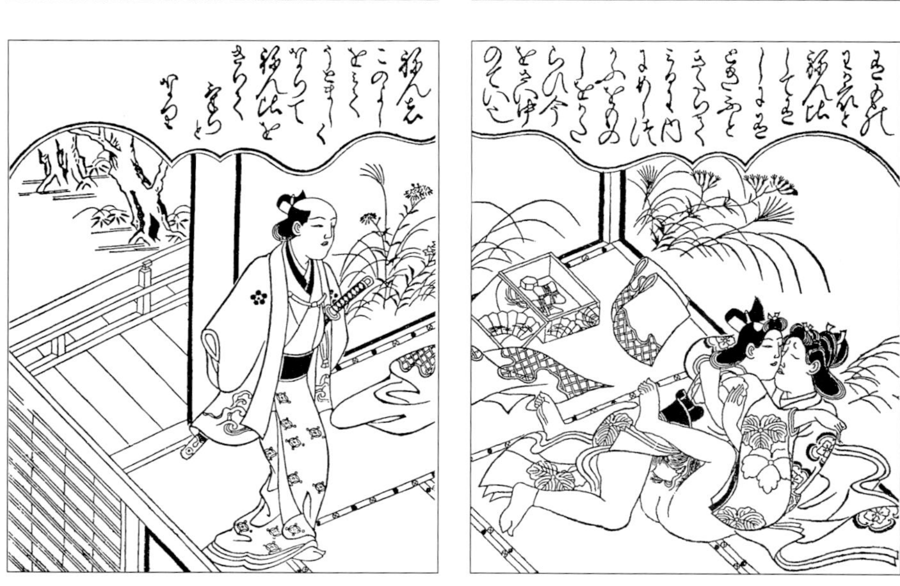

FIGURE 4.4. *Wakashu-asobi*, scene 4

> seamstress who served in the house, and they were in flagrante *(saichū no tei).* They say that when the lover *(nenja)* saw how it was, he became disgusted and severed the relationship.

Here the youngman is clearly the active one, or initiator, and the visual portrayal of the woman—with her shaved eyebrows and faced screwed up with pleasure —is far from flattering, in contrast to all the *wakashu* we have seen so far. In fact, no matter what happens to the *wakashu* in this text, no matter how forcefully or suddenly they are being taken, their faces register no emotion but maintain their almost "archaic smile." As I shall show later, the visual depiction of the seamstress is part of a general disparagement of older, married women.

Women are also active in the sixth scene, though this time neither they nor their relationship with the *wakashu* receive criticism, verbally or visually (Figure 4.5):

> When a group of ladies *(jōrō)*[16] from a certain mansion went to a certain temple, they stayed overnight together . . . there was no one else there but the pages. These ladies, thinking there must be something worth seeing in the temple's garden, had the pages guide them and accompany them here and there. After a little while, they emerged from the shadow of a hill, with their faces flushed and their hair disarrayed. What pleasant thing were they doing, I wonder?

As in the previous scene, *wakashu* are here engaged in heterosexual acts. Moreover, it is clearly the ladies who are presented as the active agents. What is most important about this example, however, especially when paired with the previous one, is that it presupposes that the reader will find this situation titillating. In other words, these episodes seem to be responding to some presumption of heterosexual desire in the reader, with the *wakashu* serving as the man's substitute (as we shall see more literally later).

Both young women and a *wakashu* are presented in scene 8 (Figure 4.6):

> A certain man had too much wealth: he employed many pages and concubines *(mekake),* and spent his time in various amusements. This is something about which it goes without saying: no one would find this unpleasant, however, it is the way of this floating world not to fulfill our desires, and all one can do is simply be envious *(urayamashi).*

Unlike the picture of the seamstress, here both the *wakashu* and the concubines are portrayed as attractive. The text's assumption is that all male readers would enjoy this situation—if only they could afford it. The virtue of deep feeling in general and the feelings of *wakashu* in particular seem to have been forgotten. This scene clearly portrays the presumed pansexual fantasies of the adult male reader, and it is in a sense paradigmatic of the libidinal structure of this work.

The text of the following scene, however, presents women as competitors for the affections of *wakashu* (in contrast to the seamstress episode, which concerns the fickleness of *wakashu*) (Figure 4.7):

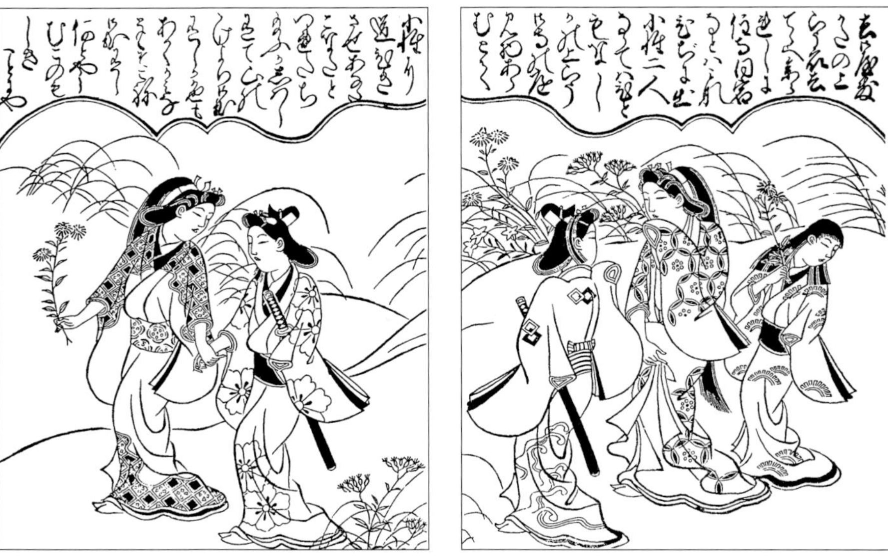

**FIGURE 4.5.** *Wakashu-asobi*, scene 6

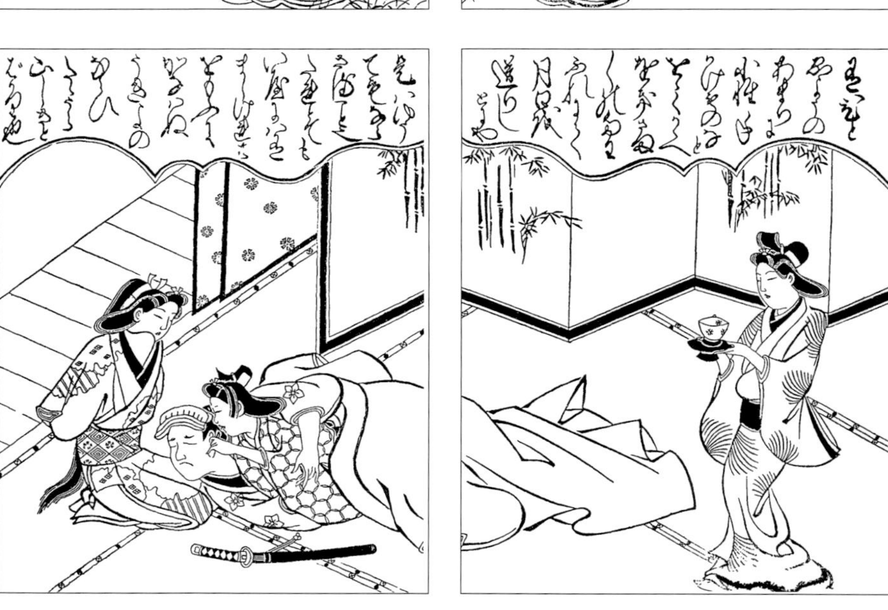

**FIGURE 4.6.** *Wakashu-asobi*, scene 8

A certain man constantly visited Yoshiwara. His youngman was jealous of this and went with him. A prostitute *(jōrō)* of the place fell in love with the page, and they talked about many things. His "older brother" ignored this, and the page started secretly visiting constantly. The prostitute, looking to come together with him, went out to the road leading to the teahouse and

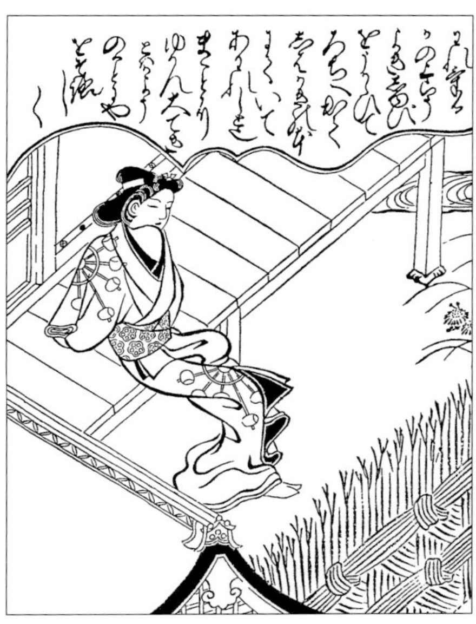

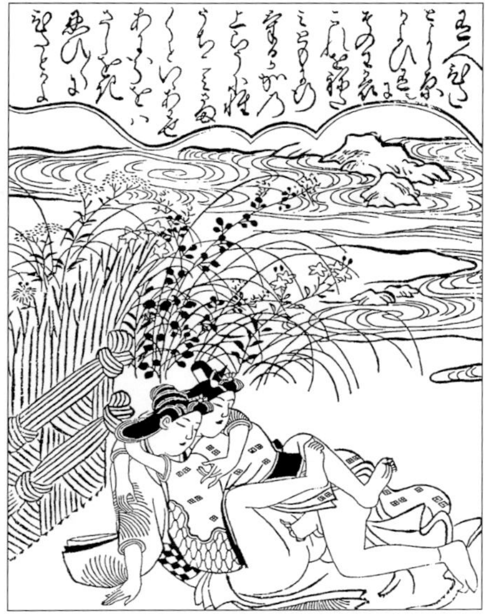

FIGURE 4.7. *Wakashu-asobi*, scene 9

> was met by the page behind a brushwood fence. Truly, the expression "inattention is the greatest enemy" refers to this kind of case. How dreadful!

Again, the text makes no presumption or condemnation of the older man visiting the Yoshiwara licensed district. And while the text seems straightforward in its condemnation of the prostitute's actions, again, the visual depiction is quite another matter: the women are clearly presented as desirable, and the fornicating couple is provided a poetic backdrop of autumn flowers such as bush clover and Chinese bellflowers. Indeed the depiction of their action is endearing, with the youngman clinging to the woman's more supportive posture. Nor does the youngman's posture provide a point of access for a male viewer who would "insert" himself into the action. Nonetheless, we must assume that the picture was meant to arouse the male viewer, despite the verbal text's condemnation. Since the "older brother" is not depicted, this picture serves as a direct contrast to the seamstress episode, and the youngman is presumably serving as the male reader's surrogate, possessing a desirable young woman.

Several other scenes present men and women as competitors for the affections of *wakashu*, calling the women "cunning enemies," as in the following (Figure 4.8):

> The honored son of a virtuous man and an amply affectionate *wakashu* of around the same age were always intimate with each other, but suddenly the

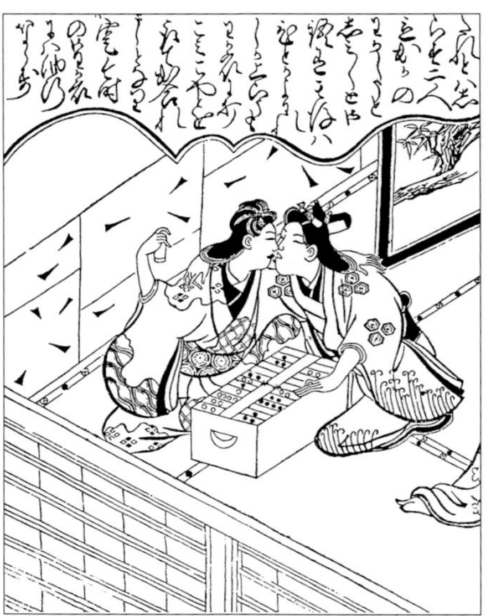
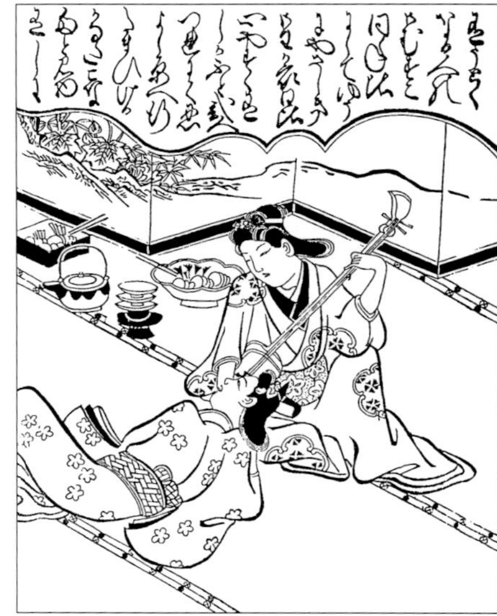

FIGURE 4.8. *Wakashu-asobi*, scene 14

> two went together secretly to Yoshiwara. They looked around here and there, when two people they did not know rushed out and had an intense conversation with the youngmen. After that, the day passed, and the ladies *(jōrō)* too fell deeply in love with the youngmen and took them out to a small lodge, where they came together. Truly, [such ladies] are cunning *(yudan narazu)* [opponents] for the esteemed *wakashu (on-wakashu)* of these times.[17]

In other words, the ladies compete with adult men for the affections of worthy *wakashu*. Nonetheless, the ladies in this scene are not depicted visually in a degrading fashion. Nor, however, is their "coming together" explicitly depicted.

The issue, not surprisingly, appears to be power and class. In fact, rather than using the term "woman" as I have been, I should make a distinction between "women" *(onna)* and "ladies" *(jōrō)*. *"Onna"* is in this text synonymous with "wife" *(nyōbō)*. "Women" are depicted visually two different ways: (1) negatively, with shaved eyebrows and their hair up, or (2) with their hair long, in the *neyui-suberakashi* style, with or without eyebrows (eyebrows were shaved on women after they had borne their first child).[18] *Jōrō* are high-class prostitutes, concubines, or maids. Those from Yoshiwara are typically shown with their hair up; those who are established concubines *(mekake)* in residences have their hair down. *Jōrō* from residences are allowed in the text to become involved with *wakashu* and are condemned neither verbally nor visually for it. *Jōrō* in Yoshiwara are seen as direct competitors for the affection of *wakashu* and termed "enemies." Yet the fundamental structuring contrast is between wives and *wakashu*.[19] There is not one scene of an adult man engaged in sexual intercourse with his wife—obviously, this text is not designed to offer what its readers took for granted but rather purveys fantasies. Moreover, *wakashu* and woman can sexually join, as long as it is under the direction and control of a man (Figure 4.9):

> Toward a certain man's house, from a certain mansion, came a good-looking woman *(mime yoki onna)*. The man had her couple all day with his devoted *wakashu*. The *wakashu* too was happy and battled with her to the point of crisis. The man, thinking to make a good end to a good beginning *(shubi)*, engaged the *wakashu*, when a sincere *wakashu (makoto no wakashu)* arrived and tried to pull the man away. But when the lady's maid also rubbed her hands [in supplication] toward the second *wakashu*, he too had a good idea and took her like that. Truly, it was a great arrangement! *(makoto ni, yoki shikumi nari)*.

The text here mirrors but exceeds the controlling direction of the man within it: the expression *"shikumi"* might even suggest a theatrical event, here staged ultimately for the reader—the "omniscient consumer," he might be called.

However, if the man in the text is not in control, the judgment of the text, both visual and verbal, is reversed (scene 11, Figure 4.10):

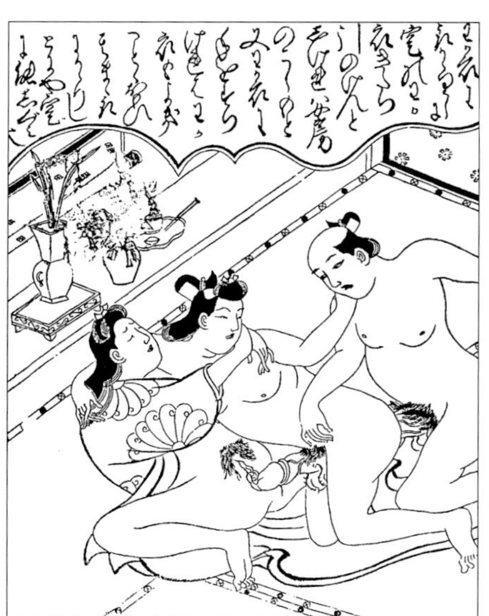

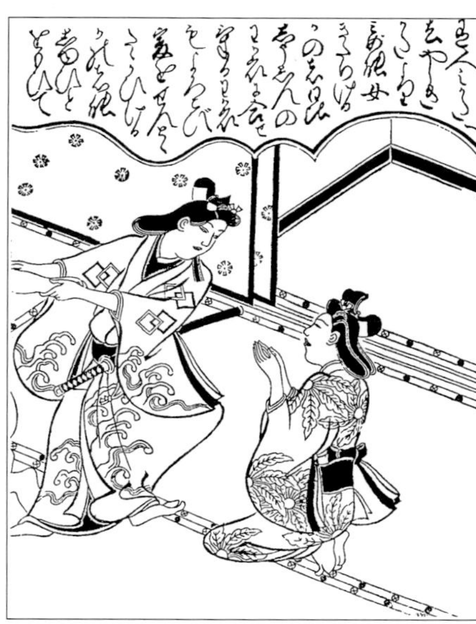

**FIGURE 4.9.** *Wakashu-asobi*, scene 10

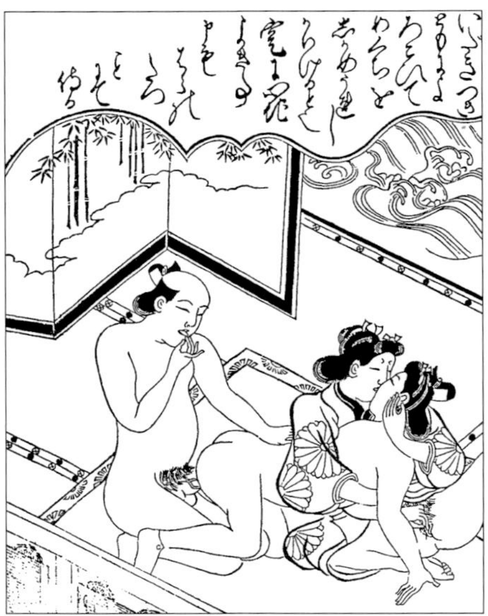

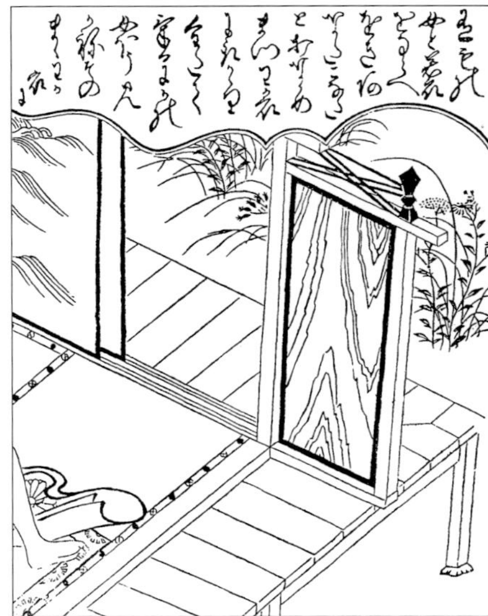

FIGURE 4.10. *Wakashu-asobi*, scene 11

> A certain man lined up his woman *(onna)* and a *wakashu*, gazed at this one and that one, and when he attempted at first to take the *wakashu*, his wife could not bear to watch and embraced the *wakashu* just like that, pleasured with him, with her mouth and eyes screwed up tight, and seemed very happy. Truly, even something that feels good is something that raises one's ire *(makoto ni, kokochi yoki koto mōsu mo hara no tatsu koto nite haberu)*.

In other words, here the wife's pleasure, while not physically interfering with that of the man, is angering because it is unauthorized.

Inversely, the text takes great pleasure in frustrated women: while there is one scene of a woman who finds her husband in bed with a youngman and discreetly withdraws "so as not to interrupt his pleasure" (Figure 4.11), the more frequent scene is of women leaving in a jealous rage (Figure 4.12) or panting with desire (Figure 4.13). In this latter case, the man insists on having them watch—he is "guarding both gates well," we are told, and the situation is described as "amusing" *(womoshirokaran)*.

Despite what is said in the preface about *wakashu* status not being determined by age, the visual text gives no examples of aged *wakashu* (and the few aged *otoko* are objects of ridicule). And despite what the text says about deep feeling and devotion, sex is largely a commodity, as seen most clearly in scene 21 (Figure 4.14), where the youngmen promise to satisfy the teaware dealers' desires if they get the price being asked for the teawares. Paul Schalow argues that "Saikaku depicts

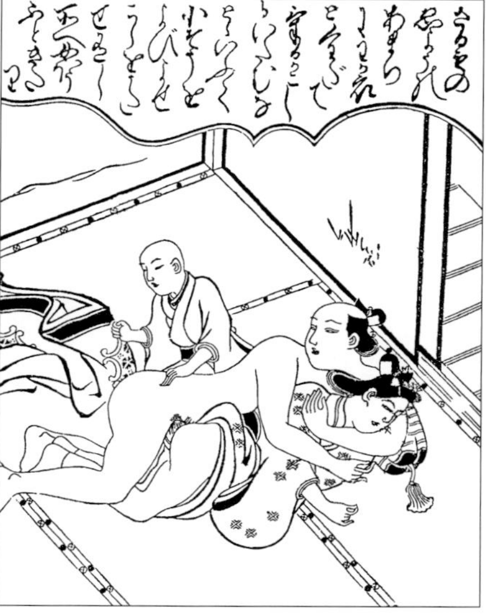

FIGURE 4.11. *Wakashu-asobi*, scene 20

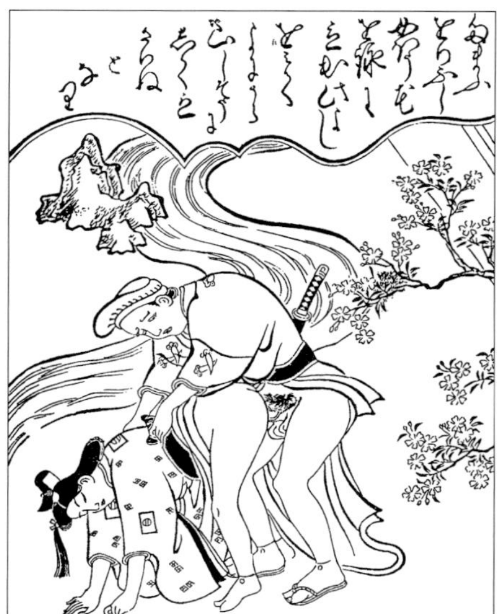

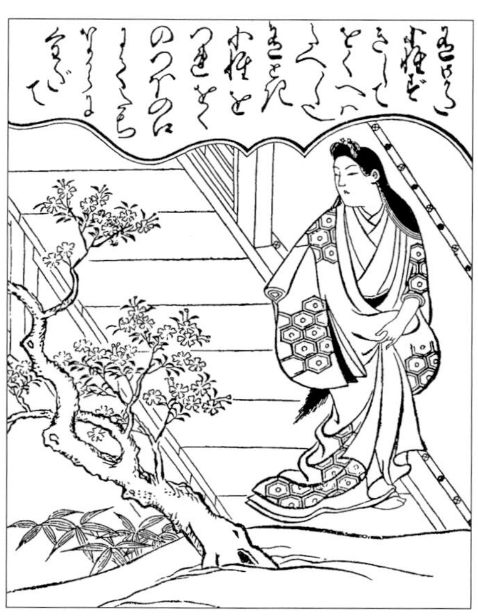

FIGURE 4.12. *Wakashu-asobi*, scene 18

two types of men in the pages of *Nanshoku ōkagami*: connoisseurs of boys *(shōjin-zuki)* and women-haters *(onna-girai)*."[20] Yet the *Wakashu-asobi* gives no suggestion of connoisseurship, in tea or sex.

The *wakashu* are all portrayed as attractive, but so are young women—only older women are portrayed in an unflattering manner. (Interestingly enough, truly absent here are virginal young girls—there is not one example of a daugh-

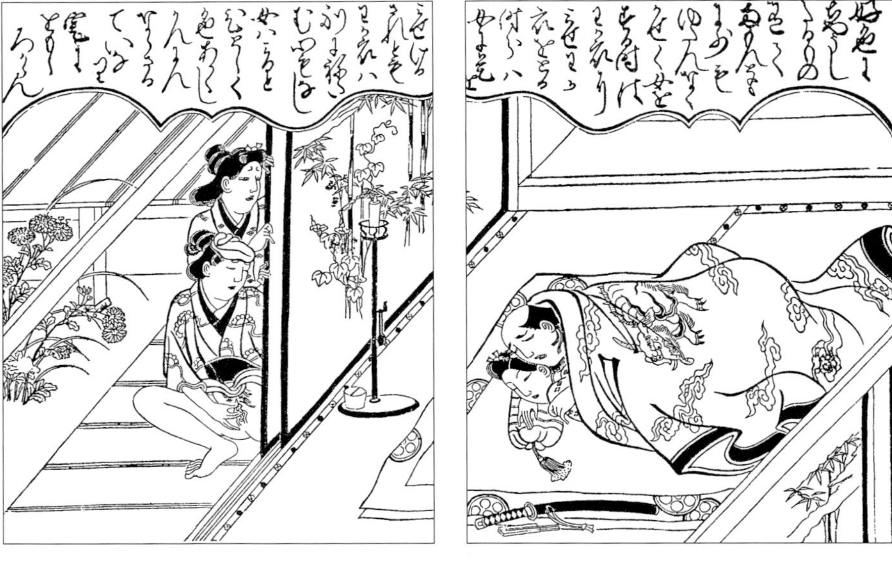

FIGURE 4.13. *Wakashu-asobi*, scene 17

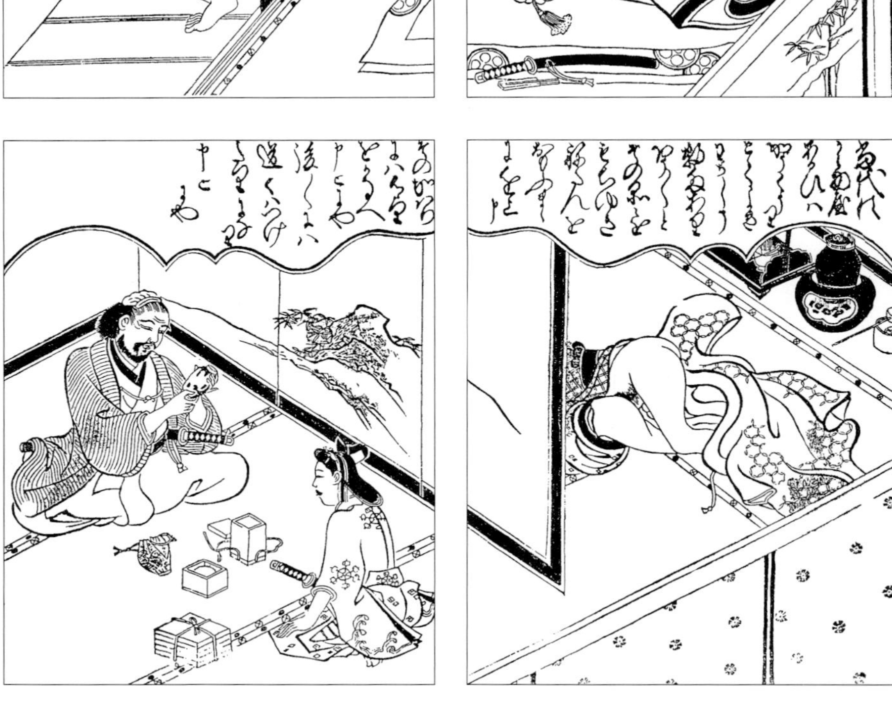

FIGURE 4.14. *Wakashu-asobi*, scene 21

ter or nonprofessional young woman in the text.) *Onna* past a certain age invariably had their eyebrows shaved off—beautiful eyebrows being considered a charming feature on women. In all his works, Moronobu conventionally portrays older women with wrinkles or frown lines in lieu of their missing eyebrows, but this is to say no more than that women past a certain age were not thought of as attractive. The text above describes the wife as having "her mouth and eyes screwed up tight" *(me-kuchi wo shikame),* but actually she looks no different from the seamstress or other nonprofessional women. And the idealized *wakashu* and prostitutes show no emotion in the faces at all. In other words, *onna* are degraded visually by showing them as aged, frustrated, and, when they dare to be proactive, disfigured by their (inappropriate) pleasure.

The text, then, is typically misogynistic, in a general patriarchal way, but it is far from exclusively homosexual, and presupposes both "heterosexual" and "homosexual"—or "bisexual"—desires on the part of its readers. Hence, *wakashu* should be understood as a gender: both men and *wakashu* are assumed to have bisexual desires (just as it is implicitly assumed in the text that women's desires are exclusively heterosexual), but there is seen to be an explicit structuring competition between men and women for the third gender, *wakashu.* Or rather, this paradigm suggests that we must think of at least four genders: men (*otoko*), wives (*onna*), prostitutes *(jōrō),* and youngmen *(wakashu)* (see Charts 3 and 4). Even in our own society, it has been suggested that mature women and young women—given how men respond to them (or, rather, don't)—are in essence different genders,[21] and in general they are distinguished by differences in dress and, for instance, hair style. In addition, the charts should factor in class, as it is clear that, at least from the standpoint of the *chōnin* reader apparently posited by the *Wakashu-asobi*, socially superior women are allowed behavior that is condemned in women of lower classes (that is, high-class *jōrō* are permitted *wakashu* and a proactive sexuality, while other women are condemned for it).

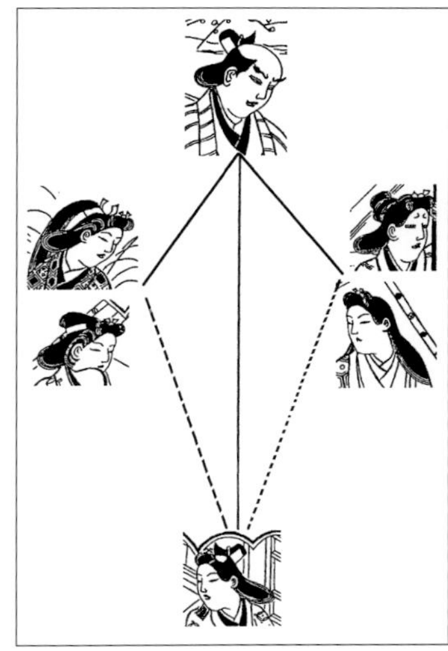

**CHART 3.** Visual Representations of the Four Genders

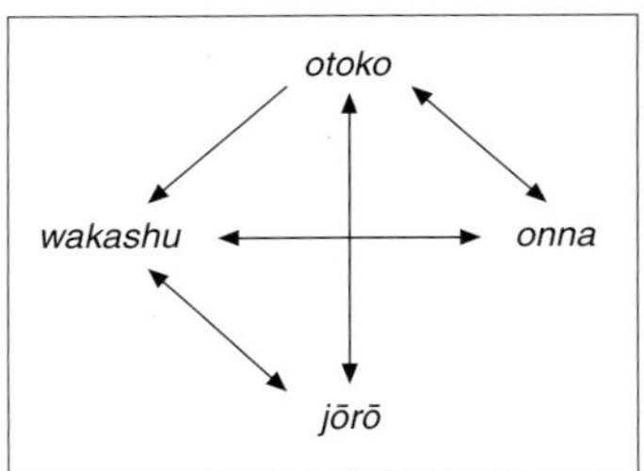


**CHART 4.** Gender/Sexuality System in the *Wakashu-asobi*

## *Shunga* as Historical Documents

Regardless of how many genders exist, the more important issue is that of representation. Any suggestion that there is in such a text as the *Wakashu-asobi* a representation of either the female viewpoint in love or that of the *wakashu* is, if I may be excused the pun, phallacious. I have offered the *Wakashu-asobi* not as a document of social reality but as a representation of social ideology or fantasy.

Robert Darnton writes on the question of how we are to read books published hundreds of years ago:

> The problem does not concern the availability of the forbidden best-sellers; they can be found in most research libraries. Nor is it a matter of accessibility; they are [no] naughtier, funnier, bolder, or bizarrer than most of the books on the best-seller list today. The difficulty lies with reading itself. We

hardly know what it is when it takes place under our nose, much less what it was two centuries ago when readers inhabited a different mental universe. Nothing could be more misleading than the assumption that they made sense of typographical signs in the same way that we do. But they left little record of how they performed that feat. Although we have some information about the external circumstance of eighteenth-century reading, we can only guess at its effects on the hearts and minds of the readers. Inner appropriation—the ultimate stage in the communication circuit that linked authors and publishers with booksellers and readers—may remain beyond the range of research.[22]

There is an even stronger tendency, however, to view pictures as self-explanatory. Several scholars have used fictional texts, both visual and verbal, as evidence of historical realities. Paul Schalow, for instance, uses tales from a collection of humorous stories, *Today's Tales of Yesterday (Kinō wa kyō no monogatari)* from the seventeenth century, to extrapolate how women of the era felt about *nanshoku*. Many of the roles he discusses are similar to those in the *Wakashu-asobi*: the jealous wife, the accepting wife, the female prostitute who must compete with boy-prostitutes, the woman who herself desires *wakashu*. Yet Schalow ends his article (published in Japanese, the translation below is mine) with a specific discussion of ménage à trois as seen in scene 10 (Figure 4.9), under the heading "Women and *Nanshoku* as Portrayed in *Ukiyo-e*" *(ukiyo-e no kataru josei to nanshoku):*

> In *ukiyo-e*, there are many *shunga* that take the scene of a man and woman joined together as their theme. Occasionally one sees *shunga* that depict a man and *wakashu* joined together. Although there is a difference in taste, I think we can pretty easily understand either image. However, how should we interpret *shunga* that have three people—a female, a man, and a *wakashu* —joined together? The positions of the three are pretty much determined: the woman on the left faces the *wakashu* directly. The "sex" [penis] of the *wakashu* has been inserted into the woman's body, while the man embraces the *wakashu* from behind, and the man is inserting his "sex" into the *wakashu*. Somehow it seems that the *wakashu* and his experience have become the focus of the *shunga*. The *wakashu* receives pleasure from both directions—the fact that he is an object at the same time he is being a subject is fascinating.
>
> However, when we think of the man's experience as the focus of the *shunga*, he is embracing the *wakashu* directly, but isn't he at the same time

> embracing the woman, through the body of the *wakashu*? Savoring the flesh of two people at one time, the man's pleasure is surely doubled. Then, when we think about it from the standpoint of the woman's experience, she is clearly holding the *wakashu*'s "sex" in her body, but she must also be fully feeling the man's "sex" from the *wakashu*'s body. The woman is being embraced by two men at the same time, so isn't it the woman's pleasure that is doubled? A woman is someone who cannot help colliding with *nanshoku* with her own body. It is this that is probably the female "discourse on *nanshoku*" in the early Edo period. Woman, *wakashu*, man, and this colliding together. Isn't this the distinctive feature of Japanese *nanshoku*?[23]

Schalow starts with the assumption, which I hope I have gone some way already to refute, that the visual images in Japanese premodern pornography are easily read and interpreted. In fact, such images very often include a written text, which can radically change our understanding of the action depicted. Regardless, Schalow is ready to admit that at least in the case of ménages à trois there may be some interpretive ambiguity. However, he claims that the composition of these images is relatively set, an assertion I would again dispute, based on what we have seen in the *Wakashu-asobi*. In addition, Schalow's use of verb forms in this description is very interesting—something I have attempted to maintain in the translation. While seeming determined to allow agency or subjectivity for the women and *wakashu* in these pictures (he is speaking in the generic, and without a specific image it is difficult to engage him at a visual level), Schalow grammatically denies them any subject position at all: "The 'sex' [penis] of the *wakashu has been* inserted [note the passive] into the woman's body, while *the man embraces* [active] the *wakashu* from behind, and the man *is inserting* [active] his 'sex' into the *wakashu*." Yet he suggests that somehow the *wakashu* "has become the focus of the *shunga*." As I have argued above, this is clearly an anachronistic reading, since the text seems to be designed for an adult male reader/viewer, who, being an adult, would not want to imagine himself being penetrated by another man.[24] However, while Schalow's reading here is anachronistic, his use of the grammatical concepts of subject and object seems entirely appropriate: indeed, the penetrator is the grammatical subject and the penetrated always the grammatical object here. Moreover, it is clear, at least in the *Wakashu-asobi*, that the *wakashu*'s insertion serves as no more than an extension of the adult male: when a *wakashu* is being penetrated by a man (Figure 4.15), the youngman's penis (erect or flaccid) is never depicted, unless it is serving as an extention of the controlling man. *Wakashu* erections not author-

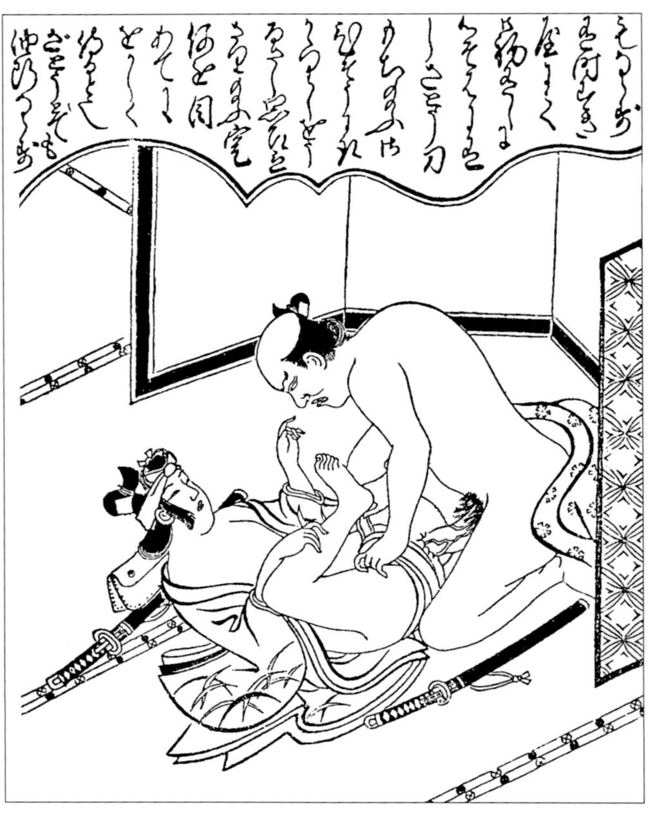

FIGURE 4.15. *Wakashu-asobi*, scene 12

ized by an older man are without exception condemned by the verbal text. The discrepancies between the verbal and visual texts allow the reading *otoko* to identify with a visual surrogate in penetrating, while the verbal text provides the "proper" patriarchal judgment.

The same kind of anachronistic reading is seen in Hayakawa's interpretation of scene 11. The last sentence of this text is ambiguous: "Truly, even something that feels good is something that raises one's ire" *(makoto ni, kokochi yoki koto mōsu mo hara no tatsu koto nite haberu).* Hayakawa asks who it is that has "something that feels good" and who it is who criticizes and whose ire is raised. While admitting that the *wakashu* in the picture is essentially functioning as a sex toy for the couple, Hayakawa nonetheless believes that this final statement should be attributed to the *wakashu.*

However, the picture gives absolutely no evidence of any pleasure on the *wakashu*'s part: his penis is not visible, and he holds himself up with one hand while stimulating the wife with his other hand. There was in fact no assumption on the part of Edo-period readers that the *wakashu* would find his situation arousing.[25] As Pflugfelder has documented: "In contrast to vaginal coitus, however, popular discourse construed only the inserter role in anal intercourse as intrinsically pleasurable, while taking it for granted that the anal insertee allowed himself to be penetrated only out of duty, affection, coercion, or the prospect of material reward."[26] Such an attitude is not unique to Japan or even East Asia; as John R. Clarke has written: "Modern authors repeatedly point out the 'phallic' construction of sexual activity in ancient Rome: all the texts that come down to us frame sexual experience in terms of the freeborn, elite male who inserts his penis into the body of another, whether that other be male or female."[27]

Finally, Chart 4 shows how wives are excluded from the triangle of desire formed by men, prostitutes, and youngmen. The phallocentric pleasure of the text is predicated on the absolute blindness to the possibility of female homoerotic pleasure. As Hitomi Tonomura has said in regard to medieval Japan: "The sexual experiences of women are [portrayed as] limited, singular, and dependent on men."[28] This view is reconfirmed in another rare work of Moronobu's *Toko no okimono* (Display-piece for the bedroom—a work set in the imperial harem): all of its main twenty-four scenes depict women masturbating (Figure 4.16), but only one is shown masturbating without a dildo *(harigata),* and there is not one example of either cunnilingus or mutual masturbation without a dildo.[29] In fact, the text is so anxious about even the possibility of women having sexual pleasure without men that each page has an upper register—completely unrelated to the main picture—showing a man and a woman in coitus, serving as a kind of normative talisman to counteract the exclusion of the phallus in the lower register. In Moronobu's pornography, the phallus is the sole source of pleasure, and, as in most Edo-period texts, masturbation is considered a very poor, and inherently demeaning, substitute.[30] This phallocentrism, then, accomplishes two interdependent things: first, it allows for the degradation of mature women, showing their "comic" frustration when displaced from the role of insertee by *wakashu;* and second, it precludes the possibility of female-female sexual gratification, which would render the phallus redundant.

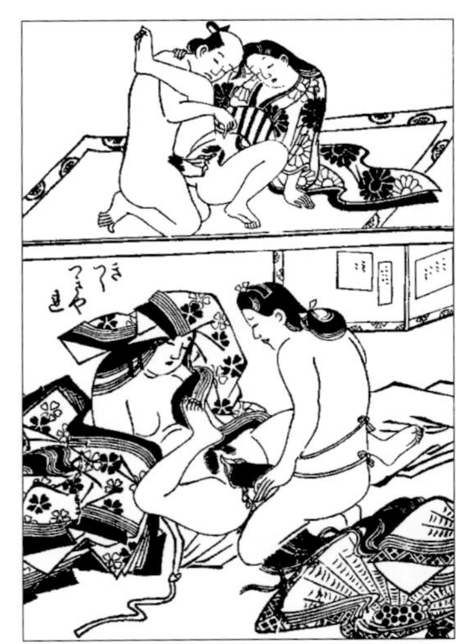

**FIGURE 4.16.** Hishikawa Kichibei (Moronobu), *Toko no okimono* (Display-piece for the bedroom), scene 9. *Ehon,* 24 pages, *ōhon* format. Edo: Kashiwa-ya, n.d. At the International Research Center for Japanese Studies Library.

## Conclusion

Limiting discussion to the *Wakashu-asobi* and extrapolating from it for only one particular milieu in Edo in the first half of the 1670s, one can say that the rhetoric of *shudō* loyalty was hyperbolic window dressing for a phallocratic pansexuality. It does not seem useful to "insert" this text into the discourse of modern homosexuality, or even "bisexuality," if the latter term is understood as opposed to a mandatory bimorphic structure of sexuality,[31] for the actions and desires it portrays are clearly meant to be taken as normative. Yet the *Wakashu-asobi* represents only one dialect of the grammar of desire, limited by time, location, and class. For instance, Shirakura Yoshihiko has remarked that the appearance of such ménage à trois as Schalow discusses is limited to *shudō* texts produced in Edo, and he has seen no example of such "bisexual" scenes in *shudō* texts produced in the western, Kamigata region.[32]

We need to try to bracket our own binary thinking and to approach Tokugawa-period "sexuality," if we may call it that, in a more holistic or systemic fashion. While there are obvious and important present-day historical and political reasons why the scholarly study of the sexual activity of the Tokugawa period has developed the way it has—political reasons that I support in the context of antihomophobic education—I think we now need studies that look critically at the whole range of sexual activity and desire in the Tokugawa period.

CHAPTER FIVE

DAVID POLLACK

# Marketing Desire: Advertising and Sexuality in Edo Literature, Drama, and Art

No doubt in part because of the understandable attention lavished on its more notorious pornographic arts, relatively little attention has been paid to what might be called the more quotidian *continuity* of erotic life in Edo-period Japan. To be sure, a part of this deficit may represent a tenacious side-effect of the Edo authorities' persistent efforts to suppress, or at least to confine to restricted urban areas, the most overt manifestations of the nation's public erotic life—efforts that, at least in theory, left available for human intercourse in the private realm little more than the manufacture of progeny.

Something of the regime's hope of segregating the erotic and private from daily public life—and the sheer futility of that hope—is both symbolized and satirized in a contemporary painting of a legendary holy man named Kume (Figure 5.1). The fall of lofty and abstract Chinese ethical values in the face of base and concrete Japanese reality is depicted in the literal tumble from heaven of this Taoist saint, painted by Kanō Terunobu in the best classical Chinese mode, rendered unable to fly by the sight of native beauty, in the shape of a pretty young washerwoman flashing her legs, as painted by Nishikawa Sukenobu in the contemporary *ukiyo-e* style. The inscription, by no less serious a Confucianist than Hayashi Hōkoku (1721–1773), fifth official philosopher to the shogun *(daigaku no kami),* identifies and rather plaintively epitomizes this dilemma in a citation from the canonical Confucian *Book of Rites:* "Eat, drink, man, woman—these are our greatest desires. Beware them! Fear them!"[1]

Even as this painting earnestly cautions against human sexual passion, it cannot help parodying the impossible hope of its repression—the usual response during the Edo period to this profound ideological contradiction. The real problem that is pointed up here is that only a saint, a man who had never entertained the actual complexities of human desire, could be so completely undone by the sight of something as commonplace as a pretty young woman. In an ethical world polarized into a rigid distinction between saint and whore, his fall is guaranteed. To redress this calamitous view of the Edo world, a more subtle description is needed of what might be called a general "economy of desire" of the period, one that is better equipped to account for the complex and diverse articulations between the ways that goods and services were actually produced and consumed. That is, we can understand the operation of a more complete range of erotic life by extending the idea of "the erotic" to the manifold ways in which desire in general was conceived of, packaged, motivated, stimulated, and catered to in various realms of Edo social life.

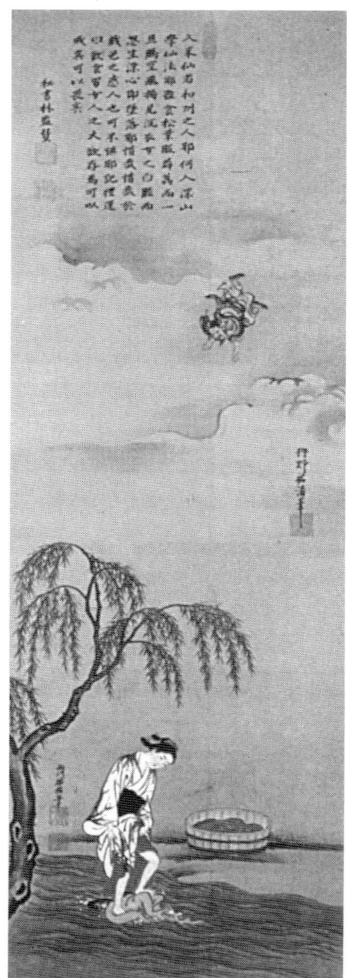

FIGURE 5.1. *Kume sennin no zu* [Portrait of Saint Kume]. *Nikuhitsu ukiyo-e* (painted *ukiyo-e*), figure of woman by Nishikawa Sukenobu (1671–1750); *suiboku* figure of Kume Sennin by Kanō Terunobu; calligraphic inscription by Hayashi Hōkoku. From Nakano Mitsutoshi, *Nihon no kinsei* [Early modern Japan], vol. 12: *Bungaku to bijutsu no seijuku* [The maturation of literature and art] (Tokyo: Chūōkōronsha, 1993), color plate 1.

One way to promote an understanding of a general economy of desire is to consider art, fiction, and drama—that is, the various genres used to represent desire—as more narrowly focused modalities of the comprehensive set of practices of what we have come to think of as the more specialized domain of advertising. Here I am using the word in its broadest sense, meaning all representation employed for the purpose of stimulating desire. The central subject and driving force of the bourgeois-oriented arts during the Edo period is, after all, the representation of desire in all of its multifarious aspects. The desire for money, the desire for goods, the desire for social status, and the desire for sex do not exist separately in a vacuum but rather represent nexuses along an unbroken continuum of social activities and their representations.

Any nice distinction between an elite "high art" and a plebian "vulgar advertising" that a beleaguered bourgeoisie might once have felt it necessary or possible to maintain was effectively blurred long ago, the two having all but coalesced in our present world of "infomercials" and "edutainment." It therefore comes as little surprise to find the burgeoning mobilization of desire in the conjunction of commercial and artistic practices in the cultural milieu of eighteenth- and nineteenth-century Japan.[2] What is surprising, no doubt, is just how dense, widespread, and sophisticated those practices actually were. The same matter-of-fact synthesis of commercial advertising, eroticism, and art had a profound impression on the work of European artists like Henri Toulouse-Lautrec nearly a century later, in which a fascination with things Japanese is so apparent—especially with all the things that could be bought and sold, women not least among them. Gustave Courbet and Utagawa Kuniyoshi may have given modern urban man his first anatomical close-up look at what Courbet apotheosized as *L'origine du monde* (Figures 5.2, 5.3); but it was the work of artists like Toulouse-Lautrec (Figure 5.4) and Kitagawa Utamaro (Figure 5.5) that showed him exactly where in the big city it was located and just when showtime began.

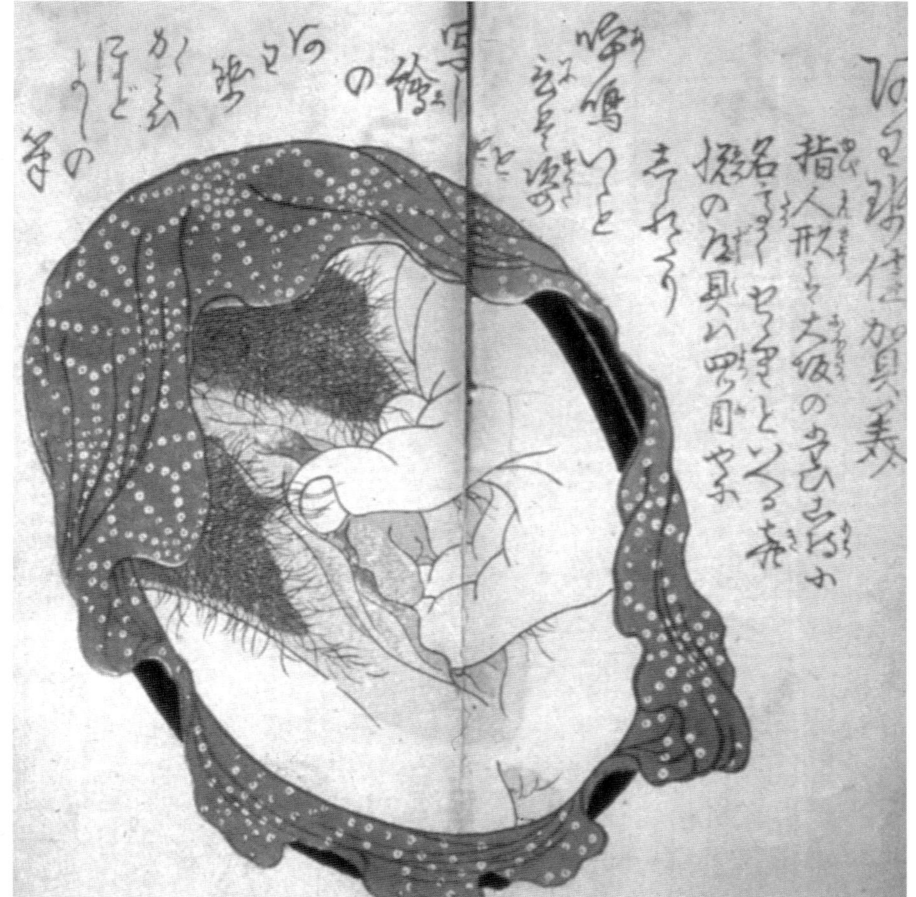

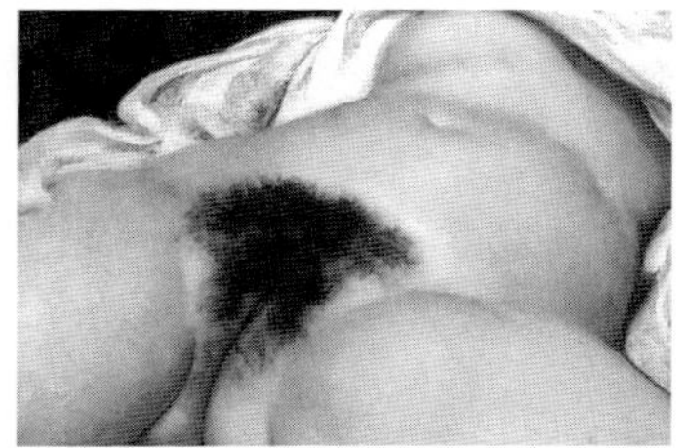

**FIGURE 5.2.** *(Above)* Gustave Courbet, *L'origine du monde,* 1866. Private collection.

**FIGURE 5.3.** *(Left)* Utagawa Kuniyoshi (1786–1861), *Awase kagami* [Facing mirrors] from *Makura kagami* [Pillow mirrors]. Private collection. From Fukuda Kazuhiko, ed., *Fūzoku ehon ukiyo-e* [Illustrated genre books of *ukiyo-e*] (Tokyo: Kawade Shobō, 1991), 139.

Most investigations of the articulations between commerce and art begin by noting that the popular Edo artists, writers, and actors, with their proven appeal to large audiences, were in constant demand by merchants for advertising purposes. Early evidence of this demand is demonstrated by the abundance of advertising leaflets *(hikifuda)* and promotional items *(keibutsu)* that were churned out at a phenomenal rate by the most popular authors of the day.[3] Writers like Santō Kyōden, Shikitei Sanba, Takizawa (Kyokutei) Bakin, Ryūtei Tanehiko, Tamenaga Shunsui, and Ota Nanpo (Shokusanjin), among many others, capitalized on their literary skills and reputations by turning out ads for medicines, cosmetics, foods, clothing, and shops of every sort selling nearly everything. Even such unlikely figures as Motoori Norinaga and Watanabe Kazan are known to have written advertising copy.[4] To be scandalized by this information is to miss the point: to be

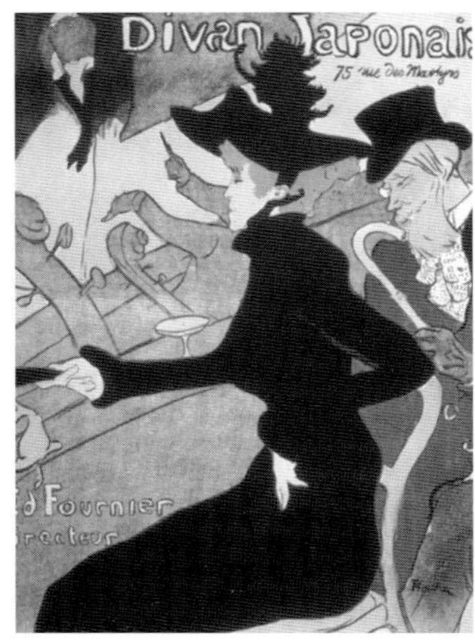

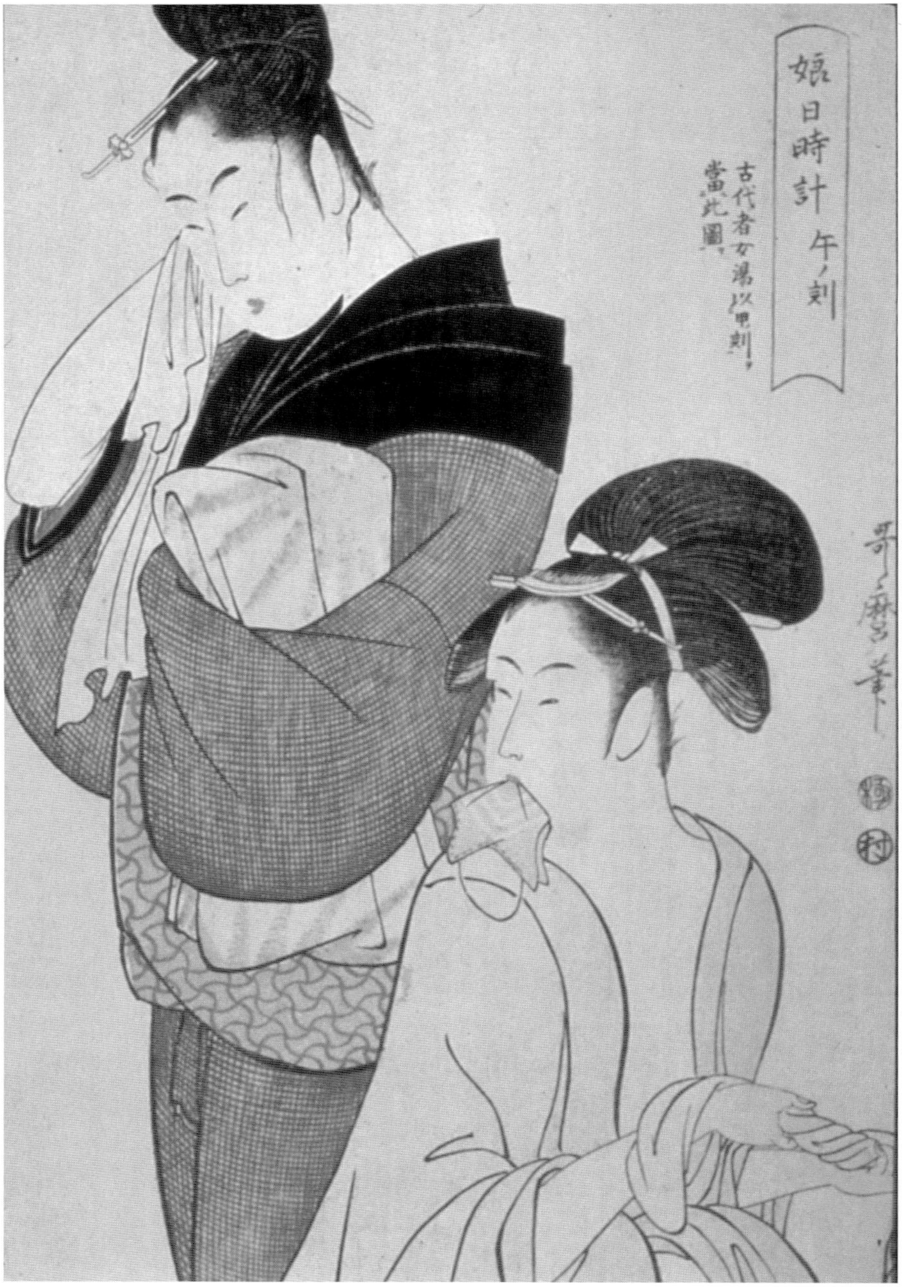

**FIGURE 5.4.** *(Above)* Henri Toulouse-Lautrec, *Le Divan Japonais,* 1893. Museum of Modern Art, New York. From Riva Castleman and Wolfgang Wittrock, eds., *Henri de Toulouse-Lautrec: Images of the 1890's* (New York: Museum of Modern Art, 1985), 185.

**FIGURE 5.5.** *(Right)* Kitagawa Utamaro (1754–1806), *Musume hidokei: ushi no koku* (The hours of women: 1:00 to 3:00 p.m.). From Masao Ishizawa et al., eds., *Heritage of Japanese Art* (New York: Kodansha, 1981), 142.

knowledgeable was to be held in high regard as a *tsū*, a well-informed producer and consumer of both goods and information.

Santō Kyōden (1761–1816) once cautioned his younger friend Bakin (incorrectly, as it turned out) that, if he persisted in writing only *gesaku* fiction, he would never be able to amass enough money to marry a woman with decently blackened teeth—anyone, that is, better than a prostitute.[5] Copywriting, in contrast, was clearly profitable work, as can be seen from a typical diary entry by Shikitei Sanba: "Bunka 9 (1812), 5/9: wrote and delivered ads *(hikifuda)* for Hassei's Saltwater Bath sold by Igaya, wrote more ads for Unomaru-zushi and Futabaya Kihachi-zushi in Asuka Tamachi Itchome, and delivered them, together with drafts."[6] Kyōden's scolding notwithstanding, Bakin would eventually become one of the very few writers to support himself solely by his fiction; by 1830 he was earning over thirty *ryō* a year as a writer—a sum that, at the rate of one *ryō* to one *koku* of *genmai* rice, while no fortune, still amounted to a comfortable living. Even so, ads by the renowned Bakin were everywhere. Kyōden might equally well have pointed out, following the events of 1791 that landed him under house arrest in manacles for fifty days, that writing ad copy in an age of unpredictable censorship was also a great deal safer than writing fiction.

The lively demand for ad copywriters was a function of the flourishing commercial atmosphere of the great cities of Japan in the decades leading up to 1800 and beyond. Indeed, in the view of the ever-observant Ota Nanpo, by 1820 there were so many shops in Edo that the public (a concept created as much by advertising as by drama, fiction, and publishing) was becoming hopelessly confused as to what was available and where it could be bought. It was for this reason that this supremely knowledgeable man (whose actual profession, it is rarely remembered, was statistician for the bureaucracy) compiled his *Edo kaimono hitori annai,* or "Your Personal Guide to Shopping in Edo" (published in Osaka by Nakagawa Hōzandō in 1824, one year after Ota's death), a comprehensive reference work to some 2,622 merchants, craftsmen, and eating and drinking establishments organized by goods and services.[7] The question of which women were available in which brothels—the real subject of all those lovely *bijinga* as well as of the ever-popular guides to the quarter—is after all simply a narrower form of the broader question that concerned all consumers of which goods were available in which shops. If few writers could, like Bakin, aspire to make a living entirely by their fiction, there was always a pressing need for copywriters to help them make ends meet.

Hiraga Gennai's miscellany *Hika rakuyō* (Flying blossoms and falling leaves,

1769, published posthumously in 1783), contains among other things several of his own advertisements for a wide variety of products, including "Sōsekikō," a tooth powder invented by this remarkable jack-of-all-trades, which he touted, centuries before his time, as "the convenient tooth powder in a box." It was sold at the shop of one Ebisuya Heisuke, where, Gennai tells the reader, "there is no charge for browsing, friends, no compulsion to buy—I shop there myself." These ads often assume the guise of formal announcements then popular on the stage, complete with the customary theatrical opening "laaaydeez aaand gentlemeeeen" *(tōzai tōzai),* and ending appropriately with the written "clack-clack" *(kachikachi)* of the clappers used to signal the end of a performance on stage. Very similar ads were in fact being delivered right from the stage by actors during performances. Gennai's style sets the tone for much of the advertising copy of the day, a rich self-referential *gesaku* prose overlaid with theatrical flourishes and full of irreverent parody: "Its efficacy soars higher than Mt. Fuji—but even if it didn't, it won't kill you, and besides, it's so inexpensive that if you don't like it you can feel free to throw it away." The Sōsekikō ad goes on to inform readers how resentful the proprietor will be if they don't buy his product, and if they do, how happy he'll be to leave his present life of poverty and move to a shop on a main street with a gleaming golden shop sign.[8]

To be sure, such extremely playful language is only to be expected from Gennai; by far the greater number of ads consisted merely of the usual highflown prose in praise of the person, shop, or product for which it was commissioned.[9] What Tani Minezō calls "Japan's first collection of advertising copy" *(kopī)* appeared in the form of a miscellany titled *Hirougami* compiled in 1794 by Honzentei Tsubohira, a restaurateur and disciple of Santō Kyōden.[10] Of the fifteen advertisements included in *Hirougami*, all written between 1792 and 1793, four are ascribed to Kyōden and eight to Tsubohira; the remaining three bearing no name. Since they all employ the colorful, complex, and playful language of *gesaku* prose, Tani hypothesizes that such ads were being written and collected as model *gesaku* exercises, though he does not address the perhaps even more important fact that they were also successful examples of how to produce income as a writer. One of the shops advertised in this collection, incidentally, is the Shirokiya, one of several well-known establishments known to the general public today through their appearance in Hiroshige's famous *Meisho Edo hyakkei* (One hundred famous views of Edo) series—another form of advertising that will be discussed below.[11]

Authors regularly took the next obvious step up from writing ad leaflets by including or inserting advertisements for their own and their friends' shops and

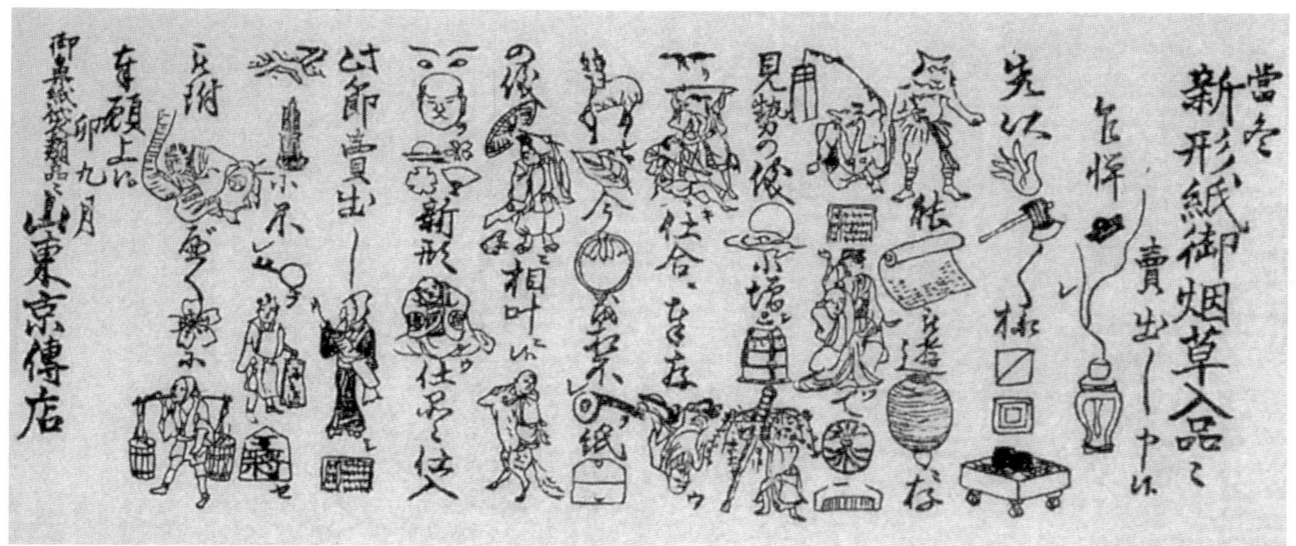


products in their popular fiction. The *gesaku* writer and artist Santō Kyōden, perhaps the most prolific of all, frequently depicts his own smoking-accessory shop in his works. His best-known ad is a complex and playful (that is, *gesaku*) acrostic puzzle of 1795 (Figure 5.6), printed on a special type of paper tobacco pouch sold exclusively at his shop. In an obvious attempt to enlarge his own readership, Kyōden also sold "Literacy Pills" *(dokushogan),* which were advertised as also "good for strengthening and improving memory, curing physical and nervous prostration, stress, hangover, and stomachache."[12] A plug in his story *Mikenjaku sannin namaei* (A winnow measure of three drunks, 1794) is typical of the ads that pepper his fiction: "My, what a large place! Why, this must be the new paper tobacco pouch shop of that fellow Santō Kyōden that everyone is talking about, where you can buy tobacco products at such low, low prices!"[13] The same text shows up as well in a scene from Kyōden's *Ikkoku atae manryō kaishun* (To have your youth back for thirty minutes is worth ten thousand in gold).

FIGURE 5.6. Santō Kyōden (1761–1816), "Shinkei kami on-tabako-ire shinajina" (New types of paper tobacco pouches). Tobacco shop ad acrostic. Nakada Setsuko, *Edo Meiji Taishō Shōwa kōkoku no naka no Nippon: kōkoku wa jidai no nagare o utsusu kagami da* (Japan in advertising during the Edo, Meiji, Taishō, and Shōwa periods: advertising as a mirror of the passage of time) (Tokyo: Daiyamondosha, 1993), Figure 14.

In Bakin's *Kyokutei ippū Kyōden-bari* (Kyokutei puffs while Kyōden curses), Kyōden (easily identified by his well-known stub of a "Kyōden nose") is shown seated at the till of his busy shop among his various pipes and smoking accessories, preparing to inscribe a blank fan—another common way by which celebrities supplemented their incomes.[14] In *Azuma-ori sumō taizen* (The great compendium of Eastern wrestling, 1809, illustrated by Utagawa Kunisada), Shikitei Sanba (1776–1822), another popular writer cum shopkeeper, depicted his shop's

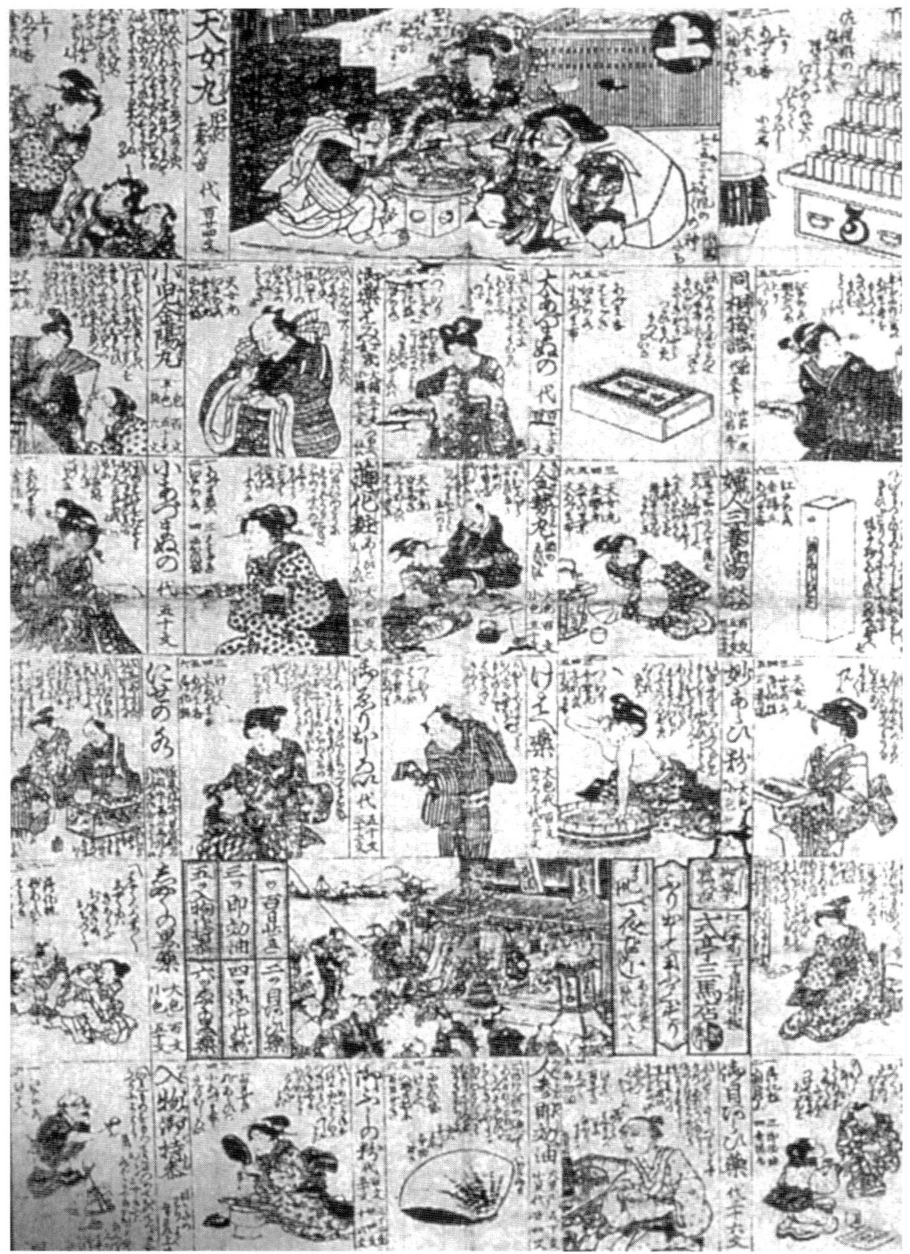


FIGURE 5.7. Ko-Sanba, *Shikitei han'ei sugoroku* (Papa's prosperous parcheesi), a *keibutsu* (promotional item) depicting Shikitei Sanba's medicinal products arrayed in the form of the popular board game *sugoroku*. From Nakada Setsuko, *Edo Meiji Taishō Shōwa kōkoku no naka no Nippon: kōkoku wa jidai no nagare o utsusu kagami da* (Tokyo: Daiyamondosha, 1993), Figure 17.

trademark on a shop curtain along with an advertisement for one of his most popular cosmetics, Water of Edo (Edo no Mizu, which is also plugged in his *Ukiyoburo* [The Floating-World Bathhouse, 1809–1813] and is the subject of his story *Edo no Mizu saiwaibanashi* [The happy tale of "Water of Edo," 1812]).[15] Sanba's son, known as Ko-Sanba or "Sanba Jr.," continued to profit from his father's fame, and his *Shikitei han'ei sugoroku* (Papa's prosperous parcheesi) shows his father's medicinal products arrayed in the form of a popular board game (Figure 5.7). Sanba also depicted his own shop in the story *Nyōbō katagi otsunaeshi* (Racy stories of housewives, 1815, illustrated by Utagawa Kuniyoshi). And Jippensha Ikku's (1765–1831) *Kane no waraji* (Sandals of steel, 1813) contains an advertisment for the special millet sweets *(awa-ame)* sold in his confectionary shop.[16]

The practice of including advertising in fiction, whether as separate inserts or as part of the work itself, is a natural extension of the merchant mentality into the typical elite cultural practices of the *ren*, the group frame of reference that served as the focal point of social and artistic practices since late medieval times. In the Edo period, the *ren* took the form of all manner of affinity groups of mixed social caste that came together, formally and informally, to produce poetry and art ranging from "serious" works that were formally judged to "playful" works that were often the product of drink and hilarity. Advertising would begin to disengage from this mixture as a separate technological medium only during the Meiji period, when the ideological functions of mass media underwent fundamental changes.

As might have been expected of a merchant culture, the same impulse that produced literary, art, and drama groups also produced clubs devoted to collecting and trading various popular items, including trading cards. Such items include and came to be symbolized by *senjafuda*. Originally personal calling cards left during visits to temples and shrines *(senjamōde),* these soon evolved into a stylized small-format graphic art form that functioned as a cross between business card, advertisement, tagging, and art. Adopted as logos by individuals, groups, and clubs, *senjafuda*, which might be thought of as a lower-class version of the more elite practice of *surimono*, occupy an important position in the history of Japanese graphic arts (Figure 5.8).[17] Thus, advertising as a larger frame of reference joins specific practices ranging from straightforward ads, to the inclusion of products as integral parts of art and fiction, to art representing goods and services, and to the Edo equivalent of today's so-called urban art of tagging; it was in no small part through such new advertising practices that a new concept of a "public" and its space is both reflected and created in this period.

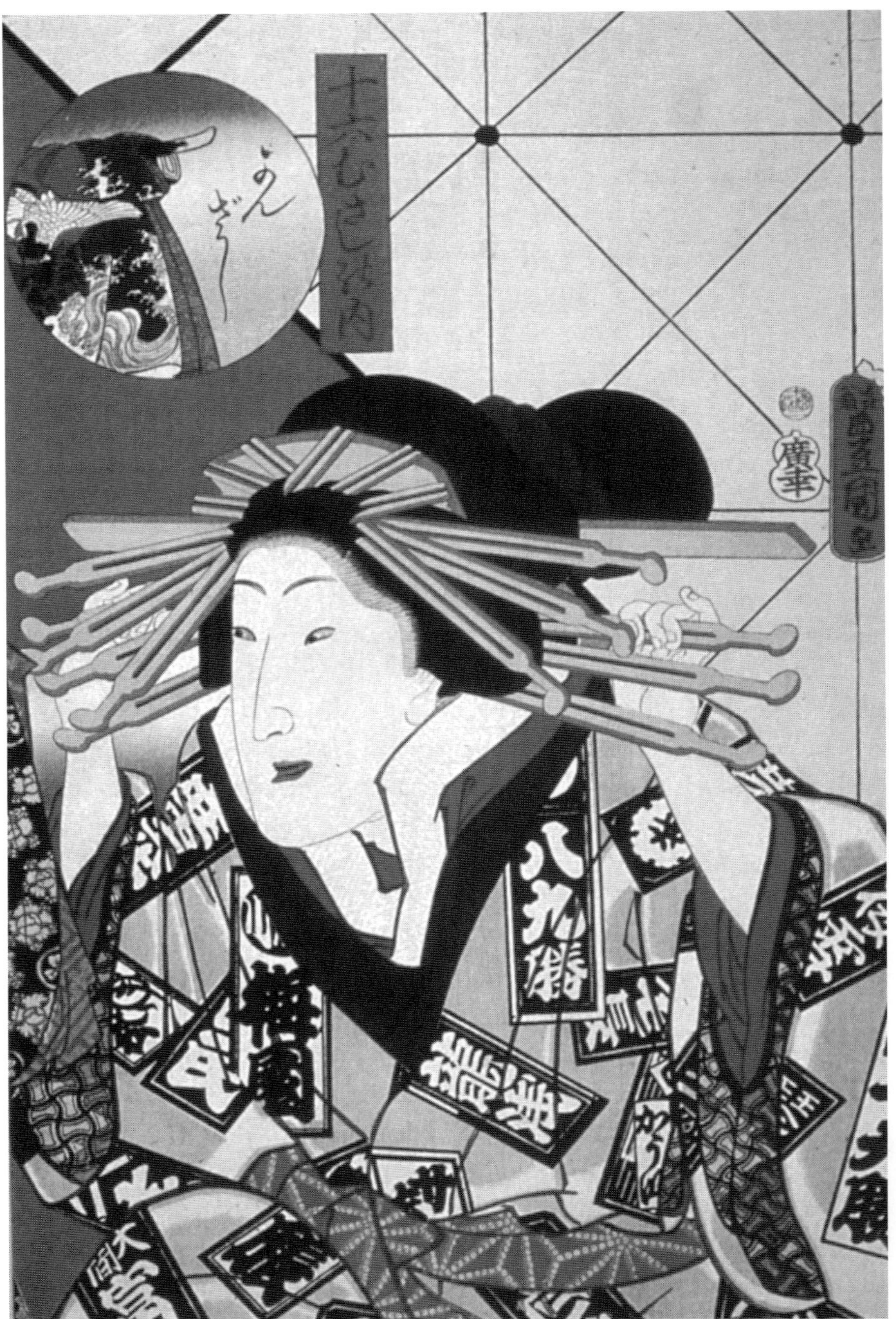

FIGURE 5.8. Utagawa Toyokuni III (Kunisada II, 1823–1880), *Kanzashi* (Hair ornaments), 1861. *Senjafuda* from the series *Jūroku Musashi.* From Nishiyama Matsunosuke and Sekioka Senrei, eds., *Senjafuda* (Tokyo: Kodansha, 1993), Figure 196.

Advertising in Edo literature was not restricted to occasional insertions in works of fiction. As in the case of Sanba's *Edo no Mizu saiwaibanashi,* entire works of fiction often consist of little more than entertaining advertisements for particular shops and goods.[18] The earliest known instance of advertising employed as the subject of a work of fiction is usually thought to be Koikawa Harumachi's (1744–1789) *kibyōshi* titled *Mimasu masu Uroko no hajime* (How Mimasuya got the better of Urokogataya, 1777), which concerns the competition between the moxa merchant Mimasuya Heiemon and his neighbor, the *ezōshi* merchant Urokogataya Magobei (the publisher of the work had a financial stake in this moxa shop, where the popular Danjūrō-mogusa was sold).[19] Santō Kyōden wrote *Onna Masakado shichijin-geshō* (The Female Masakado: seven made-up women, 1792) for the cosmetic Kumoinokō sold by Tamaya Kyūbei;[20] Jippensha Ikku's *Irozuri shinsomegata* (Sexy prints of newly dyed patterns) was composed for the Tokiwaya kimono shop's winter sale; Shikitei Sanba's *Wata onjaku kikō no hikifuda* (A broadside on the marvellous efficacy of the padded warming stone, 1802) was created as an advertisement for a heating plaster sold by Fujita Kinroku of Odenmachō (the ad for *Wata onjaku* appears right beside one for the author's own recently published fictional work *Yakusha setsuyō kyōgen-bukuro* [The actor's seasonal story bag]).[21] And Takizawa Bakin wrote *Oisenukado keshō no wakamizu* (Never grow old! The cosmetic water of youth, 1807)] for Yorozuya Shiroemon, a well-known dealer in hair oils and cosmetics.

A popular subject for contemporary fiction was the founding stories of well-known commercial establishments, told as a variant on stories about the founding of shrines and temples, or *engi-mono.* One such story, *Genkin kakene-nashi tsurizao no yurai* (The story of the "no-extra-charges-when-you-pay-cash" fishing pole, published 1764 by one Washō), recounts in legend form the founding in 1673 of the famed Mitsui Echigoya kimono store in Surugachō by Mitsui Hachirōbei Takatoshi (1622–1694). The honest well digger Hachiemon (nicknamed *kakenenashi* or "No Extra Charges" Hachiemon) and his wife Oichi, having prayed to the goddess Benzaiten for children, are blessed with a daughter, Oben, and three sons, Jirōkichi, Sankichi, and Shirōkichi. Just as Oben, a beauty, is about to be seduced by the evil well digger Kanzō, she is rescued by the two gods Ebisu and Urashima, who appear in the guise of fishermen. Ebisu fixes Oben up with Urashima and presents Hachiemon with a turtle as a wedding gift. Oben then assumes her true form as Benzaiten, and the gods instruct Hachiemon, Sankichi, and Shirōkichi in the Way of the Merchant *(akindō no michi).* Kanzō and Jirōkichi, in cahoots but not very clever, use the bamboo poles given to them by the gods

FIGURE 5.9. Suzuki Harunobu (1725–1770), *Edo san bijin* (Three beauties of Edo). Ofuji of the Motoyanagiya holding a fan decorated with the *hachi-mimasu* crest of Ichikawa Yaozō, *left;* the actor of women's roles Segawa Kikunojō, *center;* and Kasamori no Osen, *right.* Tokyo National Museum. From Nakamura Shinichirō et al., eds., *Harunobu: bijinga to enpon* (Harunobu: beauties and erotica) (Tokyo: Shinchōsha, 1992), 28.

to earn their living as sedan-chair bearers (*kumosuke* were among Edo's most despised tradesmen). Hachiemon becomes Mitsui Hachirōbei Takatoshi; Sankichi, who was given a sea bream, becomes Ebisuya (the bream and fishing pole are the symbols of Ebisu, the god of merchants); and Shirōkichi, given a turtle, becomes Kameya. This story thus accounts in legendary form for the founding of three great Edo kimono shops.[22] The expression "*genkin kakene nashi*," which originated with Mitsui, immediately caught on and became the basis of a merchandizing revolution in Edo.

So far I have restricted myself largely to the rather blatant sorts of advertising found in leaflets and *kibyōshi* that were accompanied by simple black-and-white *(sumizuri-e)* illustrations, as the law required. The advertising that appears in colorful *nishiki-e* woodblock prints, however, is considerably more subtle and sophisticated. Suzuki Harunobu, the famous neighbor of Gennai's who initiated the *nishiki-e* technique in 1765, portrayed several of Edo's many famous shop-girl beauties. Ofuji, one of the best known, worked in the Motoyanagiya dental prod-

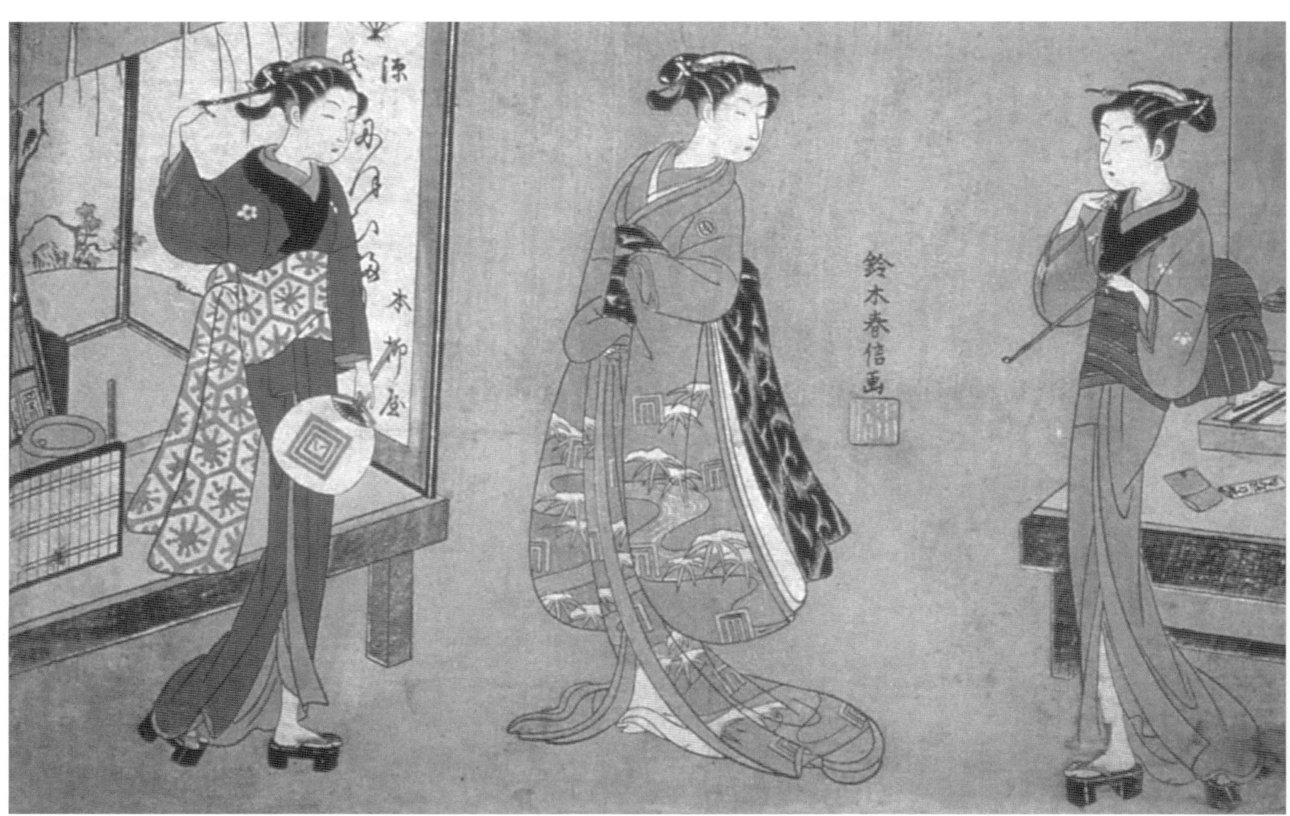

ucts shop in the Nakamise, or the long row of facing shops in the Asakusa Kannon shrine, where she is shown surrounded by her various wares;[23] another Harunobu print shows Ofuji's famous rival, the beautiful "tea-girl" *(chakumi musume)* Kasamori no Osen (fl. 1764–1771), whom Ota Nanpo judged the more beautiful of the two (Figure 5.9).[24] These pretty young women, popularly known as "billboard girls" *(kanban-musume),* were well-known public attractions and were often portrayed by artists of the day.[25]

One popular genre of actor prints shows actors costumed as itinerant sellers of various wares, as, for example, in Okamura Toshinobu's (fl. 1716–1751) series showing fans, cosmetics, kimonos, hair ornaments, and so forth (Figure 5.10). Yet another actor genre depicts actors delivering customary ritual speeches *(kōjō)* from the stage. One such print from about 1825 by Utagawa Toyokuni (Figure 5.11) depicts Ichikawa Danjūrō in the role of the night watchman Kichiroku in the middle of delivering such a *kōjō*, except that it is in the form of an ad, with the *onnagata* Iwai Murasakiwaka, in the role of Kichiroku's wife, posing demurely at his side helpfully brandishing a signboard that reads "Cosmetics and Toothpastes available from Yorozuya Naosuke at the Aeidō in Kawata-kubomachi, Ushigome."[26]

This practice of actors delivering advertising speeches on stage was already in full swing by 1715, when for the first time actors performing at all three major theaters were inserting into each performance *kōjō* advertising kimono patterns currently available at the Echigoya in Nihonbashi. This vogue demonstrates one aspect of how advertising served to link the otherwise ostensibly disparate worlds of commercial merchandising and the theater. It was not enough that actors and courtesans, in their important function as human billboards, should be seen wearing the latest designs and fashions, and that artists, like paparazzi, should seek to depict them that way for devoted fans avid for every last shred of information about them. Actors, courtesans, sumo wrestlers, shop girls, restaurants, and teahouses worked together with the artists who depicted them in much the same lucrative constellations of advertising practices that have been used by Japanese media and department stores in recent decades, continuing the old practice of using popular sumo wrestlers, actors, singers, models and other *tarento* (and now famous foreigners) to sell all manner of goods.

In 1718, a few years after the stage announcement ads for the Echigoya, the actor Ichikawa Danjūrō II (1688–1757) began inserting his wildly popular tongue-twisting patter from the play *Uirōuri* (one of the plays included by Danjūrō VII among the *Jūhachiban,* or "eighteen kabuki plays of the Ichikawa family") into

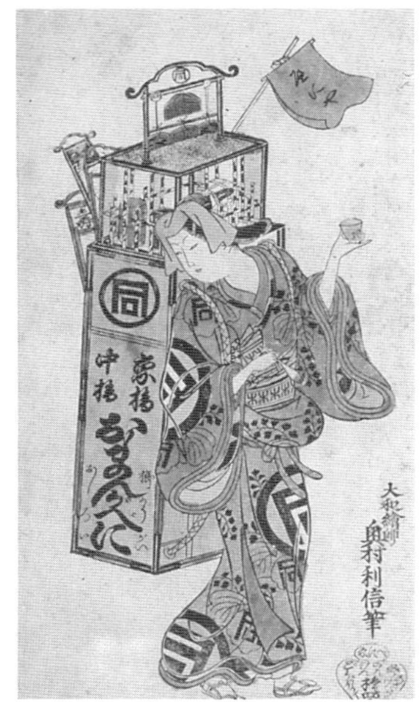


FIGURE 5.10. *(Above)* Okamura Toshinobu, *Sannogawa Ichimatsu as the Cosmetics Vendor Oman.* Tokyo National Museum. From *Tōkyō Kokuritsu Hakubutsukan shozō: Matsukata korekushon ukiyo-e hin ten* (Holdings of the Tokyo National Museum: exhibition of *ukiyo-e* art from the Matsukata Collection) (1991), 48.

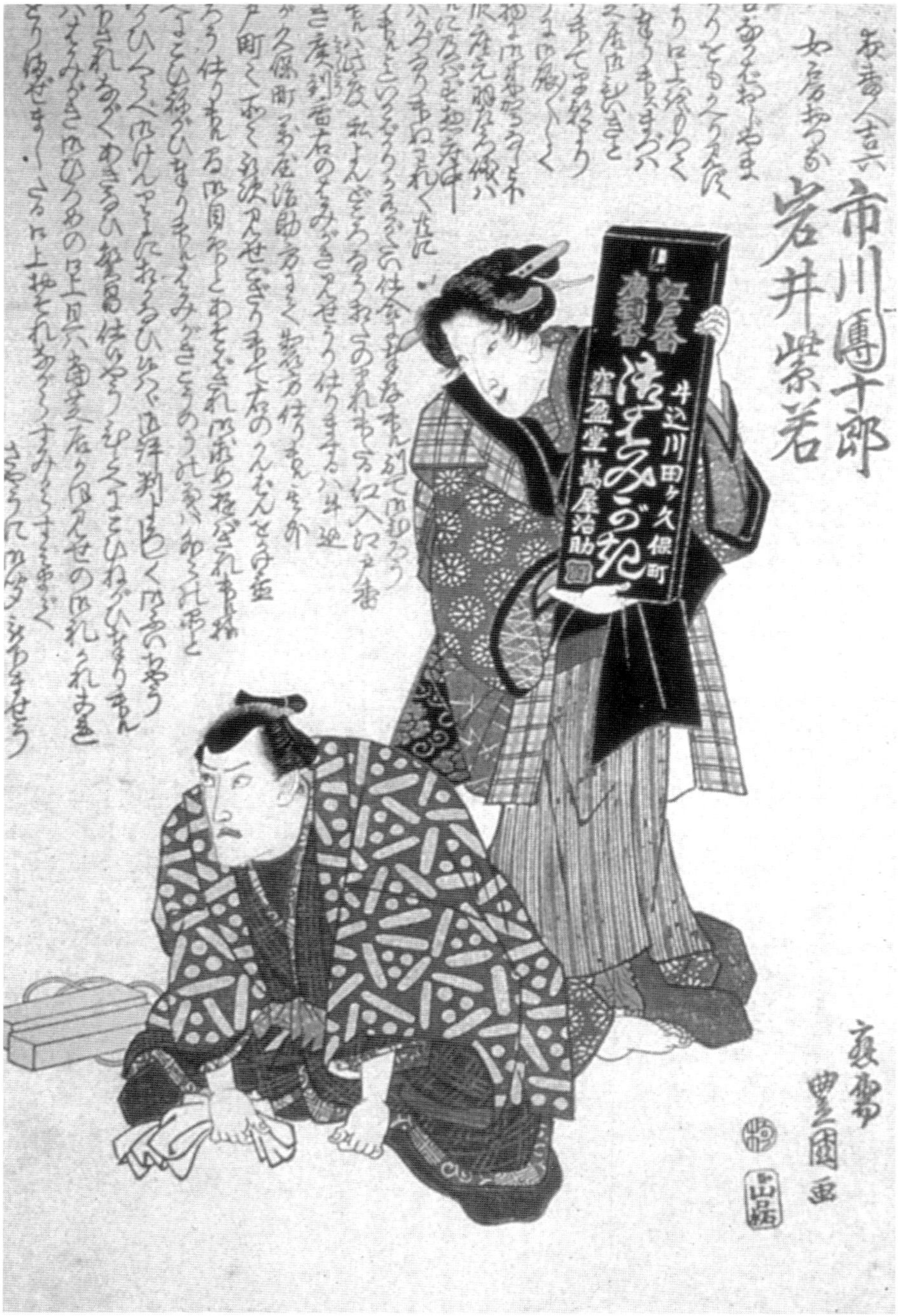

FIGURE 5.11. *(Right)* Utagawa Toyokuni, Ichikawa Danjūrō as Kichiroku, and Iwai Murasakiwaka as Otsuchi. From Nakada Setsuko, *Edo Meiji Taishō Shōwa kōkoku no naka no Nippon: kōkoku wa jidai no nagare o utsusu kagami da* (Tokyo: Daiyamondosha, 1993), frontispiece.

performances of *Wakamidori no ikioi Sōga* (Fresh young forces of the Sōga clan). Included in the patter was the information that the Yuan-dynasty medicinal oil known as Tonchinkō, "for sale by Toraya Fujiemon at Rankanbashi in Odawara," had, among its other alleged powers, responsibility for the great oral fluency being demonstrated at this very moment by the actor himself.[27] Danjūrō II, the story goes, suffering from a bad cough and hoarse throat, was cured by this medicine and in gratitude worked the ad into his role. Perhaps largely as a result, little of the play but the tour-de-force tongue twister is still performed today and that usually only as part of a bravura *kōjō* delivered on the occasion of an actor's assumption of the name of Ichikawa Danjūrō.[28] Danjūrō II, like most famous actors, also lent his name and *mimasu* trademark for use in commercial tie-ins, which in his case included the popular moxa "Danjūrō-mogusa."

Although Danjūrō II's *Uirōuri* patter is undoubtedly the most famous example, it is hardly the first, for the recorded history of stage advertising stretches back some two decades earlier. As early as 1697, his predecessor Danjūrō I is reported to have inserted an ad into the play *Daifukuchō sankai Nagoya* (Nagoya enters the ledgerbooks) at the Nakamura-za that was repeated by Danjūrō II at the Morita-za in 1717 in the "Daifukuchō" scene of *Hōnō taiheiki* (An offering of the *Taiheiki* [Chronicle of the Great Peace]). Danjūrō II himself not only incorporated a plug for his own brand-name moxa in *Keisei hibariyama* (The prostitute's mountain of swallows), performed at the Yamamura-za in 1709; among other products, he is also on record as having included one for "Shirazake" liquor in *Hanayakata aigo no sakura* (Cherry blossoms beloved of the great houses), performed in 1713 at the Yamamura-za, using a speech that would later be included by Danjūrō VII in *Sukeroku yukari Edo no sakura* (Sukeroku dyed by the cherries of Edo).[29] Such reports suggest that the practice by actors of inserting product-placement speeches into their lines was so commonplace as to be nearly unremarkable.

Advertising is also an integral part of *ukiyo-e* print art. Many prints by Kunisada, Kuniyoshi, and Eisen, among others, for example, depict beautiful women using such well-known cosmetic products of the day as "Senjokō" (or "Sennyokō"), "Kumonoue," and "Kumoinokō" white base ointments *(oshiroi)*.[30] The name Senjokō derives from the stage name (Senjo) of the famed *onnagata* Segawa Kikunojō III, whose own cosmetics shop was only one of the eighteen such shops recorded in 1774 as being owned by actors. As late as 1859, Senjokō was even the subject of a *kibyōshi* story, Santei Shunba's *Senjokō shichihen geshō* (Fairy maiden: semen transformations in makeup) illustrated by Utagawa Kunisada, given out as a promotional item to customers. And it is featured prominently in many contemporary prints, where its characteristic blue and yellow wrapper is usually left conspicuously in sight as a standard fixture of boudoir scenes. In one print by Eisen, *Gorishō musubu no ennichi: Bishamonten* (Fair day at the Bishamonten Shrine: receiving Buddha's blessings, 1823) (Plate 3), Senjokō even appears as the subject of a *senryū* fan-poem whose language seems to portend that of today's TV ads:

| | |
|---|---|
| *Yamamomo mo* | Even the blossoms of the |
| *yosōu hana ya* | mountain peach wear makeup— |
| *Senjokō* | Senjokō[31] |

Despite its ostensibly religious theme, this print offers a good example of how advertising is used to create a mood of eroticism, for everything in the print, and not least this appeal to literary eroticism, connotes sex: the large "male" half of the paired his-and-hers teacups *(meotojawan)* is placed conspicuously by the woman's bedside to suggest a partner within, while she, dressed in negligée and holding in her mouth the *misugami* paper that invariably signals sexual activity, prepares to slip under the mosquito netting and join her partner in bed. The implication is that she will be blessed with the good fortune she has prayed to Buddha for—and getting lucky tonight is assured by her choice of the right cosmetics.[32] Again, the sixth of Eisen's *Ukiyo bijin jūnikagetsu* (Floating world beauties of the twelve months) series (1835) (Figure 5.12) depicts the Tennō Matsuri in Kyoto (the banners are inscribed Gion Gozu Tennō (Ox-Headed Heavenly King of Gion), with a poem that reads:

| | |
|---|---|
| *kesshō suru* | Makeup |
| *oshiroi mo yoku* | and lots of powder, too, |
| *nori o shite* | are the rule |
| *ukaremi ni deru* | when getting dolled up |
| *Gion funahoko* | to go out to see the Gion floats |

The poem turns on the pun on *nori*, meaning both "paste" (as *oshiroi* was used) and "Buddha's Law" (the ostensible theme of the festival).

Most familiar are the huge number of prints showing famous courtesans wearing kimonos or carrying umbrellas bearing the trademarks of well-known brothels or popular shops such as Ebisuya, Daimaruya, Matsuzakaya, or Echigoya; sipping the tea or saké of certain shops; or dining in certain restaurants (Figure 5.13).[33] Some of these reveal their advertising intentions at a glance, while others are more subtle. Which goods and places were currently in fashion was,

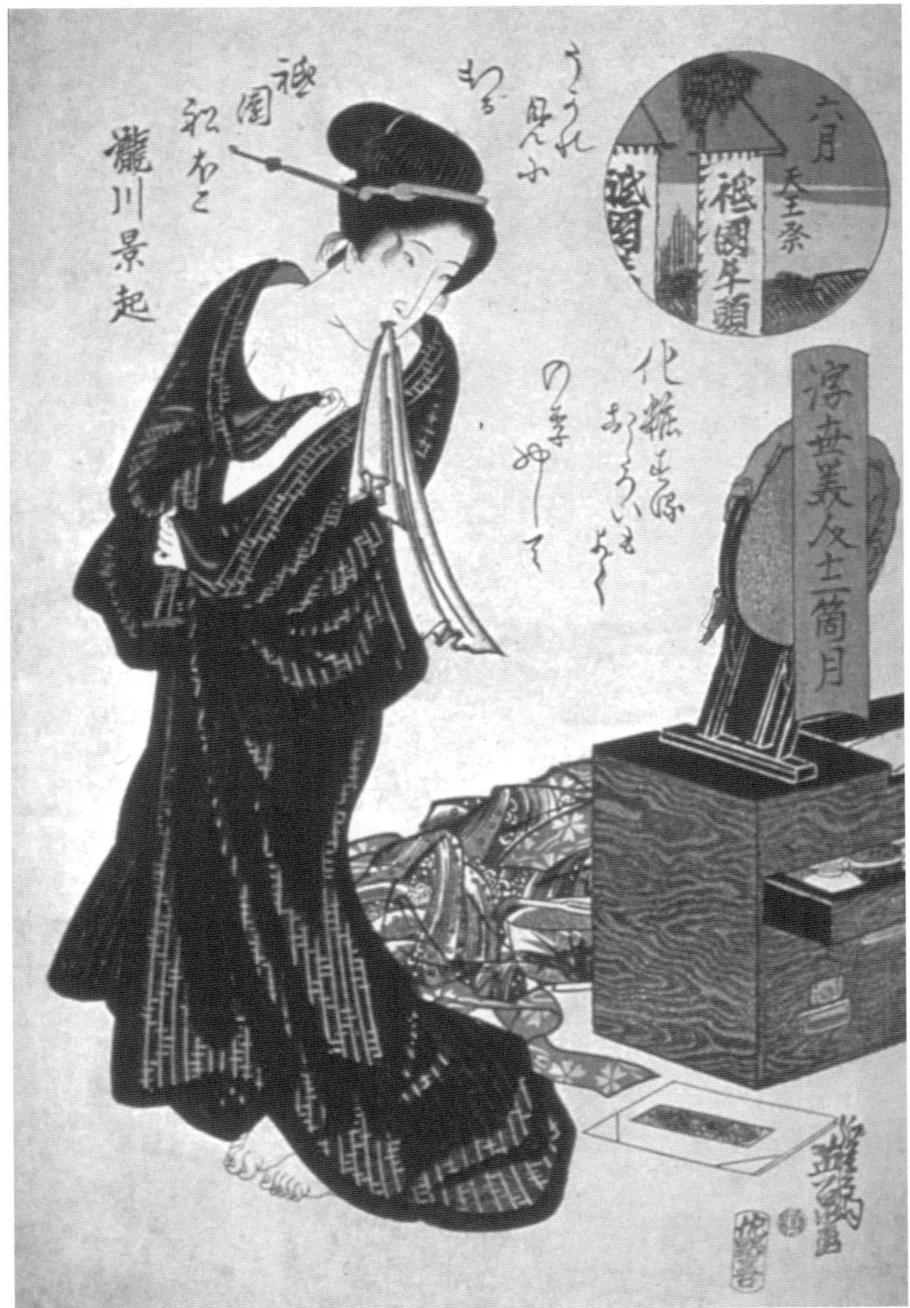


**FIGURE 5.12.** Keisai Eisen, *Ukiyo bijin jūnikagetsu: Tennō matsuri* (The hours of the women of the floating world: the Tennō Festival), 1835. From Takahashi Hakushin, *Ukiyo-e zanmai: Kunisada to Eisen* (Absorbed in pictures of the floating world: Kunisada and Eisen) (Obihiro: Arita Shobō, 1980), 219.

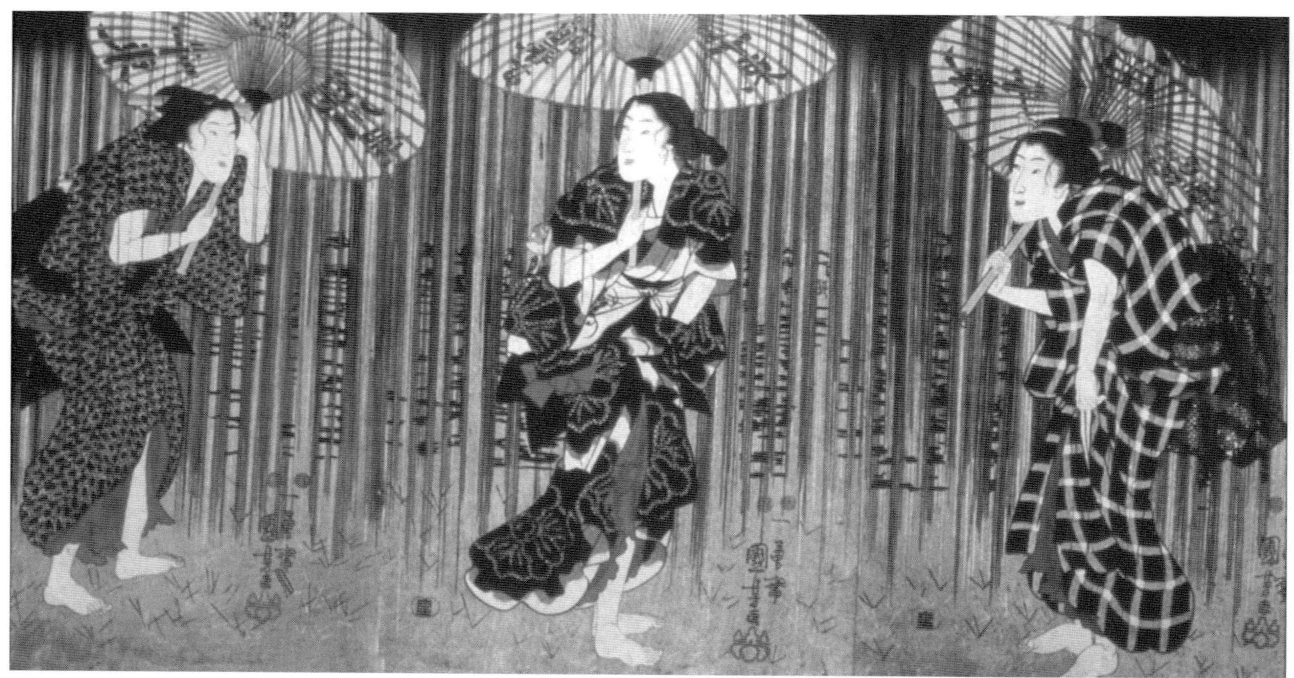

**FIGURE 5.13.** Keisai Eisen, *Summer Evening Rain,* depicting umbrellas advertising the Tagawaya teahouse and the Chūshuntei restaurant. From Suzuki Juzo, *Kuniyoshi* (Tokyo: Heibonsha, 1992), 261.

with the aid of such advertising, as much a matter of common knowledge among the cognoscenti of that time as of our own.[34] The detailed portrayals of actual brothels, prostitutes, and connoisseur products in art, fiction, and the theater call for a reevaluation of a play such as *Sukeroku* (another of the "Eighteen Plays," performed by the endorsement-minded Danjūrō II in 1713, 1716, and 1749) in the context of their advertising function—whether directly underwritten or not—for the myriad commercial aspects of the pleasure quarters.[35]

These advertising practices, which were ubiquitous and pervasive in their time, are all part of the intricate operation of what I have called a larger "economy of desire," which forms the context for what are usually now seen as the more remarkable manifestations of the erotic life of the Edo period. In this light, the familiar pornographic Edo prints can be understood as stylized icons of increasingly enlarged production and consumption in which sexual intercourse becomes a matter of genitalized clothing not so much worn by as framing its wearers. In these erotic prints, men are reduced to stylized representations of a prodigious ability to expend and women, to an equally prodigious ability to consume.

CHAPTER SIX

NORMAN BRYSON

# Westernizing Bodies: Women, Art, and Power in Meiji *Yōga*

The Rokumeikan must have been an interesting place.

By the 1880s it was becoming apparent to the Meiji elite that the opening of Japan to foreign influence was going to require a far greater measure of social integration between Westerners and Japanese than had been anticipated in the first years of the new era. There could be no question of continuing the old policy of confining foreigners territorially to the port centers. The setting up of new industries to be run at least initially by foreign supervisors, the endlessly ramifying process of bringing Japan into line with Western countries in the fields of international law and commerce, and the sheer volume of trade meant that the presence of foreigners en masse was going to become an inevitable, and very likely permanent, feature of the national landscape. In a country that had warded off foreign contact for two and a half centuries, the prospect of an actual influx of Westerners through the length and breadth of the nation must have been particularly daunting. During Japan's seclusion, the distance between Japanese and Westerners had been absolute. In Nagasaki images of foreigners going about their business, playing their music, eating, drinking, and wearing their exotic clothes, the gap between the two sides had expressed itself as an unbridgeable optical interval, a glass wall through which the images peered with a kind of zoological curiosity (Figure 6.1). What would the foreigners think of Japan, its customs and way of life, once they had broken past the barriers that had always confined them? What would it be like to have foreigners as visitors, acquaintances, colleagues? And what about their wives?

It was Inoue Kaoru, foreign minister from 1879 to 1887, who seems to have been most exercised by this issue. He had more experience of Western living than most of his peers: an early student of Dutch studies with a particular interest in Western armaments and ballistics, he had been sent together with Itō Hirobumi to study in England; he had traveled in Europe from 1876 to 1878 to in-

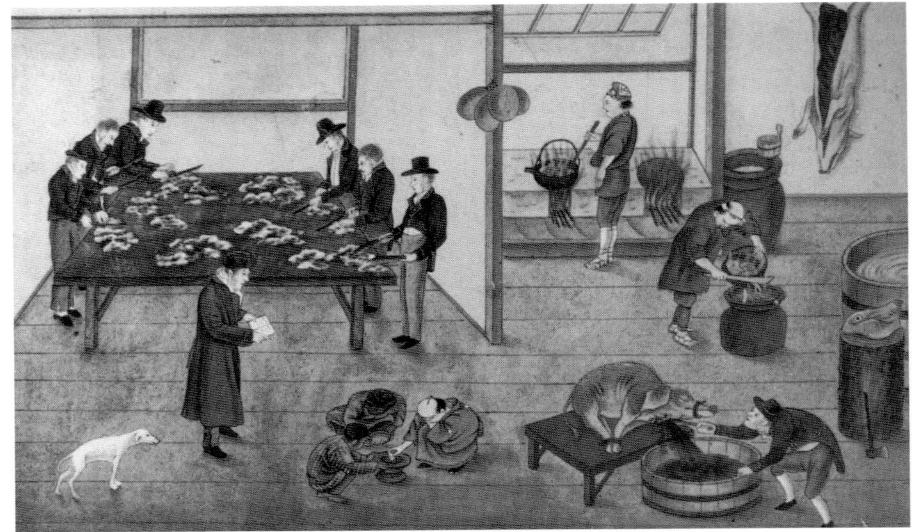

FIGURE 6.1. Kawahara Keiga, *Scroll of the Dutch Factory: A Kitchen,* early nineteenth century. Nagasaki City Museum, Nagasaki.

vestigate matters of finance and taxation, and as foreign minister he was on the front line of negotiations concerning treaty revision and the overhauling of the legal system. He was determined that the government play a leading role in directing the next stage of modernization, when Westerners would come to interact with the people directly. His announcement of the Rokumeikan project was couched in terms that present it as a forcing house, an irritant in the social body that nevertheless will generate new kinds of national force and confidence:

> The Japanese must achieve a system of self-government and a vigor of conduct sufficient to assure the creation of a strong people and a powerful and effective government. . . . How can we impress upon the minds of our thirty-eight million people this daring spirit and attitude of independence and self-government? In my opinion, the only course is to have them clash with the Europeans, so that they will personally feel inconvenienced, realize their disadvantage, and absorb an awareness of Western vigorousness. . . . I consider that the way to do this is to provide for truly free intercourse between Japanese and foreigners.[1]

The instrument devised for this purpose, the Rokumeikan, was enormously influential: it gave its name to the whole era between 1884 and around 1889. Designed by the British architect Josiah Conder, it was essentially a club where high-placed Japanese could mix freely with Western visitors in an atmosphere comparable to what was imagined to be the glittering social whirl of London or Paris.

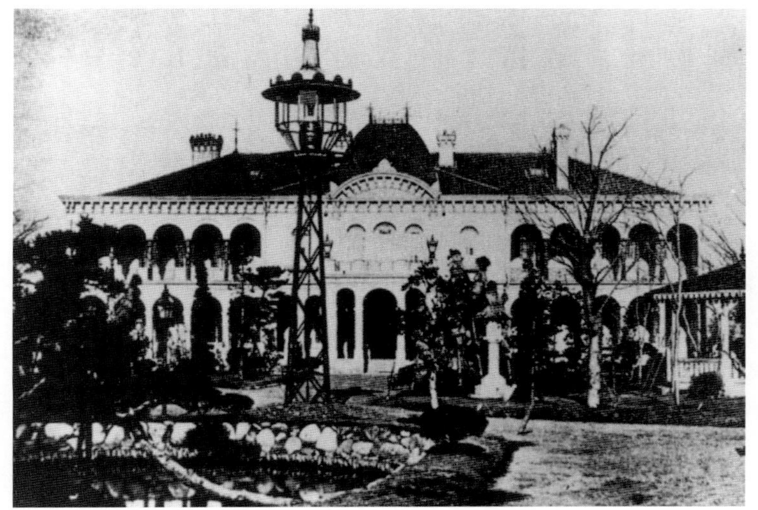

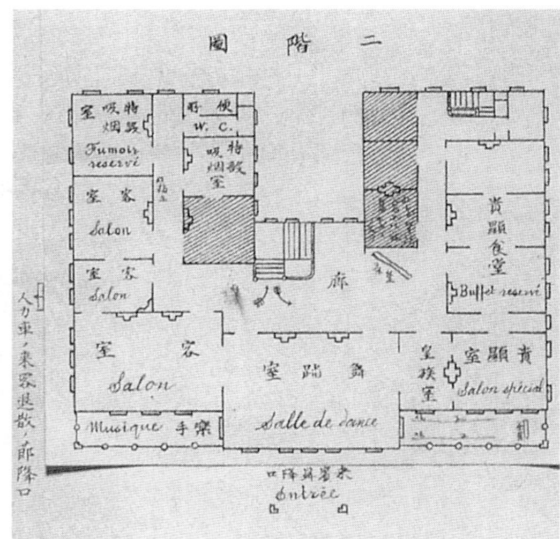


Building the Rokumeikan was costly and difficult; three years and perhaps 180,000 yen were needed to complete it (Figures 6.2 and 6.3). Conder seems to have been sensitive to the pan-European sensibility of his patrons in avoiding too direct an association with any one European national style. The Rokumeikan could not appear too French, English, or Italian, but should be equidistant from—or equally close to—all the nationalities of its guests. With its Louvre-like roof, the upper level invokes Paris; the open arcading on two stories suggests a generalized sense of Renaissance Italy; the high voids of the porch resemble those in grand entranceways of British architecture in the East. Perhaps American visitors found it American, and French visitors French; that, at any rate, would be the desirable effect. Inside were drawing rooms, a library, a billiard room, a music room, quarters for official visitors, a dining room catered by a French master chef, bars, and a ballroom. It was the background to the principal events and social occasions that the government and the visitors together were able to devise: concerts of Western music, charity bazaars, banquets, tea dances, and balls.

The visitors declared it altogether a success: "The Rokumeikan is so excellently planned that even a monster entertainment like that of last evening presents no difficulties. Its capabilities have now been repeatedly tested, and we imagine that the hospitable people of Tokyo must often congratulate themselves on possessing a handsome and stable building so admirably adapted for the accommodation, distribution, and easy circulation of large assemblages of guests."[2]

**FIGURE 6.2.** *(Left)* Josiah Conder, Rokumeikan, photo 1883. From Takasugi Mikitarō, *Meiji Taishō kenchiku shashin shūran* (Collection of Meiji and Taishō photographs of architecture) (Tōkyō Kenchiku Gakkai, 1936).

**FIGURE 6.3.** *(Right)* Floor plan of the second floor of Rokumeikan. Gaimushō Gaikō Shiryōkan, Tokyo.

A subject of frequent remark among all nationalities was the successfully Western appearance of the Japanese women present and their honorable acquittal on the dance floor. "In the dancing last evening the Japanese ladies took a large share. Indeed, it has now become difficult to distinguish them from their sisters of the West, so thoroughly have they adopted European costumes, and so perfectly versed are they in the usages of Western society" (Figure 6.4).[3]

The foreign visitors might well be surprised by this craze for the crush bar and the dance floor. The goings-on at Western diplomatic receptions had met with considerably less enthusiasm when first witnessed in Washington, D.C., by members of the Japanese delegation to the United States in 1860. The leader of that embassy, Deputy Ambassador Muragaki, took pains to record in his diary his disapproval and shock at the absurd proceedings laid on during his visit by Secretary of State Lewis Cass. His entry is extremely revealing and worth examining at length:

> We arrived at Cass's residence. I wondered about the nature of the ceremony we were going to perform on this occasion, since it was an invitation from the Prime Minister. To our great surprise, however, we found that the hall, passages, and rooms were all packed with hundreds of men and

**FIGURE 6.4.** Hashimoto Chikanobu, *Picture of Dignitaries Dancing*, 1888. Photo, Shōgakukan.

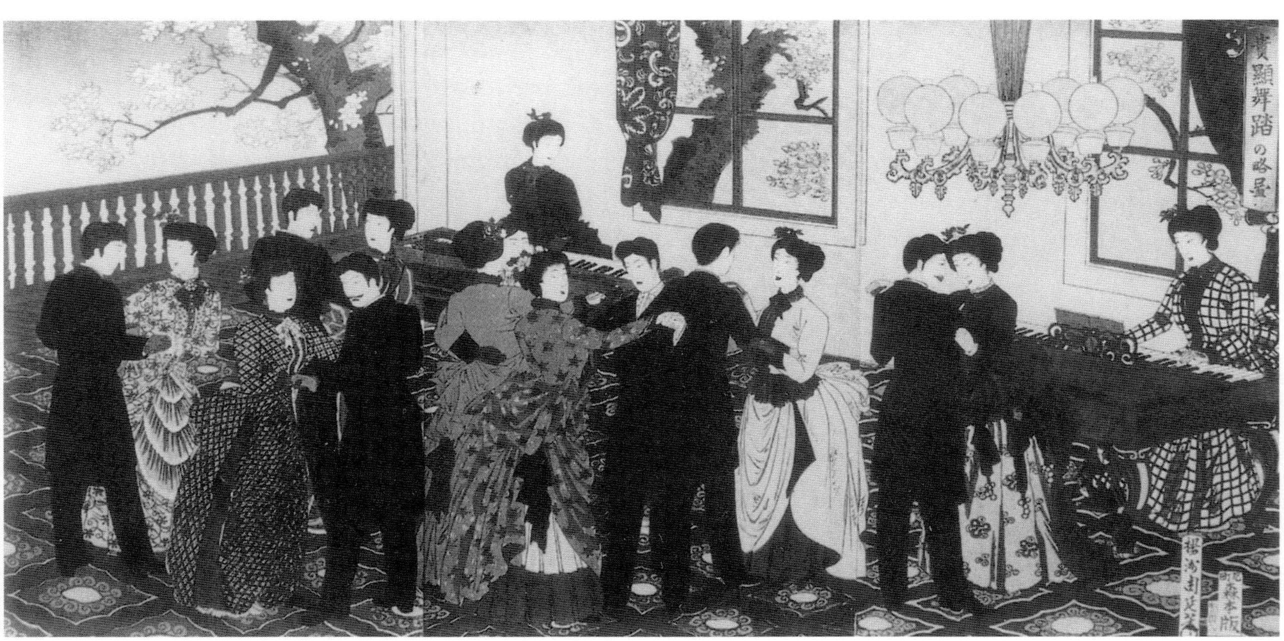

women. . . . At the center of the table were Japanese and American flags to express friendship. We had some drinks and food at the table. Soon we were led away to another large room; its floor was covered with smooth boards. In one corner there was a band playing something called "music" on instruments that looked like Chinese lutes. Men were in uniform with epaulets and swords, and women with bare shoulders were dressed in thin white clothes. They had those wide skirts around their waists. Men and women moved round the room couple by couple, walking on tiptoe to the time of the music. It was just like a number of mice running around and around. There was neither taste nor charm. It was quite amusing to watch women's huge skirts spread wider and wider like balloons as they turned. . . . As for myself, I was astonished by the sight, and wondered whether this was dream or reality. We asked DuPont to say good-night to the host for us, and left for the hotel. Admittedly, this is a nation with no order or ceremony, but it is indeed odd that the Prime Minister should invite an ambassador of another country to an event of this sort! My sense of displeasure is boundless: there is no respect for order and ceremony or obligation. The only way to exonerate them is by recognizing that all this absence of ceremony issues from their feeling of friendship.

All is strange,
Appearance and language,
I must be in a dream-land.

Women are white and beautiful, and they are handsomely dressed with gold and silver decorations. Although I am becoming accustomed to their appearance, I find their reddish hair unattractive, and their eyes look like those of dogs. Now and then, though, I see a black-haired woman who also has black eyes. They must be descendants of some Asian race. Naturally they look very attractive.[4]

Why was Deputy Ambassador Muragaki so displeased in 1860—and why were Japanese men and women whirling round the Rokumeikan dance floor with such gusto in 1885? Perhaps the first question is easier to address. The Cass reception must be counted as a unique moment of intercultural collision. Not only Muragaki but all the members of the Japanese mission were appalled by the evening's entertainments. Hidaka Keizaburō Tameyoshi, a middle-ranking officer, complained in his diary that "women and maidens were nude from shoulders to arms . . . the way men and women, both young and old, mixed in the dance, was simply insufferable to watch."[5] Morita Kiyoyuki, too, found it an unnerving sight: "Although there was very little that was licentious or lewd, it was unbearable to watch."[6] Ono Tomogorō declared the dancing of the American women was "a bore that dragged on and on" and that the singing resembled the "gibberish scream of a bewitched woman."[7]

The idea that women should be present at all at a major official function lay quite outside the visitors' cultural experience. In Japan a foreign ambassador would be received only by men, at least during the crucial phases of the proceedings. Perhaps afterwards women might be brought in to supply a little diversion, but these would be professional entertainers, trained for the purpose, not wives and daughters. The element of confusion introduced by the dancing of men and women together ("like a number of mice running around and around") seems to have been especially disquieting to Muragaki. As Masao Miyoshi has pointed out, the deputy ambassador quickly reaches for the watchwords of order to recover his composure (ceremony, *rei*, and obligation, *gi*). At the end of his account, he has recourse in the same way to *waka* verse, as if to purify himself from the contamination he has been forced to endure. At least part of his sense of pollution is evidently sexual. For a man filled with disapproval, his gaze and his description dwell on a surprising number of visual details concerning the foreign women: their bare shoulders, their thin white clothes, their waists, their ballooning skirts. Once his mind has calmed down thanks to his exercise in *waka* therapy, he seems able to address this aspect of his perturbation more directly. After the lines of verse his entry bounces back and forth between sexual interest and sexual refusal. The women are white and beautiful, he is getting used to them—but their reddish hair and their eyes remind him of "dogs." Even so, some of them—the ones with black hair and eyes, that is—are naturally "very attractive." To permit himself this realization, however, it is necessary for Muragaki first to annex these more beautiful ones to an Asian physical type, to endogamy, and thus to understandable and licit attraction.

The one point, then, at which Muragaki seems to lower his guard and to permit a current of feeling to work its way past the severity of his reserve is sexuality. Even he, and in the same moments when he is moved to place the alien physique on a par with canines, is thinking of hair, eyes, and a racial fantasy of Asiatic ur-Europeans that will allow him to indulge his evident interest in the bare shoulders, arms, and whirling gowns. The Rokumeikan will take this crack in the samurai armor and elaborate it into a cultural concourse. It is through the presence of women, the dance, and the spectacle of bare shoulders and turning crinolines multiplied to infinity that the Rokumeikan will build and bind the international fraternity.

It took hard work for Japanese women of the Rokumeikan years to achieve fashion parity with their "sisters of the West." The convenient twentieth-century idea of simply choosing from the racks had not yet made its appearance. Instead, one had to select a model from fashion plates and magazines (of which there was by now an abundance), have a seamstress copy it in a chosen material or do so oneself, and then make the creation personally unique by varying the details, drapery, and accessories. The fashions of the 1880s must have presented a particular challenge. The hooped skirts that so interested Muragaki in 1860 had given way to the bustle, with its elaborate infrastructure of whalebone or steel, and its over-mantle and inset cushions surmounted by wasp waist and ample bodice. The costume was difficult to make and difficult to manage. Ideally the figure would glide in space, like a train on its track; turnings could not be too abrupt or sudden, since in effect the body had attached to itself a cumbersome protrusion with its own center of gravity and inertia. Sitting down was an art in itself. The *queue de Paris* had to be deftly pushed to one side so that it sat next to one on the sofa, almost by itself.[8] Getting up was not much easier: the bustle had to be returned to its correct alignment without this problem appearing to preoccupy the wearer.

Then there was the whole question, given this unwieldy doppelganger, of appropriate movement. The narrow skirts of women's kimono required steps to be short and rapid, with the foot never raised much above ground level and the toes slightly turned in. The habitual movements and rhythms evolved around Edo women's kimono must have been hard to cast aside or to transform into the smooth majestic glidings that hooped and bustled gowns assumed. In Western clothes, too, the female body had to express itself as a volumetric, statuelike form. The kimono is flat; it folds flat, like paper, and of itself it makes no particular accommodation to bodily contour. Nineteenth-century European dress, in contrast, is premised on the molding of fabric to the underlying form; the styles of the 1880s were strictly tailored, with the bodice fitting tightly all around. In terms of bodily outline or silhouette, the contrast between Paris and Tokyo was perhaps never greater than in the 1880s. In her proclamation of 1866 urging Japanese women to adopt Western dress, the empress emphasized that the new costumes were actually close in spirit to those of the past ("If we look at contemporary Western women's wear, we find that it combines a top or jacket and a skirt in the manner of our ancient Japanese system of dress").[9] But the adjustment must have required considerable agility and practice. It must have sometimes been consoling, at Rokumeikan, to think that one could at any rate escape the fatiguing occidental gear on at last returning home.

Despite the difficulties, Rokumeikan worked. Here is Pierre Loti, a guest at a ball held at the Rokumeikan in the mid-1880s:

> I stop in surprise in front of a person with a distinguished and refined face, wearing shoulder-length gloves, impeccably coiffed in a suitable manner; her age indeterminate, obscured by white rice-powder; a long satin train of very pale lilac colour, very discreet, decorated with garlands of little forest flowers, of deliciously varied nuance; her bodice forming a slim sheath and covered with a stiff embroidery studded with pearls: in short, an attire that would do very well in Paris and is really worn very smartly by this astonishing parvenue. So, I take her seriously and offer a polite greeting. She, in turn, is equally polite and above all courteous, and she offers me her hand in American fashion with a self-confidence that quite devastates me.
>
> In passing, I quickly inspect the other two women as well. The first is a petite darling all in pale rose with camellias on her train. And then the last of the group, on whom my eyes would have lingered voluntarily, the Duchess Arimasen,[10] a young person from the old aristocracy married to the Emperor's grand master of ceremonies: jet-black hair, pulled up very high in a chignon *à la clown*, as is the fashion this winter season; pretty velvet eyes like an adorable little kitten; attired in ivory satin in the style of Louis XV. It is an unheard of effect, this mixture of Japan and eighteenth century France, this pretty Asian face wearing hoop skirt and tight bodice, just as at Trianon.
>
> Oh! Very well done, ladies; my sincere compliments to all three! Your attitude is most amusing and your disguises are brilliant.[11]

It is perhaps difficult to avoid being irritated by Loti's tone of supremely discerning condescension. With its air of cosmopolitan nonchalance, Loti's reaction to Rokumeikan seems light years away from Deputy Ambassador Muragaki's perplexed response to the Cass reception in Washington in 1860. But it is in fact quite similar. If a Japanese woman meets with Pierre Loti's approval, as does the "Duchess Arimasen," she is paid the compliment of being assimilated—elevated—to Loti's own culture. The Duchess Arimasen—it is quite remarkable—is just like a fashionable woman of Paris! In the same way that Muragaki had tried to absorb the figure of the black-haired and black-eyed American women he found attractive into the ranks of some imaginary ur-race of Asiatic Europeans, so Loti annexes the "Duchess Arimasen" to the type "Pompadour." In the same moment that Loti elevates "Arimasen" to the exalted imaginary status of a court lady at the Trianon, he also belittles her with a vocabulary of sickening cutesiness: her companion is a "petite darling," she herself is an "adorable little kitten" (with Muragaki it was much the same: the women are "white and beautiful"—but they are also like "dogs"). Loti seems sincere in his praise of the ladies' brilliant artifice, itself a compliment to Rokumeikan as a whole; he congratulates the Rokumeikan ladies on their brilliant disguise. At the same time, he finds the whole theater of Rokumeikan absurd: it is, he says, like a second-rate casino at a French spa town.

In fact, the complex, absurd, weirdly entertaining world of ballroom diplomacy effectively equalizes and neutralizes both sides. Foreign Minister Inoue—and Secretary of State Cass—presumably knew exactly what they were about. The actual political and diplomatic situation was perilous. Inoue was concerned that, unless the Japanese made "the Empire like the countries of Europe and our people like the peoples of Europe," Japan could not hope to withstand the impact of the West or prolonged competition with the Western powers. The stakes could hardly be higher. In Inoue's view Japan had to achieve a system of self-government and a "vigor of conduct sufficient to her new circumstances," or the country would remain forever behind the foreigners whom the *Hōchi shinbun* described, in 1885, as evidently "more industrious, better educated, more courageous, and more intelligent."[12] To neutralize the situation, the presence of women from both sides was highly desirable.

In place of an outright clash between two antagonists poised for a fight, each side now reconfigures around the third (and excluded) term, woman. It is not that love conquers all—that the spectacle of so many Countess Inoues or bare white shoulders simply makes the men lay down their arms, like Mars conquered by Venus. Rather, the interaction that the presence of women as quasi-available sexual objects permits is such that each side starts to assimilate the other through the milieu of sexuality, localized in the bodies of their attendant females. Muragaki confesses, after his *waka* self-cleansing, to finding that the women are "white and beautiful," and he ends by fantasizing a hybrid erotic creature, half European and half Japanese. Pierre Loti may be dying to impress his reader with his polish and urbanity, and he is at pains to show how much he thinks the Rokumeikan crowd are simply (like himself) arrivistes. But he ends by imagining the countess as one of his own kind, an elegant Parisian hostess who has befriended him and takes his hand in the trusting, American way, and by putting "Arimasen" through a series of complex metamorphoses that conclude in her absorption back into his own nation ("Louis XV," "just as at the Trianon").

The women of Rokumeikan, Japanese and non-Japanese alike, were the great equalizers of the show. By virtue of their attendance and their efforts, they took a situation of potentially extreme antagonism and converted it to one of male fraternity: men of different nations, as men, could close ranks around the women of Rokumeikan. In a sense the Rokumeikan ladies were the heirs to the salon tradition of the previous century. Why did the *philosophes* flock to the gatherings of the madames de Lambert, du Deffand, and d'Epinay? Did their hostesses really possess such devastating ideas? Were the women who presided over the salons the true stars in their world? Or were they rather catalysts: able to end the competition between men, with their struggles over rank and position, by providing a milieu in which they were, with regard to the hostess herself, equally men, just as she was, to them, and equally, a woman?

In any case, the women were not thereby empowered in any way the men of either side would recognize. It would be more accurate to say that they were made over as a medium of intramale exchange. The circulation of women accompanied and stimulated the general traffic of goods and ideas that made up the larger context of modernization in the Rokumeikan years. It was because of their association with men that they were valued, not because they were starting to acquire the same power that the men had. Perhaps women like the "Duchess Arimasen" might be best described as counters in a game of intermasculine identification. The declared goal of Foreign Minister Inoue in establishing Rokumeikan had been to "make our people like the people of Europe." It was for exactly this reason that those opposed to Rokumeikan modernization objected: "Current education is a matter of plastering Western civilization on one's person—and not merely plastering, either, for they are not satisfied until the body itself changes into that of a Westerner. Moreover, we have reached the point where some people advocate not only changing the body into that of a Westerner, but also turning the spirit into that of a Westerner, so that in the end all human races will turn into Western races."[13] In this process whereby middle (and later) Meiji Japanese "became" Westerners, women played a crucial role in the cultural imaginary. It was not necessarily because Japanese men found that their wives and daughters looked more beautiful that way that the latter had to start wearing bustles and bonnets and dance the polka. It was because they thought that this was what Western men desired. By possessing what Western men desired, they could enter into the orbit of the West through identification: in possessing the desire of the other, they could assimilate the Other to the order of the Same. Rokumeikan was a theater of identification, a *salon des glaces* in which a European face was returned by the mirror as Asian, a Japanese face as Western. In itself the mirror is without qualities: it simply reflects what the men are or want—a "woman."

Perhaps the most elaborate game of mirrors was the masquerade ball hosted by Count Itō on April 20, 1887. Four hundred guests were invited; it was probably the most extravagant, the most extreme, of all the Rokumeikan nights. The count himself appeared in the costume of a Venetian nobleman. His wife wore a Spanish-style dress with mantilla. Ten days later the following account appeared in the *Japan Weekly Mail:*

> The first Fancy Dress Ball given in the capital came off on Wednesday evening, and was a brilliant success. The handsome salons of Count Itō's Nagata-chō residence were rapidly filled, after nine o'clock, with a gay and motley throng of warriors and peasants, gods and devils, kings and nobles. Much forethought had evidently been expended on the different costumes, which were shown to advantage in the brilliantly lighted ballroom. This spacious apartment, now in its first winter, is decorated in white and gold, and is lighted with electricity. The floor, of seasoned *keyaki*, was, on Wednesday night, in excellent condition for dancing.
>
> . . . Several ladies, one an Imperial princess, appeared as Night, and did the character full justice. . . . Britannia, in coat of mail and burnished helmet, was there in state. An American Republic in stars and stripes was also represented from Yokohama. . . . A lady of the Imperial court appeared in an exquisite Persian costume of crimson and white with pearls, and a French lady from Yokohama was charming in Egyptian dress.
>
> . . . A Japanese gentleman had donned the conical corded hat and the tight-fitting habits of a Tyrolean peasant. No country was better represented in the ballroom than the pleasant land of France. Louis Quatorze and Louis Quinze court dresses were favourites both with ladies and gentlemen, with Westerners and with Japanese. Prince Kita-Shirakawa appeared in a bright and becoming French Court costume. Most charming in every respect was the costume of an English lady who appeared in the rich embroidery and piquante collar of Marie Antoinette.
>
> . . . Of the success of the ball and the thoroughness of the satisfaction of the guests there can be no two opinions. The experiment was a bold one,

> but the result showed that in a pageant of this sort Japanese taste and fancy are inimitable. The one regret in connection with the affair is that it revived our recollection of the delightfully picturesque costumes which Japan has discarded for Western swallow-tails and bell-tops.[14]

This was identification with a vengeance! One might perhaps want to think of Itō's ill-fated masquerade (the furor that erupted when the details of the ball became known was a factor in the abrupt ending of treaty negotiations and in Foreign Minister Inoue's resignation) as a transposition into the terms of fantasy of the harder realities of Japan's absorption of economic, technological, and military expertise—as the expression, in a playful accompanying superstructure, of the serious business of modernization occurring in the base. But one could equally think of it the other way around: that the masquerade reveals the extent to which Meiji modernization unfolded as a fantasmatic process, centrally dependent on a cultural imaginary in which self-identification with the West was played out; as a systematic attempt at "protective mimicry" in which the threat posed by the Other was countered by absorbing differences into the category of the Same.

To that extent, the modernization denied difference, in fact, was built on denial of difference. It occurred as the assimilation of the West into Japan and as the assimilation of Japan into the West, in a mirror economy of mimesis and internalization. By the same token, the cultural imaginary expelled and abjected from itself whatever sites of difference might disrupt the smooth interlocking of Japan and the West. Prominent among these was Edo. Rokumeikan culture was determined to minimize, where it could not altogether erase, the traces and cultural forms of premodern Japan. As Okakura Tenshin later put it: "To the advocates of the wholesale modernization of Japan, Eastern civilization seems a lower development compared with the Western. The more we assimilate the foreign methods, the higher we mount in the scale of humanity. They point out the state of Asiatic nations and the success of Japan in maintaining a national existence by the very fact of recognizing the supremacy of the West. They claim that civilization is a homogenous development that defies eclecticism in any of its phases."[15] At the center of the culture of the Same, there can stand one subject, that of modernity taken as a homogeneous and global whole. Hence, at the same time, the need to exclude from the central enclosure of modernity the principle of sexual difference: the members of the enclosure are masculine only. The women have only a catalytic function, to express what the men of one camp sense the men of the other camp desire and to act as tokens, demonstrations, of the extent to which the men of one side now identify with their mimetic rivals. The Paris-style elegance of the Rokumeikan women is living proof of the degree to which the men who modernized Japan were capable of internalizing the desire of the other.

The women at Rokumeikan were, then, shape-shifters in more sense than one. For their own part they had to remake their clothes, their movements, their bodies in the image of the West. Yet this was accomplished not in order to turn them, but to turn their men, into the subjects of modernity. What they acted out physically, through their transformed bodies, was an expression of the more important transformation that was supposed to be occurring in the hearts and minds of the men who would be masters of the modern world. What the women expressed objectively, as spectacle, the men were to experience subjectively, as a style of consciousness. The men were modernity's subjects, women its objects, satellites, mirrors. However much the women modernized, they could never inhabit the core enclosure of the Subject-without-difference. As women they could only, perhaps, threaten it.

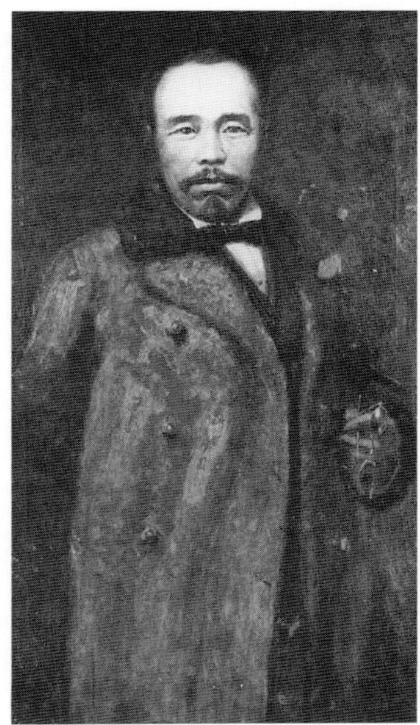

FIGURE 6.5. Koyama Shōtarō, *Portrait of Kawakami Tōgai*, 1881.

## Early Western Oil Painting (*Yōga*)

The development of the nude as a branch of Meiji Western painting was in the first place a result of the pedagogy introduced by the European academicians at the Technical Art School in Tokyo in 1876. Detailed anatomical knowledge of the human form was essential to Western painting—even when the figures to be depicted were clothed. Early *yōga* paintings such as the *Portrait of Kawakami Tōgai* by Koyama Shōtarō (1881; Figure 6.5) might earnestly strive for illusionistic effects, but without a solid grounding in anatomy it remained impossible to resolve fully all of the problems posed by naturalism. Koyama's work is keen to register such striking "reality effects" as the reflections on the rims and lenses of Tōgai's spectacles; the accurately observed reflections are a kind of promise of the Western style's ability to record visual appearances with scientific objectivity, as though the capacity of lenses to correct the shortcomings of vision stood for the Western style's heightened accuracy as a whole.[16] But other passages in the painting suggest that this promise lies rather ahead of itself. The representation of Tōgai's fingers, for example, requires more knowledge of foreshortening than the painter has evidently yet acquired, and the handling of Tōgai's costume seems unable to follow the molding of the shirt, waistcoat, and jacket on the underlying structure of bones and muscles. A prime goal of academic instruction was to impart to students the anatomical skills they would always have to draw on, whatever the genre they worked in: the figures in a landscape or an urban scene would have to demonstrate confidence in the treatment of the body quite as much as a portrait or the nude itself. Throughout the European academies the formula was the same: junior students would begin by learning to draw from inanimate objects and plaster casts, then as seniors would graduate to the figure, employing direct observation through study in the category of apprentice work traditionally known as the "academy" (painting from the living model) and copying.

The speed with which Japanese painters became proficient in the new techniques is impressive. The time-honored tradition of working with the picture surface laid out on the floor was replaced with easels aligned to casts. Students working in the format of the "academy" became familiar with the harsh, tenebrist lighting that placed the greatest demands on their representational skills. A work such as Hyakutake Kaneyuki's *Reclining Nude* (ca. 1881; Fig. 6.6) may seem to the Western viewer an unusual reflection of a taste for chiaroscuro, combined with a sense of mid-century realism, but the painting is better understood if placed in the context of student instruction. Professors of painting knew well the sort of shortcuts and evasions that students might be drawn into when painting the human form. With shadowless illumination it was always possible for the neophyte painter to simplify or avoid the problems of contour and depth; or a student might be able to create a plausible enough likeness by concentrating on a dramatic outline for the body. But the intense chiaroscuro that the "academy" entailed made any bluffing impossible: the strong light-dark contrast forced attention onto the figure as a complex set of volumes in space, and in pedagogic terms this stricture ensured that the figure would be firmly imprinted on the student mind as a solidly three-dimensional form.

What the training in Tokyo could less easily supply was the background thought necessary to idealization of the human form. The academies had always stressed that painting and sculpture, as liberal arts, involved much more than the mechanical copying of the surfaces of things. In Reynolds' phrase the grand manner pursued "central forms"—those typical or recurring aspects that the artist abstracted from the welter of visual experience. To create such forms required a shedding of sensory particulars and a quest for Platonic or ideal forms, whose relation to particulars was essentially dialectical: the painter or sculptor recognized, in any given model or pose, the higher level of generality with which it might be associated; this higher or ideal type was then referred back to its instantiation in the individual case. In learning to grasp the academic *eidos* two ingredients were

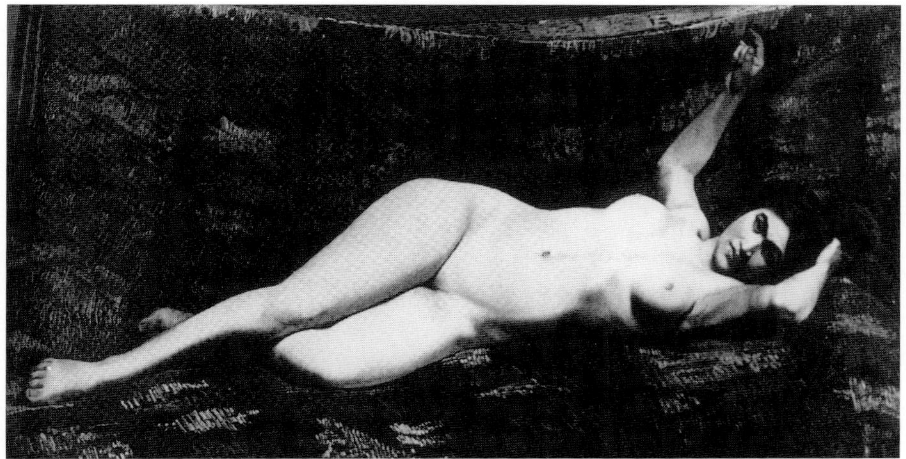

**FIGURE 6.6.** Hyakutake Kaneyuki, *Reclining Nude*, ca. 1881. Oil on canvas. Ishibashi Museum of Art, Fukuoka.

considered essential: extensive experience of the human figure, based on actual observation of the living model; and familiarity with the forms stored within the classical and Renaissance traditions, enabling the student to refer any given model or pose to canonical forms (*Aphrodite Anadyomène, Niobe*, *Apollo Belvedere*, and so forth). In Tokyo these latter conditions were especially difficult to reproduce. Students needed prolonged and systematic instruction in the life class and access to extensive collections of works of art from the West. Neither was yet available (Kuroda is said to be the first to introduce the living model in Japan, after his return from Europe in 1893).[17]

It is perhaps this factor that gives to a work such as the *Nude* by Yamamoto Hōsui its distinctive mid-Meiji cast (ca. 1880; Figure 6.7). The execution of the figure is highly accomplished by academic standards. Nevertheless, by those same standards the painting is strangely devoid of those associations with canonical European images that were supposed to act as a filter between observation and the final image. The model herself is unusually individuated, closer to portraiture than the conventions of the nude normally allow, conveying the sense of the model as a particular person rather than a Zeuxian type, an actual Western woman whose expression and features have not been generalized toward the bland, anonymous mask preferred by the academy. One result is that the painting seems to be the record of an individual encounter in the studio with a specific model, an encounter unmediated by the Western-classical mystique (or mystification). Instead of being a composite of classical or old-master echoes, she is simply a modern European woman, without her clothes.

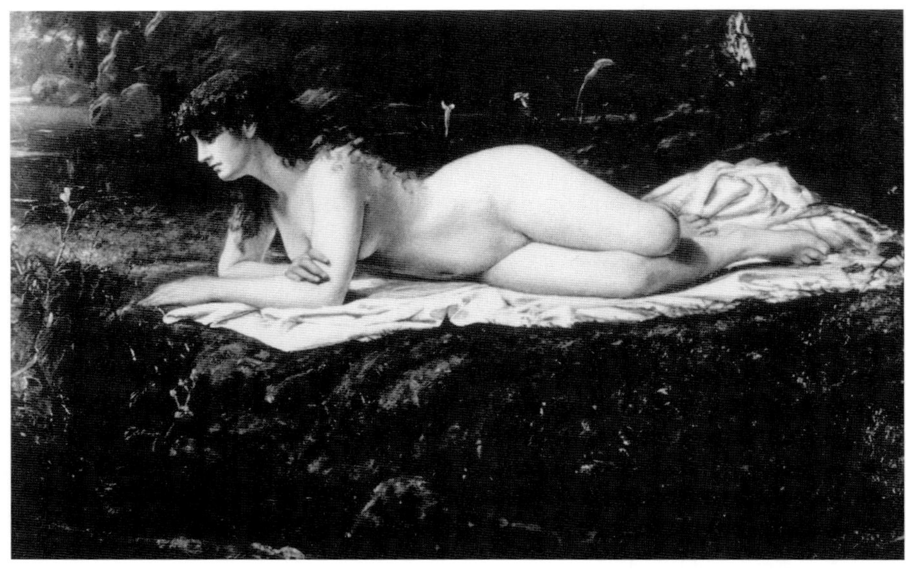

FIGURE 6.7. Yamamoto Hōsui, *Nude*, ca. 1880. Oil on canvas. Private collection.

At almost any previous time in the nineteenth century, this lack of familiarity with the academic echo chamber would have proved a handicap to Japanese painters in the final stages of their formation. As it happened, the first European journeys of Japanese artists coincided with the rapid breakup of the whole academic apparatus of canonical allusion, neoclassical reference, and "central form." The work of Gérôme, whose studio Hōsui joined in the 1880s, is instructive as a barometer of the changing climate. In the 1880s Gérôme sought more than ever to rationalize his sensationally voyeuristic scenes by grounding them in classical precedent. Sculptural reference could cast a mantle of respectability over his female figures more effectively than almost any other device, and increasingly Gérôme worked directly with statuary.[18] Yet the kind of sculpture he created, though still in the idiom of antiquity, could not have been further from the chaste marble generalities favored earlier in the century by neoclassicism. Turning in the spirit of the Pompeian revival to the polychromatic sculpture whose existence in antiquity had been proved by antiquarian scholarship, Gérôme began to use new media—brightly tinted surfaces, mixtures of ivory and bronze—that looked back to the "chryselephantine" (ivory and gold) statues of sculptors such as Phidias. Yet there the resemblance probably ends. The use of polychrome materials gave Gérôme a classical pretext behind which he could mask, or at least diminish, his development of poses that dramatically deviate from the monumental forms of Greece and Rome. His sculptural work came to possess an immediacy and freeze-frame specificity quite unlike the dignified immobility of the classical canon. Earlier in the century, an artist like Hōsui would have been obliged to spend years building up a visual repertoire corresponding to the academy's notions of the *eidos*. But by the 1880s even Gérôme, pillar of academic standards though he was, had come to abandon this outlook.

The new tendency in the work of Gérôme, as of the art around him, was to pursue the ephemeral, the fleeting movement and the particularized expression. Hōsui's *Portrait of a European Lady*, painted in Paris in 1882, deliberately hovers between the portrait and the sketch (Plate 4). The image takes what is in fact one of the most immobile and formal approaches to the portrait likeness—a full profile, with the features outlined against the background in silhouette—and then shakes free of its fixity and frozen delineation by dramatizing the play of a rapidly moving brush. Though the painting shows every sign of compositional deliberation, especially as a design whose internal balance is governed by the frame, Hōsui presents his work as a casual *fa presto* improvisation, whose rapidity and informality are advertised by the irregular scribble in the corner at the lower right. Unencumbered by the weight of academic precedent, the painter is able to join immediately the newest tendency of French painting, the pursuit of the spontaneous. The light and rapid brushwork gathers into itself and expresses in visual terms the fleeting and informal nature of the social occasion it invokes. The painter has not detained his sitter for hours and days in his studio, while gradually building up a definitive gestalt (like Ingres and his patient sitter Madame Moitessier, whose portrait in London Ingres took years to perfect). Instead, the rhetoric of spontaneity establishes the sitter as an individual whom the painter has encountered appreciatively, memorably, and in passing. The authoritarian relation whereby a painter such as Ingres established an enormous social and epistemological distance between painter and sitter gives way here to the idea of a social conviviality in which painter and sitter are equally members of the polite society of Paris, in one another's company like guests at any reception. The lightness of brushwork stands here for urbanity, civility, and enjoyment of the passing encounters of metropolitan life. One sees how much the social and cultural distance between the Japanese painter and European society has narrowed. Where, earlier, Hōsui had approached the figure as a technical problem, staged in the unnatural conditions of the studio, now the goal is to neutralize the social and cultural distance, and to present the Japanese visitor as an insider within Europe, on the same footing as his painting's subject.

At their warmest, Meiji portraits of Western women convey most vividly the

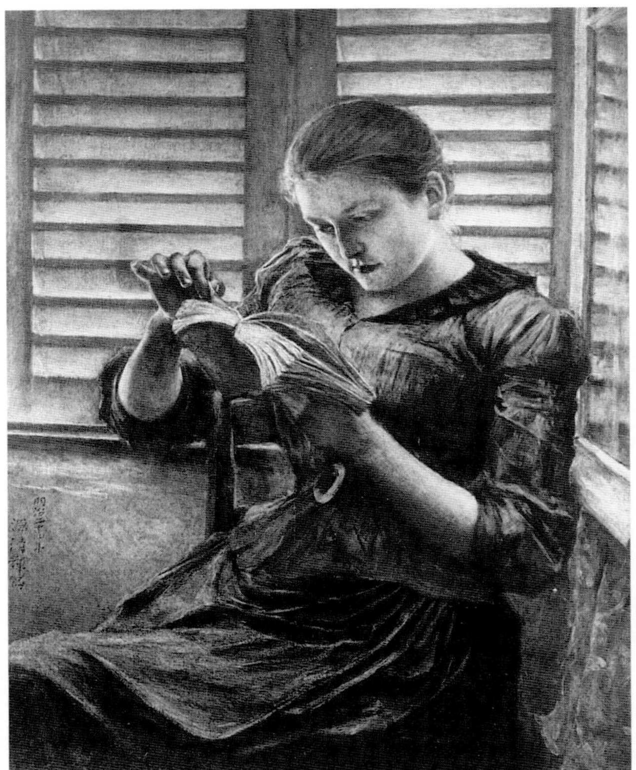

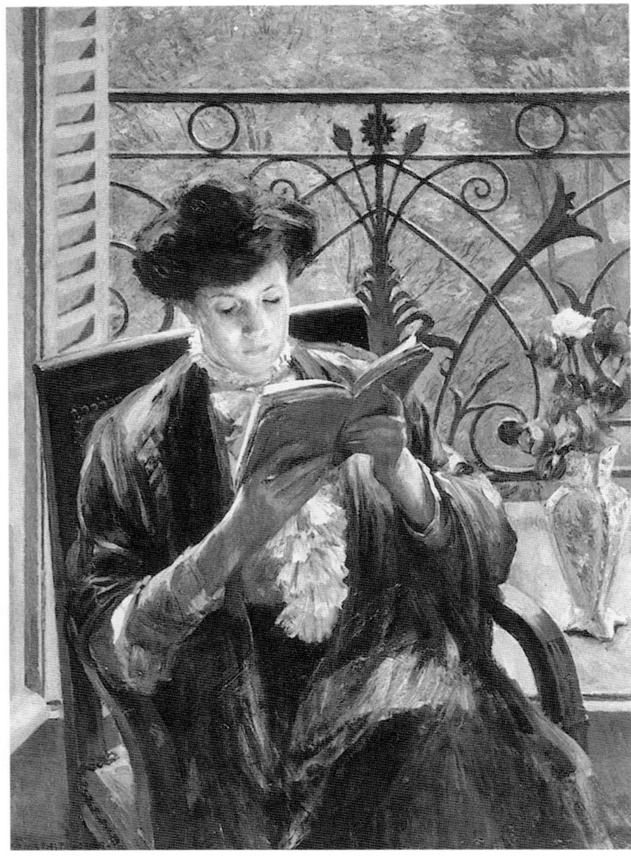

**FIGURE 6.8.** *(Above)* Kuroda Seiki, *Reading,* 1891. Oil on canvas. Tokyo National Museum.

**FIGURE 6.9.** *(Right)* Yamashita Shintarō, *Reading,* 1908. Oil on canvas. Bridgestone Museum of Art.

sense of cultural distance overcome, a feeling of intimacy all the more valuable for the obstacles and barriers now surpassed. Two images can stand here for a whole category of work: Kuroda Seiki's *Reading* (1891; Figure 6.8) and Yamashita Shintarō's *Reading* (1908; Figure 6.9).

Kuroda's *Reading* is a painting careful to minimize the sense of the painter's intrusion into his sitter's personal space. The device of the book is used, as always, as a practical means of keeping the sitter occupied while the painter goes about the time-consuming task of making the portrait. But Kuroda uses this always serviceable prop to suggest something unusual in the iconography of portraits invoking books, the sitter's genuine and fascinated absorption into the subjective space the book opens up (one could think of a whole gallery of European portraits in which books make an appearance, but are ignored, as decorative tokens of learning or culture). In part it is an effect of the sitter's right hand, poised to turn the page, as if she wished to avoid the least interruption to the flow of the text. In part it is a question of her position in the room, in the corner where the shutters let in the most light, as though for her reading is a serious pursuit that needs its own consecrated corner. To be sure, the sense of absorption is heightened by the condition of the book itself, with its spine broken and the pages well thumbed, again suggesting a style of reading indifferent to the book's appearance (combined with the sitter's plain and unadorned costume, it suggests as well a personal style indifferent to appearance in general). The impression of deep absorption is conveyed, too, in Kuroda's careful weighing of the pose, so that reading seems for her not a matter of perching the eye lightly on the page but of settling the whole body around the book's center of gravity, and for a lengthy period (the head sunk toward the chest, the shoulders tilted in a position that would be uncomfortable if the reader were not so drawn inside what she reads).

What counts still more, in the evocation of the sitter's subjective space, is the light flooding her face and her surroundings. In fact the area is cramped, the angle of a room, with a small, unupholstered chair, but Kuroda's handling of light opens it out into spaciousness and air. Technically, the use of white is crucial: the blue and red of the costume, and the tints of the sitter's complexion, are touched everywhere with passages that mix the colors with large amounts of white pigment—so much so that there is almost a break with realism, since light falling on these surfaces would not in fact bleach the colors to this extent (it would also alter their hues).[19] Kuroda's palette keys all the hues to the brightest register, treating the colors spectrally, as refractions of the underlying whiteness. Taken up into the scene's content, this all-pervasiveness of white suggests a kind of transfiguration, not spectacular but everyday, a space of confinement opening on to another, more expansive and luminous space, the larger world that the woman brings into being as she reads. By the same means—by conveying the sense of another space and another light traversing the actual space and light—Kuroda suggests an intense empathy with the sitter's subjectivity.

In fact the whole situation is asymmetrical, presenting a danger of the painter and sitter assuming opposite poles, with the sitter caught up in mental and inward space while the painter remains fixed in the objective world, gazing at his sitter as object. Kuroda's handling of light and color succeeds in warding off this possibility of polarization, since the technical problem that most engages him as a painter, the evocation of brilliant light, seems so much to be a metaphor for the sitter's expansive and illuminated state of consciousness. The result is a suggestion of friendliness, of *en famille*, so that both individuals are free to pursue their present interests to the full (reading, painting) without encroaching on each other's privacy: two parallel kinds of absorption that nevertheless seem to converge at a point of friendship and respect rooted in domestic familiarity.

Yamashita Shintarō's *Reading* is similar in its atmosphere of intimacy and ease in domestic space. In fact the scale of the figure within the frame is such that, for her to be painted in this way, Yamashita's easel would have to be virtually on top of the sitter; she would have to try to read, or pretend to read, with the back of the easel only a few feet away.[20] The problem is a recurrent one in naturalistic portraiture: that of harmonizing the unnatural conditions of the actual portrait session with the spontaneity that the portrait ideally seeks. Yamashita's solution involves considerable finesse in his handling both of space and of the signs of interpersonal exchange. Compensating for the cramped stage of the foreground, the background view recedes into a prospect of autumn colors. And the sitter is presented as absorbed in her book, yet not so much as to seem lost to the world, like the woman in Kuroda's *Reading*; rather she reads in awareness of the painter's presence (she might look up), and the formality of her costume, which suggests a certain social distance (she is much more elaborately dressed than Kuroda's sitter), counters the potential invasiveness or incursiveness of the painter's easel and gaze.

Personal intimacy is presented as a force strong enough to dissolve the barriers separating Japan from the outside world: that, at any rate, is the utopian aspect of these paintings, their promise—or their lure. For it is also clear that such works are self-conscious, even ostentatious *displays* of familiarity and intimacy with European culture: they assert their intimacy with pride, as proof or credentials of cosmopolitan identity. In fact the viewer has no way of knowing whether such intimacy with the European women depicted in the images was ever actually attained; all that is certain is the images' intense desire to make it seem so. Yamashita's *Reading* and Kuroda's remarkable *Reading*, like Hōsui's *Portrait of a European Lady*, are striking in the way that the value of intimacy with European culture that they express with such assurance turns on the presence of the female sitter. It is through a focus on the bodies of women rather than men that proximity to and intimacy with the West are evoked. Such a high degree of assimilation into European visuality cannot have been easy for any of the Meiji artists to achieve. Yet in a sense there was always a place carved out for them in advance, by virtue of the fact that the European visual régime they were embarked on entering was centered squarely on the masculine subject of vision—one had only, so to speak, to step into his shoes.

Interestingly, the studios that Meiji artists tended to join were headed by men who had made their career depicting women. Yamamoto Hōsui's teacher was Gérôme himself. By far the most sought after studio was that of Raphaël Collin, whose scenes of naked females in woodland settings departed from academic conventions of the nude by breaking the spell of the ancient world that still prevailed at the studio of Gérôme. One perplexing result of this move is that Collin's figures, though livelier and more agile than Gérôme's, tend to lack narrative justification or rationale and can look placeless and stranded. Gérôme would have made sure they were recognizable at once as dryads, bacchantes, or other of the denizens of the legendary erotic landscape of antiquity. Gérôme was always careful, at any rate, to establish that the reason the viewer is now being treated to the spectacle of females unclad is that some "they" have required it—oriental or Roman slave merchants, sultans, emperors, or Areopagite judges. By divesting his figures of narrative as well as clothing, Collin drops most of the alibis and pretexts that enabled Gérôme to navigate his way through bourgeois respectability—and hypocrisy. With Collin the only reason one can think of for the nudity is that this is "art"; art itself is now a sufficient cause for the unveiling of the female form before the masculine gaze (Figure 6.10). In Collin the basic visual power relation between the male subject of the gaze and the female object for that gaze emerges with unqualified directness. Though Collin may be a somewhat forgotten figure among historians of French art, it would be wrong to underestimate his influence on Meiji painters working in Paris: besides Kuroda, Yamashita Shintarō, Kume Keiichirō, Wada Eisaku, Okada Saburōsuke, and Kojima Torajirō all worked in his studio, and Collin's hedonistic sense of female beauty, now brought down to earth and at the same time considerably refined, is an influence throughout the work of Kuroda. Renoir, too, was eagerly pursued: Umehara Ryūzaburō was one of Renoir's last students when the latter was in his sixties, and Umehara's later developments of the nude can be thought of as premised on the example of Renoir's fantasies of large-limbed and voluptuous beauties (Figure 6.11). And in the field of sculpture, the example of Rodin exerted an enormous influence on Meiji artists, who developed still further his feeling for vigorous massing and freedom of pose.

From a Western perspective the decisions of Japanese artists concerning whose studio to join (and whose not to join) seem strange, if consistent. And doubtless there were many factors in play. Renoir, for example, was one of the few great Impressionists still teaching in 1910. Collin's popularity may partly be attributed to the Japanese tendency in international arrangements to favor al-

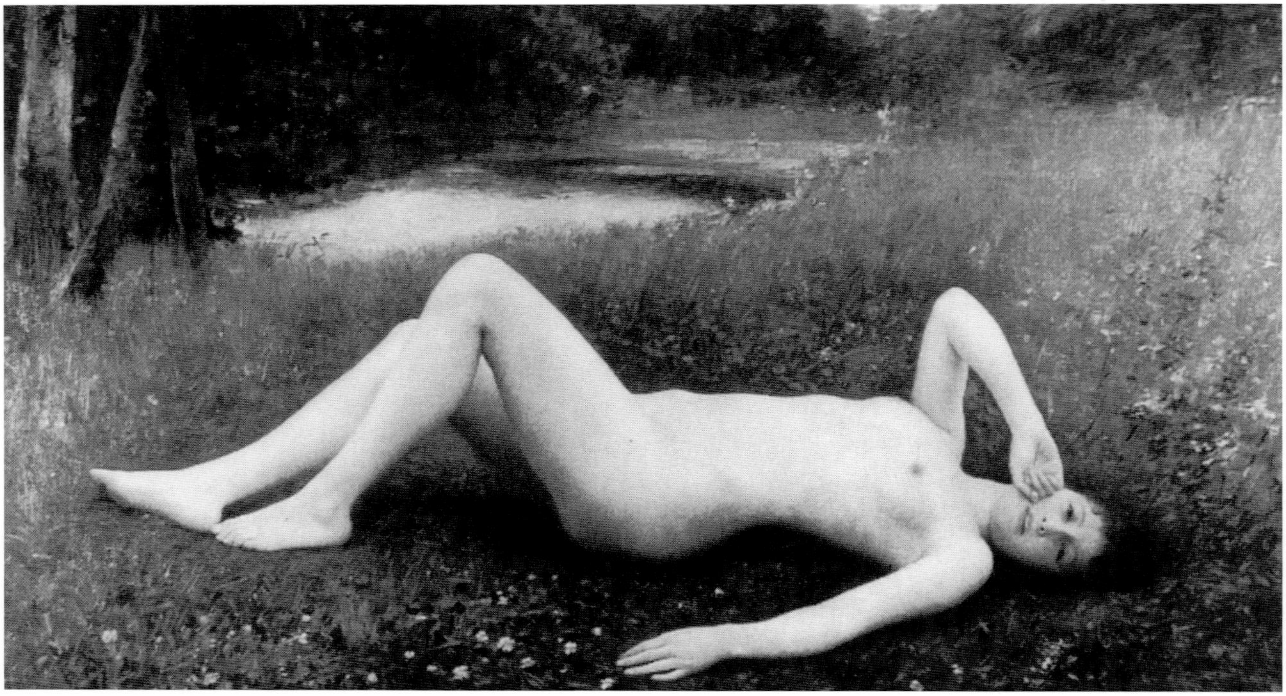

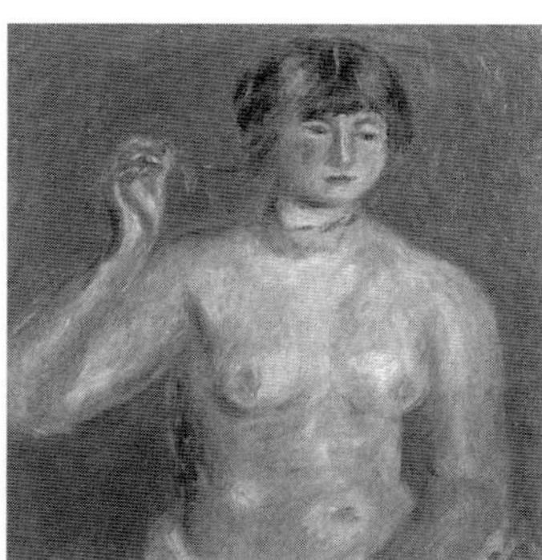

FIGURE 6.10. *(Above)* Raphaël Collin, *Floréal,* 1886. Oil on canvas. Museum of Fine Arts, Arras.

FIGURE 6.11. *(Left)* Umehara Ryūzaburō, *Necklace*, 1913. Oil on canvas. The Museum of Modern Art, Tokyo.

ready established introductions and networks over ad hoc contacts. All the same, there is a clear pattern of choice, one that orients the visual field to the female as preordained target of the gaze.

It is interesting in this regard to consider the effect on artists from Japan, as from other countries, of the late-nineteenth-century myth of Paris as the mecca of *la vie bohème*. To become a painter in Paris in, say, 1815 was to enter a profession much like any other—architecture, medicine, law. Painters, like architects or lawyers, might have their own style of behavior, but it was not of absorbing interest to the public at large, not yet the great legend of bohemia it would become after the Romantics and the Impressionists. By the turn of the century, fiction about artists set in a world of dandified poverty and free-wheeling improvisation, with complex erotic intrigues among artists and models and mistresses, had become a genre in itself, the *Künstlerroman*.

For Japanese painters, to study art in Paris was to enter a play where one already knew the sets, the characters, and the likely plot. Painting was, in fact, the most exactly scripted of all professions—what it meant to study law or medicine was by comparison far less codified. Bohemia provided a secure and preestablished identity; this may have made bohemianism especially attractive to those who acutely felt the need to find a viable Western role for themselves, not just because this was Meiji ideology but as a solution to the feelings of culture shock that many of them must have experienced.[21]

Bohemian life centered, all were agreed, on eros, and eros' representative in art, the model. For Japanese artists the model might be the first naked Western body they had seen, and her presence at the life class ensured that a student from even so distant a land as Japan would be absorbed, together with his fellow students, into the masculine camaraderie of the studio. The libidinal currents of the life class spelled fraternity, the comradeship between men as men, equalized before the naked woman who was there for all of them in the same way. When the students had their photograph taken, they rallied round her as though round a mascot or trophy. Students from Japan were no exception: Kume Keiichirō is as high-spirited as his classmates—more so (Figure 6.12). (Kume Keiichirō appears in the top right of the photograph, jokingly peering out from under a shawl). For students of art, libidinality was the key to cultural assimilation in ways it could never be for Meiji students of law or engineering or economics. Their whole endeavor centered on the human body, and in the studios of Gérôme, Collin, and Renoir on the body of the female as the key site of modern, avant-garde visuality.

Developing an iconography of the eroticized Western body is central to the work of Kuroda in the early 1890s. *Woman with a Mandolin*, from 1890–1891 (Figure 6.13), belongs to the new bohemian ethos of the nude in that the model is no longer given any of the traditional narrative pretexts for her nudity or her sensual allure—Kuroda has even dispensed with the "arcadian" conventions that gave to the work of Raphaël Collin a last, residual alibi. Instead, the eroticism of the figure belongs to the new narrative of bohemian Paris and the pleasures of the artist's life. The figure appears not as a creature of fiction (Phryne, odalisque, dryad) but as a model, and she has about her an air of the studio and studio theatricality. Though one can perhaps imagine her (just about) as recently playing on her musical instrument, essentially the mandolin is a prop, and like any other property of the studio or the stage, it establishes a performative distance between the subject of vision and vision's spectacular object. As such, it conveys the idea of a woman whose nudity is professional and does not necessarily con-

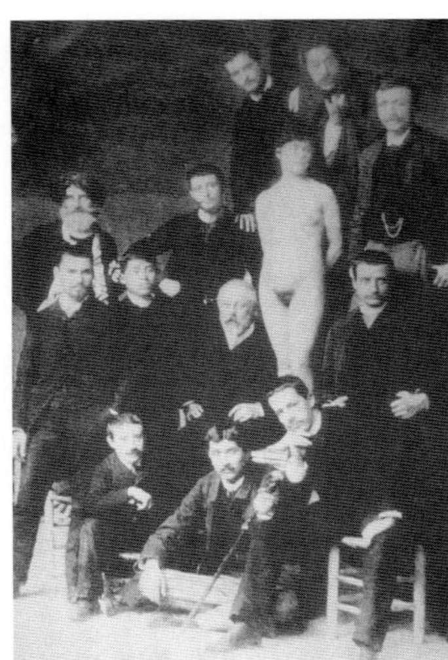

**FIGURE 6.12.** Kume Keiichirō and fellow students with their model. Photo. From Takashina Shūji, J. Thomas Rimer, and Gerald D. Bolas, eds., *Paris in Japan: The Encounter with European Painting* (Tokyo: The Japan Foundation, 1987).

note sexual availability. What undoes this impression, however, and elides the figure of the model with that of a sexual partner, is the pillow—that, and her swimmingly languorous pose. These belong to another dimension than the mandolin, to a dimension of erotic liaison where nudity denotes sexual availability. The distance of the studio props now collapses in the encounter between lovers, in an implied milieu where the line between model and sexual partner is exactly blurred (this being the crux of the "bohemian fantasy"). And it is perhaps possible to trace the outline of a further fantasy, that of the woman who is usually paid for her services but now offers them for nothing—a wish fulfillment especially gratifying in a male-centered dispensation, since it does away with the idea of an actual economic structure of power in which men rule over women and makes the arrangement seem voluntary (she freely chooses the position of object in the sexual and visual régime).

One hesitates to speak of Kuroda's *Morning Toilette*, from 1893 (Figure 6.14), since the original is lost; it is likely that the interaction of colors (on the chair, on the bearskin rug, and in the scene reflected in the mirror) would have considerably qualified and complicated the stark impression conveyed by black-and-white photography. But there can be little doubt that it is among Kuroda's most voyeuristic works. The mirror in the painting could be said to be a delegate or double of the painting itself, giving an even more intimate and close-up presentation of the model's body than the picture itself provides. Though the mirror seems to relay the model's gaze upon her own body, from the angle of vision that structures the picture, the reflection in the looking glass is far more for the spectator than for herself. (Imagine the following experiment: look in the bathroom mirror and trace the outline of face and body with soap; the figure is in fact tiny, half life—sized. That would be the scale of the looking-glass reflection, from the model's point of view. But the reflection in the painting is only slightly smaller than the model herself. Her outlook, her center of vision are taken from her, in the very place they should be hers, and routed toward the spectator's vantage point).

To this extent, the figure has only partial control over the image that comes from her to the viewer: the frontal view shown in the mirror she is able to arrange according to her taste, but the view from behind remains outside her knowledge —which gives the viewer more command over her image than the figure possesses herself. Though it is entirely natural for her arms to move into the positions shown in the picture in order for her to pull her hair into the fashionable knot of the 1890s, it is evident that the pose has also been selected with the aim of displaying her breasts in the most glamorous way compatible with realism. In

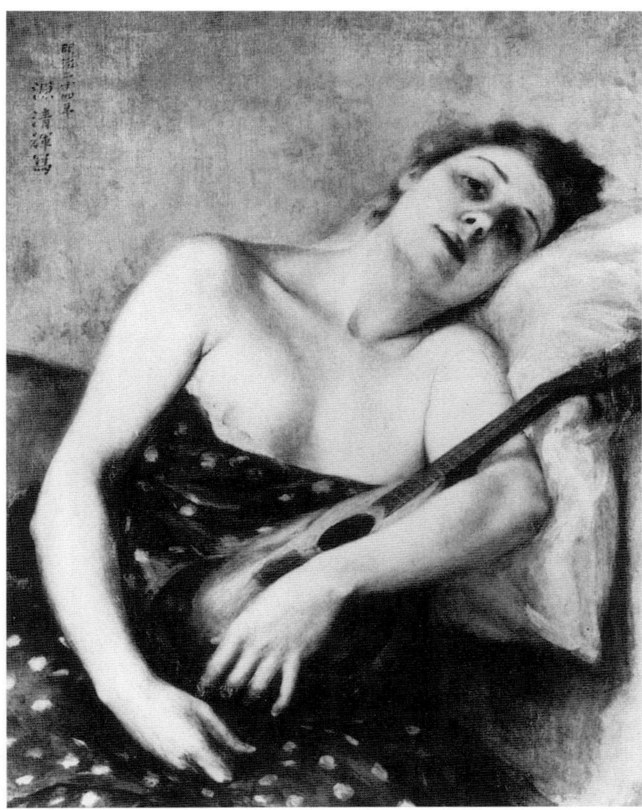

FIGURE 6.13. *(Above)* Kuroda Seiki, *Woman with a Mandolin*, 1890–1891. Oil on canvas. Tokyo National Museum.

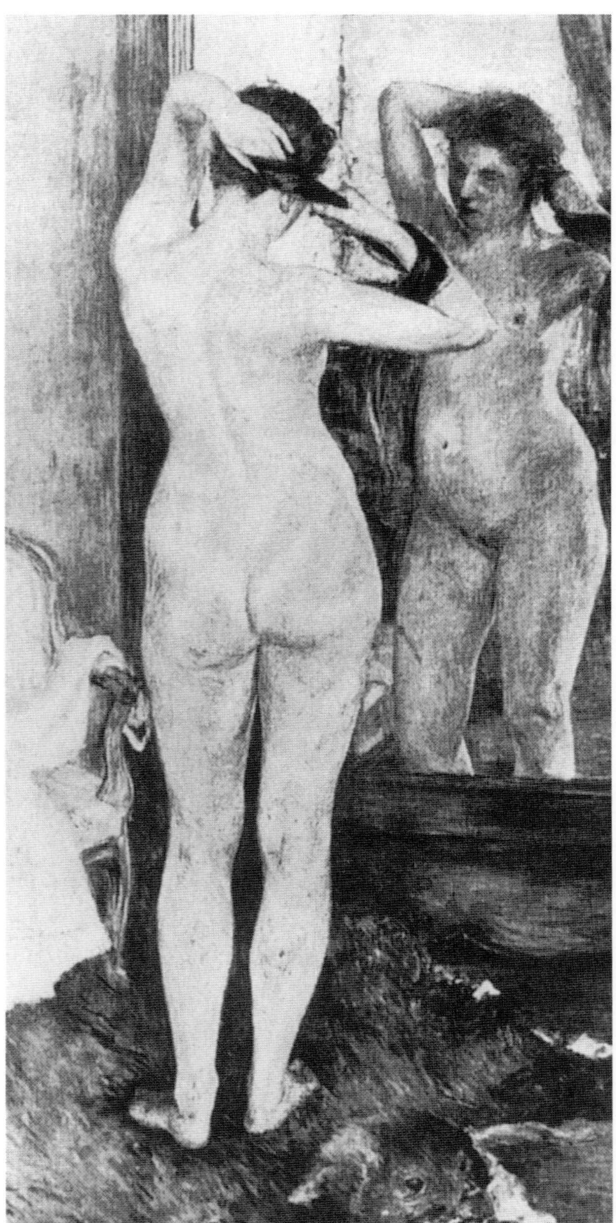

FIGURE 6.14. *(Right)* Kuroda Seiki, *Morning Toilette*, 1893. Oil on canvas. Original destroyed.

a tradition as old as voyeurism itself, the display of a woman's body before the male is attributed to her own desire to be beautiful, to her vanity or narcissism, following once again the pattern whereby a structure of power in which the male gaze dominates is naturalized and made to seem voluntary by the woman's presentation of herself primarily as an object of spectacle. And the atmosphere of the work is the daring, modern spirit of bohemian freedom, in which the female form inevitably goes naked through the world (in the studio of Rodin, models were paid to range freely through the atelier without their clothes until a pose they struck might happen to trigger the master's inspiration).[22] The device of the coiffure positions the model at the threshold between public space (in which she will appear with her hair correctly in place) and the space of intimacy and privacy (where letting down her hair connotes sexual accessibility): the threshold of seduction itself (does the artist add a note of self-mockery in the bearskin rug, which seems to growl under her feet?).

In the male-centered visuality given a new lease on life by Gérôme, Collin, Renoir, and Rodin, the model herself was not the visual order's mistress, merely its humble servant. The imagery of Western women produced by Meiji artists working in France reveals much the same pattern of male-female power relations as that of European modernism as a whole: what constitutes the modernity of the paintings is inseparable from representation of the supremacy of men over women.[23] What makes the Japanese case more complicated is that this mode of vision also involved the process of cultural assimilation of Japan to the West and the West to Japan, within the overall context of Meiji modernization. As at the Rokumeikan, it was women whose participation as the excluded term of power enabled the assimilation to proceed: Japanese artists joined ranks with European artists over the subordinated figure of woman. The positioning of women as the inferior subjects of modernity was as integral to the economy of the arts as it was to industry: models, like textile workers, provided a dynamic that was indispensable to modernization yet unrecognized and shabbily rewarded.

It is interesting to see the evolution of this visual structure when transplanted from the West back to Japan. In 1893 Kuroda came back from ten years of working in France. When he showed his *Morning Toilette* at the Fourth Industrial Fair, the picture caused an uproar: there was no precedent for this kind of public display of nudity in Japan. With the category of the nude apparently blocked, at least for pictures intended for public exhibition, Kuroda turned to "traditional" women of Japan (in quotation marks: what constitutes the tradition is exactly in question here). His painting *Maiko* (Figure 6.15), from the same year as the *Morn-*

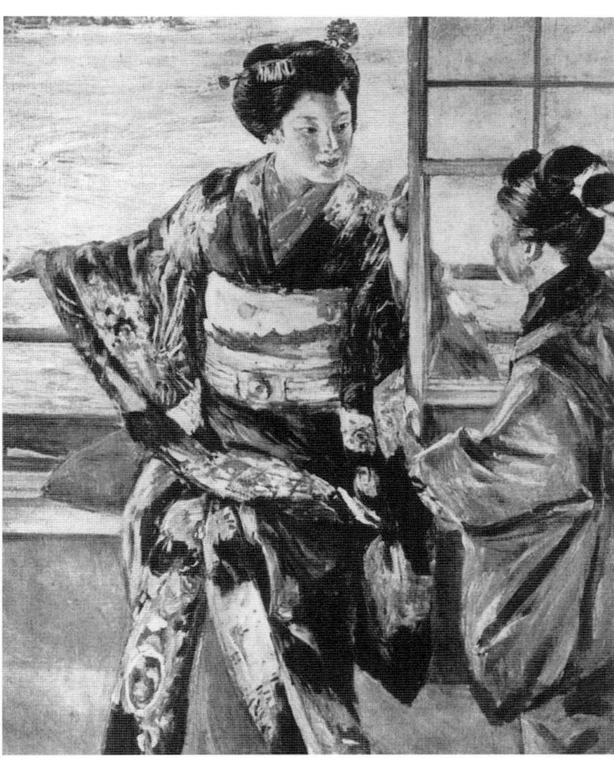

**FIGURE 6.15.** Kuroda Seiki, *Maiko,* 1893. Oil on canvas. Tokyo National Museum.

*ing Toilette*, takes as its subject an exchange between two women entertainers in a house probably in Kyoto, overlooking the Kamo River—the epicenter of Kyoto's geisha activities. It is strange to see the elements of the classical Japanese costume handled in the broad, generalizing strokes of Impressionism. The clarity and sharp edges of the kimono patterns are dramatically changed in the process, becoming blurred and indistinct; and the head and features of the principal figure, given complex illumination and volumetric handling, belong to a different universe from the shadowless flatness of the traditional *ukiyo-e* schema. One cannot overlook the gendered nature of Kuroda's assimilation of Europe and his return to Japan. He is the cosmopolitan subject, Westernized but also Japanese; the *maiko* remains outside this cosmopolitan process, the traditional women who never left Japan, who wait behind in premodern loveliness, the limit against which the male artist's modernized subjectivity is defined.

Kuroda's personal journey, from law to painting and from Japan to France and back, might have stayed just that, a private odyssey or biography, like those of so many artists and writers caught up in the cultural movement between East and

West. What is significant about Kuroda's career, however, is the immense prestige with which he was and still is honored in Japan (in Tokyo he has his own museum, like the Musée Delacroix or the Musée Rodin in France). From the beginning, Kuroda was associated with glittering prizes, first in France (*Reading* was accepted by the Société des Artistes Françaises, the *Morning Toilette* was shown at the Société Nationale des Beaux-Arts) and then in Japan, where the White Horse Society, which he founded, became a principal center for advanced painting in the Western style. Where *yōga* painters in previous decades had often been ignored or opposed by the state, Kuroda's success came at a time when the Meiji government had begun to realize that distinguished painting in the Western style could serve both nationally and internationally as proof of the extent to which the Japanese had mastered the methods and the outlook of the West. In 1907 an appeal made to Makino Nobuaki, minister of education, by Masaki Naohiko, director of the Tokyo Art School, together with a member of the faculty of Tokyo Imperial University and Kuroda himself resulted in the organization of an official, state-sponsored Salon—the Bunten—showing Western-style painting alongside *nihonga*. Kuroda, and *yōga*, had the full support of the establishment.

One might well ask why. It could by no means be said that Western-style painting reigned supreme in the art world—Japanese-style painting also received official support, and the Bunten showed the two schools side by side. But *yōga* mattered to the state. It was important to display the Western style alongside *nihonga*. No other cultural enterprise could demonstrate so conclusively to the Japanese public the extent to which Japan had successfully assimilated Western culture—not just superficially, through mastering its operational techniques, but to its depths, its way of being in the world, its phenomenology, its style of consciousness. The Bunten exhibitions and Kuroda's example proved internalization: the Meiji government had arrived at the furthest reaches of Western modernity and had brought the results back to Japan.

In the process, a structure of sexual difference was installed in visual representation that paralleled the structures of sexual difference in industry, commerce, and education. The subject of Meiji modernization was resolutely male. The images of European women and Japanese women might differ in function. With representations of European women, the female body marked a path of entry to the West, a route of access and familiarization, sometimes softened by friendly intimacy, often energized by a frank libidinality. With representations of Japanese women, the female body marked the limit that the modernizing male consciousness had surpassed. But in both cases the outcome was the same: the process of cultural assimilation was figured through a female iconography; the relationship between the men who ruled the modern world was visualized across the bodies of women whom modernity excluded.

In 1882, 66 percent of workers in Japanese industry were women. Modernization centrally depended on women's labor. In Japan as in the West, women formed an invisible infrastructure in the elaboration of modern culture, essential but placed in the disadvantaged position, in the lower reaches of modernity's hierarchy. Was the situation in the arts so different? In *yōga*, too, their presence was essential in giving visible form to the new order of Japan. Yet they were ancillaries, mere handmaids of modernity. At the apex of the hierarchy stood the heads of the studios and the art associations: Gérôme, Collin, Rodin, the leaders of the Technical Art School, the Meiji Fine Arts Society, the White Horse Society. At the bottom of the studio hierarchy stood the model. Art, like industry, was men's business. Like business, it involved the exchange of techniques and commodities between masculine subjects. The difference was that, with the arts, what was exchanged was the image. As images, women acquired in *yōga* an importance they never had in the studio or the factory. How?

To pursue the analogy with the commodity, in the exchange between two masculine subjects, the objects of exchange acquire a "plus value," a supplement that gives those objects a value that they do not possess in themselves, away from the structure of exchange.[24] It is through being entered into the circuit of exchange between men that the object comes into "its own." Yet it is not as itself that the object now stands in the exchange. To its original state is superadded another form that derives from its position in the intermale economy. This second form is exclusively the product of men's work and interaction. It is for this second body, superimposed upon the original body, that the commodity is valued. This second body has a radiance, an aura, a glamour that does not center in itself but is passed to it from the outside. Placed in the circuit of exchange, the object is energized and lights up, as though with electricity.

Modernity required women's bodies to be transformed, occidentalized. Under the bright lights of the Rokumeikan, the women appeared and moved like Westerners. But the purpose of the Rokumeikan's transformation scene was not to turn traditional women into the sovereign subjects of the modern era. Rather its aim was to add to women's bodies a new value, a brilliance, a modernity that passed to them from the outside and flowed across them from one side of the exchange to the other.

*Yōga* resembles the Rokumeikan in that it, too, is a theater of bright illumination. The women of *yōga* are placed in a field of vision that floods their bodies with light and displays them with a precision and acuity only possible in the modern age. Perspective, color, and focus give them an enhanced visibility, a quality of spectacle that allows the state of modernity now to manifest before the gaze of modernity's actual makers. It is not with their own radiance that the images shine. But for that very reason they are able to represent the "enlightenment" that the masters of modernity cast upon them, in its purest form.

CHAPTER SEVEN

DORIS CROISSANT

# Icons of Femininity: Japanese National Painting and the Paradox of Modernity

After the opening of the country, Japan found itself in a dilemma: whether to incorporate European art education along with technological modernization or, contrarily, to reorganize native art production as a guarantee of cultural independence. Although in 1876 Western-style painting—*yōga*—was made part of the educational reforms, after 1882 the decision was made to promote native painting—*nihonga*—instead. As an academic discipline *yōga* was not rehabilitated until 1896.

It is generally believed that the *nihonga* reform owed its theoretical basis to the American philosopher and japanophile Ernest Fenollosa. In the 1880s he had ventured to predict the birth of a universal modern painting style, provided that Japan's efforts to catch up with Western realism were abandoned. With the rise of art nouveau and postimpressionism, it turned out that the impact that Japanese traditional arts had exerted on Western visuality posed intricate problems in the establishment of a *nihonga* identity. At the end of the Meiji period, it became clear that the definition of a national aesthetics could no longer resort to a seemingly natural antagonism between the arts of Japan and of the West.

*Nihonga*'s discourse of modernism is demonstrated by the activities of a group of painters and art historians who gathered around the art historian Nakai Sōtarō in Kyoto from 1912. This chapter focuses on the painter Tsuchida Bakusen, the leading figure of this *nihonga* group.[1] Making paintings of beautiful women *(bijinga)* his specialty, he created veritable icons of Japanese femininity. Already during his lifetime Bakusen was hailed for having achieved a synthesis of French postimpressionism with traditional Japanese painting. However, his attempt to revitalize native painting and subject matter reveals a paradox, inherent in modernism itself: the impact of Japanese art on postimpressionist painters like Cézanne, van Gogh, and Gauguin provided "Japanese" painting with a model of aesthetic self-identification that encouraged the return to early modern *ukiyo-e* aesthetics and subject matter.

## New Visions of Eroticism

In 1910 a handful of progressive young *yōga* and *nihonga* artists gathered in Kyoto at the art club Chat Noir (Kuroneko Kai), which one year later became reorganized as the club La Masque (Kamen). The spiritual leaders of the group were the art historians Tanaka Kisaku (1885–1945) and Nakai Sōtarō (1879–1966), who lectured on modern French painting and acted as critical advisors.[2] The most prolific *nihonga* painters were Tsuchida Bakusen (1887–1936), Ono Chikkyō (1889–1979), Murakami Kagaku (1888–1939), and Nonogase Banka (1888–1965).

Bakusen graduated in 1911 from Kyoto City University of Arts with a painting on silk, showing a woman dressing her hair in front of a vanity table (Figure 7.1). The blank background, the flat pattern of the kimono, the wavy outlines, and the balance of the deep black of the woman's hair and the table, are indebted to *ukiyo-e* prints (Figure 7.2), though a sense of corporeality is augmented by the sensuous rendering of arm and hands, allowing a glance beneath the woman's armpit.[3]

In 1907 the Ministry of Education inaugurated an annual art exhibition, known as Bunten. By confining the *nihonga* and *yōga* exhibits to separate sections, the qualitative standards of judgment were also kept apart. As Bunten awards were crucial to an artist's career, most painters worked through the year to produce pieces that would find the judges' approval. Bakusen established his fame at the sixth Bunten exhibition in 1912 with a pair of screens called *Island Women (Shima no onna)* (Plate 5). The work was awarded a prize and purchased by the Ministry of Education.[4]

FIGURE 7.1. Tsuchida Bakusen, *Hair,* 1911. 79.5 × 86 cm, color on silk. Kyoto City University of Arts.

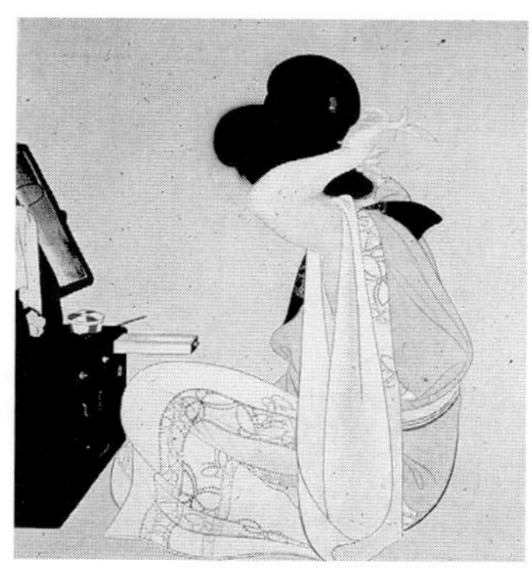

*Island Women* was conceived during a ten-day trip through the Inland Sea to the Pacific island of Hachijōjima, where Bakusen arrived at the beginning of July 1912.[5] The two screens show a coherent composition with four women in a courtyard, sheltered under the rich foliage of a tree. On the right screen a crouching young woman is combing her hair, while a girl in the background carries a water tub on her head. On the left screen two peasant women are pounding something with mortar and pestle. The sturdy bodies show no shading but are voluminously structured by swelling outlines, typical of the Edo-period Rinpa style. An iconographic innovation not previously seen in *nihonga bijinga* is the exposure of the women's bodies, shown bare to the waist.

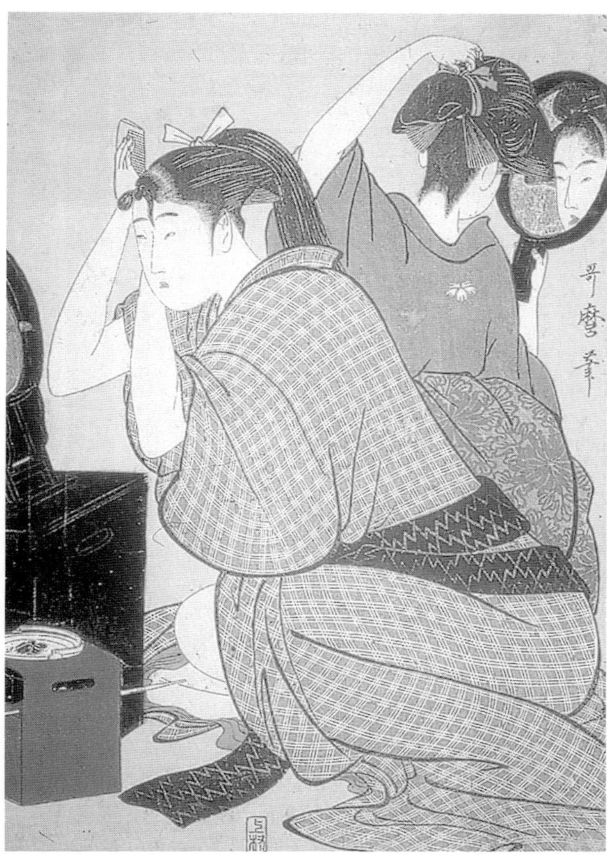


FIGURE 7.2. Kitagawa Utamaro, *Kamisuki bijin*, (Beauties dressing their hair), 1794–1796, from *Bigan Jūni-tate* (Series of twelve beautiful faces). Charles Steward Smith Collection, Miriam and Ira D. Wallach Division of Art, Prints and Photographs, The New York Public Library, Astor, Lenox and Tilden Foundations.

Since 1911 a debate about antinaturalism and postimpressionism had raged among Tokyo artists and intellectuals who gathered at the so-called Shirakaba Group, named after the illustrated journal *Shirakaba* that promulgated the art of Cézanne, van Gogh, Gauguin, and Matisse.[6] The sudden change of style in 1912 is usually attributed to Bakusen's fascination with the life story of Gauguin and the paintings he created in Tahiti after 1891.

It has been argued that parallel to Gauguin's impact on Bakusen, an increasing interest in rural folklore made Bakusen model his figures after illustrations in the ethnographic journals of his day.[7] It appears, however, that Bakusen got his inspiration less from the reportage of lithographs than from Edo-period painting. The woman combing her hair on the right screen is frequently found within *ukiyo-e bijinga* and erotic paintings that feature a courtesan washing her hair *(kamisuki bijin)*. An abbreviated type of the same figure is shown in a print by Utagawa Kunisada (1796–1865) of 1853 (Figure 7.3).

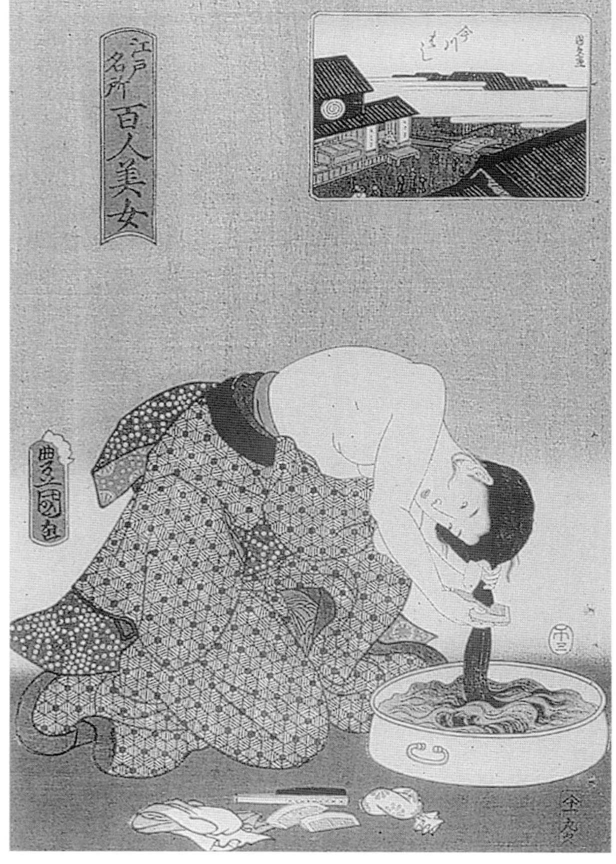


FIGURE 7.3. Utagawa Kunisada (1796–1865), *Imagawabashi* (*Edo meisho hyakunin bijo*) (Imagawa Bridge [Famous places of Edo compared with one hundred beautiful women]), 1858, *Nishiki-e*. Private collection. From Sebastian Izzard, *Kunisada's World* (New York: Japan Society, 1993), cat. 94.

An erotic meaning can also be associated with the women with the mortar on the left screen. Peasant women pounding with a mortar for husking rice formed part of harvest scenes as depicted, for example, by Hanabusa Itchō (1652–1724) (Figure 7.4). In the scroll sequence *Six Jewel Rivers (Mu Tamagawa)* by Sakai Ōho (1808–1841), the motifs of women pounding a mortar or beating clothes on a fulling block *(kinuta)* allude to love poems associated with the *tetsukuri* and *kinuta* scenery.[8] The pornographic allusiveness of "pestle" *(kine)* and "mortar" *(usu)* as well as "fulling block" eventually extended to erotic parody *(mitate)*. In a *shunga* scroll painting by Tsukioka Settei (1710–1786), the frontispiece alludes to the scroll's title, *Copy of Tamagawa (Mosha Tamagawa),* by showing a riverbank framed by mortar and fulling block.[9]

The possibility that Bakusen conceived *Island Women* as an analogy to the erotic connotations of the "Island of Women" in Saikaku's famous prose fiction

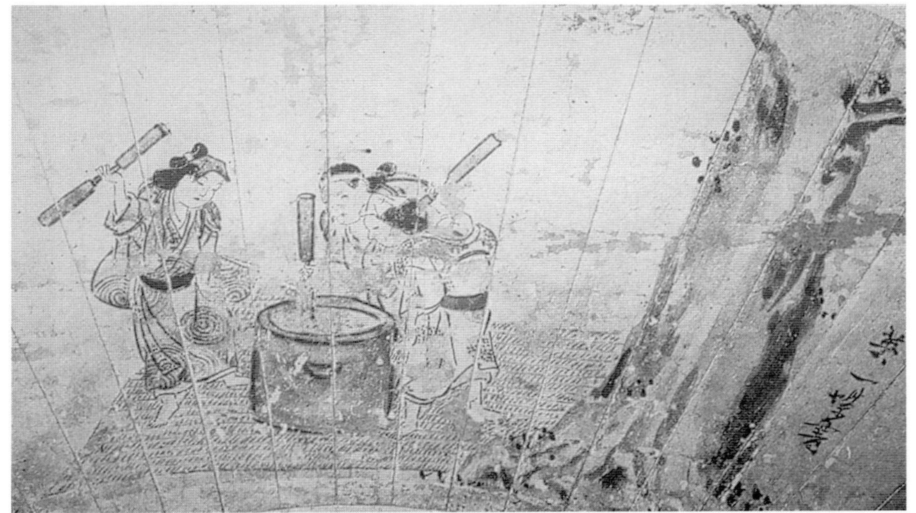

**FIGURE 7.4.** Hanabusa Itchō, fan painting, 1710s. Collection unknown. From Richard Lane, "Kaigai no nikuhitsu, ukiyo-e ippin sen: Hanabusa Itchō to sono ryūha" (A Gallery of *ukiyo-e* paintings [XVIII]: Itchō and his school), *Ukiyo-e,* 74 (1978), Figure 669.

*Life of an Amorous Man (Kōshoku ichidai otoko)* can be taken as a further link to erotic imagery (see below). However, the incongruous combination of peasant women with the young beauty on the right screen suggests instead a symbolic meaning alluding to the antagonism of work as opposed to leisure.

In Bakusen's large screen paintings *Abalone Divers (Ama)* of 1913, the subject itself derives from *ukiyo-e* erotic imagery while the social significance of labor is again stressed by the figures' activities (Figure 7.5). This time the figures on the right screen are shown at work, while the women on the left screen enjoy rest.

The genesis of the *Ama* screens is revealing: in July 1913 Bakusen traveled to an island named Namikiri in the Pacific Ocean, east of Izu Peninsula. In a letter to his patron, Nomura Kazuyuki (1881–1963), he commented on his plan for creating a painting to be sent to the seventh Bunten exhibition in October 1913.[10] He writes that his first design showed three or four fisherwomen—*ama*—lying on the beach "like softly meandering snakes." Behind them a giant fisherman was arrving with two companions on a boat and stepping ashore. In preparation for this work, Bakusen kept watching abalone divers and made sketches of three women who visited him in his lodgings.

Although Bakusen had indulged since 1911 in doing life sketches of the apprentice geisha of Gion who would later become his spouse or of models recruited with the help of newspaper advertisements, there is strong evidence that in his final version of *Ama* he again referred to *ukiyo-e* prints rather than to the sketches he had made on the spot.[11] Significantly, in the final version, the male

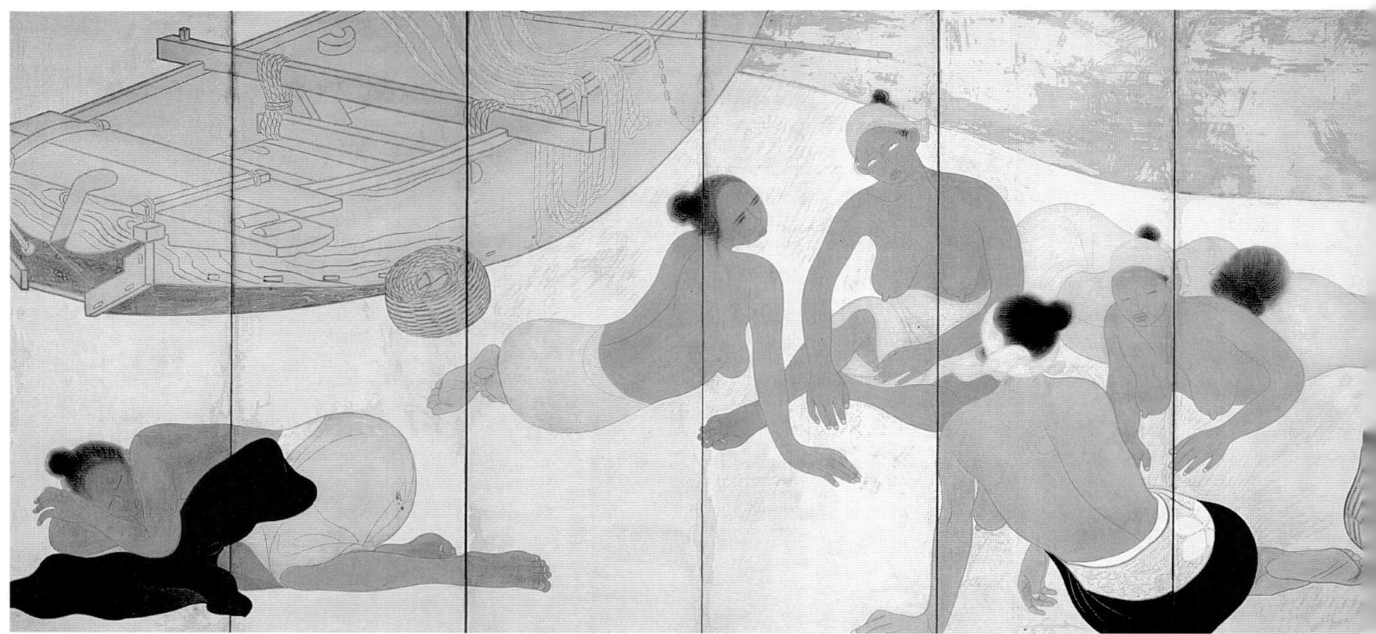

**FIGURE 7.5.** Tsuchida Bakusen, *Abalone Divers*, 1913. Pair of six-fold screens, 170 × 366 cm each, colors on silk. The National Museum of Modern Art, Kyoto.

figures were all replaced by women. Reminiscent of printing techniques are the glistening background covered with mica powder, the forceful colorism of the women's brownish-yellow skin, the deep blue in their loincloths and in the sea, and the accents of green in the plants on the right screen.

Ever since 1913, when a Japanese art critic had compared the figures' deformed shapes to Gauguin's Tahiti women, the *Ama* screens have been associated with Gauguin's primitivism.[12] The half-naked, dark-skinned, and dark-haired figures in Gauguin's Tahiti paintings resemble Bakusen's fisherwomen in their basic postures, but there were other works of Western symbolists to attract the Japanese painter's attention.[13]

Bakusen most probably knew Ferdinand Hodler's monumental painting *The Night* (1889–1890, Kunstmuseum Bern), exhibited at the World's Fair in Paris in 1900 (Figure 7.6). In Hodler's painting male and female figures symbolize the dreams and nightmares that haunt humans in sleep. The sleeping woman in the left *Ama* screen resembles the reclining woman in Hodler's painting in posture and outline. This correspondence leads one to assume that both artists had independently made use of prototypes found in erotic art. The conspicuous figure of a reclining woman, penetrated from behind, is frequently met with in erotic

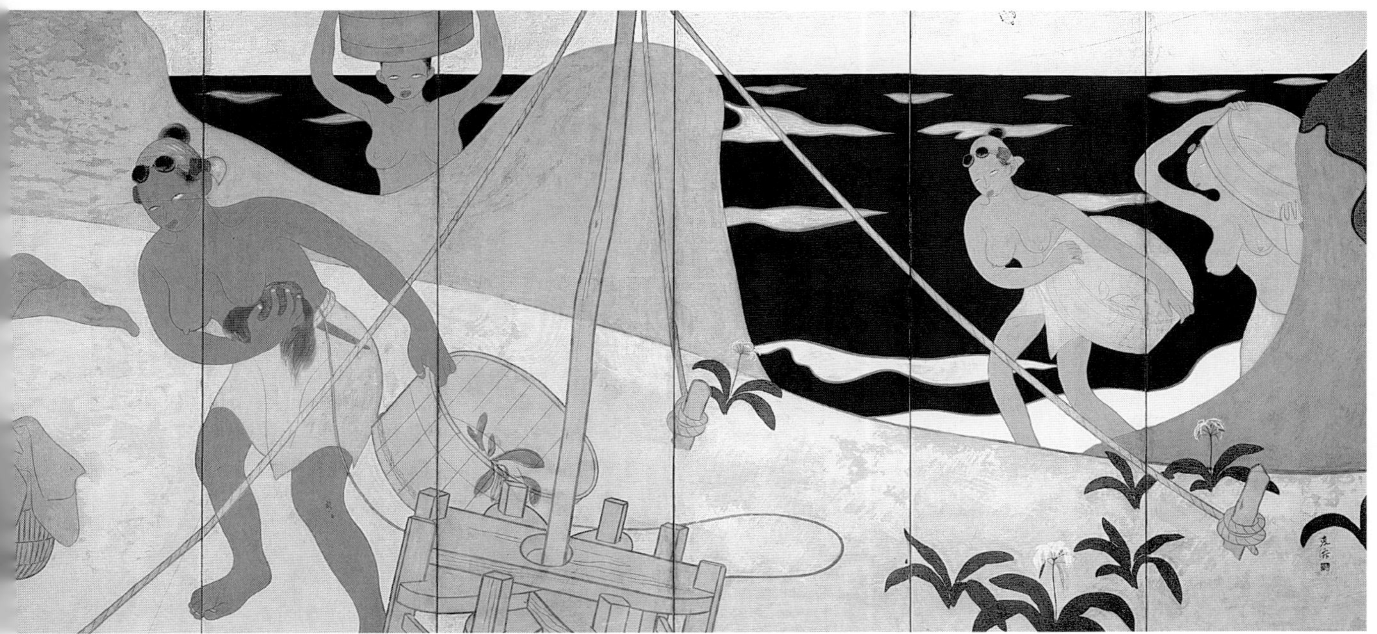

paintings of the Edo period, a late example being a masturbating fisherwoman in a scroll painting by Taisō Yoshitoshi (about 1873) (Figure 7.7).

Bakusen no doubt knew Utamaro's famous print of the 1790s that shows a courtesan with divers in front of the sanctuary of Enoshima (Figure 7.8). He may also have been familiar with the erotic connotation of the word "fisherwomen"—*ama*—which can pun with the near-homophone *amma*, or "masseuse."[14] But, in the *Ama* screens, eroticism again comes in the guise of a metaphoric meaning associated with labor and rest.

By erasing the masculine figures from his origianl design, Bakusen avoided hinting at an encounter between the opposite sexes. Counteractive to an erotic reading, moreover, are the dark and malformed female bodies. In fact, the figures were perceived as extremely "ugly" by a Bunten critic in 1913.[15] In the *Ama* screens the juxtaposition of moving and resting women suggests again that the painter's ambition was to compose an allegory of labor and leisure.

The admittance of *Island Women* and *Abalone Divers* to Bunten signaled without a doubt a change in the judges' expectations. As neither of these works is listed among the *bijinga* exhibits, they were probably exhibited as *joseiga* (paintings of women), another, smaller category of *nihonga*, comprising historical subjects and

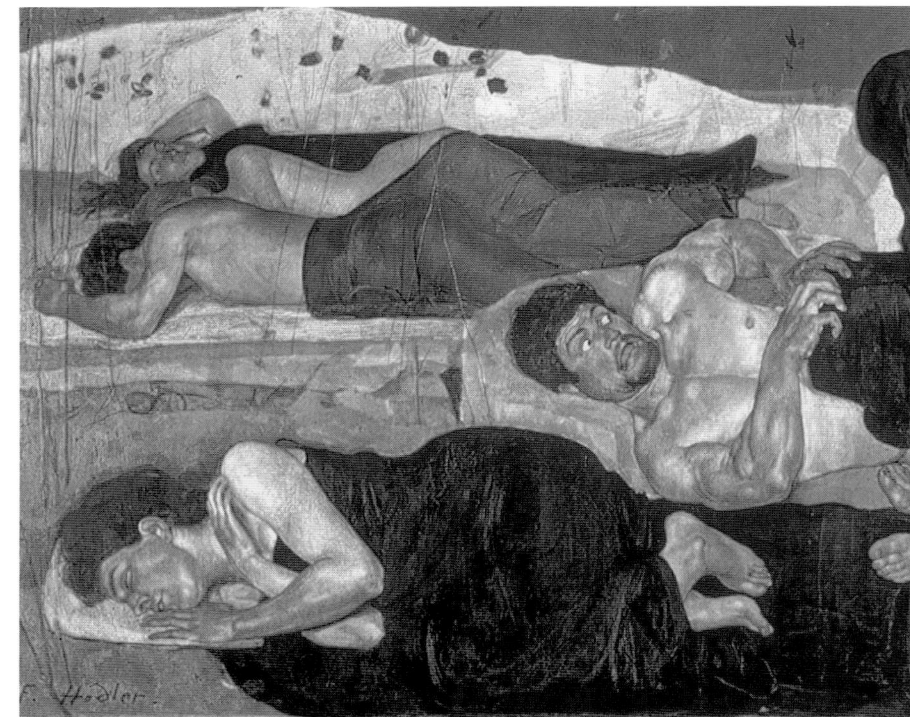

FIGURE 7.6. Ferdinand Hodler, *Die Nacht*, detail, 1889–1890. Kunstmuseum Bern. From Nationalgalerie Berlin, ed., *Ferdinand Hodler* (Katalog 1983) (Kunsthaus Zürich and Benteli Verlags AG., Bern, 3d edition, 1998), 220.

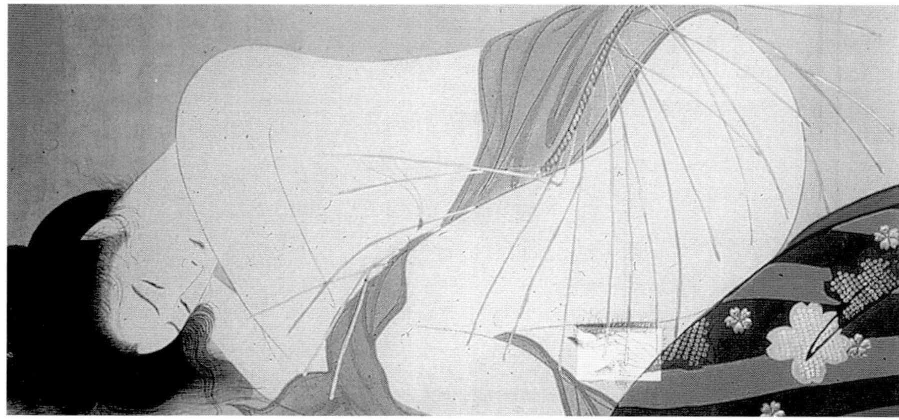

FIGURE 7.7. Taisō Yoshitoshi (1839–1892), *Enjo jūnitai* (Twelve types of voluptuous women), after 1873. Scroll painting, private collection. From Fukuda Kazuhiko, ed., *Nikuhitsu fūzoku emaki* (Painted genre scrolls) (Tokyo: Kawada Shobo, 1988), 133.

rural scenes with peasant women.[16] This was certainly the case with Bakusen's contribution to the Bunten of 1915, which showed three neatly dressed peasant women from the village of Ohara, north of Kyoto, rushing downhill with bundles of firewood on their heads.[17] Here the emphasis on labor precludes an erotic interpretation, showing Bakusen's interest in a traditional motif from Kyoto folk-

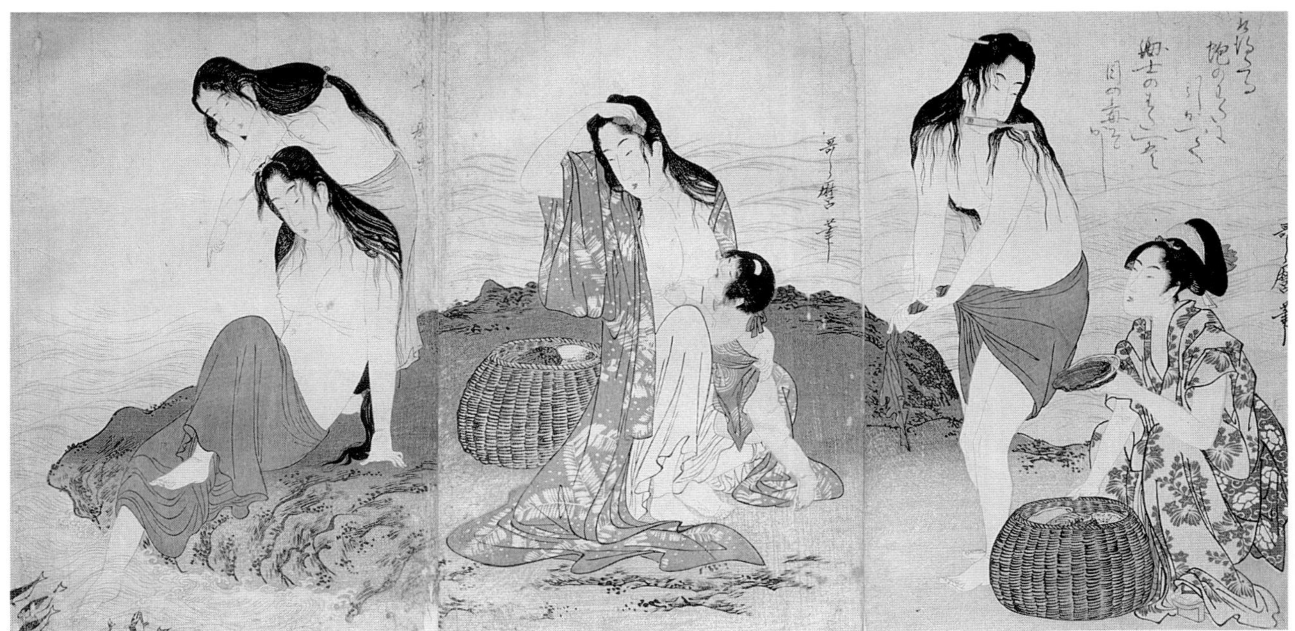

FIGURE 7.8. Kitagawa Utamaro, *Ama* (Abalone divers), 1790–1800. *Nishiki-e.* Musée Guimet, Paris. © Photo RMN—Thierry Olliver. From Asano Shūgō and Timothy Clark, *The Passionate Art of Kitagawa Utamaro* (London: The British Museum, 1995), 189.

lore. The painting was praised as a successful synthesis of postimpressionism and Edo painting styles of the Shijō and Kano schools. It is possible that the unbalanced composition as well as the motif of white head scarves were related to Gauguin's women of Brittany.[18]

When planning *Three Maiko Girls (Sannin no maiko)* for the tenth Bunten of 1916, Bakusen again dealt with a motif with erotic connotations.[19] In search of models for this painting, he made sketches of apprentice geisha living in Gion's renowned teahouse Ichiriki, but the actual composition of a triad of *maiko* playing cards is again taken from Utamaro.[20] Confirming Bakusen's concern that his work might—contrary to his intent—be considered *bijinga* (a genre still associated in his mind with erotic *ukiyo-e*), the painting was in fact displayed in the Bunten's *bijinga* room and hailed for the sweetness and innocence of the girls' faces and the splendor of the kimono design.[21]

Starting in 1916, Bakusen worked passionately on *Serving Girl at a Spa (Yuna)* (Figure 7.9), which highlighted his grappling with the genre of the nude.[22] The last version, finished in 1918, shows a lascivious woman in a transparent red bathrobe lying on a veranda, partly hidden behind the foliage of a pine tree, densely overgrown with wisteria flowers. Inside the house a figure of indistinct gender is playing the shamisen, his or her face hidden by the roof in a way simi-

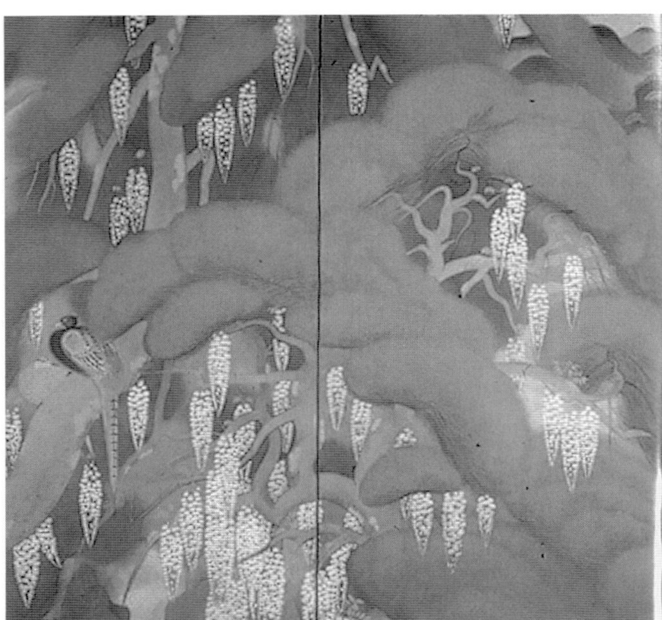
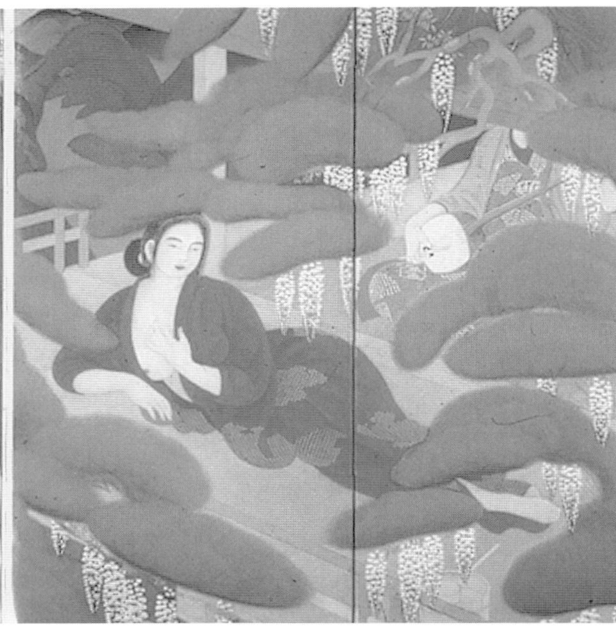

**FIGURE 7.9.** Tsuchida Bakusen, *Serving Girl at a Spa (Yuna),* 1918. Pair of screens, each 197.4 × 195.6 cm. Collection of The National Museum of Modern Art, Tokyo.

lar to the convention of hiding the emperor's face in *yamato-e* iconography. According to Bakusen the painting was meant to symbolize "the power of life" *(iki)* in natural surroundings.[23]

In spite of the many sketches that Bakusen made of a bathhouse prostitute *(yuna)* in the hot springs of Arima in preparation for his work, art historians today mention Goya's *Maya* and Manet's *Olympia* as possible models for *Yuna.*[24] In a letter to his sponsor written in April 1916, Bakusen confessed his fascination with the erotic paintings and prints that he tracked down in several collections in the Kansai region.[25]

## National Painting as "Pure Art"

*Yuna* was first shown to the public in the first exhibition of the Association for the Creation of National Painting (Kokuga Sōsaku Kyōkai), which opened on November 1918 in the Tokyo department store Shirokiya (Nihonbashi).[26] Out of dissent with Bunten, the association had been founded in 1918 by former Chat Noir members, including Bakusen, their teacher Takeuchi Seihō (1864–1942), and the art historian Nakai Sōtarō.[27]

The society's declaration of principles *(riyūsho)* was written by Bakusen's brother, the philosopher and art historian Tsuchida Kyōson (1891–1934). It starts: "What should be considered the spirit of our society is our aim of promoting Japanese art by creating and promulgating 'pure art' *(junshin naru bijutsu)*."[28] The declaration goes on to argue that further participation in Bunten exhibitions would spoil the very aim of creating "pure art." Accordingly, art—that is, *nihonga*—was not only of individual concern but amounted to a social movement *(shakai undō)* to which Takeuchi Seihō had given his blessing, urging the members to subordinate individual preferences to the advantage of the entirety of Japanese painting.[29]

The term "pure art" had already been coined by the advocates of *nihonga* revivalism in the late 1880s. While "pure art" *(junsui bijutsu)* was at that time contrasted with "applied art," the obvious affiliation with the "essence of national polity" *(kokusui)* tinged it with a patriotic flavor. Clearly, in Meiji *nihonga* "pure art" was not yet conceived of in the sense of *l'art pour l'art* but referred to a claim for the ethnic purity of national painting.[30] The Kokuga Sōsaku Kyōkai declaration is commonly thought to witness the birth of a *l'art pour l'art* spirit and the decadent aestheticism of Kyōto *nihonga*, but the argument that an artist's self-concern could do harm to the production of "pure art" sheds doubt on the political disengagement of the association.

Much in tune with the responsibility of a "social movement" are the works Bakusen and Nonogase Banka created for the association exhibitions after 1918. For the exhibition of 1919, Nonagase choose to depict mothers and children in a peaceful, natural setting, suggestive of leisure and recreation (Figure 7.10). Sharing a frescolike flatness with Bakusen's *Spring* of 1920,[31] and showing a mother with her baby enjoying springtime in a flowering garden, Nonogase's figural composition epitomizes rich harvest with the mother offering her baby a breast, a peasant woman with fruits, and children playing music and collecting flowers in a rural scene. These works lack the taste for decadent eroticism that characterizes other Kyoto painters like Kainoshō Tadaoto (1894–1978) and Okamoto Shinsō (1894–1933), who exhibited with the association as guests.[32]

The linkage of female beauty to rural life derived from the earthly paradise located in Arcadia, splendidly pictorialized by Puvis de Chavanne in monumental pastorals of antiquity before unfolding in the glorification of country life at home—and in Gauguin's Tahiti. No wonder this imagery ended up in the visions of a golden future prophesized by fascism.[33] Clearly, the Golden Age motif was a challenge for *yōga* and *nihonga* artists who aimed at idealizing life on native soil, too.

With future fertilization through the study of Western art in mind, Bakusen embarked in April 1921 on a two-year excursion to Europe. Together with four

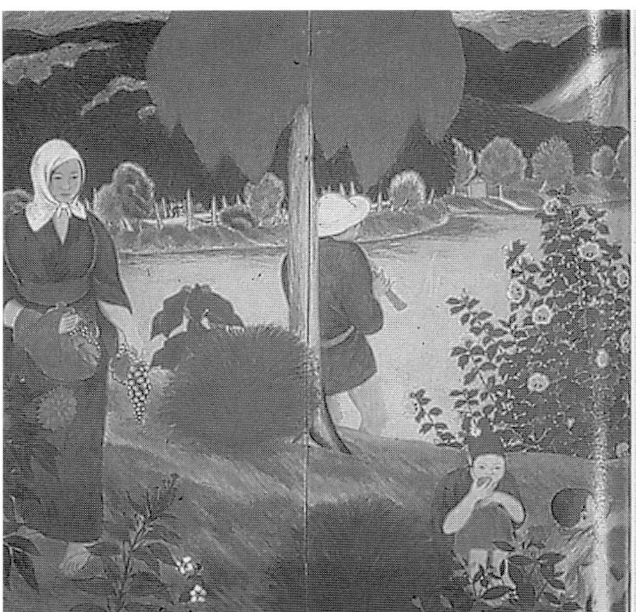
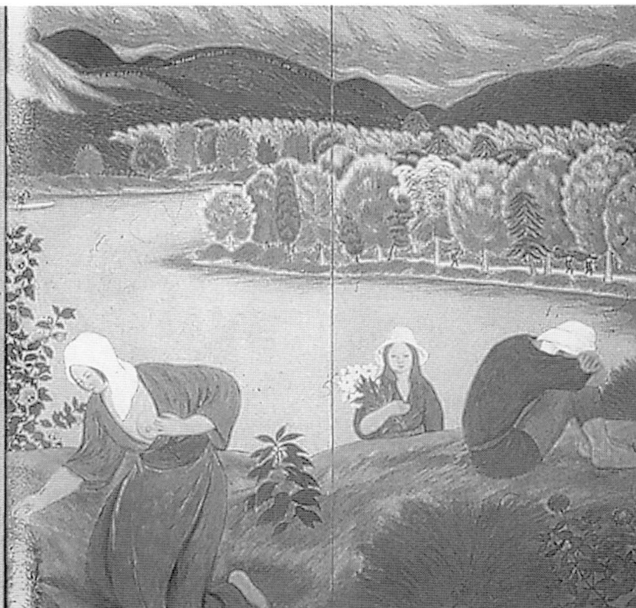

**FIGURE 7.10.** Nonogase Banka, *Recess (Yasumi toki),* 1919. Pair of two-fold screens, color on paper, private collection. From *Kokuga Sosaku Kyokai Retrospective*, ed. Kyōto Kokuritsu Kindai Bijutsukan (1993), plate 15.

colleagues, among them Ono Chikkyō and Nonogase Banka, he toured cultural sites all over Europe, taking back home in the summer of 1923 a large collection of oil paintings and prints by modern masters like Gauguin, van Gogh, Cézanne, Renoir, and Henri Rousseau.[34]

In 1924 Bakusen exhibited *Maiko Girl in a Garden (Bugi rinsen),* showing an apprentice geisha in a costly kimono, sitting on a rock in a stylized garden landscape reminiscent of Kyoto's temples and palaces (Figure 7.11). Posing like a painter's model, the girl looks timidly at the beholder. This painting too was hailed for synthesizing Cézanne and Renoir with the decorativeness of Tosa painting. Recently, however, it has been suggested that *Maiko Girl in a Garden* has a counterpart in Leonardo da Vinci's *Mona Lisa* (1504, Louvre), though the Gioconda's sensuality differs considerably from the introverted maidenliness of the *maiko*.[35]

Bakusen's endeavor to challenge Western masterpieces becomes even more apparent when one holds *Ohara Maidens* of 1927 (Figure 7.12) against Manet's *Déjeuner sur l'herbe* (1863) (Figure 7.13), which Bakusen certainly did not miss seeing on his visits to the Louvre. The pose of the naked woman in Manet's painting recurs in the left figure of *Oharame*, although her enigmatic "look out of the picture" has been turned into meditative engrossment. The frivolous encounter of naked women with fashionably dressed gentlemen is transfigured into innocu-

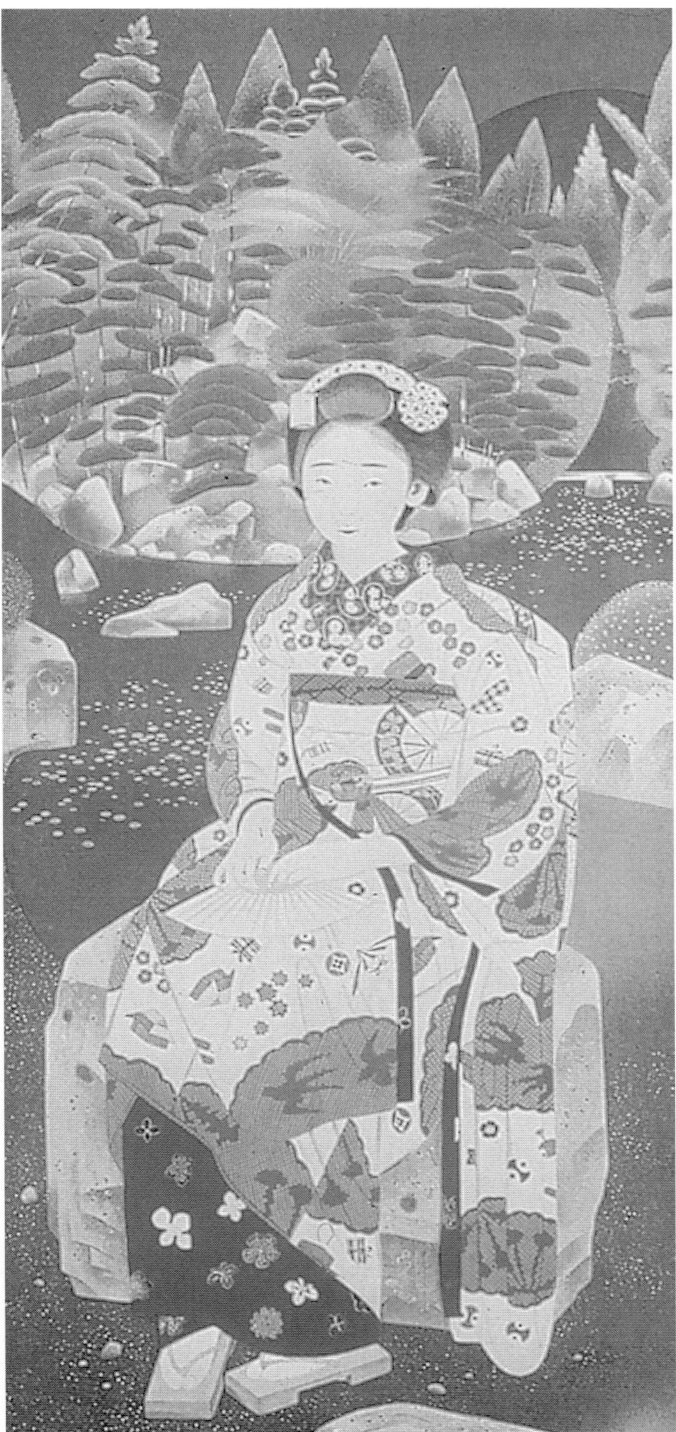

**FIGURE 7.11.** Tsuchida Bakusen, *Maiko Girl in a Garden (Bugirinsen),* 1924. Collection of The National Museum of Modern Art, Tokyo. From *Tsuchida Bakusen ten* (Tsuchida Bakusen: a retrospective) (Tokyo: National Museum of Modern Art, 1997), 93.

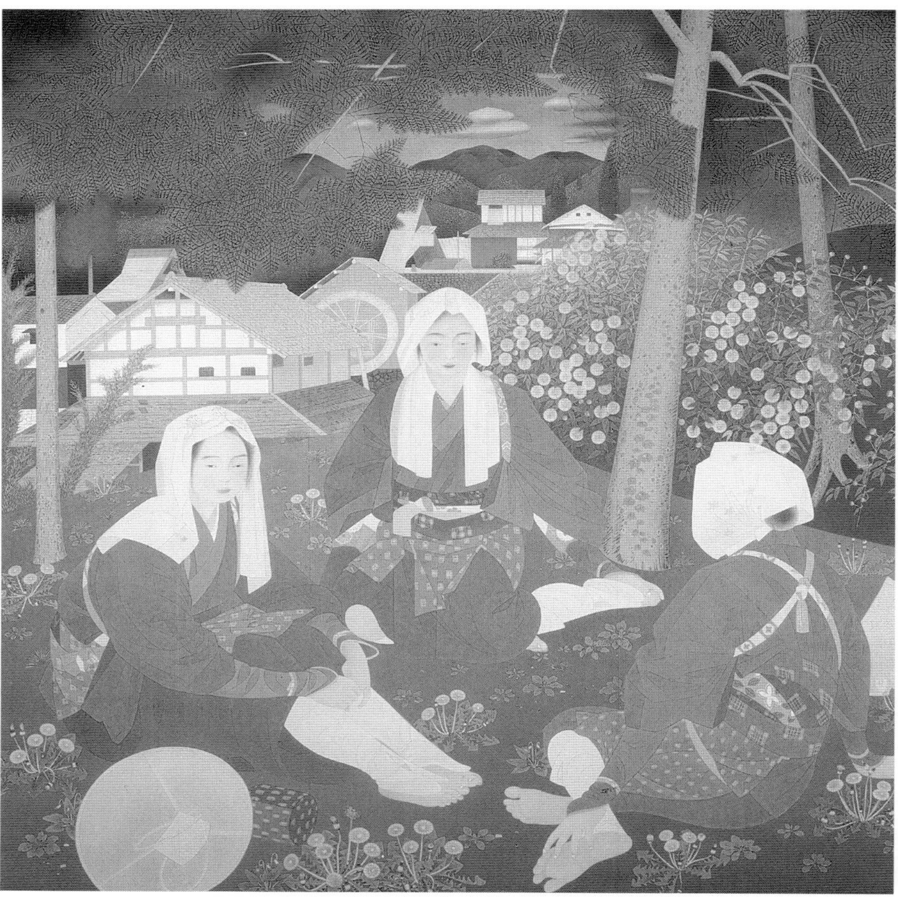

**FIGURE 7.12.** Tsuchida Bakusen, *Ohara Maidens (Oharame),* 1927. The National Museum of Modern Art, Kyoto.

ous folklore. Again the mixing of males and females is consciously avoided. Leisure seems to redeem the hardship of work.

Significantly, the *yōga* painter Ishii Hakutei criticized *Maiko in a Garden* and *Oharame* for a lack of the linearity that he thought essential in *nihonga* style.[36] In fact, at the end of the Taishō period, *nihonga* and *yōga* tended to converge to the point where it was solely material and techniques, rather than compositional format, that attested to their opposition. In 1925 the Kokuga Sōsaku Kyōkai even established a *yōga* division, frequented by painters who strove for a synthesis of *yōga* colorism with decorativeness, such as Umehara Ryūsaburō (1888–1986).[37] However, when in 1926 Bakusen forced Kainoshō to withdraw a portrait of a barely clothed women by calling it a "dirty picture" (*kitanai e*), he may have been reprimanding the work's stylistic hybridity as well as its obscenity.[38]

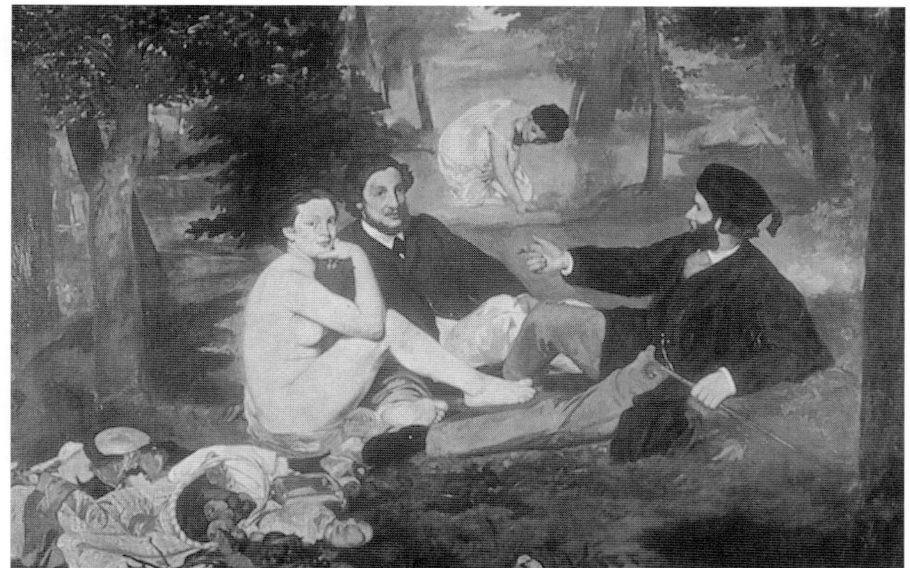

FIGURE 7.13. Edouard Manet, *Déjeuner sur l'herbe*, 1863. Paris, Musée d'Orsay, donation Etienne Moreau-Nélation, 1906.

In July 1928 the Kokuga Sōsaku Kyōkai was dissolved, presumably for economic reasons. Bakusen was already counted among the painters whose works were found suitable to represent modern national painting at *nihonga* exhibitions internationally, such as in Paris (1929) and Rome (1930).[39] The question arises as to why Bakusen and other Kokuga Sōsaku Kyōkai members aimed at counterbalancing eroticism by creating images of femininity that would stand for the claimed moral and aesthetic integrity of National Painting.[40]

## *Ukiyo-e* as a Paradigm of Modernism

In his letters written from Hachijōshima, Bakusen called the "expression of life" *(iki)* the ultimate goal for the art that he sought to achieve with all his physical and spiritual energy.[41] His complaints about the uncivilized life on the island resonate with the romantic idea that starvation would lead to creativeness. Experiencing hardship was essential for creating "primitive art" *(yaban na geijutsu)*. Likewise, Bakusen argued that the Bunten judges would refuse his *Abalone Divers* as "heresy" *(jadō)*. When describing his studies on the island, he claimed "to portray the wondrous mystique lurking in the depth of nature."[42]

Although Bakusen may have fancied himself on the tracks of Gauguin's escape to Tahiti, back in Kyoto he evidently discarded the sketches that he had made on the spot and modeled *Island Women* with the help of prototypes taken from *ukiyo-e* and Western painting. What is more, when traveling to Hachijōshima, he may have drawn a parallel between Gauguin and a Japanese paragon of withdrawal from the world: in Ihara Saikaku's erotic novel *Life of an Amorous Man* (1682), the hero Yonosoke puts an end to his erotic adventures in Japan by sailing away to the "Island of Women" *(nyōgo no shima)*. Ironically, this fictitious island of love was identified with Hachijōjima.[43] The conjunction of Gauguin's amorous adventures in Tahiti with Yonosuke's journey is not extraordinary when seen in the context of *mitate*, the device of conflating phenomena of different times, cultures, or classes by virtue of visual or textual parody.[44]

The francophile art historian Nakai Sōtarō had acted since the days of the Chat Noir as the spiritual leader of Kyoto painters. In his book on modern art published in 1922, he hailed Cézanne, van Gogh, and Gauguin as the predecessors of Expressionism *(hyōgen shugi)*. Especially Gauguin's struggle for true art provided the model for a "new civilization" *(atarashiki bunmei)*, set against the materialism prevailing in Western culture.[45]

By calling the "expression of life" the essence of modern art, Nakai reiterated the concept of *l'art pour l'art (biteki seikatsu)*, proclaimed as early as 1890 by Takayama Chōgyū (1871–1902), one of the first Japanese advocates of Nietzsche's aesthetics of vitalism. It appears that to Nakai the "expression of life" was equivalent to a native *principe vitale* that a *nihonga* painter was called on to produce from individual experience as well as from tradition.[46] In the closing sentences of the chapter dedicated to the founders of modernism, Nakai writes:

> [Art] must be stigmatized by the soul *(tamashii)* of living human beings, demonstrating the differences of race and time. Only by returning to the homeland of the soul will the truth of tradition spread its light. I believe that the complex meaning of Gauguin consists in the fact that he is unsurpassed as a primitivist. That is what the long-awaited art of Gauguin is giving to us. He awaked the soul fitfully sleeping in the shallowness of naturalism, he made the nerves of people living in our times recover from fatigue, he poured healthy spring water on our decadent minds, and he taught us how to return to our homeland *(furusato)*. Being the forerunner of Expressionism, he is the painter who possessed what art in our times needs most. Clearly, he is the fountain of mystery, a magnificent artist who dips deep into a grand source of light.[47]

Nakai's eulogy amounts to the canonization of Gauguin as the father of modernism in the Japanese "homeland." While attesting to Gauguin's deep love for the heritage of his own culture, Nakai declares the stylistic connotation of "primitivism" the paramount principle of *nihonga.*

In the 1920s the philosopher Nishida Kitarō (1870–1945) came to stress Cézanne's role as a mediator between Eastern spirituality and Western materialism. While calling Cézanne as a witness against the materialism of European culture, Nishida did not bother to claim idealism as the basis of Japanese aesthetics.[48] In the essay "An Explanation of Beauty," published in 1900, Nishida compared the disinterested delight in "beauty" *(bi)* to the Zen concept of "no-self" *(muga)* or "ecstasy" in self-effacement.[49] In his thoughts on art and ethics published between 1920 and 1923, he maintained that the expression of "life force" must be controlled, as only the union of truth *(shin),* morals *(zen),* and beauty *(bi)* would constitute the criteria of true art.[50]

The philosopher Kuki Shūzō (1888–1943) left for France in the same year as Bakusen. In Paris in 1926, he finished the manuscript for *Iki no kōzō* (Anatomy of chic).[51] Kuki saw no difficulty in declaring the *ukiyo-e* ideal of aesthetic refinement—*iki*—the very essence of Japanese visual arts and culture. Significantly, Kuki sensed in the prints of the Yoshiwara painter Utamaro a high-class feminine taste that revealed a "heroic affinity" with modernity.[52] By assigning *ukiyo-e* artists the consciousness of *l'art pour l'art*, Kuki suggested in a talk given in 1928 in Pontigny, France, that the decadent flavor of "modernity" emerged in *ukiyo-e* independently of and prior to modernism in Western art:

> Les choses honteuses et répugnantes au point de vue moral étaient parfois le sujet des estampes de la période Tokugawa (1600–1850). Avec quelle ardeur pure et sereine sont-elles traitées! On se trouve ainsi avoir pratiqué, depuis plusieurs siècles, la théorie de l'art pour l'art, cette théorie de l'idéalisme absolu dans l'art.
>
> [Things that are shameful or repugnant from a moral point of view are sometimes the subject of prints from the Tokugawa period (1600–1850). With what pure and serene ardor are they treated! It happens thus that we have been practicing, for several centuries, the theory of art-for-art's-sake, the theory of absolute idealism in art.][53]

Kuki attributed the origin of modern art to the impact of a genre from the very bottom of the aesthetic value system of Japan's feudal past—*ukiyo-e*. This entitled him simultaneously to claim *l'art pour l'art* the basis of the refined lifestyle in Edo pleasure quarters and to contrast it to the vulgarity of modern life.[54]

Kuki shared a love for *ukiyo-e* with other Japanese travelers touring Europe during the 1920s. To them, however, the reconciliation of *ukiyo-e* imagery with the idealistic definition of art posed a more serious problem. While formal simplification, deformation, and distortion in postimpressionistic painting opened their eyes to the similar nonrealistic qualities of Edo-period painting, the vulgar connotations of *ukiyo-e bijinga*, not to mention the indigenous concept of the human body in *shunga*, prohibited this genre's classification as "art" for them.

When the philosopher Abe Jirō (1883–1959) studied in Heidelberg in 1922, he presented his landlady with a print by Utamaro, showing two courtesans being dressed (see Figure 7.2). In 1930 he remembered his embarrassment on commenting on the print's aesthetic refinement in view of the subject's moral dubiousness.[55]

Similar to Abe, but again quite different from Kuki, Bakusen valued *ukiyo-e bijinga* as a cultural asset that had to be purified in order to stand comparison with Western concepts of female beauty. During his stay in Paris, Bakusen got a clearer idea of his attraction to *bijinga* and Japanese women. On January 8, 1922, he wrote to his spouse:

> Since I arrived here I feel the strong desire to study *ukiyo-e* more intensively. Moreover, I have decided to study Japanese women in order to become a real painter of women.
>
> Actually, our Utamaro, Harunobu, and others have created fairly nice pictures of women. I want to study these *ukiyo-e* painters, look sharply at the object, and thus express the essence of Japanese femininity so that I can outdo all Japanese painters from the past. (These remarks might sound alarming to you, but for the sake of art I have to ask for your permission, all the more so as for me there is no other way but to paint women. I think there is a real need for painters of women in Japan, and there is good reason for creating a new *ukiyo-e* made of brilliant colors and line drawing).[56]

In spite of his admiration for the Yoshiwara beauties of Harunobu and Utamaro, in *Maiko Girl in a Garden* Bakusen substituted the innocence of an apprentice geisha, still awaiting her first erotic encounter, for erotic seductiveness.[57]

## Woman for the Nation-State

While elevating "woman painting" to the level of "pure art," Bakusen confirmed the *nihonga* painters' mission of expressing the essence of Japanese aesthetics

*(Nihon no bi)*. Tomi Suzuki has pointed to the fact that the gendering of literature prepared for the cultural fundamentalism of prewar Japan.[58] Correspondingly, by eliminating all male figures from the visual field, the iconology of Bakusen's *bijinga* was in keeping with the tendency to make femininity into the quintessence of Japanese aesthetics as opposed to the masculinity of Western civilization.

In 1922 Nakai Sōtarō held Gauguin up as an example to *nihonga* artists who aimed at expressing native spirituality in nonnaturalistic form. By calling "primitivism" a denominator common to Gauguin and *nihonga*, Nakai ingeniously recognized that national painting was capable of beating Western art at its own game. It seems plausible that a similar idea caused Bakusen ten years earlier to make use of *ukiyo-e* figural types in creating his own "primitive art" *(yaban no bijutsu)*. It is also possible that since the days of the Chat Noir, Nakai had encouraged Bakusen to develop *bijinga* into a genre that would represent a true alternative to the *yōga* nude. However, in order to grasp the policy behind the promotion of "woman painting," the correlation between stylistic innovation and subject matter must be taken into consideration.

In terms of subject matter, a fundamental difference between Bakusen and Gauguin lies in the fact that the French artist explored the exotic charm of a tribal culture, whereas Bakusen glorified native women of the countryside, making them into a symbol of rural life as opposed to Western civilization. Consequently, the antinaturalistic and therefore antiacademic rhetoric of primitivism lost the purpose of visually alienating a foreign race. It appears that even though in the Taishō period the Western idea of the "noble savage" may have been projected onto Japan's colonies, this very myth more fundamentally provided a model for cultural self-identification.[59] Not the exotic world at the borders but the Japanese homeland itself was cast in the part of the "country innocent" who suffered exposure to metropolitan corruption. On top of this, in the context of *nihonga* revivalism, the reception of primitivism helped to avert the danger of self-alienation that illusionism had enforced on Japanese painting. When seen in the framework of Bunten exhibitions, the flatness of Bakusen's peasant women and fisherwomen counteracted the arousal of sexual desire, so forcefully incited by contemporary *yōga* nude painting.[60]

In contrast to the voyeuristic delight in *yōga* nudes, *nihonga bijinga* directed itself toward edifying female viewers. In Meiji-period *bijinga* the ideal of female beauty had lost its formerly overt association with the erotic culture of Edo pleasure quarters. Echoing the new "civilizing" ideal of "good wives and wise mothers" *(ryōsai kenbo)* as proclaimed in women's magazines of the Meiji and Taishō periods, *bijinga* had been transmuted into a genre for female consumption.[61] Uemura Shoen (1875–1949), Kaburagi Kiyokata (1878–1973), Itō Shinsui (1898–1972), and many more *bijinga* specialists translated *ukiyo-e* figural types into *nihonga* realism, creating images of "ideal woman" that conflated elegant behavior with a sweet persuasiveness of commercial advertisement that supported female desire for kimono fashion and urban commodities.[62]

Depicting peasant women or abalone divers in a primitivist mode, Bakusen deliberately discarded the fashionable sensualism that he was still after when painting *Hair* in 1911. His familiarity with symbolism and postimpressionism inspired him to ascribe to *ukiyo-e* figural types a sense of corporeality that made the female body into a vehicle of allegorical meaning. The monumental format of paired screens lent itself to the juxtaposition of figures that hinted at the opposing activities of leisure and labor.

But around 1915 the growing male demand for pornographic allusiveness encouraged *bijinga* painters in this direction to the extent that measures had to be taken to ban obscene works from Bunten.[63] Bakusen's *Yuna* of 1918 seems to reflect the ongoing sexualization of *bijinga*, but being aware of his mission as a *nihonga* painter, he refrained from expressing the carnal splendor of nudes painted with oils. Complaining about the constraints imposed on *nihonga*, he alleged: "If I were allowed to use oil pigments, I probably would have aimed at expressing the whole of my admiration for the splendor of female bodies like the ones of the women of Goa."[64]

As a whole, Bakusen perceived only three categories of women: urban beauties of the pleasure quarters, peasant women and fisherwomen, and, though represented by only a single painting, mothers. This categorization restricted women to the brothel, the countryside, and the home, confirming thereby male dominance in terms of sex, labor, and procreation. In this respect *Ohara Maidens* of 1927 epitomizes the "agrarian myth" as advanced by the ethnologist Yanagita Kunio (1875–1962), who set rural timelessness against the decadence of modern life *(modan raifu)* and metropolitan coffee girl *(moga)* entertainment.[65] Resonating with the aesthetic idealism in the 1920s, Bakusen denigrated eroticism by connecting feminine beauty to diligence and virtuousness. Significantly, in 1930 Bakusen exhibited *Oharame* and *Maiko rinsen zu* in the Exhibition of Feminine Art (Josei bijutsu tenrankai) organized by the Yomiuri Newspaper.[66]

In a time of increasing industrialization and exploitation of female labor, Bakusen managed to create an image of native womanhood that fit the cultural essentialism of imperial Japan. When displayed abroad, these works could not fail to corroborate the impression that the national painting was as undefiled, modest, and beautiful as the women it depicted. Bakusen's icons of Japanese womanhood encoded the sanctimonious message that imperial Japan had successfully withstood the temptations of modernity as it kept its art and its women in a pristine condition.

CHAPTER EIGHT

KIM HYESHIN

# Images of Women in National Art Exhibitions during the Korean Colonial Period

The history of the modernization of Korea is fraught with emotionally charged issues and contradictions. The thirty-six-year period from 1910 to 1945 that Korea spent under Japanese imperial rule as the colony "Chosŏn" (in Japanese, Chōsen)[1] is also Korea's period of modernization. Japan, which put Korea under direct government control after it annexed it, brought about this modernization through a variety of colonial policies. Thus, Korea's modern period was started by its colonizers, who created a situation where Koreans were unable to make decisions of their own volition and were limited by the psychological stress of being under colonial control.

The field of art was no exception. All the members of what is now known as the first generation of modern Korean artists went to Japan to study or apprentice under famous Japanese artists in the period before and during annexation. For them, Japan was a window to a new civilization, and it influenced them throughout their careers, from training to production to gaining recognition as artists. The Korean Fine Art Exhibition (Chosŏn misul chŏllamhoe or Chōsen bijutsu tenrankai, hereafter referred to as "Sŏnjŏn"), institutionalized in 1922, played a central role in this process. Sŏnjŏn was established by the Japanese governor-general as one link in its colonial policy of so-called Cultural Policy *(Bunka seiji seisaku)*. The exhibition along with the judging regulations and administrative methods were modeled on the Imperial Art Institute Exhibition (Teikoku bijutsuin tenrankai), the official government exhibition in Japan at the time. Until the twenty-third annual exhibition in 1944, Sŏnjŏn held absolute authority as the official exhibition and controlled all initiatives in the Korean art world. From this, the "Sŏnjŏn picture" was born, and what can be called Sŏnjŏn tendencies or trends took shape.

During the Sŏnjŏn period as a whole, representation of the colonial landscape as lonely and impoverished and of figures in traditional dress as submissive was common. Until recently, even in the Korean art world, art displaying this tendency has been explained away as "art exhibiting a weak form of lyricism or localism that is no longer in existence" or collectively dismissed as "products from the dark colonial period" and let alone. In direct opposition to this tacit avoidance, the journal *Quarterly Art Magazine* printed an article in 1983 that announced the artworks and the real names of artists who cooperated with the Japanese fascist government during the war at the end of the colonial period, or from the last half of 1930 to 1945. This article caused a fierce debate, now referred to as the "Pro-Japanese Art Dispute." Unfortunately, this dispute ended with a head-on collision between the artists who argued for an art-for-art's-sake approach and the *Quarterly Art Magazine* side without any analysis of the actual paintings.[2]

That the debate did not open a discussion of colonial period art or the context of its production is disappointing, because I believe that Sŏnjŏn art has the distinctive feature of allowing the "colonized Chosŏn" to be seen. This is particularly obvious in works that contain representations of women. In this essay, from the viewpoint that art is a part of government structure, I will do a reading of the power politics apparent in the images of women in the paintings selected for Sŏnjŏn. As Wakakuwa Midori has stated, images of women from a certain period can show how women at that time were regarded in that culture and society.[3] When the authorities exert their influence and a work is given an appraisal based on a set standard, a place to be shown, and resulting honors, the painted image becomes legitimated, which censors the viewer's gaze. Bryson calls this process "vision structuralized by power,"[4] where art strengthens the operation of power and closely follows the power structure that is being set up. Based on the above assumptions, I will examine the Sŏnjŏn exhibit to ascertain the function it served in terms of cultural policy and analyze some of the works selected for *Sŏnjŏn* that contain images of women.

## The Character of Sŏnjŏn

At the outset of colonial rule, the "Military Rule Policy" was used to establish a system of governance. Resistance to annexation was suppressed by the military police; Korean military, government, and cultural activities were all strictly forbidden. Yet independence movements survived and finally in 1919 came the large-scale uprising now called the "March First Movement." Like most first-stage national independence movements in colonies, the March First Movement was initiated by the intellectual class and then spread rapidly into a nationwide movement. This uprising was brutally suppressed by the military, but afterwards Japan instituted a new policy that ostensibly relaxed the intensity of military rule. Under the new post–March First governing policies, the publishing of magazines and the two national newspapers, the *Chosŏn ilbo* and the *Tonga ilbo*, were allowed, and Keijō Imperial University (now Seoul National University) and technical colleges specializing in Korean traditional arts were established. But the real purpose of this so-called Cultural Policy remained the disruption and weakening of the influence of national independence movements by getting people to focus on culture rather than on the hopes for independence raised by the March First Movement.

The governor-general appointed after the March First Movement, Saitō Makoto, early on instituted a number of policies to foster pro-Japanese feelings at a vocational level as one method to combat Korean nationalist movements. This move proved to be very effective, and many cultural intellectuals became pro-Japanese.[5] The Cultural Policy's concrete effects on the art world appeared in the form of two exhibitions. One was the Korean Painters and Writers Association Exhibition (Chosŏn sŏhwa hyŏphoe chŏllamhoe, or Hyŏpchŏn), which was formed by Ko Ŭidong, the first Korean to study Western art at Tokyo Art University, and a group of Korean traditional artists. In April of 1921 the first Hyŏpjŏn exhibition (which was also the first public group exhibition) was widely publicized by the newspapers and attracted much interest among the general population. But the following year, when the government-sponsored Sŏnjŏn exhibit was initiated, things became difficult. It soon became evident that, in the sparsely populated Korean art world, Sŏnjŏn needed the Hyŏpjŏn artists to participate, and the government acted to induce the members of the Painters and Writers Association to switch to Sŏnjŏn. One of the main Sŏnjŏn artists, Yi Chong'u, stated: "At the time, the government mass-mailed a kind of announcement letter addressed to the members of the Writers and Painters Association. The content of the letter was something to the effect that next time an exhibition like the Imperial Exhibition in Tokyo was to be established in Keijō and our positive participation would be appreciated."[6] Thus, in June of 1922, many of the Writers and Painters Association members had their work shown at the first Sŏnjŏn exhibit. From then on, owing to the government's powerful influence and support, Sŏnjŏn was seen as the main exhibit.[7]

Sŏnjŏn, the jewel in the crown of the Cultural Policy, was under the administration of the Ministry of Education. Judges in the first year included Kawai Gyokudō and Okada Saburōsuke and, in the second year, Wada Eisaku, Komuro

Sui'un, and Fujishima Takeji—all Bunten (Japanese Ministry of Education exhibition) and Imperial Exhibition–level artists. The power of appointment was held by the Japanese colonial government; furthermore, many government ministers who had no connection to the fine arts were appointed as judges. In the early period of the Sŏnjŏn exhibits, the only Korean who participated in the judging was the high ranking pro-Japanese government official Yi Wanyong, the former prime minister and Korea's signator to the annexation agreement. From the fourteenth Sŏnjŏn (1935), a "recommendation system" was established, and those who had repeatedly had works selected for exhibit at Sŏnjŏn were given special dispensation to show without going through open competition. Also, from 1937, a "participation system" was established whereby artists who were further selected from among those in the select "recommended" group were granted license to become judging assistants.

Over the entire history of the Sŏnjŏn exhibits, however, only three Korean artists received such a title: Kim Ŭnho, Yi Sangbŏm, and Sim Hyŏnggu. This tokenism exemplifies the tactics of the Cultural Policy. Based more on political considerations than on artistic merit, rising to the "recommendation" or "participation" level, in effect, meant that an artist had been recognized for faithfully following the policy aims of the colonial government. Also, Sŏnjŏn, through its essentially Japanese judging monopoly, was able to create and direct the abovementioned Sŏnjŏn trends by choosing works that conformed to the standards it set. Art conspicuously avoided showing the real situation of the Korean nationals, their pain, or any resistance to the government. This tendency, through a steadily increasingly powerful Sŏnjŏn, was strengthened by the artists who valued the titles of "recommended artist" and "participating artist" as an honor and a proof of success.

The cultural policies from before and during annexation that created such institutions as Sŏnjŏn also have direct parallels to the historical views of Korea held by the Japanese. For example, the "Stagnation Theory" stated that Korea at the end of the Chosŏn dynasty (1910) was suspended at the stage that Japan had been at during the early Heian period (approximately 794–898)—which is to say that the Koreans appeared to be unable to develop on their own. The "China-Korea One Body Theory" stated that Korea had never had its own history but rather had only experienced the effects of Chinese history (and therefore was not a "country" that deserved independence), while the "Heteronomic History Theory" stated that Korean history was only a history documenting the influences of foreign powers such as China and Japan.[8] The following quotation describing an important debate in the Japanese newspapers during the annexation refers to these historical viewpoints: "The contemporary view of Korea is visible in the contempt for Korea, or 'Backwards Chōsen' as it was called. It was spoken of in this manner as if it were given, common knowledge. And furthermore, because Korea has from the start been seen as a satellite of Manchu China, its independence has been denied, and solely owing to heteronomous power, Koreans are portrayed as lazy and passive."[9]

Of the various biased historical views, cultural policy was based most strongly on the "Japan-Korea Common Ancestor Theory." This theory justified Japan's control of Korea by saying that Japan had been leading Korea since far back in time, when the Japanese and the Koreans had common ancestors. This thinking engendered the assimilation policy "unifying" the colony of Chosŏn with the Japanese "homeland." According to his writings, Governor-General Saitō claimed that a plan for the cultural assimilation of Korea with Japan and the various reforms this would allow would be the best way to meet the goal of annexing Korea.[10] His thinking was based on the assumption that the colonizer was intrinsically superior to the colonized. As historian Kang Sangjung states, the annexation of Korea was based on "a self-righteous cultural mission that put Japan in the role of the 'strong advanced cultural country' that would save the inferior Korea through contact and the idea that assimilation was the best form for such contact to take."[11] In an assimilation/annexation where both parties are not equal, a two-tier relationship is formed whereby the side with the power of the gaze also has the power to represent the object it gazes at and to protect it, while the side that is the object of the gaze is the object of representation and protection. If this equation is applied to Sŏnjŏn paintings, it presents an interesting view of colonial geography. Add this to Fukuzawa Yukichi's metaphor of Korea positioned between China and Japan being like a sexually free woman ("who will even flirt with Chinese men") rather than being a proper (monogamous) wife, and the sexism inherent in that geography and those paintings becomes apparent also. The terms "man" and "woman" become trapped in representations of power positions as the "man" who represents "woman" becomes the colonizer and the empire, while the represented woman is the colonized and backward country needing "help."[12]

If the underlying assumptions of the Cultural Policy are seen as matching those of the orientalist power politics of the Assimilation Policy, then it follows that Sŏnjŏn held the same purpose as well. The basis for a gender analysis of Sŏnjŏn paintings lies in the general concept that the images in the paintings selected for Sŏnjŏn emphasize sexual difference, the "male" and the "female," in reference to cultural and social values.

## Images of Women at Sŏnjŏn

The first Sŏnjŏn exhibit opened on June 1, 1922, at the Keijō Eirakucho Commodity Exhibition Hall and was launched as the foremost official government-sponsored Korean art exhibition. From the very beginning, Sŏnjŏn paintings had a noticeable thematic cohesion. They tended to show the colonial landscape as lonely and impoverished, and often contained submissive figures in traditional dress. Such paintings also fit categories such as "lethargic and obedient," "undeveloped," "inferior," and "feminine" that Said finds to be characteristic of those used by its colonizers to describe or represent "the Orient."[13]

Here I will focus on and analyze works selected for the exhibit that contain images of women. No Suhyŏn's painting *A Sunny Spot* (Figure 8.1) was selected for the fourth Sŏnjŏn exhibition. It shows an old woman and a young boy in a rural setting. The old woman is trimming grass that she has picked from the field and has spread out on her lap. Beside her is a young boy who could be her grandson. He has put down a rake and is lying down in the field, staring at the sky. This image of a woman eking out a living by laboring in a poor farming village fits well into the main Sŏnjŏn themes, "proving" that Chosŏn is indeed, as the Stagnation Theory states, "heteronomous, stagnant, and therefore needing someone to represent it." In Itō Akiune's *Light and Dark* (Figure 8.2), the woman is wearing what is called a *"ssŭgaech'ima,"* which Korean women wore to cover and hide their heads and the top half of their bodies when they went outside. Women were not allowed to show their faces to people, especially men other than their husbands, in the light outdoors and so were hidden in the dark shadows. Women, who, because of the strict patriarchal social structure based on Confucian ideas present from the Chosŏn dynasty, were always and only represented by their husbands or men, fit perfectly into the "feminine" image that helped the colonizers justify their actions. Chino Kaori has argued that, from the Heian period on, Japan had seen the great cultural nation of China as "masculine" and had chosen to describe its own identity as "feminine," but after the Meiji Restoration, as China was taken over by the West, Japan learned to take on the masculine role and attempted to lock its Asian colonies into the "feminine" one.[14] From this point of

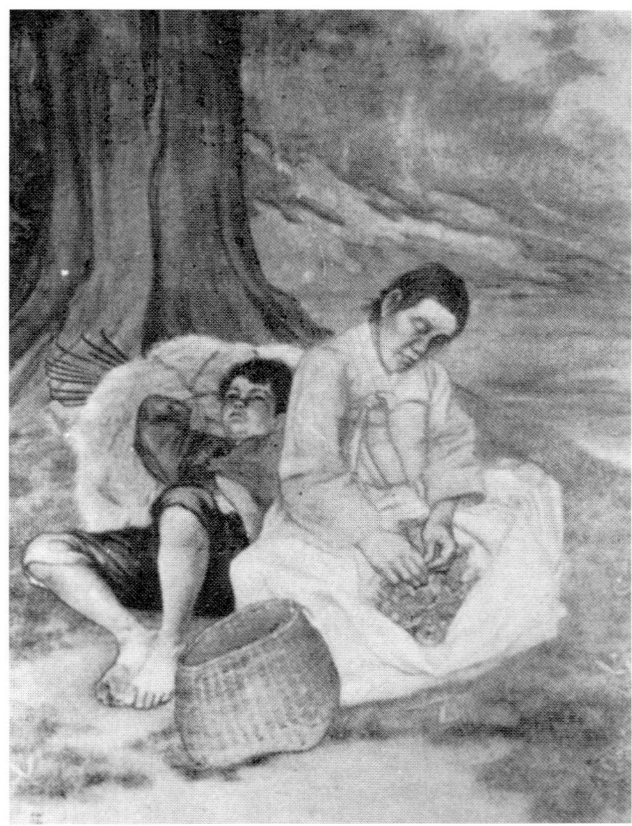

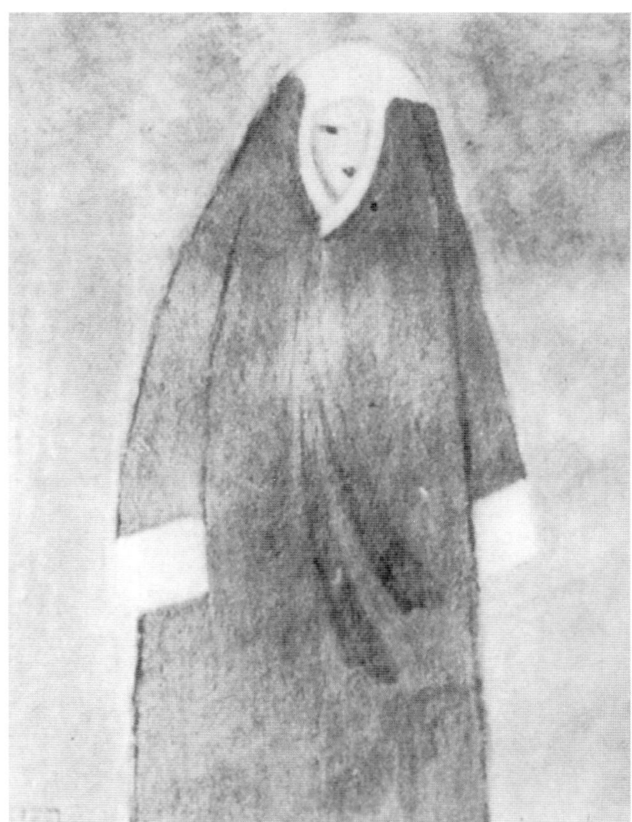

FIGURE 8.1. *(Left)* No Suhyŏn, *A Sunny Spot. Sŏnjŏn Exhibit Record,* 1925.

FIGURE 8.2. *(Right)* Itō Akiune, *Light and Dark. Sŏnjŏn Exhibit Record,* 1926.

view, the image of the woman in the *ssŭgaech'ima* can be said to represent the Japanese colonizer's image of the Chosŏn colony.

Kim Chongt'ae's painting *Pose* (Figure 8.3), which was selected in 1928 for the seventh Sŏnjŏn exhibit, shows a young girl kneeling in undergarments worn with traditional clothing. In Japan, this kind of sitting is called *"seiza"* and is considered polite or proper, but in Korea, it is only used by prisoners or people who are about to be punished or scolded. The girl is thus sitting in a *seiza* posture that has now become Korean—the proper way to sit in a colony with a Japanese education system—in traditional clothing that is soon to become not proper. The stasis in this painting is evident in many other Sŏnjŏn paintings. Okada Saburōsuke, one of the judges for the first Sŏnjŏn exhibit, had this to say after he viewed all of the paintings: "In general, they all have a feeling of sleepiness about them."[15] Sleeping people appeared in many of the paintings in Sŏnjŏn. The same Kim Chongt'ae painted *Bathing in the Spring Sun* (Figure 8.4). Other paintings of sleep-

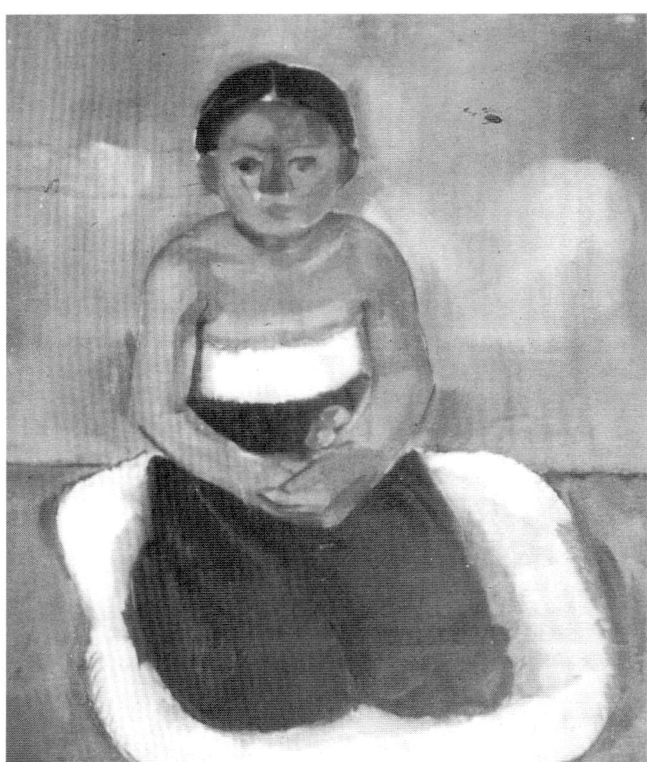

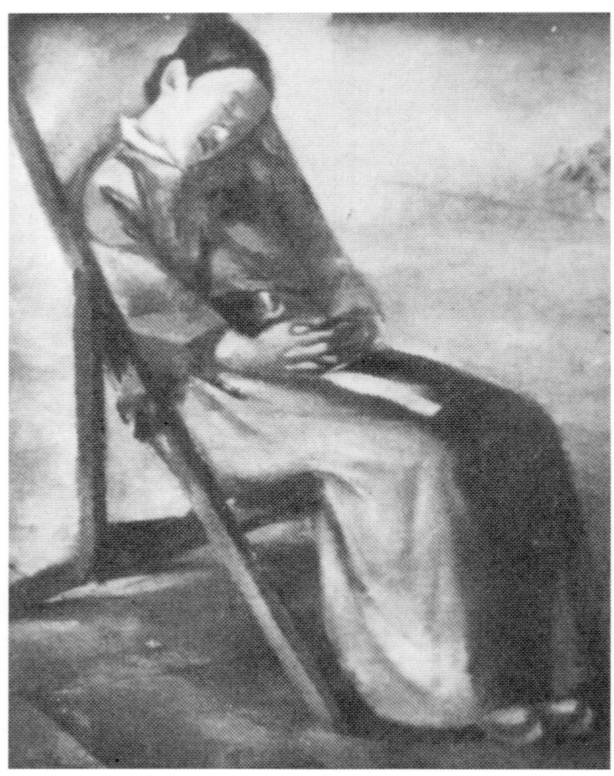

FIGURE 8.3. *(Left)* Kim Chongt'ae, *Pose. Sŏnjŏn Exhibit Record*, 1928.

FIGURE 8.4. *(Right)* Kim Chong-t'ae, *Bathing in the Spring Sun. Sŏnjŏn Exhibit Record*, 1930.

ing people were titled *The Nap, Afternoon Sleep, No Worries,* and *Light Tiredness.* Not only would dozing, inactive, or lazy subjects be easier to control, but they also made justifying colonization that much easier.

When women were represented outside of the house, they were mostly shown taking care of children. Yi Yŏng'il's *Country Maids* (Figure 8.5) shows a girl with a baby on her back and another little girl with shoulders hunched against the cold and picking up gleanings. The hem of the girl's skirt is lifted and the grass is swaying in what seems like a very cold wind. The same artist's *A Break for Nursing* and Chŏng Ch'anyŏng's *A Young Girl* (Figure 8.6), together with works such as Matsuda Shōei's *Shiragi Fields,* are examples of Sŏnjŏn paintings from the late 1920s containing depictions of women in rural or natural settings. These settings are one of the reasons that Sŏnjŏn art has come to be known as nativist art,[16] and they contribute to one of Sŏnjŏn's main themes—connecting natural scenes and manners of the colony's rural areas lyrically. But, as Ueno Chizuko has said, "this 'rural ideology,' having come from reactionary thinking where 'modern' has been born of a nostalgic image of a past that never was and as part of an orientalism

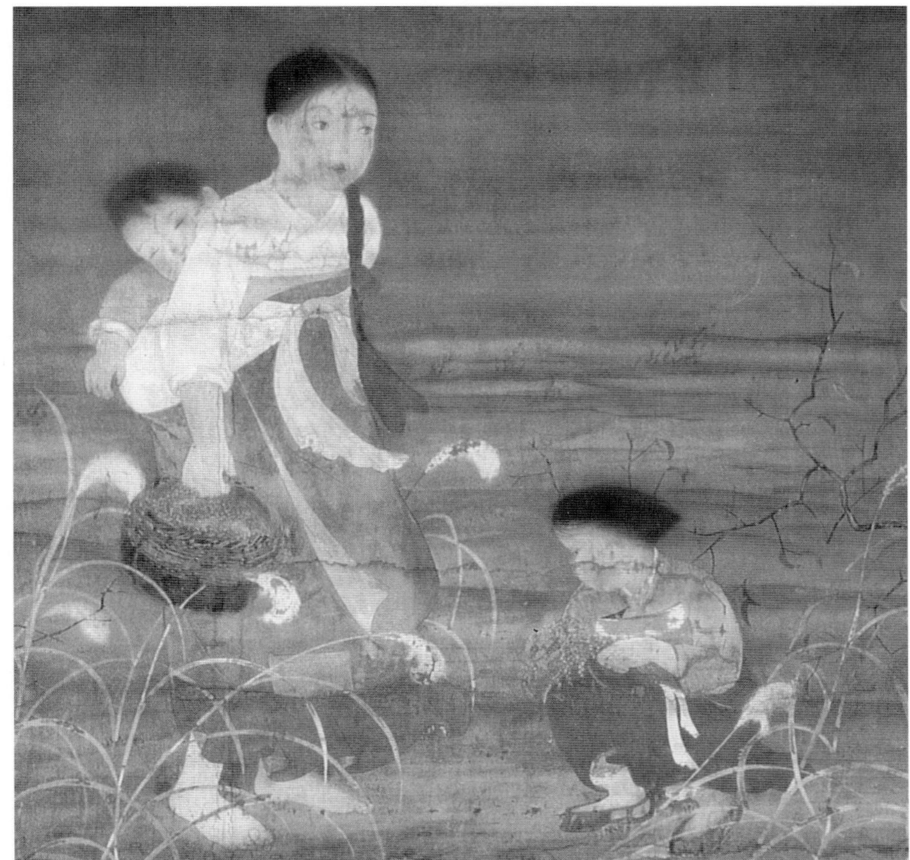

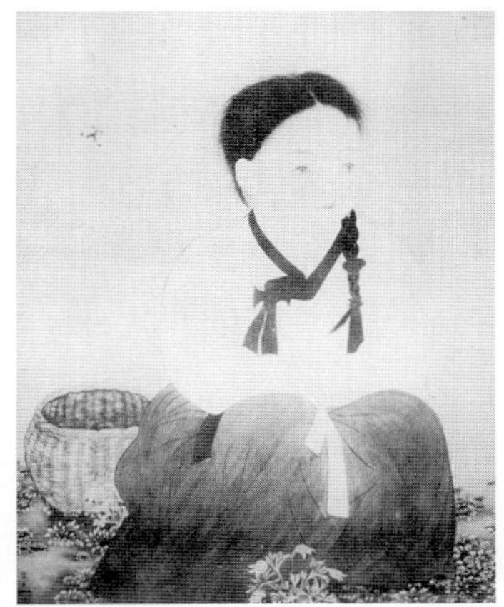

FIGURE 8.5. *(Left)* Yi Yŏng'il, *Country Maids.* Korean National Museum of Modern Art, 1930.

FIGURE 8.6. *(Above)* Chŏng Ch'anyŏng, *A Young Girl. Sŏnjŏn Exhibit Record*, 1935.

where the 'west' represents 'modern,' fits very well into Japanese orientalism."[17] This is why modern Japan, having been forced to walk the anti-Asia path, found solace in a backwards Asia in which time had stopped.

Another example of this point of view is the very interesting painting *Afterglow* (1923) by Asakawa Noritaka (Figure 8.7). As a member of the Society for the Appreciation of Korean Arts and Crafts, Asakawa was involved in the appraisal of folk crafts and wrote articles about Yi-dynasty pottery. Many of his paintings were inspired by these artifacts. This painting shows an old man and a young girl standing next to a large and a small piece of pottery. The swelling at the bottom of the small pot-shaped piece of pottery matches the swell of the girl's *chi'ma*, and the shape of the knob on the lid of the large piece echoes the shape of the man's hat. Both people have their eyes closed, and there is no feeling of movement at all—they have been completely objectified.

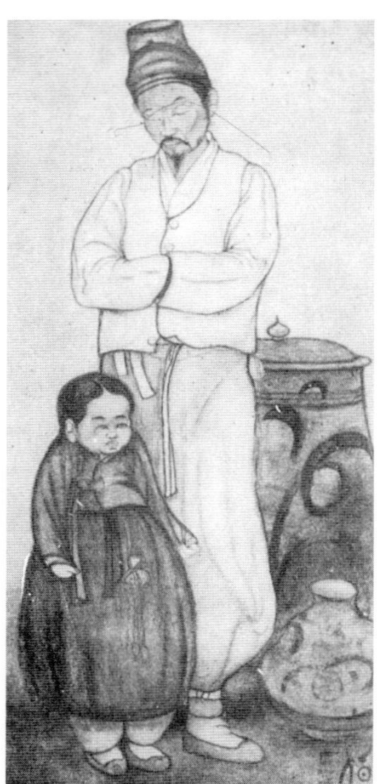

FIGURE 8.7. Asakawa Noritaka, *Afterglow. Sŏnjŏn Exhibit Record,* 1923.

These images demonstrate and problematize the close relation between colonialism and the opinion that Korean traditional art is mainly arts and crafts. A clue to the importance of this hypothesis lies in Yanagi Sōetsu's aesthetic theories about the characteristics of Korean art based on the concept of "the beauty of pathos." Yanagi, a close contemporary of Asakawa, felt that Korea's natural environment and history gave its art the special characteristic of "the beauty of sorrow and grief" and contained the unstable geographical position of the peninsula and the unrest and hardship of its history.[18] Meanwhile, in 1937, the Sino-Japanese War started, and Japan moved into a period of intense militarization that the Sŏnjŏn works reflected. The Assimilation Policy reached its peak at this time with "imperial subjectification," which marked an attempt to Japanize even the soul of the Korean people. Koreans became imperial citizens via the "National Language (Japanese) Daily Use Act" (1938) and the "Name Order" (1939),[19] and were sent out as imperial soldiers to the battlefields of the "Sacred War." The "Japan-Korea Common Ancestor Theory" that formed the basis for the Cultural Policy was used very effectively and insistently during this period of fascist rule.

During this period, the so-called home front woman appeared in paintings. In the painting *Chosŏn Enlisted Soldier* created by one of the Sŏnjŏn authorities, Yamada Shin'ichi, for the 1939 Sacred War Art Exhibit, a mother is shown sending her son off to the front with a young girl beside her holding a Rising Sun flag. As the art world also fell under the wartime Assimilation Policy, the public service in charge of art became more powerful. Here, the central roles were played by the main painters from Sŏnjŏn who had received "recommended" or "participant" status. When "participant" artist Sim Hyŏnggu published his opinion that art should have service to the state as its conscious objective, his painting *Costume for the Battle Dance* (Figure 8.8), which shows a woman in a traditional Korean costume used in dances depicting battle scenes, had already been accepted for the 1938 Sŏnjŏn exhibit.[20] A painting that much more clearly epitomizes the role of women at the time is *An Illustration of Golden Offerings* (Figure 8.9) by Kim Ŭnho, another of the "participant" artists. It shows the leaders of the patriotic women's club busy working for the National Defense Fund by presenting Governor-General Minami Jirō with their gold hairpins or other patriotic donations. In the painting *Harmony* (Figure 8.10) painted by Kim Ŭnho for the last Sŏnjŏn in 1944, a young boy is playing the harmonica while a girl sings and their mother watches over them smiling. This work was first judged to be lacking "the consciousness of the times" and was refused entry. But, because one of the judges defended the

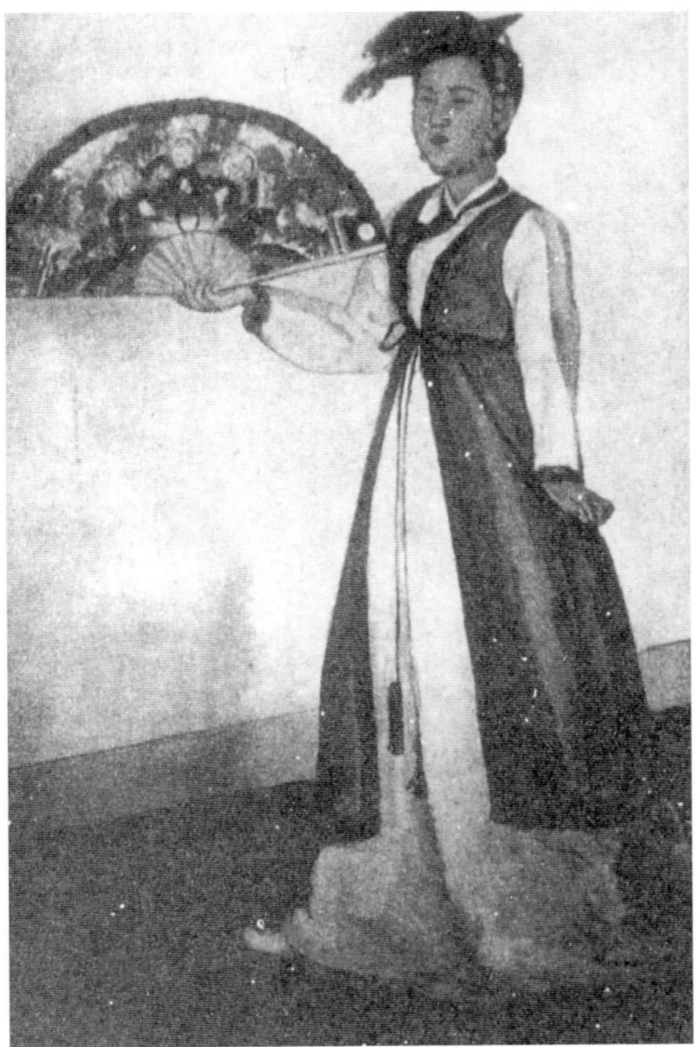

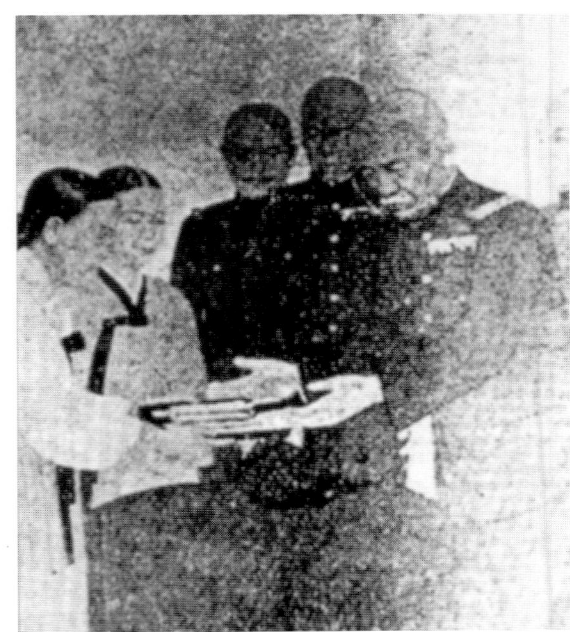

FIGURE 8.8. *(Left)* Sim Hyŏnggu, *Costume for the Battle Dance. Sŏnjŏn Exhibit Record*, 1937.

FIGURE 8.9. *(Above)* Kim Ŭnho, *An Illustration of Golden Offerings. Sŏnjŏn Exhibit Record*, 1937.

painting by commenting that a picture of a family living peacefully might give the soldiers in the "Sacred War" the state of mind they needed to press on, it made it in as an unjudged work.[21] This perhaps would never have happened had the artist not already been officially recognized as the painter of *An Illustration of Golden Offerings.*

At the time, the group of pro-Japanese artists raised under the Cultural Policy who had become faithful to the empire grew rapidly and became very active. For example, the poet Mo Yunsuk shouted out at the December 1941 meeting of the Chosŏn Women's Wartime National Service League in Keijō: "We need to

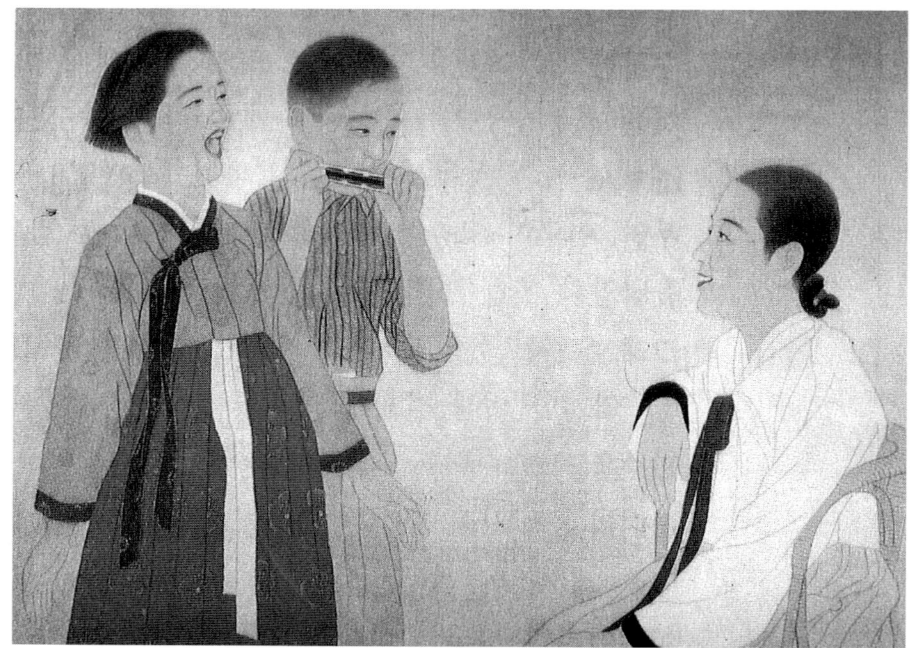

**FIGURE 8.10.** Kim Ŭnho, *Harmony*. *Sŏnjŏn Exhibit Record*, 1944.

become conscious of ourselves as Asian women, fill our hearts with the Yamato spirit, and carry our bamboo bayonets. Even if we get forced out of our homes, we can become wives that cannot be forced out of the homeland."[22] The images of women as brave, manly, and bright, seen at the end of the colonial period, came about because of the two-tiered structure of the fascist regime of colonial rule. These images fit Wakakuwa Midori's analysis that, during the war period, in order to complete the "Sacred War," women were expected to behave in a way that contradicted what had, hitherto, been considered feminine.[23] The image of women as weak and obedient that came out of the early Sŏnjŏn exhibits was also extremely useful during the war period, with its fascist art policy. From there, the role of Korea as a whole as the colonized in Japan's imperial colony in a period of unequal power relations can be seen.

## Conclusions

I have used gender as a point of view to try to read power politics from the images of women that occur in the paintings selected for Sŏnjŏn exhibits. Sŏnjŏn was created and run as an official exhibition by the colonizers as part of their overall colonial governing policy. This policy shifted over time from takeover to colonization, assimilation, amalgamation *(naisen ittai),* and, finally, Japanization: the dream of an imperial Japan at the center of the culturally homogeneous new Asian order in the Greater East Asian Co-prosperity Sphere. As the historian Ōe Shinobu has stated, the special characteristics of Japanese colonial rule were "not just the political and economic suppression of the former colonies, but the infliction of psychological pain by trampling on racial pride and culture."[24]

For Japan, Korea was not a faraway exotic country or a perfect paradise like the colonies were for the orientalist West. Korea and Japan are not just geographically close—their landscape, customs, and physiology are similar also. The hegemonic relationship that is stereotypical of orientalism is apparent in the process of the colonizing or "othering" of Korea by Japan—making the colony out to be inferior, undeveloped, and feminine. But from the Korean point of view, the colonizer and the colonized were both from Asia, so the "Western" identity Japan needed to turn away from Asia and become European had to have been just pasted on. In this interchange, imperial Japan and its vacillation between a sense of inferiority to the West and a sense of superiority to Asia, comes into view. In order for Japan to forget its geographic origins, "an image of a wretched Asia" became necessary to allow Japan to differentiate itself from its backwards neighbors.[25] The Korean colony played the role of the mirror in the cultural imagination of the Japanese in the process of turning themselves into the West. The images of women that were painted during the colonial period are contained in that mirror.[26] But these images also function as a metaphor for the twisted form of orientalism that Japan planted in the soil of its colonies.

Because it is impossible to escape from the fact that paintings are produced by living beings who are full of hopes and complications, it must surely be impossible to find one exclusively true reading of a work of art from this period. And especially because this time was full of violence, uprising, and madness, it is highly unlikely that the images in this mirror would be of still and misty mornings or full of fresh lines and colors. This essay is an attempt to explore the idea that it is both necessary and possible to see the art from the colonial period from different viewpoints.

CHAPTER NINE

CHIGUSA KIMURA-STEVEN

# The Otherness of Women in the Avant-Garde Film *Woman in the Dunes*

*Woman in the Dunes (Suna no onna),* directed by Teshigawara Hiroshi, is one of the most highly acclaimed avant-garde films to emerge from Japan. As well as winning the Critics' Award at Cannes in 1964, its screening drew an enthusiastic response from around the world.[1] In Japan, according to the film critic Sawa Kōzō, the success of this film initiated a new trend in the representation of women in cinema: in his 1964 article Sawa wrote that "since the director, Teshigawara Hiroshi, used the body of the actor Kishida Kyōko as an *objet*, displaying bold female nudes became a popular feature even in mainstream cinema [as opposed to pornographic films]."[2] Sawa was also of the opinion that the use of female nudes on screen could be a sign that "men are regaining power" and that "women's power is waning, even though others say that what have become stronger [in the postwar era] are socks and women."[3] Sawa's concern over both the objectification of women's bodies in mainstream cinema and the shifting gender balance in the wider community is historically important, especially in view of the recent development in feminist film theory that focuses on such issues as "visual pleasure" in cinema and its social/cultural implications.[4]

My research, however, indicates that the 1960s gender relationship was much more complex than that perceived by Sawa in his 1964 article, and in *Woman in the Dunes* this complexity is reflected in the portrayal of the protagonist Niki Junpei's relationships with two women: his wife and the woman living in the dilapidated house at the bottom of the sandpit who becomes pregnant by Niki—a role played by Kishida Kyōko. Neither of these characters is named: Niki refers to his wife as *"omae"* (you), and the woman is simply referred to throughout as *"onna"* (the woman). Perhaps because of their anonymity, Niki's relationships with these women have until now received little critical attention—the existence of Niki's wife has been totally ignored in critical discourse—even though an understanding of the roles of both women is essential if one is to comprehend fully Niki's quest, which is the film's central concern. Indeed such neglect might be a reason why most critics and reviewers have been puzzled by Niki's quest, despite their appreciation of the film: an American reviewer described it as "one of the weirdest adventures ever invented for the screen,"[5] while a well-known Japanese critic commented, "This is truly a strange film. . . . We do not understand what the characters are doing. But perhaps life is just as unfathomable."[6] It is probable that the publication of an English translation of the screenplay, including still photographs of some scenes from the film, was prompted by a desire to understand the plot, that is, Niki's quest, although the screenplay does not explain such matters as shot sequences or camera angles, which are essential parts of the cinematographic language system or the narrative system of a filmic text.[7]

In the absence of a critical study of the narrative system of Teshigawara's film, I will examine not only the gender-related issues, but also the narrative system of the film itself, including the shot sequences and camera angles, in order to unravel some of the issues that have puzzled the critics. Methodologically, I will adopt a similar analytical method to that advocated by Janet Bergstom—a contributor to the book *Feminism and Film Theory* (1988)—who emphasizes that "to study a textual system . . . is to analyze a film in the organization of, ideally, all its codes, specific and non-specific."[8] She suggests that the following approach, advocated by Roland Barthes in his book *S/Z* (1970), could be useful for film analysis:

> To study this text down to the last detail is to take up the structural analysis of the narrative where it has been left till now: at the major structures; it is to assume the power (the time, the elbow room) of working back along the threads of meaning, of abandoning no site of the signifier without endeavoring to ascertain the code or codes of which this site is perhaps the starting point (or the goal); it is (at least we may hope as much, and work to that end) to substitute for the simple representative model another model, whose very gradualness would guarantee what may be productive in the classic text.[9]

If one adopts such a method in analyzing *Woman in the Dunes,* the complexity of its textual system—consisting of both real and fantastic elements—becomes apparent, and one is able to discern that important messages, including those relating to the roles of the two women and their relationships with Niki, are mostly conveyed through fantastic elements.

Teshigawara's film is, in fact, a close rendition of Abe Kōbō's novel *Suna no onna* (1961)—the title of the English translation of this novel is *The Woman in the Dunes*—which can be regarded as a version of "magical realism," and the film's complex textual system derives from the novel. The term "magical realism" was initially used to describe "narratives by contemporary Latin American writers that blur 'the traditional realist distinction between fantasy and reality,' "[10] but in recent years the application of this terminology has extended to works by non-Western writers that display similar characteristics. Susan J. Napier first used the words "magical realism" to describe some Japanese writers' works, including Abe's *Woman in the Dunes*.[11]

Napier does not specify what constitutes the "magical" realm in this novel, but if one adopts Barthes' analytical method, it becomes clear that the "magical" realm is Niki's unconscious world. Possibly Abe, who was a clinical psychology graduate of Tokyo University's Faculty of Medicine, was inspired by Freud when he wrote this novel: in the first chapter of the novel, he uses Freudian expressions such as "Oedipus complex" to describe an aspect of Niki's unconscious desires.[12] Abe might also have been inspired by the French Surrealist movement to explore Freudian theory in *Woman in the Dunes*: he was a member of an avant-garde group, Yoru no Kai, and a keen admirer of Surrealist art—although applying Freudian ideology had also been a popular practice among the prewar avant-garde movement.[13] The depiction of the "magical" in Abe's writing might also have derived from his study of Surrealism, just as magical realist writers in Latin America were influenced by Surrealists, and I will discuss this point in the final section of this chapter. Abe would have been unfamiliar with Lacan's study of Freud (although Lacan in the 1930s was close to the Surrealists), because the latter's work was not introduced to Japan until the late 1970s. Yet Abe's understanding of Freud seems to have been similar to Lacan's, because he also depicts Niki's unconscious desires as possessing their own logical structure, and his plot is organized according to the dynamic of those unconscious desires. This arrangement means that if the reader were to ignore the "magical" or the symbolic aspect of the novel and focus exclusively on the external events, the plot would seem bizarre and incomprehensible.[14]

Likewise, the plot in the film is organized around the dynamics of Niki's unconscious desires—which constitute the "magical"—probably because Abe wrote the screenplay and worked closely with Teshigawara (also a member of Yoru no Kai) during production. The main difference between the plot's depiction in the two media is that, while the novel focuses primarily on Niki's desire to become an important member of his community, with his wish to regain his virility as the second priority, the importance of these two themes is reversed in the film. Otherwise, the film portrays the magical aspects of the novel effectively through skillful use of imagery, shot sequences, and camera angles.

## Is the Woman Niki's Jailer?

There is a general consensus among reviewers and critics that Niki Junpei (played by Okada Eiji) is a victim who has been imprisoned by the villagers and the nameless woman in the sandpit (played by Kishida Kyōko); some in fact call him "her prisoner."[15] But defining him as such is problematic.

It is certainly true that on a "real" level the villagers refuse to release Niki from the sandpit, and the woman herself admits that the villagers brought him to assist her because the job of clearing the sand is too great a burden for one person. Yet when one examines Niki's desires, which constitute the "magical," the situation is more complicated than it first appears. Niki has two desires, and in the film his need to regain his virility (the main theme) is first explained through the portrayal of his relationship with his wife, which in turn determines the nature of his relationship with the woman.

Structurally, the scene in which Niki's wife appears begins in the following manner: after searching the vast sand dunes for rare insects, Niki discovers a boat stranded in the midst of the dunes and decides to rest in it. While resting, he recalls an argument with his wife in the city, and as he articulates their argument aloud, a horizontal image of his wife's face appears from the depths of the dunes. The camera returns briefly to Niki, and in the next instant his wife, now a full figure dressed in elegant city attire, walks across the dunes toward him to sit silently beside the boat. Unmistakably, she is a phantasm, or the projection of the image conjured in Niki's mind, and this scene is the first clear indication that "real" and "magical" realms coexist in the film. The phantasm remains silent throughout (a common aspect of phantasms), but the contrasting expressions of hostility and sadness in her eyes illustrate the couple's strong mutual animosity. Niki confirms this throughout his monologue, in which he blames her for his unhappiness, saying: "You criticized me for arguing too much. But this is a fact," implying that she is a nagging wife; the phantasm, of course, cannot contradict him.

Another important aspect of this scene is that, while these events are occurring, Niki remains seated in the boat and the wavelike patterns on the surrounding sand give the impression that he is at sea. In fact, his wife's face first appears horizontally amidst the sand dunes with these wave patterns superimposed upon her, creating the illusion that she is emerging from beneath the sea. When combined, these scenes convey the message that Niki is escaping from his nagging wife and sailing to another land.

A husband's flight from his nagging wife has always been a popular theme, depicted in numerous stories, such as "Rip van Winkle." The novel is slightly different in this regard, as the woman is not represented as Niki's wife but as a lover: he refers to her as *"aitsu,"* that is, "that woman," and they argue constantly about his lack of commitment to their relationship. By presenting them as a nagging wife and a persecuted husband, the film evokes the popular myth in viewers' minds, an effective way of winning them over to Niki's side at his wife's expense. It is therefore possible to say that at this moment the dominant discourse of the film, which until now has been less gender specific, becomes patriarchal and masculine.

At the same time phallic symbols are used to indicate what Niki wants to accomplish on this trip: at first, while resting in the boat, he places a thermos flask between his legs, and as he speaks of his problems with his wife in the presence of her phantasm, the flask is dwarfed by his bent knees, suggesting that her coldness and constant nagging has had a castrating effect on him. This is not an extreme interpretation, because in the novel Niki states that his partner's clever but unsympathetic remark that he has "a psychological venereal disease" has "made him impotent."[16] After the departure of his wife's phantasm, Niki, still in the boat, lies supine with his legs spread wide and is filmed from a very low angle so that the flask stands tall in the center of the screen, indicating that freedom from his wife is already helping him regain his virility. In the next scene, as Niki dozes, a long shot is taken at a distance from the boat in such a way that the tall bow, which is a much longer and more threatening phallic symbol than the thermos flask, appears to rise from between Niki's outspread legs with the flask now concealed behind it. This image clearly indicates that not only does Niki wish to regain his full virility but he will realize this dream during this trip to the dunes.

In the following scene, three men from the village appear out of nowhere and awaken Niki. This sequence of dozing and abrupt awakening is typically Freudian, indicating that what occurs hereafter is part of Niki's dream and that the villagers are there to help him achieve his desires. This message is reinforced by the number of the villagers present—three—because three is a magic number in myth and religion as, for example, in the doctrine of the Trinity in Christianity. In addition, the fact that the eldest man, the authority figure and spokesperson, is old enough to be Niki's father, while the two younger men are closer to Niki's age, indicates that the libidinal or Freudian father will assist his "son," Niki, to regain his virility.

The old man's advice to Niki, however, is prosaic rather than mysterious. He simply informs him that the last bus to town has already left. This conversation serves to place the village in the realm of the "real," because, as Freud notes in his article "The 'Uncanny,' " if a text is depicting "uncanny" ("magical") phenomena, it must leave the reader/viewer uncertain as to whether a particular figure or place is "real" or "uncanny"; otherwise those who are not interested in the "uncanny" will find the text less diverting.[17]

In the next scene the old man offers to find accommodation for Niki and, when the latter accepts, takes him to the woman whose house stands at the bottom of a deep sandpit. Both the sandpit and the house are carefully constructed to appear real so that life there also appears "real," but the warm, moist, and dark sandpit is a "magical" element, embodying a kind of archetypal womb. In many parts of the world, the earth was worshiped as Great Mother or her womb, and a similar worship of Great Mother and her womb existed in Japan.[18] I am certain, however, that Abe's creation of the sandpit/womb was inspired by Simon de Beauvoir's book *Le deuxième sexe,* which was translated into Japanese in the late 1950s, because his descriptions of the sandpit and Niki's fear of it are uncannily similar to Beauvoir's description of the myth.[19]

Beauvoir states that because "the cult of germination has always been associated with the cult of the dead," a man fears that "the Earth Mother engulfs the bones of her children."[20] Thus he perceives that "under his feet there is a moist, warm, and darkling gulf ready to draw him down; in many a legend do we see the hero lost for ever as he falls back into the maternal shadows—cave, abyss, hell."[21] In his novel, Abe skillfully re-creates similar circumstances for Niki. For example, in Chapter 1, he states that an "unusual preoccupation with insect collecting frequently indicates an Oedipus complex," suggesting that Niki has an unconscious desire to return to the mother or the mother's womb. And after sending Niki down to the maternal cave, that is, the sandpit, Abe informs the reader that the woman's husband and daughter were engulfed by falling sand during a storm, and their remains are still buried somewhere inside the sandpit. In the film, the woman also tells Niki this story about her husband and daughter.

But what necessitates Niki's return to the womb, which is also associated with death? Generally, in myth, including Japanese myth, "initiatory death is indispensable for . . . birth to a higher mode of being."[22] Probably because of such a belief, Abe decided to depict Niki's aspiration to regain virility as the death of the old Niki and his rebirth as a new person. (I will discuss the issue of symbolic death and rebirth further when analyzing Niki's second quest.)

Who then is the woman Niki finds in the womblike sandpit? Is she his jailer? In the realm of the "real," the woman tells him that she needs a man to assist her in the maintenance of her house, but the Freudian sequence has already informed the viewer that Niki's own desire has brought him to the sandpit, and if he is to regain his virility, he requires a woman as his mate.

According to Clare Johnstone, a female character in patriarchal cinema usually serves as the signifier of male desire.[23] Similarly, the woman in the sandpit is endowed with all the appropriate qualities to fulfill Niki's needs. For example, the villagers refer to her as "Bāsan" (old woman) or "Kāchan" (mother), though she is still young (in the novel she is about thirty), and she tells Niki that she is a widow who has also lost her daughter, all of which indicate that she is sexually experienced and fertile, as well as having a nurturing quality. Surely these qualities would be useful for a man wanting to regain his virility and have his wounded ego nurtured. Indeed later in the novel Niki refers to her as a "true woman,"[24] implying that she is the ideal woman to satisfy his desires.

If the woman exists as Niki's mate, are the villagers his jailers, as suggested by the critics? In the realm of the "real," they may appear so, but if one focuses on the "magical" part of the narrative, it is clear that the villagers, that is, the Freudian father and his sons, remove the rope ladder from the sandpit the following morning because Niki has not yet regained his virility. Although Niki is fearful of entrapment in the sandpit and angry at the villagers, the latter's actions are in fact regulated by the logic of Niki's unconscious desires, just as are the woman's actions. Abe was probably inspired by both Freud's theory of unconscious desires and Beauvoir's study of the myth of the Earth Mother's womb in devising this complex plot in which Niki wishes to return to the womb but fears entrapment in it—because Niki has begun to regard the womb as a place of death as well as rebirth after hearing the woman's story of the death of her husband and daughter in the sandpit/womb—and this fear is projected onto the villagers, that is, the Freudian father and his sons.

In both the film and the novel, the villagers return the ladder in the end. According to the logic of Niki's unconscious world, this should indicate the realization of his desires. In the following sections I will examine whether this is the case.

## The Headless Naked Body

Although Niki outwardly shows scant interest in the woman during his first night in the sandpit, his sexual desire for her as well as the type of relationship he wants with her are symbolically represented in the film by the image of her sleeping naked with a towel covering her face, exactly like the illustration produced for the novel by Abe's wife, Machi, who was a well known avant-garde artist (Figure 9.1).

As I mentioned earlier, Sawa has noted that this nude scene changed the representation of women and initiated a popular trend in Japan's mainstream cinema of displaying brazen female nudes. In reality, no woman would sleep in such a defenseless manner when a man she has just met is sleeping in the same room. Indeed, the film, through another Freudian sequence, informs the viewer that the vision of this faceless/headless naked woman is not "real" but a projection of Niki's own desire: at the outset Niki is again asleep, then awakens (just as in the previous Freudian sequence) and sees the contours of a naked female form (whose is not made clear) emerging from the sand in the same manner as his wife's phantasm. He gazes at it briefly then falls asleep again, but this figure with the familiar wave-patterned sand superimposed on it continues to float across the screen, indicating that she is part of his dream. As he begins to stir, the floating figure solidifies, and when he opens his eyes, he sees the statuesque naked woman lying on the floor beside him. This sequence is the "magical" part of the narrative, based on the following description in the novel:

> She was stark naked.
>
> She seemed to float like a blurred shadow before his tear-filled eyes. She lay face up on the matting, her whole body, except her head, exposed to view.

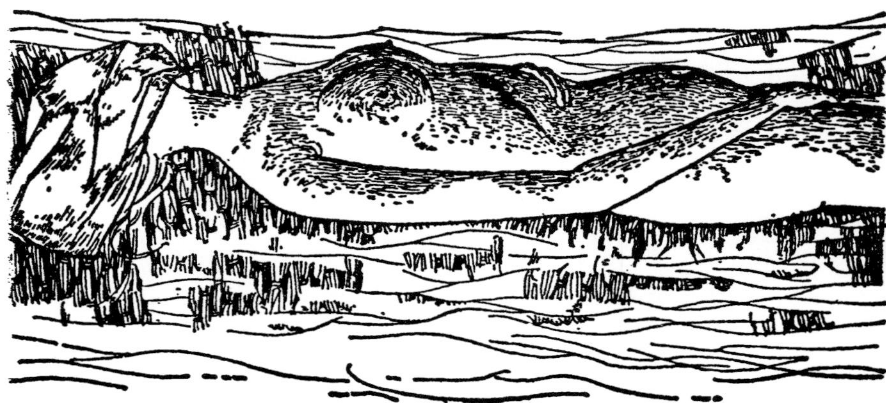

FIGURE 9.1. Abe Machi, illustration to *Suna no onna* (Woman in the dunes).

> . . . The whole surface of her body was covered with a coat of fine sand, which hid the details and brought out the feminine lines; *she seemed a statue gilded with sand.*[25]

Abe's original script and the English translation of the screenplay also say: "The woman is stark naked; only her face is covered with a towel. Covered with sand, she looks like a sand statue."[26] The image is faithfully re-created on the screen, as the actor, whose naked body is coated with a thin layer of sand and whose face is covered by a towel, lies motionless like a statue. It is probable that it is because Abe's script as well as his novel describe the woman as a "sand statue" that Teshigawara commented that he presented the actor Kishida Kyōko's body as an "*objet*." Furthermore, the Japanese title of both the film and the novel—*Suna no onna*—literally means a "sand woman'" or a "woman made of sand," just like the *"suna no oshiro"* (sand castle) that children might build on the beach. In other words, the title indicates that this faceless/headless naked body is a creation of Niki's imagination, or "the signifier of his desire."

But why does Niki desire a woman who is a faceless/headless naked body or a mere sexual object devoid of intelligence? The answer becomes clear if one recalls his relationship with his wife/lover in the novel. In the novel, his lover is portrayed as a negative example of a highly educated and intelligent woman with a responsible job: she has a razor-sharp tongue, lacks empathy, and places her career above his needs. As a result, Niki claims that he has become "impotent."[27] In the film only the wife's phantasm appears, and she remains silent. Yet her hostile gaze combined with Niki's monologue indicate that she is too argumentative, too critical, and too cold, and the thermos flask is used to convey the message that she has a castrating effect on him. He therefore wants the woman to be sexually available but faceless/headless, or a silent and unintelligent being.

Is the woman silent and unintelligent? Not in the beginning: she argues with him too much and places her work above his needs, just as his wife did. For instance, while serving the meal, she undermines his ego by constantly challenging his views, especially about sand and insects, the very areas in which he thinks he has expert knowledge. He tries to dismiss her views as utter nonsense, but she remains skeptical. Furthermore, she places her job above his needs just like his wife: immediately after the meal, she begins her work of clearing away the sand, and the evident strong affection between her and the young men who come to collect it arouses Niki's jealousy. In the novel, the narrative states that he is interested in her "body concealed beneath the coarse work trousers,"[28] and he impatiently says to her: "Oh, let it go. The rest can wait until tomorrow."[29] In the film he simply asks in a nagging/pleading tone: "How in the world long do you intend to work?" The woman simply replies, "Until the morning," because "the sand doesn't rest for us." Clearly, for her, her work is more important than Niki's needs. Thus he retreats dejectedly into the house and falls asleep, and during his sleep the Freudian sequence of the headless nude occurs, indicating that he would like to reduce her to a mere sexual object without brain or independent mind.

Eventually Niki manages to reduce the woman to a "headless" and submissive being during his stay: he constantly undermines her confidence through verbal domination, until she ceases to argue against him. He also uses physical violence: he ties her hands and legs, gags her with a towel, and leaves her lying helplessly on the floor. He tries to justify his brutal actions by saying that he is merely trying to gain bargaining power with the villagers, but the villagers ignore his demands to be freed from the sandpit. This comes as no surprise, since he has not yet regained his virility.

The villagers then send down a parcel containing cigarettes and alcohol; the libidinal father is apparently trying to help Niki relax so that he can act out his desire. Sure enough, after smoking some cigarettes and drinking alcohol, he unties the woman who is now visibly weak and submissive.

In the following scene Niki suddenly provokes the woman to fight by attacking her most valued possession, her house. Perhaps his entrapment makes his violence against the woman appear more acceptable in the viewer's eye, but if one recalls Niki practicing boxing outside the house before this action, it is clear that he simply wants to test his physical domination over her as a part of the process of regaining his virility. When he succeeds in overpowering the woman, his hand accidentally slips into the woman's kimono top and touches her bare breast. That finally gives him the courage to initiate sexual intercourse. Of course, in terms of the mechanism of his desire, touching the woman's breast is not an accidental but a logical step. Furthermore, in the novel, just as he is about to have sex with her, he refers to her as a "true woman," an apt and timely remark, as he has finally managed to reduce her to a "headless naked body." Although the film lacks such verbal confirmation, its message is equally disturbing, because verbal domination and physical assault—not affection—are portrayed as necessary for the restoration of man's virility.

Niki's sexual act with the woman is not an expression of love but an aggressive assertion of his virility. In the novel it is also intended as a revenge against his lover, so that even during intercourse he continues to be brutal and misogynistic toward the woman and compares his sexual appetite to "the appetite of meat-eating animals."[30] William Currie comments that although Niki is "decent at the beginning of the book, [he] becomes frighteningly animal-like and inhuman in his treatment of the woman,"[31] and I agree with his comment. In the film the revenge theme is omitted, and Okada Eiji's acting emphasizes a gentleness that is lacking in Niki's portrayal in the novel. Nevertheless the film also celebrates Niki's virility in an aggressive manner through the manipulation of the camera. In her essay "Visual Pleasure and Narrative Cinema," Laura Mulvey states that in the cinematic tradition the "masculinization" of the spectator position occurs through the camera's eyes, regardless of his or her actual gender. A similar phenomenon can be observed in Teshigawara's film: the moment Niki touches the woman's body, the camera zooms in to focus on her ecstatic face as well as her fingers gripping Niki's buttocks and her toes pressing into the sand in extreme pleasure. Clearly the woman is framed by the camera as the object of the gaze. On the rare occasions when the camera is not focused on her, it portrays the movement of several streaks of sand, one of which is shaped like a penis, suggesting penetration and ejaculation. This is no doubt to indicate Niki's full recovery from his impotence, and the woman's ecstatic response is to highlight the magnitude of his virile power.

But why is Niki's pleasure not shown? With respect to the pleasure of viewing, another feminist critic, Linda Williams, states that in a film even when such pleasure is "constructed for masculine spectators," "it is the female body in the grips of an out-of-control ecstasy that has offered the most sensational sight."[32] *Woman in the Dunes* is also constructed within such a cinematic tradition, although if one considers that it was produced at the beginning of a so-called sexual revolution in Japan, one cannot rule out the possibility that the resistant female spectator might have identified with the woman and found her lack of inhibition liberating.[33]

After the restoration of his virility, Niki understandably plans an escape. This is in fact his third attempt, and because three is a magic number, as noted earlier, one can expect a special event to occur. Indeed, before his escape, he performs a ritual to reaffirm the restoration of his virility by drinking saké with the woman and having her wash his entire body. On the "real" level, Niki avers that these actions are intended to exhaust the woman so that she will sleep soundly and not alert the villagers when he escapes, but partaking of saké and cleansing one's body are common ingredients in many Japanese rituals, although asking the woman to wash his body instead of washing his own body is a deviation from traditional ritual. Another deviation here is that the woman washes him with her hands to show her pleasure in touching his body. She also washes starting from his toes, a most unusual way of washing someone, and no sooner does she touch them than she becomes aroused, which indicates to the viewer that even the most remote part of his body is charged with an irresistible virility and attraction.

After the completion of this ritual, Niki manages to climb out of the sandpit using a rope, which he has been secretly making. His success is a logical progression in terms of the mechanism of his unconscious world. Interestingly, in the novel, during his escape he thinks of a mirror when thinking of the woman, which comes as no surprise, since her main function up to this point has been to "mirror" his desires. In the film there is no such reference to a mirror, but the above ritual amply demonstrates his success in molding her to act as his reflection, or if one takes a hint from the title and the Freudian scene, one could say that Niki has successfully molded her into the headless and naked sand statue on whom he can project his own desires.

Niki's freedom, however, is short-lived: he loses his way and falls into quicksand. He is soon rescued by the villagers and returned to the sandpit. The villagers' action in returning him to the sandpit is not cruel, however, but a logical step since Niki's second aspiration has not yet been fully realized.

## Alienation

Niki comes to the dunes to escape from both his wife and the city. But in the film his life in the city is not depicted in detail, probably because it is reduced to a secondary theme. I will therefore refer to the novel, because one cannot fully understand Niki's relationship with the woman and the villagers without knowing why he has left the city.

The novel begins with the news of Niki's disappearance and the reactions of his colleagues and his lover, all of which reveal his alienation from his job, his colleagues, and his lover. Abe then shows that Niki's alienation stems mainly from the fact that he lives in a huge and highly industrialized urban community. There he is merely one of a faceless mass who must carry many different certificates to prove his identity. Abe emphasizes the anonymity of his protagonist by referring to him simply as "the man" until the last page of the text; for clarification, I have referred to him by name throughout.

It is possible that Abe, who was a socially conscious writer, intended Niki's frustration and alienation to mirror the experience of those living in the rapidly expanding urban communities around Japan at that time. Unlike Europe, where large-scale industrialization and urbanization occurred during the late nineteenth and early twentieth centuries, in Japan a major population movement to urban areas only began around the mid-1950s, when the Japanese economy started to flourish and major industries were being developed. As a result, between 1955 and 1960, the workforce in Tokyo and its surrounding areas increased by about 1,675,000, while the population of Tokyo reached almost 10 million.[34] Such rapid demographic change and the high population concentration in urban areas—much of which was also new to an urban environment—would have been conducive to the type of alienation suffered by Niki. Indeed, the literary critic Akiyama Shun states that *Woman in the Dunes* brilliantly captures urban dwellers' ontological awareness of becoming "mere grains of sand."[35]

Abe presents Niki as a typical modernist hero who is alienated from his job, colleagues, and society, and in Chapter 2 he reveals that Niki turns to seeking rare insects because, although he has a strong desire to be an important member of his community, he is unable to fulfill this dream through his job:

> The true entomologist's pleasure is much simpler, more direct: that of discovering a new type. When this happens, the discoverer's name appears in the illustrated encyclopedias of entomology appended to the technical Latin name of the newly found insect; and there, perhaps, it is preserved for something less than eternity. *His efforts are crowned with success if his name is perpetuated in the memory of his fellow men by being associated with an insect.*[36]

The above passage, which has not been considered by Abe's critics, including Akiyama, indicates that Niki goes to the dunes either in search of a new identity or to be reborn as a new person who will be appreciated by his community. In the film, although Niki's alienation from the city is only depicted by his eagerness to escape the city as quickly as possible, Niki explains to the woman, shortly after his arrival in her house, why he wants to find a new type of insect, expressing a similar sentiment to that described in the novel.

Thus the question that should be addressed, in both the novel and the film, is, does Niki find a new identity or a way to become an important member of his community? The answer in both the novel and the film is yes; in fact Abe clearly states in the final chapter of his novel that Niki finds "a new self,"[37] although critics have not remarked on this.

Perhaps, critics of both the novel and the film have overlooked the positive outcome to Niki's second aspiration, because they considered the village a type of distopia. Yet if one focuses on the "magical" elements, it is clear that the village is essentially a utopian space for Niki, because it is there he is able to fulfill all his dreams. It is true that the village is poor owing to the barrenness of the land, and the constant threat from the sand also makes everyday life hard and miserable. As a result there has been an exodus of young people from the village to the big cities.[38] Nevertheless it is portrayed as a place where a primitive but pure type of communism flourishes: the villagers have formed a cooperative and work together to collect sand to sell to the surrounding cities. They also share the profits from it in the fairest possible manner.

Niki is at first unaware of this and thinks that in clearing the sand the woman is simply performing a meaningless and mindless task. But in the second half of the novel and the film, after his rescue from quicksand by the villagers during his escape and his return to the sandpit, the woman tells him that the sand sold to cities is the source of the village's livelihood. She also informs him that "buying and selling the sand is done by the union," and she emphasizes that "anybody who was rich enough to have boats or anything got out of here long ago,"[39] indicating there are no capitalists with private means of production. She then declares: "You and I have been treated very well. . . . Really, they weren't unfair to us. If you think I'm lying, get them to show you their records, and you'll see right away."[40] In the film, although the woman's speech is less forceful and her comment about the records is not included, the fact that the village is a primitive communist society is made clear. Furthermore, through their joint efforts, the villagers are also able to save their village from being engulfed by the sand.

The villagers' motto—at least for those who have remained—is "Love Your Village,"[41] emphasizing the high value accorded to communal spirit, and the woman demonstrates her love of the village through her actions: when Niki tells her to stop clearing the sand, she refuses, saying, "If this house is buried, then the house behind will be in trouble." She is genuinely concerned for the survival of the village and wishes to make her contribution, indicating that the villagers operate from a completely different value system than the competitive and individualistic value system to which Niki has been accustomed in the city.

Fredric Jameson calls this type of primitive communism a "nostalgic-Utopian triad" and states that, although it "is handily identified as the Marxist 'vision of history,' " it is "a feature of the right-wing critique of capitalism which preceded Marx."[42] In Abe's case, however, his vision of the village is deeply rooted in Marxism. He joined the Japan Communist Party in 1949 and remained an active member until his expulsion in 1962.[43] Judging from *The Woman in the Dunes*, however, his expulsion from the Communist Party did not cause him to abandon communism immediately, although his own experience with party authorities might have been reflected in his negative depiction of the village authorities, who are shown as keeping a constant watch on Niki's movements from their watchtower. When he refuses to work, they also cut off his water supply so that he has no choice but to work against his will. Although many critics seem to give undue emphasis to this aspect of village life and regard it as symbolic of an authoritarian state, the villagers' conduct is not totally negative.[44] At the "magical" level, they all, especially the old man, function as protectors of Niki's interests, and in being forced to work, Niki, an alienated urban intellectual who has been brainwashed by the individualistic and competitive culture of capitalist society, rediscovers the joy of physical labor and the importance of collective work.

It is also in this village that Niki discovers the means to achieve his desired goal of becoming an important member of the community. This occurs when he finds pure water in the barrel—aptly named "Hope"—that he had buried in the sand with the intention of catching a bird after he was rescued from the quicksand. At first he is puzzled to find water in the barrel, but the realization that water has accumulated there through the capillary action of the sand gives him the confidence to invent a better device to collect more water. Such an invention would be of little use in the city but most useful for the village, where the shortage of water has long been a major problem. The indications are that he will be able to use his scientific training for the betterment of the community, a far more fulfilling task than chasing elusive rare insects. In other words, Niki indeed finds "a new self," as Abe states in his text. If so, it is logical that Niki decides not to return to the city even though the villagers leave the rope ladder for him.

## The Dispensable Womb

The woman's role in Niki's second quest is first to teach him the values of the village, particularly their work ethic and community spirit, but Niki initially refuses to listen to her, because he is influenced by the ideology of an affluent, competitive, and individualistic society, and he resents being "dictated to" by a woman. The latter attitude is already apparent from his relationship with his wife.

Although Niki's appreciation of village life and its value system is a gradual process, it accelerates after he experiences a ritual of death and rebirth: his death is a symbolic act and part of the "magical," which occurs when he loses his way in the village and falls into quicksand during his attempt to escape. In the novel, Niki's symbolic death is emphasized by such expressions as "no one will even turn around to look at his death spasm" or "one was on the point of death,"[45] while in the film the villagers who rescue him simply say that many have died there.

When he is returned to the sandpit because he has not realized his second dream, the narrative in the novel states: "A rope was passed under his arms like a piece of baggage, he was again lowered into the hole. No one said a word; it was as if they were at *interment.* The hole was deep and dark."[46] In the film, no such explanation is given, but the camera angle causes Niki to resemble a seed or a plant being planted into a hole in the ground or the womb of the Earth Mother.

What is the woman's function in this myth? According to Beauvoir, the Earth Mother is usually personified by a woman, and the only information Abe gives regarding the woman is that she has been a mother. The title *Suna no onna* also indicates that she is a "sand woman," that is, a part of the earth, and this aspect—that she is an extension of the earth and a personification of the archetypal mother—is reinforced in the film by the inclusion of the Freudian scene referred to earlier where she is shown emerging from the sand.

The clearest answer to why the woman is assigned such a mythical role is given in the scene where the old man (the libidinal father) tells Niki that, if he wishes to be allowed out of the sandpit, he must have intercourse with the woman in front of the villagers. Most critics regard this scene as the ultimate degradation and dehumanization of Niki by the villagers—he could have refused as the woman had: she insists that sex is a private affair and not for public display. Yet Niki, ignoring her plea, drags her outside and attempts to rape her. He does not succeed, because she fights back. Nevertheless, as Currie points out, Niki's behavior is "frighteningly animal-like and inhuman." In the film the viewer may forgive Niki's actions because Okada's acting depicts him as pathetic and sad rather than animal-like, but the violence he displays toward the woman cannot be overlooked. It is significant that this scene is a part of the "magical": the novel describes it as a "nocturnal festival,"[47] and in the film the villagers actually arrive in festival attire and beat a festival drum, while a man wearing a sacred mask performs a ritual dance.

What sort of festival is this where Niki must perform a sexual act? If one recalls that Niki has already gone through the ritual of death in the quicksand and is beginning to accept the villagers' value system, it should be clear that this is a ritual of rebirth or an initiation ceremony. In many agrarian societies, a sexual act was performed as part of the ritual to encourage the successful germination of seeds as well as a good harvest, and in Japan in some agricultural festivals, such as the Onta Matsuri held at Asukani-Imasu Shrine in Nara, a simulation of sexual intercourse is included in the ritual.[48] Indeed, Abe makes clear that the festival is part of the preparation for Niki's rebirth by having Niki state that "everything, after all, had gone as it was written it should,"[49] even though he fails to rape the woman, because in the ritual only a simulation, rather than actual intercourse, is required. After this occurrence, Abe states in the narrative that "what remained of him had turned into a liquid and melted into her body,"[50] indicating that Niki had "melted into" the body of the surrogate Earth Mother in order to be reborn, the ultimate realization of his Oedipus complex. In the film this scene of Niki melting into the woman's body is not included, possibly because of the difficulties of re-creating it on the screen.

As I stated earlier, if one focuses on the "magical," one will find that the plot is in fact very logically constructed, and after Niki "melts into the woman's body," his rebirth follows. This is marked by his discovery of clean water in the barrel, aptly named "Hope": in the novel the narrative states that "along with the water in the sand, he found a new self,"[51] while in the film it is simply marked by his gesture of triumph. At this point Niki has finally solved all his problems. It is therefore logical that in the novel the narrative states, "He was still in the hole, but it seemed as if he were already outside,"[52] whereas in the film, the same sentiment is expressed by Niki wearing a traditional kimono with the pattern of a large white flying bird on the back.

In respect to the woman, according to the logic of Niki's unconscious world, her importance should diminish from this point, since he has become a new person and is enjoying the full recovery of his virility. Indeed, the plots of both the novel and the film evolve toward the woman's exit from the sandpit and his life: she suddenly begins to suffer acute pain shortly after Niki discovers the water in the barrel, and one of the villagers diagnoses her pain as an extrauterine pregnancy, adding that it is perhaps too late to save her. In the novel the villager does not make this pronouncement, possibly because the earlier description of her body covered with blood is sufficient to indicate her imminent death.

When he hears this diagnosis, Niki for the first time shows some compassion toward the woman, and the narrative in the novel says he let "her hold one of his hands, while with the other he kept rubbing her belly."[53] In the film, although Niki also does the same, his compassion toward the woman is short-lived. In fact what follows in the film is more disturbing than in the novel, because while the woman in great pain is being carried away by the villagers on a makeshift stretcher, Niki deserts her in order to fetch his notebook containing information about the water device with the intention of discussing it with the old man. Although in the end he abandons this plan, his preoccupation with his invention and his neglect of the woman's fate appears heartless, since her life is threatened owing to her pregnancy with his child.

Eventually Niki goes to say farewell to her but offers no words of comfort and even averts his eyes when she pleads, "I don't want to go." Her helpless, painful cries, "No. . . . No. . . . No. . . ." gradually fade away as she is carried from the sandpit. All the while Niki remains totally silent, which might be interpreted as a sign of shyness—Japanese men are usually hesitant to express affection in the presence of others—but his obsession with his invention clearly indicates his lack of concern for the woman's welfare.

On the question of why the woman must suffer an extrauterine pregnancy and die, Keiko McDonald suggests that "the child the woman conceives, a symbol of a better future, must be aborted," because this is "too easy a solution" in mitigating "man's alienation."[54] She also states: "The woman's miscarriage certainly signifies the difficulty of achieving a better world, but the film seems to say that contemporary man's effort to maintain love is more important than the achievement of the goal itself."[55] Although McDonald is the only critic concerned with the woman's miscarriage, this reading is problematic, because not just the child but the woman too is dying, and Niki is also more concerned about his invention than about the woman's welfare. I cite McDonald's article as it signifies an instance of the "masculinization of the spectator position," with which Laura Mulvey is concerned in her article mentioned earlier.

If one focuses on Niki's quest to regain his virility, the extrauterine pregnancy, in fact, indicates two things: Niki has proven to himself and to the world at large that he is not only virile but also fertile, yet there will be no obligation for him to support either the woman or the child in the future, as neither will survive. A plot in which Niki and the woman could have had a healthy child and raised it together would have been entirely feasible, since in reality the percentage of normal pregnancies is far higher than the percentage of complications. The only logical explanation for the woman's sad end is because Niki does not want her any more: he required her only for the restoration of his virility and for his rebirth as an important member of a community. Niki merely regarded her as a "headless, naked body," and the part of her body that he most required is shown to be her womb.

Furthermore, through his knowledge of science, Niki has discovered the way to use the Earth Mother's womb, that is, the sandpit. Abe once again seems to have borrowed an idea from Beauvoir's text: "The mother is the root which, sunk in the depths of the cosmos, can draw up its juices; she is the fountain whence springs forth the living water, water that is also nourishing milk, a warm spring, a mud made of earth and water, rich in restorative virtues."[56] The wooden barrel named "Hope" that Niki buries in the sand is indicative of the nipple of the Earth Mother, and the pure water accumulated in it through the capillary action of the sand resembles the nourishing milk of the Earth Mother. This scene is reproduced in the film, and Niki's assertion that he knows how to make a better and more effective device indicates that he will be able to control the hostile Earth Mother and use her nourishing and restorative milk for the betterment of the village.

Once Niki gains such power, and his virility and fertility are proven, the woman, whose womb has nourished him, is hoisted from the sandpit and destroyed, just as a child destroys his "sandcastle" when it is time for him to go home. The title *Suna no onna* would suggest such a reading, although Niki decides to remain in the village even though the villagers leave the rope ladder for him when they remove the woman.

Critics are generally vexed by his decision, but both the novel and the film inform the reader/viewer of Niki's desire to reveal his water device "Hope" to the villagers, and when he does, the latter will no doubt embrace him as an important member of their community. The novel ends at this point, but a new conclusion is added in the film: when Niki returns to the sandpit to check the water in the "Hope," he suddenly sees the face of a young boy reflected on the surface of the water. He looks up, and before the boy disappears, their eyes meet and there is a fleeting second of rapport between them. The message is again clear: one day Niki will have a son to whom he will pass his dreams, and he will teach him to control and use the resources of the Earth Mother. In order to have a son Niki must find a new woman, but his treatment of the woman indicates that he will never accept any woman as his equal.

## Gender Politics in the 1960s

Because the plot is complex, I have until now limited my discussion to the function of the woman and the wife/lover within the confines of the film and the novel, but an important question remains: what were or are the social and cultural implications of such female images?

As I mentioned earlier, according to Sawa, after Teshigawara Hiroshi "used the body of the actor Kishida Kyōko as an *objet,* displaying bold female nudes became a popular feature even in mainstream cinema." But the idea of using an actor's body as an *objet* probably came from Abe, because the woman in his novel (and screenplay) is described as "a statue," that is, an *objet.* The scene in which Niki gazes at the naked woman whose face is concealed by a towel also shows a remarkable resemblance to the painting by the Belgian surrealist Paul Delvaux titled *The Sleeping City* (1936) (Figure 9.2).

The difference between the painting and the novel is the setting: in the painting the woman with the covered face is standing, but in Abe's work she is lying down and only she is present. If one simply searches for an image of a naked woman with her face concealed, numerous examples can be found among other Surrealists' works. Abe might even have been influenced by two famous group photos of Surrealists taken by Man Ray: in the first photo, taken in 1924, a headless female nude figure hangs above their heads, and in the other, taken in 1929, small photos of sixteen Surrealists surround the painting of a nude by René Magritte.[57]

Perhaps the comparison of the imagery in Abe's novel (and in the film) with Surrealist art may seem tenuous, but Abe had a strong interest in Surrealism, and his earlier short story "Kabe" (A wall), depicting a man who becomes a human wall and inside whose body a vast barren field stretches away to the horizon, shows an unmistakable resemblance to Salvador Dali's work *Man* (1936), while the novel *Tanin no kao* (The face of another) contains images that show a strong affinity with several of Magritte's paintings, indicating that Abe had a special gift for spinning interesting stories inspired by Surrealist paintings. According to Amaryll Chanady, "the French Surrealists [i.e., their art] is appropriated by Latin American magical realists in their narrative strategies of identity construction."[58] I am certain that Abe also appropriated Surrealist ideology and technique in his work, and *The Woman in the Dunes* indicates how well he understood the way in which gender politics function in Surrealist art.

Since the publication of Xavière Gauthier's book *Surréalisme et sexualité* (1971),

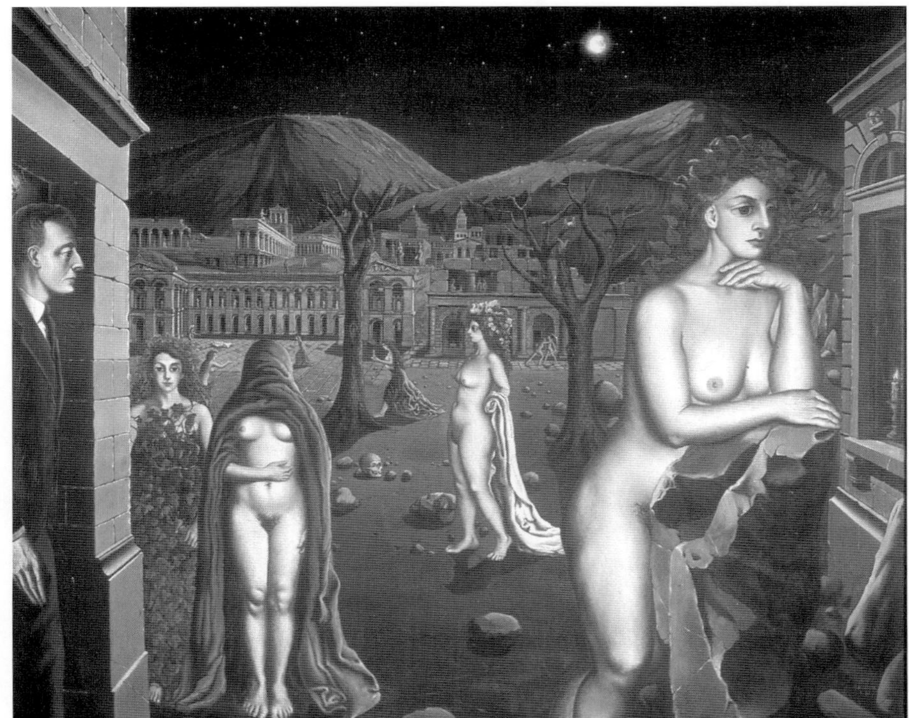

FIGURE 9.2. Paul Delvaux (1897–1994), *The Sleeping City,* 1938. Oil on canvas. Private collection.

many books and essays have noted the chauvinistic attitudes toward women found among Surrealists as well as in their actual works. In her book *Women Artists and the Surrealist Movement*, Whitney Chadwick, for example, points out that Surrealists were depicting the faceless nude and glorifying the *femme-enfant* (the woman-child) at the very point in history when women were becoming more liberated, emphasizing that after the First World War unprecedented numbers of young women had joined the work force as clerical workers both in the private sector and in government departments. Women were also making increasingly strong demands for the right to vote, although in France they did not gain this right until the end of the Second World War. According to Chadwick, during the 1920s women also became aviators and art patrons, and as a result "library and artistic circles were dominated by talk of the 'new woman,' an independent, often androgynous being who had fled the stifling domesticity of late Victorian culture."[59] Such studies suggest that male Surrealists' art of the "headless nude" captured men's uneasiness with those "new women" who were beginning to live independently of men. In my view such an interpretation is endorsed by Anthony

Penrose's comment about Man Ray's photographs of Lee Miller (Penrose's own mother): "Some of his strongest artistic photographs are of parts of her body. Her torso is devoid of her head and therefore reduced to an object which has no intelligence and cannot talk back."[60] Penrose suggests that such photos signify Ray's desire to reduce Miller, a strong-willed, independent woman and talented photographer, to "an object over which he could then exert his control, and have unchallenged possession."[61] Perhaps not all Surrealists had this possessive attitude toward their models. Nevertheless, their obsession with the headless nude and the *femme-enfant* indicates their desire to reduce woman to a creature devoid of intelligence or will.

In Abe's novel as well, the faceless/headless nude symbolizes the protagonist's desire to reduce the woman to a sexual object devoid of intelligence. When Abe was creating this image, gender relationships in Japan were similar to those in Europe in the 1920s and 1930s, when Surrealists were depicting headless nudes. Japanese women, who gained the right to vote after World War II, were particularly politically active around the late 1950s and early 1960s, and they were able to quash the government's plan to reinstate the intensely patriarchal family system *(ie seido)* of the prewar era. Although the *ie* system was abolished in 1947 as a part of the democratization process initiated by the Allied Occupation Force, in 1954 the conservative government announced their intention to reinstate it, which alarmed women, because they had suffered most under this system. They therefore organized a large-scale opposition movement throughout the country, and in 1960, after many years of struggle, they won their battle.[62] That year, many women also participated in the mass political movement that opposed the renewal of the Japan-U.S. Joint Security Pact: one female student was killed when riot police tried to disperse the demonstration by force.[63]

In other areas gender relationships were also undergoing rapid change. The opening up of university education in the postwar era, which was also a part of the democratization initiated by the Allied Occupation Force, encouraged women to study. A large number of them entered universities, particularly from the late 1950s, to the extent that men began to complain that women students were robbing men of opportunities and that this loss would eventuate in the downfall of the Japanese nation.[64] Furthermore, rapid economic growth, which had begun in the mid-1950s, was creating large numbers of jobs for women, and their employment figures doubled between 1955 and 1965.[65] Women were also becoming more socially assertive, and in popular women's magazines, debates and articles on gender issues appeared frequently, sometimes under such provocative titles as

*How to Train Men to Suit Our Needs (Dansei shiiku hō),*[66] *How to Choose a Man (Otoko no meigara),*[67] or *How to Improve Your Sex Life (Sei seikatsu no chie).*[68]

When examined within such social contexts, Niki's rejection of his wife (the lover in the novel), who is intelligent, strong-willed, and has a career, as castrating can be seen as a rejection of those "new women," while his preference for the "headless naked" woman seems to be in tune with those men who objected to women being politically active, studying at universities, or even obtaining employment.

Also relevant in the gender politics of the period is the ownership of the house at the bottom of the sandpit. Initially, it belongs to the woman, and she constantly informs Niki that "this is my house." She also refers to him as *"okyakusan"* (the guest), indicating that she is the head of the household and she represents the household in the village. If she dies, however, the house will become Niki's, as she has no relations, and he will become head of the household. In the final scene Niki is alone in the house, indicating that it has indeed become his. In the film a scene is added to indicate that Niki will one day have a son and establish a male family line. This is significant because the woman had only one daughter, who predeceased her mother, implying that the female family line could not and must not survive. If one views this plot in the light of the success of the women's movement in averting the government plan to reinstatement of the old *ie* system, which strongly favored the male family line, it is apparent that the film's ending expresses the sentiment of the conservative government. In fact, after the government abandoned their plan to reinstate the *ie* system, male writers and critics began to reiterate the need for men to regain power within their families, and both Abe's novel and Teshigawara's film convey the same message.[69]

It should also be noted that the novel and the film are phallocentric in their use of mythology. Although Beauvoir was concerned that myth makes women the Other, Abe has ignored her concern, reiterating the Earth Mother myth from the traditional male perspective and depicting the woman as the Other: once her task is accomplished, he has her biology destroy her. Teshigawara's film reproduces the same myth, and the presentation of the actress' body as an *objet* makes the "real woman" the Other.

However, the overall message in the film is less misogynistic than in the novel. This has been achieved first of all by omitting much of the highly chauvinistic monologue of the male protagonist. Also, the portrayal by actor Okada Eiji helps to soften the extremely brutal and cruel behavior of the original character, because his acting above all conveys a sense of pathos and helplessness as well as tenderness toward the woman, which makes his character appear far more humane than in the novel. In contrast, Kishida Kyōko's portrayal of the woman is more assertive: at that time Kishida was also playing a cynical and intelligent second sister who mocks and ridicules her male admirers in the popular TV drama *Otoko girai* (The man haters).[70] Perhaps given her experience in mocking men in the TV drama, when Kishida's character is required to mock Niki, her tone of voice is so subversive that it instantly undermines his authority. Thus, in the film, the power relationship between Niki and the woman appears more equal, and the warm rapport between the two actors makes the film appear at times almost like a love story, despite the very misogynistic plot. Nevertheless, the misogynistic presentation of the two female characters causes concern.

Like Abe's novel, Teshigawara's film is the story of an escape to a utopia where a man can accomplish all his dreams: dreams that have become unattainable in the urbanized modern city, where gender relationships are in a state of change. It is ultimately a male utopian vision, and the phallocentric representation of women endorses the avant-garde tradition, especially that of Surrealism.

CHAPTER TEN

GUNHILD BORGGREEN

# Gender in Contemporary Japanese Art

Since the latter half of the 1940s, contemporary artists and artworks alike have traveled to and from Japan in a constant flow of cultural exchange. Cultural exchange between Japan and other countries existed before this period, but I will limit my discussion to contemporary art, which in the case of Japan is defined as art produced in the period between 1945 and the present day. The term "contemporary art" *(gendai bijutsu)* is often associated with avant-garde art, and many trends in contemporary Japanese art are formed in close dialogue with concepts or styles of the international art scene. From the early 1980s a number of contemporary Japanese art exhibitions have been shown in the United States and in Europe, increasing the Western world's attention to the Japanese art scene and improving the possibilities for Japanese artists to pursue a career outside Japan. The shifting of geographic locations of artists makes it difficult to speak about them as "Japanese" or as of any other nationality, for that matter.[1] Other participants in the Japanese art environment emphasize the importance for artists to define a regional or national identity, often as a way of establishing a local position as opposed to the "universality" inherent in the concept of internationalism or as a response to what is seen as a dominating cultural influence from the West.[2]

These remarks should indicate that contemporary art in Japan consists of many different approaches and artistic trends and cannot be defined as a unified or homogeneous entity. Diversity also governs the motivation for artists and critics in contemporary Japan when they address gender issues, and the discussions presented here are only a few of the many approaches possible. In the first part of this chapter I will focus on how attention to female artists created the specific category of "female art" as well as a notion about a "feminine sensitivity" in Japan from the mid-1980s and into the 1990s. Such categorizations are often constructed by art critical discourses surrounding works of art. One aspect of "femininity" is related by critics to the style and subject matter applied by individual artists, for example, bright color and biomorph forms of vegetation and proliferation, while another aspect of "femininity" is connected to the notion of female artists being particularly sensitive to the female body. Male artists may apply the same styles or subject matter, but the discourses about how to interpret the images are different. In the second part of the chapter, I will focus on two artworks from the mid-1990s in which conventional gender stereotypes are being questioned and deconstructed. The works address representation of women in contemporary Japanese society as well as the issues of consumption, ethnicity, and orientalist eroticism.

## "Female Artists" as a Category

Discussions concerning gender in contemporary Japanese art began with a focus on women and were related to a general increase in the number of women on the labor market in Japan from the late 1970s onward.[3] Japanese scholars and feminists addressed feminist approaches to art history, and feminist art historical texts from the United States were translated into Japanese and published.[4] However, these early contributions to a feminist or a gender-conscious understanding of art often stood alone and did not appear to have much influence on the art environment in the early stages.

The increase in general attention to female artists from the early 1980s had the effect of promoting female artists in various publications, individually and under the category of "women artists." Several leading mainstream art magazines in Japan featured special issues about female artists. The magazines were all celebratory in tone and focused on the positive merits of those women who had managed to establish careers as artists. The attention to female artists seemed to be designed to have them serve primarily as role models for other women who wished to deal more seriously with art production and to pursue their activities further than the usual (and socially accepted) level of art as a "hobby."[5]

The most significant focus on female artists during the second half of the 1980s was triggered when *Bijutsu techō* (Art notes), a widely circulated art magazine on contemporary art, launched a special issue about the "Super Girls of art" *(Bijutsu no chōshōjo-tachi)* in August 1986. The phrase *"chōshōjo"* (super girl) was meant to celebrate a large number of young Japanese female artists, born in the late 1950s or early 1960s, who had recently graduated from art universities and were making their way in the contemporary art scene. The *Super Girls of Art* issue of *Bijutsu techō* comprised some sixty pages and featured photos of artworks by thirty-nine female artists together with short biographical information and a portrait photo of each artist.[6] Nine artists were treated in more detail with one-page articles. Two longer articles discussed works by various female artists, one of which was written by art critic Shinohara Motoaki and titled "Chōshōjo shinpen uchū" (The Super Girls' personal universe). The critic describes specific artworks by young Japanese female artists under various subtitles such as "Nuu koto" (Needlework) or "Ie" (Home). The other article, titled "Ima kakeru onna" (Women on the march), is a transcription of a conversation between literary critic Matsuoka Kazuko and creative director Enomoto Ryōichi. The two critics talk about the increasing number of young female artists on the Japanese art scene, and they try to define what is typical of artworks produced by the "Super Girls."[7]

The articles in the *Bijutsu techō* issue argue that one important trait of young female artists is that they use objects and ready-made things from household activities and everyday life as sources for their creative ideas or as basic material in their works. Female artists often use textiles, and they are praised for addressing the tactility of fabrics, not only when handling the material in the process of weaving, sewing, or knitting, but also because of the body's physical contact with clothing material. It is argued that female artists express their experiences in a direct manner, for instance, by using primary colors instead of blending or mixing them. Female artists, it is claimed, are interested in organic forms and things that grow, and thus address subject matter such as flowers and plants. Female artists use simplified biomorph patterns that are repeated and combined in color and shape to make complete and whole artworks. Enomoto connects what he calls "an ornamental disposition" *(sōshokusei)* in the stylistic expression of young female artists with ethnic or folklore art, for example, Indian art or art from Southeast Asia.[8] Mitsuoka distinguishes between abstract and concrete modes of expression, and argues that, in general, abstraction is a weak point among female artists.[9]

## "Super Girl" Style and Subject Matter

The two feature articles in the *Super Girls of Art* issue of *Bijutsu techō* mention a number of individual artists who represent one or more of the characteristics proposed. The artist Sugiyama Tomoko and her works provide a good example. Sugiyama was one of the nine artists selected for special treatment with a full-page introduction and several photos, and a view of Sugiyama working in her

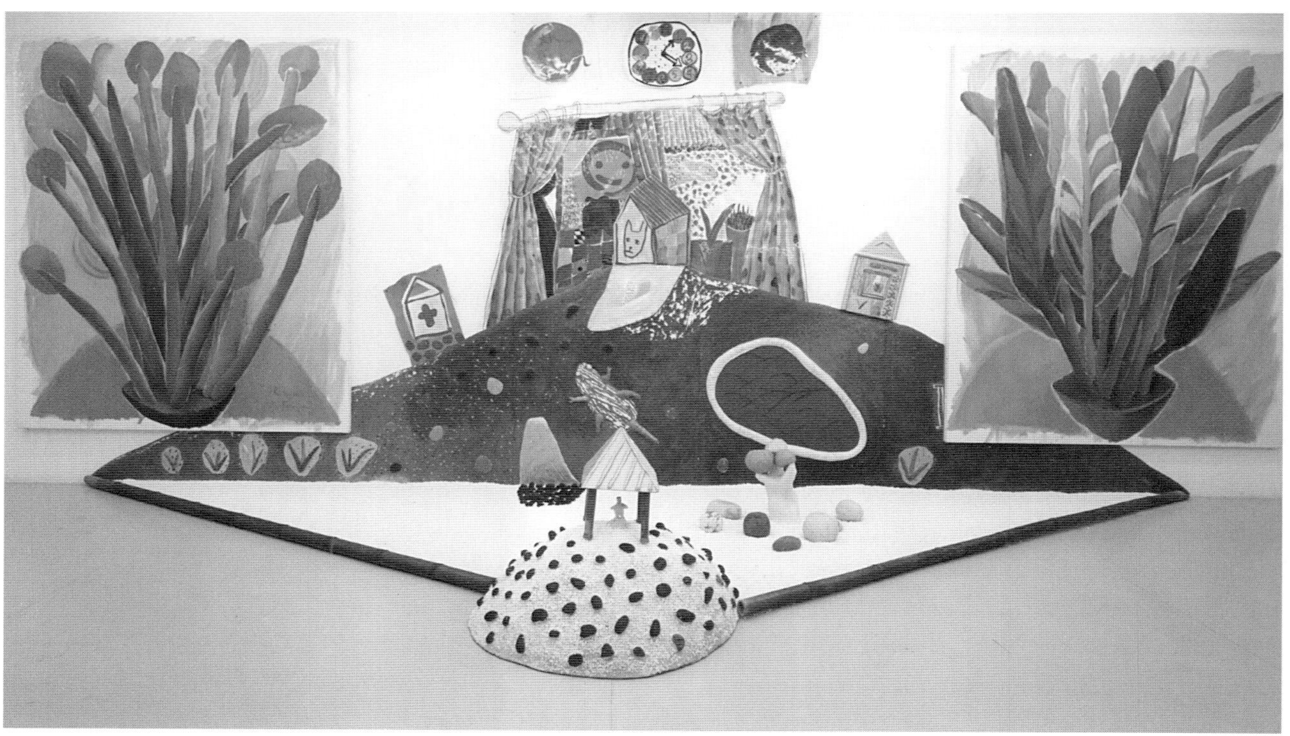

**FIGURE 10.1.** Sugiyama Tomoko, *Houses*, 1986. 680 × 240 cm, Oil on canvas, clay, bamboo, wood, ceramic, and other materials.

studio is featured on the front cover of the magazine. Sugiyama makes sculpture and reliefs that are often combined to form an installation. The figurative content of Sugiyama's work usually refers to houses and gardens, as can be seen in a work titled *Houses* from 1986, which was featured in the *Super Girls of Art* issue (Figure 10.1). On the gallery wall are two large paintings on canvas, each of them depicting a large bunch of flowers or leaves in bright colors, emerging from a diminutive bowl. Between and partly behind the two paintings, on the gallery wall, is a painted landscape consisting of a green hill on which various small plants, dots, and other elements in contrasting colors are placed. On top of the hill is painted an irregular square flanked by a pair of hanging polka-dot curtains, suggesting a window. Within the square are some flower pots and a round smiling face, and above are three round ornaments, one of them resembling a clock. Three small houses are also placed on the hill, one of which contains a cartoonlike drawing of a dog's head. The work extends into the gallery on two bamboo poles placed on the floor to form a triangle, pointing toward a small three-dimensional hill made of ceramic. The little hill, echoing the larger one on the wall, is decorated with dark stones, and on top is a miniature pavilion in which a small figure is seated.

Many of the significant characteristics of works by young female artists pointed out by the two feature articles in *Bijutsu techō* can be found in works by Sugiyama Tomoko. The style of Sugiyama's work is bright and cheerful, and it includes the aspects of home and family life that were claimed in the magazine to be a part of female artists' visual vocabulary. The homely curtain in the center part encloses a slightly disorganized but happy and colorful environment, and the dog house in front may signify both the house pet as well as the protection of the family from outside dangers. The vegetating elements of growth and proliferation are present in the flowers pots on the two large paintings as well as in many details in the work. Sugiyama applies patterns of various kinds, such as dots, stripes, or ornamental elements, and always in curved, irregular lines with no attempt to make the patterns look straight or well-ordered. Such designs can be seen as exemplifying "an ornamental disposition" in works by female artists. The visual vocabulary of children's drawings also comes to mind in the playful and illogical combination of components in different scale and the cartoonlike drawings and patterns.

## Focus on a "Feminine" Style

Considering the impact the *Super Girls of Art* issue had on later debates on gender in Japanese art, it is useful to look at the gender politics implied by the promotion of "Super Girls."[10] Although there were many direct references to specific artworks in the articles, such as the descriptions and photos of Sugiyama Tomoko's works discussed above, there are also many generalizing statements of how young female artists make art. Hereby the magazine promotes a notion of a "feminine" or "female" style and content in art, and advocates a number of gender stereotypes attached to female artists, such as, for example, that female artists do not work with abstract concepts or that female artists do not conceptualize their artworks beforehand but rather create spontaneously and intuitively, even irrationally. Being featured in the *Super Girls of Art* issue of *Bijutsu techō* most likely presented a dilemma for some of the artists involved—attention from a leading art magazine must have been encouraging, while at the same time many artists probably did not recognize themselves within these limited descriptions.

The notion of a certain type of "feminine" art is misleading not only about what kind of art female artists were actually creating in the mid-1980s and onward, but also about the art scene in general in Japan at that time. The special *Super Girls of Art* issue of *Bijutsu techō* featured plenty of female artists who create figurative, decorative, and brightly colored artworks. But the magazine gave no examples of female artists who work with abstract or formalist content, or apply materials of "cool," hard, and monochrome character, such as stone, glass, steel, iron, or other kinds of metal. By the mid-1980s, several female artists were receiving critical acclaim elsewhere for such types of work, for example, Miyawaki Aiko, a sculptor working with long flexible steel wires in motion; Kasahara Emiko, whose conceptual works include tiles, marble, and steel plates; Aoki Noe, who cuts and welds thick sheets of iron; Kikutani Naomi, who makes abstract sculpture of metal sheets; and Mikami Seiko, whose installations are made of waste material from computer circuit plates, television monitors, and other electronic devices.

Many of the styles, materials, and subjects promoted in the *Super Girls of Art* issue were also being applied by young male artists at the same time. Several special editions of *Bijutsu techō* published in the mid-1980s presented overviews and summed up new trends on the Japanese art scene. These publications make it clear that significant traits of the Japanese art scene in the 1980s in general include the application of bright colors and decorative patterns, emphasis on the tactility of concrete materials and media, inclusion of materials and elements drawn from sources conventionally not associated with art, and visual references to everyday objects as well as elements alluding to flowers and plants. This trend, which appeared on the Japanese art scene during the 1980s, was termed "new painting" or "new wave."[11] None of these special editions of *Bijutsu techō*, however, attribute the new styles specifically to female artists; in fact most of the artists discussed in the articles are male. In other words, the same art magazine can celebrate female artists in one special volume but include only a few female artists in its general overview issues. The magazine thus implies that women are to be considered as a "special case" and not incorporated into general art critical practice.

## In the Context of the "New Wave"

One example of a brightly colored and biomorphic art work by a male artist can be seen in a piece titled *Chameleon Eater* from 1985 by Tsubaki Noboru (Figure 10.2). The work was included in a *Bijutsu techō* volume about contemporary sculpture in the context of the "New Wave" style.[12] Tsubaki's sculpture is an irregu-

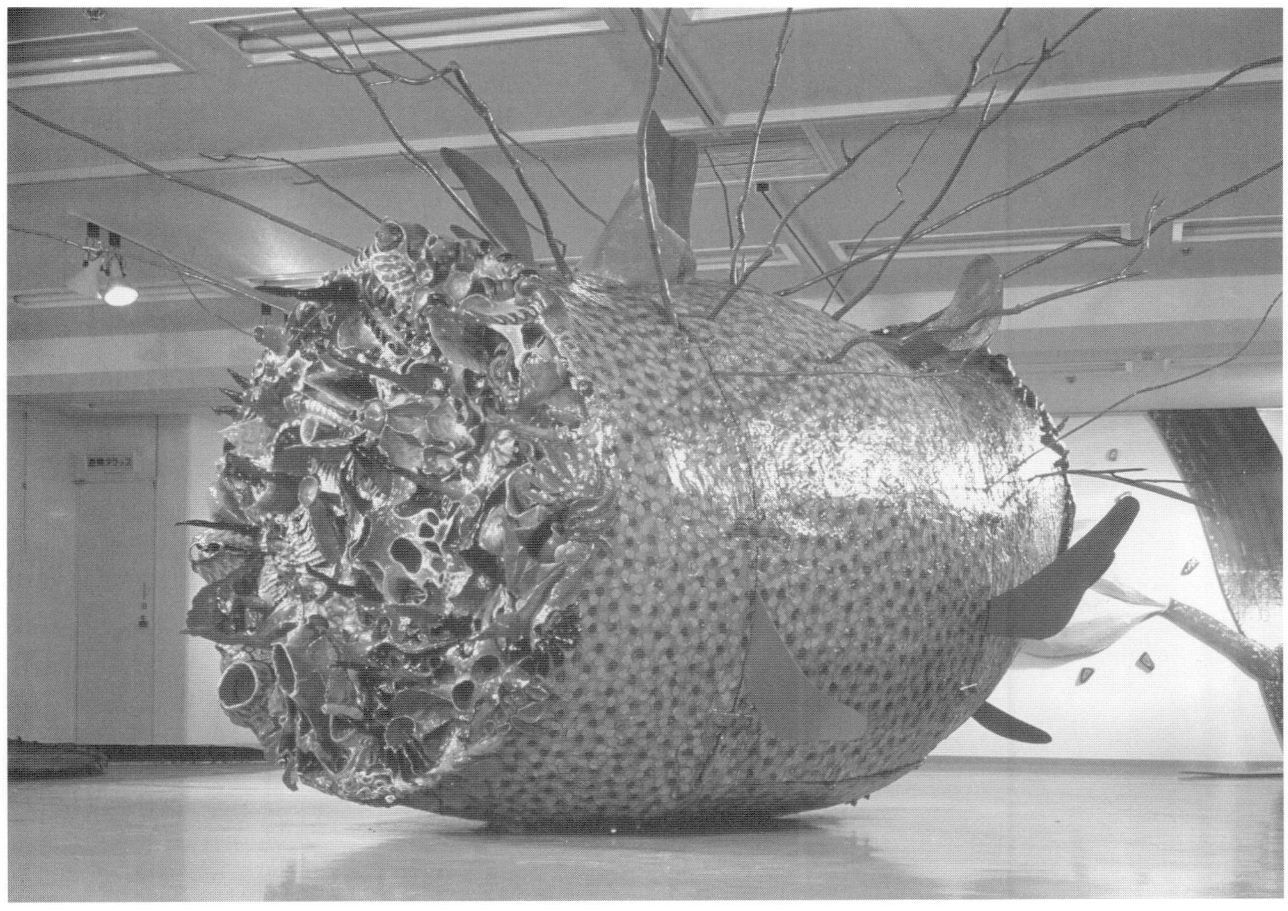

FIGURE 10.2. Tsubaki Noboru, *Chameleon Eater*, 1985. 230 × 350 × 220 cm, mixed media.

lar, oblong, container-like object four meters long and two and a half meters in diameter. The main body of the sculpture is made of glass fibers, and the shiny, reflecting surface is covered with a pattern of dots in various bright green colors, resembling ornamental leaves. From the sides and the top of the object, branches and sticks painted green protrude together with a number of green silhouette cutouts that might resemble wings or leaves. Each end of the oblong cylinder is closed by a relief of three-dimensional flower heads in strange, organic shapes, as if the flowers are proliferating from the inside of the container in a colorful vegetating abundance. The flowers and plant parts are not drawn from realistic botanical models but are grotesque and fantastic, painted in bright colors in which red and orange hues dominate. Except perhaps for the size, the object emanates a childlike playfulness and represents many kinds of tactility, such as the smooth curving surface on the sides, the bumpy and proliferating forms on the ends, as well as the protruding and sharp edges of the green fins and pointed sticks.

The sculpture *Chameleon Eater* can be seen as a humorous and slightly ironic comment on the romantic notion of a peaceful and harmonious relationship between human beings and nature. The concept of nature is increasingly conceived as bright and beautiful as more and more people move away from it to live in cities. At the same time many people feel alienated by nature at this distance, and once they encounter nature at close hand, they may feel threatened. The size of the object may allude to a certain anxiety or fear, for in a gallery space the physical expansion of the object can create a feeling of uncontrollable invasion, despite the cheerful colors, and the proliferating abundance of flowers as well as the protruding sticks may transform into clutching tentacles.

On a certain level there are similarities in style and subject matter between the work by Sugiyama Tomoko and that of Tsubaki Noboru, namely, the use of bright colors and ornamental patterns as well as the references to plants and other organic forms. On this formal level both artists are related to the New Wave tendency mentioned above. The New Wave styles emerged as a reaction against the highly conceptual and abstract formalist art that had dominated during the 1970s. The New Wave was a return to figurative subject matter as well as a revival of the notion of "real art," because it aimed at reevaluating and reinstalling the status of conventional painting and sculpture by emphasizing gestures of brushstrokes or chisel marks. Art critic Tōno Yoshiaki wrote about Japanese female artists' involvement in the New Wave movement in the 1980s, and he interprets the emergence of chaotic, formless, colorful three-dimensional installation works made by young female artists in the early 1980s as a reaction against the minimal and conceptual art of the 1960s and 1970s.[13] Tōno credits female artists for a high degree of consciousness about their artistic activities, although in the end he does not say explicitly whether the New Wave art forms in Japan during the 1980s were in fact triggered by female artists. It may be difficult to attribute the beginning of a new trend or style to any individual artist or group of artists, and international movements may also have influenced the local art scene, in this case Neo-Expressionism or the "New Wild" artists in the United States and Europe.

### The "Super Girls" of the 1990s

The idea of "Super Girls of art" continued to flourish during the first part of the 1990s along with the notion of a specifically feminine mode of expression and a particular feminine subject matter. American Tokyo-based art critic Janet Koplos interviewed a number of Japanese female artists in 1990 and reported that the "Super Girl stigma" still prevailed among some of the artists she met. The sculptor Yano Michiko, for example, admitted that she and other female artists received more critical attention and had easier access to museum and gallery space after the "Super Girl" exposure, but she still found it difficult to be taken seriously as an artist, especially by the older generation of male critics and curators. Yano reportedly had stopped attending exhibition openings and avoided interviews, because she wanted the focus to be on her artworks, not on her person. The success of another artist, Kasahara Emiko, was evident by the coverage of her in Japanese weekly magazines, which, according to Koplos, featured "not just her work but her young, pretty face."[14]

Some of the artists introduced in the *Super Girls of Art* issue of *Bijutsu techō* were doing very well in the 1990s. Naitō Rei was especially praised for her sensational evocation of the female body through the use of textiles. Naitō's tentlike installation piece titled *Apocalypse Palace* from 1985 was reproduced in the *Super Girls* issue, and art critic Matsuoka Kazuko commented on the installation by describing the act of entering the tent as "returning to the womb."[15] The image of the womb has been associated with other of Naitō's works. Figure 10.3 shows the artist herself seated in the midst of another of her installations, *Chijō ni hitotsu no basho o* (One place on earth), when the work was exhibited at Sagachō Exhibit Space in Tokyo in 1991. The installation consists of a fifteen meters long and more than five meters wide tentlike construction of fabric surrounding an enclosure, into which the audience enters one person at a time though a slit in the curtain draping. Visitors in the gallery cannot look into the tent from the outside, and since only one person is allowed at a time, visitors must wait their turn to enter. The floor area inside is covered with thick felt in shapes of different colors, and the visitor must take off his or her shoes before stepping on the felt carpet. The dimly lit space is filled with a large number of objects. In the center of the tent, for example, is a tall construction made of thin flexible bamboo wire tied together to form a netlike three-dimensional abstract form. Other objects are tiny and made of wire, thread, paper, textiles, beads, plant leaves, seeds, or other

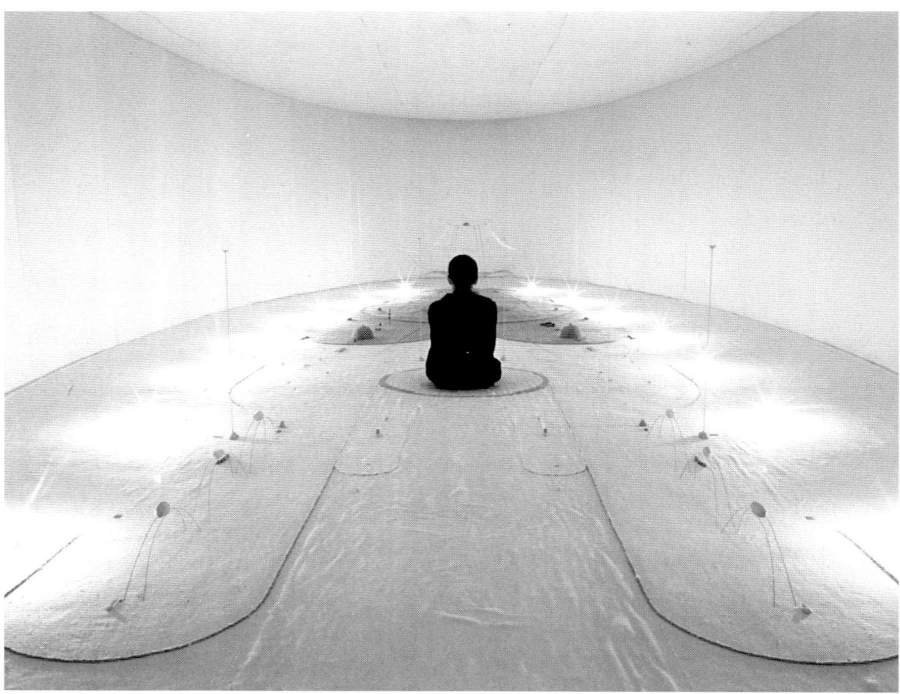

FIGURE 10.3. Naitō Rei, *Chijō no hitotsu no basho o* (One place on earth), 1991. 15 × 5.5 × 2.6 (h) m, rattan, bamboo, string, wire, woods, seeds, leaves, fruits, petals, shells, stones, sand, wax, felt, cotton cloth, fur, leather, glass, and other materials. Photo by Masayuki Hayashi.

materials. Most of these objects are nonfigurative, although some elements look as if they refer to body parts, evoking especially the female body.

Naitō Rei received enormous critical acclaim for this work in the 1990s, and many critics emphasized a "feminine" sensitivity or spirituality in the work. Naitō's art is in general conceived as epitomizing the essence of femininity. Critics focused on the use of natural and organic materials as well as the proliferating abundance of small objects, almost like a miniature landscape. Central to the notion of a "female" sensitivity is the handicraft aspect, the artist's close relationship to material during the artistic process. This relationship is seen in the miniature objects and the delicate way in which they were crafted by the artist's own hands. But more than anything, the "femininity" in Naitō's installation is linked to the symbolic representation of the female body in the installation itself when entering into the enclosed space. Many delighted critics, both Japanese and Western, evoke the image of "entering the womb" when they describe Naitō's work. One critic wrote of the work that "this quiet and purified space, which only has room for one person, is a holy womb."[16] Another critic described it as "a womb-like tent,"[17] while a third critic recalls the 1991 exhibition with these words: "Describing Naitō's tent doesn't do the work justice but the sensation was very much like walking into a womb."[18] In 1997, Naitō Rei was invited to represent Japan at the International Art Biennale in Venice, and the *Chijō ni hitotsu no basho o* installation was chosen as the sole artwork in the Japanese pavilion. In this situation, too, association with the female body and the womb was evoked at the very beginning of an introductory text about the work. "This oval-shaped tent," wrote Nanjō Fumio, commissioner to the Japanese pavilion, "symbolizes female genitalia and what it contains is a metaphor for the inside of a woman's body."[19]

In other words, a notion of "femininity" continued in Japanese art during the 1990s, exemplified by artists such as Naitō Rei. Naitō appears as an ideal model for female artists, because she is presented as strong and powerful enough to have success in the competitive art world; she is able to attract recognition and approval from critics and curators on an international scale; and yet she maintains her "feminine" integrity by making her own kind of art, which is gentle, sensitive, and nonaggressive. The aspect of the female body and sexual organs that many critics refer to in describing Naitō's work does not indicate an explicit sexuality on part of the artist; on the contrary, references to the womb seem more closely related to the idea of protective and goddesslike spiritual powers of (asexual) motherhood. Every positive quality of an "ideal woman" is summed up in Naitō's installation and is reflected in the celebration of this and other female artists' direct or symbolic representation of the womb.

## Another Representation of the Womb

The notion implicit in the appraisal of "Super Girls" such as Naitō Rei seems to suggest that women are more knowledgeable and sensitive than men regarding such an explicitly "female" subject matter as the female body and especially the womb. There are, however, also male artists who include references to the womb. Figure 10.4 is a reproduction of a work by Yanobe Kenji titled *Tanking Machine* from 1990. Yanobe's work is a two and a half meters tall sculpture of steel made as a large oval isolation tank with supportive legs. The main body is painted white, while the short supportive legs have a bulging cover of black rubber. In the center of the front end of the tank is a large round porthole with a brass frame, and from this center eight black straps extend around the tank. On the top is a lid that curves upwards in the middle, and on the front side of the lid is a face made of plaster, covered with a white gas mask. This upper part resembles a torso because of a pair of shoulders extending from under the lid. A propane gas cylinder is suspended from each shoulder of the torso, and from each gas cylinder a flame of propane is directed toward a round steel plate on the bottom sides of the tank. The tank is filled halfway with saltwater, the same kind of sodium chloride solution found in human fluids, and the propane flames on the outside are to keep the temperature of the water as close to that of the human body as possible. At the bottom front side of the tank is a water tap from which the water can be let out.

Yanobe Kenji's sculpture *Tanking Machine* was meant not just for visual experience from the outside, but also as a physical and mental experience inside the tank. When the work was exhibited for the first time in the summer of 1990 at the gallery Art Space Niji in Kyoto, the audience was invited to bring along bathing suits and to climb into the tank during their visit. Yanobe's idea was that the person entering the tank would be able to enter a state of meditation when floating in the water with a salt solution and temperature equal to that of the human body and with the lid closed.[20] The artist himself stated in an interview that he intended a metaphor of the womb: "That piece has a lot of elements to it," says Yanobe, "but on a personal level, it represents a process of rebirth by going back to the womb."[21] In the text accompanying a picture of *Tanking Machine* in an article, a bath inside the tank was described as "retracing the past as fetus in amniotic fluid."[22] Art critics have commented on the womb metaphor, as when one critic wrote about the event at Art Space Niji: "All the visitors, regardless of age and gender, who had felt the water in *Tanking Machine* with their body, came out with flushed faces as if they were children born once again. *Tanking Machine* is an artificial womb. And Yanobe, as the midwife, while renewing the water of the child's first bath, delivered one hundred babies during the week."[23] Another critic calls *Tanking Machine* "a safe, womb-like *ofuro*" (Japanese-style bath) and, referring to the way in which the sculpture directs the audience's attention to its inner self, concludes that "*Tanking Machine* is a metaphor for finding peace in mind."[24] A third critic wrote in a catalog text: "Floating inside the tank's heated salt water the spectator returns to the safe womb of the embryonic stage and can shut away the outside world."[25]

Although the artist as well as several critics recognize the spiritual and meditative aspect of the symbolic womb in Yanobe's *Tanking Machine*, my interest in the enclosure as a protection device against the outside world is in comparison to the comments on Naitō Rei's work discussed above. Other works by Yanobe during the 1990s are made to resemble large-scale sci-fi toys or echo fantasy hero figures from popular culture such as Godzilla or the *manga* figure Atom Boy.

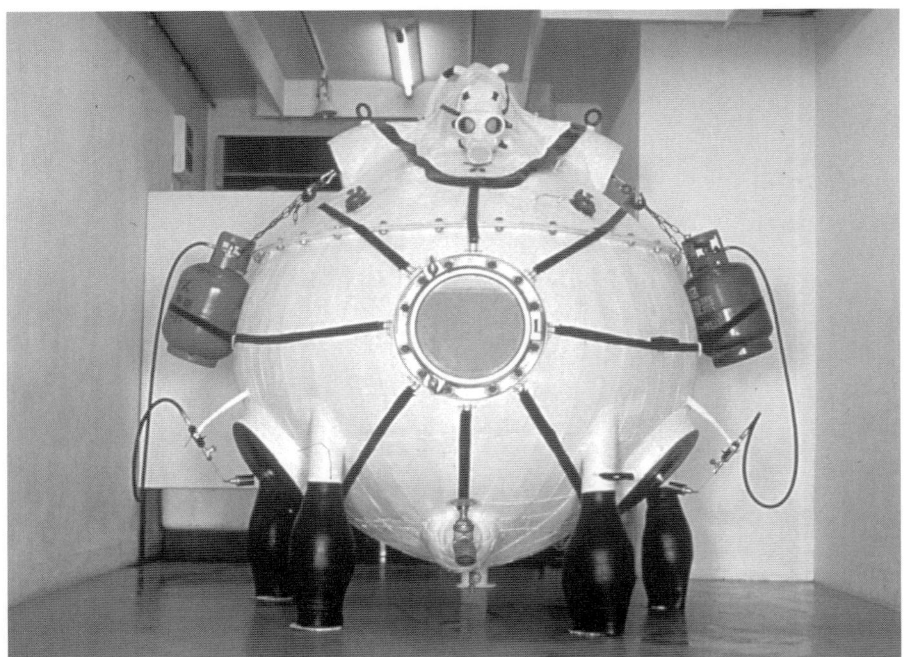

**FIGURE 10.4.** Yanobe Kenji, *Tanking Machine*, 1990. 240 × 240 × 240 cm, steel, propane gas, salt solution.

These artworks are made to be worn or manned by an actual person (often Yanobe himself), and they all address the dual aspect of isolation and defense. Several critics connect these themes as a part of the *otaku* discourse, and although Yanobe does not recognize himself as an *otaku*, his artistic vocabulary is linked closely to the icons of the *otaku* generation.[26] As many scholars of popular culture in Japan have noted, the underlying notion in the behavior of certain youth groups, such as *otaku*, in general seems to indicate isolation from or a defense against the dangers of adulthood.[27] In this respect, Yanobe's *Tanking Machine* addresses the issue to an extreme, suggesting a resistance against even being born. Other young male artists in the early 1990s engaged the same issue, for example, Nakahara Kōdai, who made a similar isolation tank installation some years after Yanobe's work. Art critic Azby Brown linked the two together under the term "techno-infantilism" in an article from 1993, in which he wrote: "Other recent work by Nakahara takes the form of isolation tanks in which, according to the accompanying drawings, the artist visualizes himself floating naked and shitting like a baby. This wish to return to the womb pairs him quite closely with Kenji Yanobe, who had exhibited a nearly identical isolation tank a couple of years earlier."[28]

The formal differences between the works of Naitō Rei and of Yanobe Kenji discussed here are numerous, but my point in relation to the idea of a specific "feminine" art should be stressed: it is misleading to connect elements of the female body's reproductive abilities specifically to female artists because of women's alleged sensitivity toward their own bodies. The case of Yanobe Kenji (and others) shows that concepts and images of the womb can be found in artworks by male artists as well. However, as indicated by the many citations, the critical discourse about the way in which to interpret the symbolic womb comes out differently. The reference to a metaphoric womb in the artworks of Naitō Rei is praised as genuine spiritual creativity and feminine sensitivity. The womb metaphor of Yanobe's *Tanking Machine* is more ambiguously interpreted, ranging from an appraisal of the meditative aspects of floating in the water to a connection to the introverted *otaku*, who after the Miyazaki incident had become a suspicious figure in contemporary Japan.[29]

I have pointed out how certain styles or subjects in Japanese art in the latter half of the 1980s and the early 1990s were associated specifically with young female artists and attributed "feminine" qualities. Although male artists might apply the same style or subject matter, their works were not perceived in the same way as expressing a "feminine" sensitivity, and if gender issues were addressed at all, interpretations would point in the direction of a male context, as in the case of *otaku*. In other words, the gender discourse surrounding contemporary artworks directly or indirectly maintained two mutually exclusive categories of "feminine" and "masculine," based on the biological sex of the artist. I will now turn to two artworks from the latter half of the 1990s to show how artworks may question or even deconstruct gender stereotypes by dismantling conventional images of women in areas of popular or mass culture such as consumption and media.

## Images of Women in Consumer Society

Plate 6 is a photographic work by Yanagi Miwa titled *Annaijō no heya 1F* (titled in English *Elevator Girl House 1F*). The work consists of two separate photos, each with a similar composition, namely, a view from one end of a moving walkway that disappears into the far distance in a vantage point at the center of the composition. In each of the two photos, showcases with large glass windows flank the walkway, and the decreasing distance between the vertical window frames emphasizes the illusion of an exaggerated three-dimensional depth in the composition. In the left-hand photo, a number of young women dressed in identical red jackets and skirts, white gloves, and hats sit or lie closely together on the entire walkway, which disappears into a black spot. The showcases on each side are filled with bunches of different kinds of flowers to which small white labels are attached. In the right-hand photo, the female figures have moved from the walkway and are now aligned in the showcases instead of the flowers, facing each other across the empty walkway. The walkway leads toward a white spot, resembling a bright light in the distance. The uniformity of the figures is more apparent in this photo. The women have identical height and physical shapes, and are all dressed alike in red skirts and jackets with two rows of golden buttons, white low-heeled shoes, white gloves, and a grayish hat adorning long loose hair. Although the postures of the figures vary, they all have the somewhat stiff pose of a mannequin.

Yanagi's works cannot be interpreted from a gender perspective without including aspects of contemporary consumer culture in Japan. In many ways women have become symbols of consumption, not only because images of women often appear in commercials to attract attention and help sell the product. Since the economic boom of the 1980s in Japan, women have also been recognized as potentially the largest group of consumers, because women often have more time to go shopping than men, and young, single women working as "OLs" ("office ladies") increasingly have more money to spend.[30] Yanagi addresses the issue from both sides in her works, namely, the representation of the female figure in the world of consumption as well as the aspect of women as consumers. In the right-hand part of this particular work, the figures with their stiffened appearance suggest mannequins in a department store window. As indicated by the title of Yanagi's work, the female figures also refer to another aspect of Japanese department stores, namely, the *annaijō*, or "information girl." Often referred to in English as "elevator girls," *annaijō* can be encountered in Japanese department stores and large shops or in the lobbies of wealthy business companies and exclusive hotels to provide service to the customers. Positions as *annaijō* are usually occupied by young females who have been selected by the management on the basis of their good looks and elegant behavior in order to "offer a decorative hospitality to the customers."[31] The large number of identical female figures in Yanagi's photo also points to the stereotyping that takes place in the employment process not only at the request of employers, but also by the women themselves.

Yanagi points out that the job as elevator girl, companion girl, or department store girl is a specifically Japanese type of occupation and represents one section of female images in Japan.[32] In an interview Yanagi relates that for a number of years she worked as a teacher at a junior college for women. It was strange for her to observe how the eighteen-year-old girls who entered college would during their two-year stay become complete copies of each other, as if it was a comfort not to have a personal identity. Yanagi did not like the way in which the young women apparently changed their appearance without any reflection.[33] In other words, although Yanagi herself does not place her works within feminist criticism, she does transmit a social message in the way she stages the models in her scenes.[34]

## The Glamour of Advertising

Yanagi's work can be seen as a critical comment on this decorativeness of female *annaijō* in Japanese department stores specifically and on consumer culture in general. In the right-hand part of *Annaijō no heya 1F*, female figures are lined up for visual display in showcase windows, a visualization of the female body as commodity. It is difficult to determine whether the female figures are human beings or not because of their stiff poses and the lines of light reflection that cover their faces as a semitransparent band. In the left-hand part of the work, the women in the showcases are replaced by flowers, as if to spell out the parallel; these too have been groomed carefully to become uniform in size, shape, and color. The female figures in the left-hand part may be symbolic of the female consumer who makes herself look like everyone else. The figures all ride on the moving walkway leading into Consumption Paradise, a dark spot not unlike a black hole in the universe that draws in and absorbs everything. But the young women are already so exhausted or bored that they need to sit or lie down. Although they touch each other's bodies with knees and thighs, they do not have eye contact, and all seem to be alienated from other individuals and absorbed only in their own thoughts.

The strong persuasive element in Yanagi's works has to do with her use of the photographic medium. The architectural spaces of urban consumption in Yanagi's works do not exist in reality but are created entirely by Yanagi in her studio with the use of photos and computer graphics software. The female figures who inhabit these spaces were not a part of the original photo but are models posing in a studio photo later placed in the space with the help of advanced computer manipulation. Details are carefully manipulated and added to the photo in order to convince the viewer of the realism of the image.[35] Yanagi relies on the common notion of photography as a documented account of reality as it takes place in front of the camera lens in the split second when the shutter is released. However, exaggerated perspective, two vanishing points in one composition, absurd narratives, and other "unrealistic" elements are added, which makes Yanagi's works uncanny and disturbing, because these surrealistic elements are confronted with the persuasive aspect of "reality" in the detail. Furthermore, the quality and size of the photos in Yanagi's work resemble large-scale professional commercial posters, and the works are often displayed as a light box advertisement with a strong light from behind that emphasizes the brilliant colors and the glamorous appearance of the young women and their surroundings.[36]

Yanagi visualizes the dual sides of present-day consumer society by displaying beautiful and luxurious icons in high-quality, large-scale, and glossy prints, while at the same time revealing the uncanny space and discomforting sense of displacement in endless arcades inhabited by superficial, clonelike females. Yanagi's work can be seen as addressing idealized standards of feminine beauty and reveals the anonymous uniformity resulting from everyone wanting to conform to the ideals. Yanagi Miwa points at the homogenizing effects of mass production and mass consumption as well as their effect on the representation and self-image of women.

## Movie Star Spectacle

Another perspective on the theme of the mass consumption of images of the female body is addressed by Morimura Yasumasa in his photographic work titled *Serufu pōtoreito (joyū) / Shirubia Kurisuteru to shite no watashi 1 (Self-Portrait [Actress] / After Sylvia Kristel 1)* from 1996 (Figure 10.5). A wicker chair with a large round back is surrounded by green subtropical plants and placed against a plain pink backdrop. A female figure dressed in white lace underwear, white silk stockings, and white high-heeled boots is reclining in the chair, her head turned back and upward. Makeup is applied to the face, eyebrows are plucked, and golden hair lies in gentle waves across the forehead. The eyes are halfway closed, and the figure looks somewhere down to the left. The mouth painted red is slightly open. The legs are spread open, with the right leg placed over the armrest, and the person's right hand relaxing on the knee, while the left hand, adorned with sparkling rings, plays with a long necklace of white pearls. The area between the legs is partly visible, partly concealed behind a corner of white lace from the skirt.

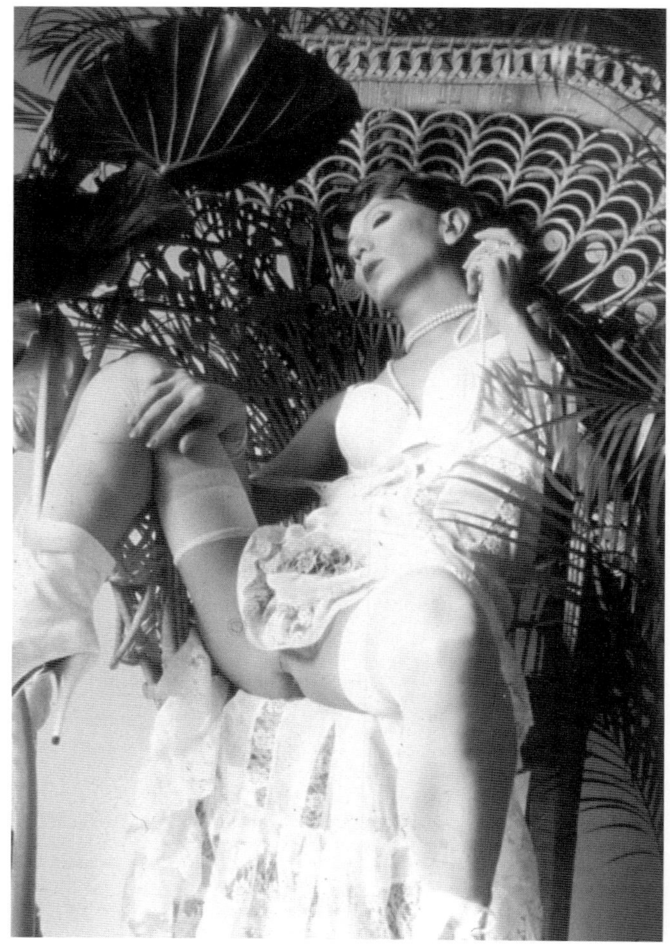

**FIGURE 10.5.** Morimura Yasumasa, *Serufu pōtoreito (joyū) Shirubia Kuristuteru to shite no watashi 1 (Self-Portrait [Actress] / After Sylvia Kristel 1)*, 1996. 120 × 96 cm, Ilfochrome, framed acrylic sheet.

The figure in the photo is Morimura himself, and the work is a part of a series, *Self-Portraits as Actresses*, in which Morimura dresses up and disguises himself as famous female movie stars in various well-known movies—most of them Hollywood stars, but also European actresses as well as a few Japanese. In the entire series, Morimura plays only women.[37] One might look at Morimura's *Actress* series from the psychoanalytic approach proposed by film critic Laura Mulvey in her essay "Visual Pleasure and Narrative Cinema" from 1975.[38] In this famous essay, Mulvey applies Freud's theory of scopophilia, which is defined as "an active taking other people as objects, and subject[ing] them to a controlling and curious gaze."[39] In Hollywood movies especially from the 1930s, 1940s, and 1950s, this kind of voyeurism often takes place within the movie theater itself, where an active heterosexual male looks at and controls a passive female object. Scopophilia also takes place in the cinematic experience when the spectator identifies himself with the male protagonist and enjoys the visual pleasure of the woman as an erotic object on display. While the woman is passive, the man is active not only by looking at the woman, but also by controlling events in the story line of the movie. The female figure's contribution to the development of the story consists of how she provokes or inspires the male hero to take action. Mulvey argues that the woman's presence in the movie can tend to work against the narrative, "to freeze the flow of action in moments of erotic contemplation."[40] Film stills of female heroines posing in front of the camera capture exactly these moments of contemplation, and the individual photo can therefore easily be taken out of the movie's narrative context. This may be one of the reasons for Morimura's exclusive use of female movie stars in his *Actress* series, for as Morimura states, his ambition was to re-create the spectacle of real movies in his photographic works.[41]

*Self-Portrait (Actress) / After Sylvia Kristel 1* may illustrate another important point of psychoanalytic theory applied by Mulvey, namely, the aspect of castration anxiety in a phallocentric system. In her essay, Mulvey points out the paradox that the passive female in narrative cinema is displayed for visual pleasure, but at the same time the female figure poses a threat to the male protagonist (as well as the male viewer), because she symbolizes a sexual difference by demonstrating her lack of the phallus. In Morimura's *Actress* series, almost all the other images feature either a dressed figure or a body whose nudity is concealed by other objects. In these images, Morimura's own male body is hidden behind layers of women's clothes and accessories, and he signifies "femininity" through gender-related attributes such as makeup, certain types of clothes and shoes, hairstyle, gesture, and so on. In this particular work, however, the genitals of the figure are both revealed and hidden at the same time; parts of the area between the legs are visible, but the lace veil effectively suggests the absence of a penis, thus symbolizing the lack of phallus in the Freudian sense. It is possible to see Morimura's work as an ironic visualization of this castration complex, because Morimura (himself a male) has taken an image from a film still from a well-known erotic movie and has exaggerated what the male spectator wants to see but also feels threatened by the sexualized female body on display.[42] At the same time, while emphasizing "feminine" accessories and attributes, Morimura blurs the biological sex that most people use as the foundation for gender identification, thus asking the viewer to reconsider on what grounds gender identification of self and other is made in the first place.

## Sexual Liberation versus Sexual Exploitation

Sylvia Kristel, the actress behind Morimura's appropriation, was a Belgian model and beauty contest winner who played the role of Emmanuelle as one of her first movie performances. The French movie *Emmanuelle* from 1974 was directed by Just Jaeckin and had great success among French audiences, as well as audiences around the world. The story line is about a young wife, Emmanuelle, who accompanies her husband to Thailand, where he is posted as a diplomat. Here Emmanuelle ventures into a number of sexual relationships with various people, Europeans as well as Thai, men as well as women, and she meets the older man who teaches her that love making should be free from moral values and social restraints. Sexual liberation seemed to be the message of the movie, promoting sensuality and eroticism in a manner that, according to film historian and critic Maitland McDonagh, emphasized prettiness and cleanliness in order to distance itself from hard-core pornography.[43] The movie *Emmanuelle* also became well known in Japan, where it was released in December 1974 and apparently was seen by a large female audience. The impact of the movie was great enough in Japan to trigger a fashion word the following year, namely, *emanieru suru*, literally, "to do Emmanuelle," meaning to have a casual and extravagant love affair.[44] The figure of Emmanuelle can thus be seen as representing, and perhaps promoting, the notion of a liberated and active female sexuality.

The female figure in the work *Self-Portrait (Actress) / After Sylvia Kristel 1* alludes to ethnicity as a parallel to the gender perspective suggested above. In his transformation into the figure of Sylvia Kristel, Morimura changes from man into woman and from Asian into Caucasian, thereby confronting power hierarchies by juxtaposing one Other (woman as man's Other) with another Other (Asia as the Other of the West). However, considering the context of this image, the identity as "Japanese" becomes a dubious position. The original movie *Emmanuelle* takes place in Bangkok and represents in both plot and imagery the stereotypes of the depraved Orient as an erotic utopia for the West where anything goes, a perfect setting for the promotion of eroticism and sexual liberation for a Western audience.[45] Such an image of Thailand would also be recognizable in Japan in the 1970s, as sex tourism for Japanese men to Southeast Asian countries was being organized regularly as part of the general boom of tourism following the economic growth in Japan.[46] In his work, Morimura includes references to the exotic location by placing the figure in a wicker chair reminiscent of Southeast Asian furniture and surrounding it with subtropical junglelike plants. The point about Thailand as an erotic paradise will probably not be lost on Morimura's Japanese audience of the 1990s, since Thailand has remained a popular tourist site, also for organized sex tours.[47] In terms of gender and power structures, many Japanese seem to have adopted the Western clichés about the hedonistic Orient rather than identifying with other Asian peoples. Morimura's merging of a Japanese figure into a Caucasian can thus be seen as a comment on transnational alliances in the exploitation of a global sex industry. In this way, Morimura's work can be interpreted not only in regard to aspects of gender relations, but also in regard to issues of ethnicity and power structures that are more complex than the simplistic dichotomy of West versus East seems to suggest.

## Conclusion

Issues of gender in contemporary Japanese art deserve attention, for as indicated in this chapter, the area has numerable entrances, and there are many ways in which to approach the topic. I have focused first on the promotion and celebration of young female artists, the so-called "Super Girls of art," which took place in Japan from the mid-1980s and continued well into the 1990s. On the one hand, such attention paved the way for a new generation of female artists and created encouraging role models for others to follow. On the other hand, the way in which the "Super Girls" were discussed in art-related media during the 1980s and 1990s formed a specific category of "female artists" to which a number of constricting sets of characteristics were attached. The categorization of "female artists" not only excluded female artists who did not conform to the prescribed "feminine" style, but also supported gender stereotypes about how men and women express themselves in art.

In the second part of the chapter, I proposed a gender-related reading of two artworks from the later half of the 1990s, in which the artists address issues of gender in close relation to other aspects of contemporary Japanese society. One work addresses aspects of contemporary consumption patterns and mass media, and by including images that are at the same time both glamorous and slightly unpleasant suggests some of the dark sides of Consumer Paradise. The other work relates to popular culture and can be seen from a number of approaches, from a perspective of the visual pleasure of scopophilia, to a focus on gender and ethnicity in complicated power structures of global economy, tourism, and sexual exploitation. These and many other artworks indicate not only that gender issues are related to other social and political factors in contemporary Japanese society, but also that contemporary Japanese artists are aware of these relationships and engage in addressing the issues by means of their art.

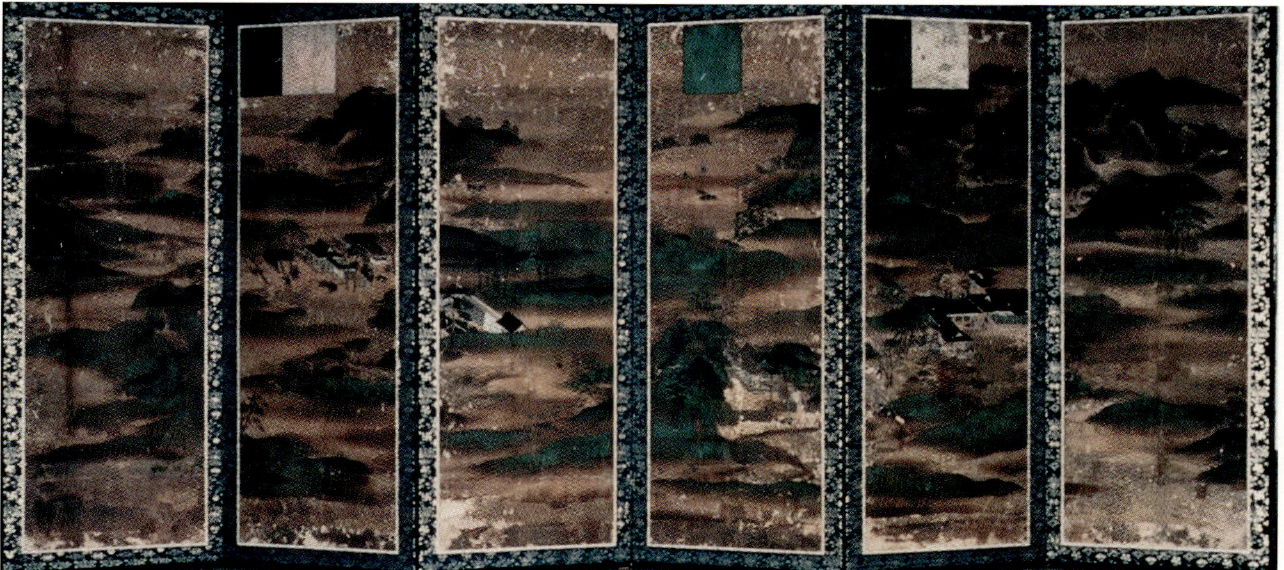

**PLATE 1.** *Jingoji Landscape Screen (Jingoji senzui byōbu),* end of the twelfth to beginning of the thirteenth century. Each panel 110.8 × 37.5 cm, colors on silk. Jingoji Temple, Kyoto.

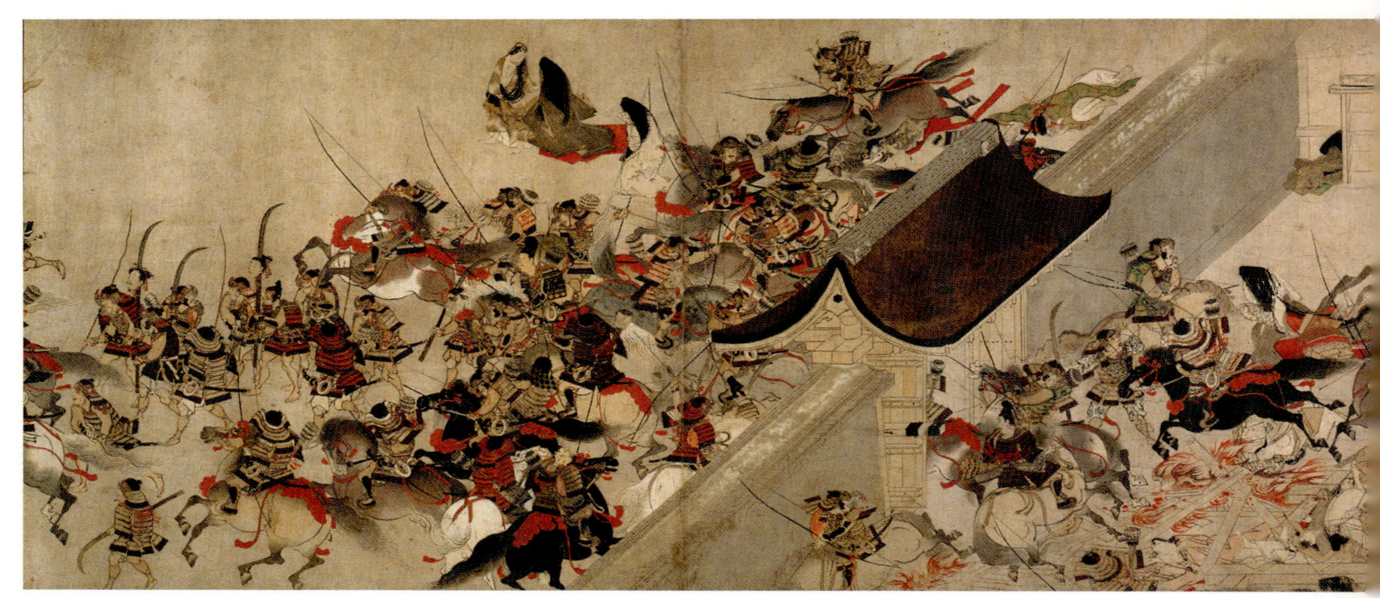

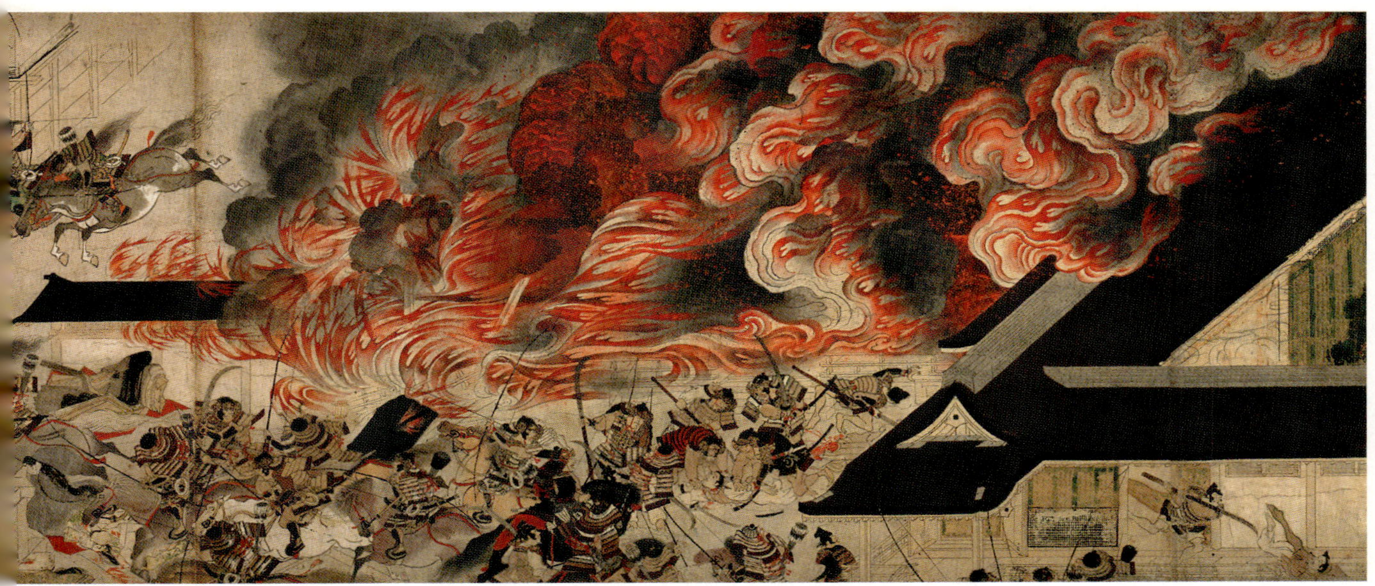

**PLATE 2.** *Night Attack on the Sanjō Palace* from the *Illustrated Scrolls of the Tale of the Heiji Era (Heiji monogatari emaki),* mid–thirteenth century. Handscroll. Museum of Fine Arts, Boston.

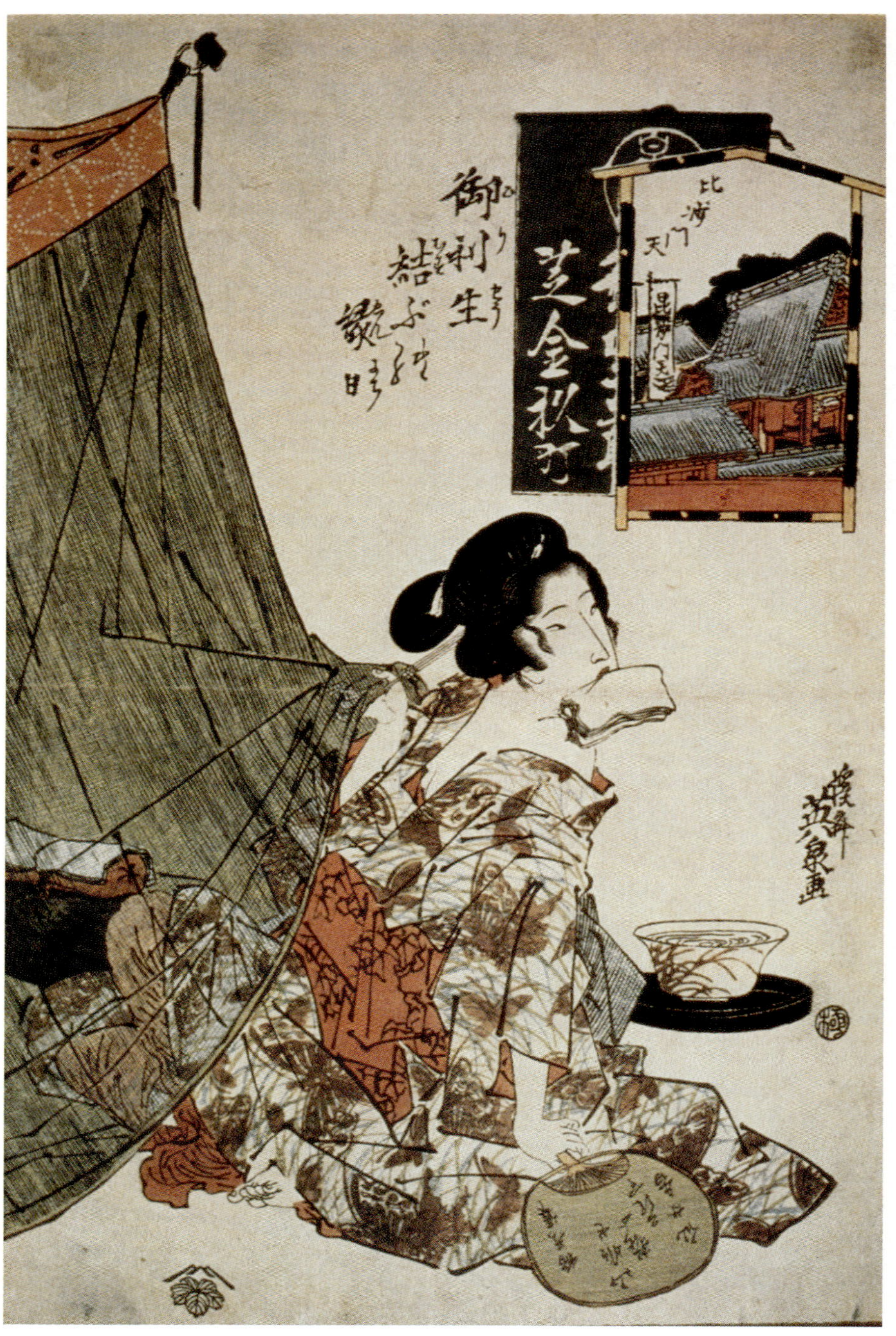

**PLATE 3.** Keisai Eisen, *Gorishō musubu no ennichi: Bishamonten.* (Fair day at the Bishamonten Shrine: receiving Buddha's blessing). From Takahashi Hakushin, *Ukiyo-e zanmai: Kunisada to Eisen* (Tokyo: Arita Shobō, 1980), 181.

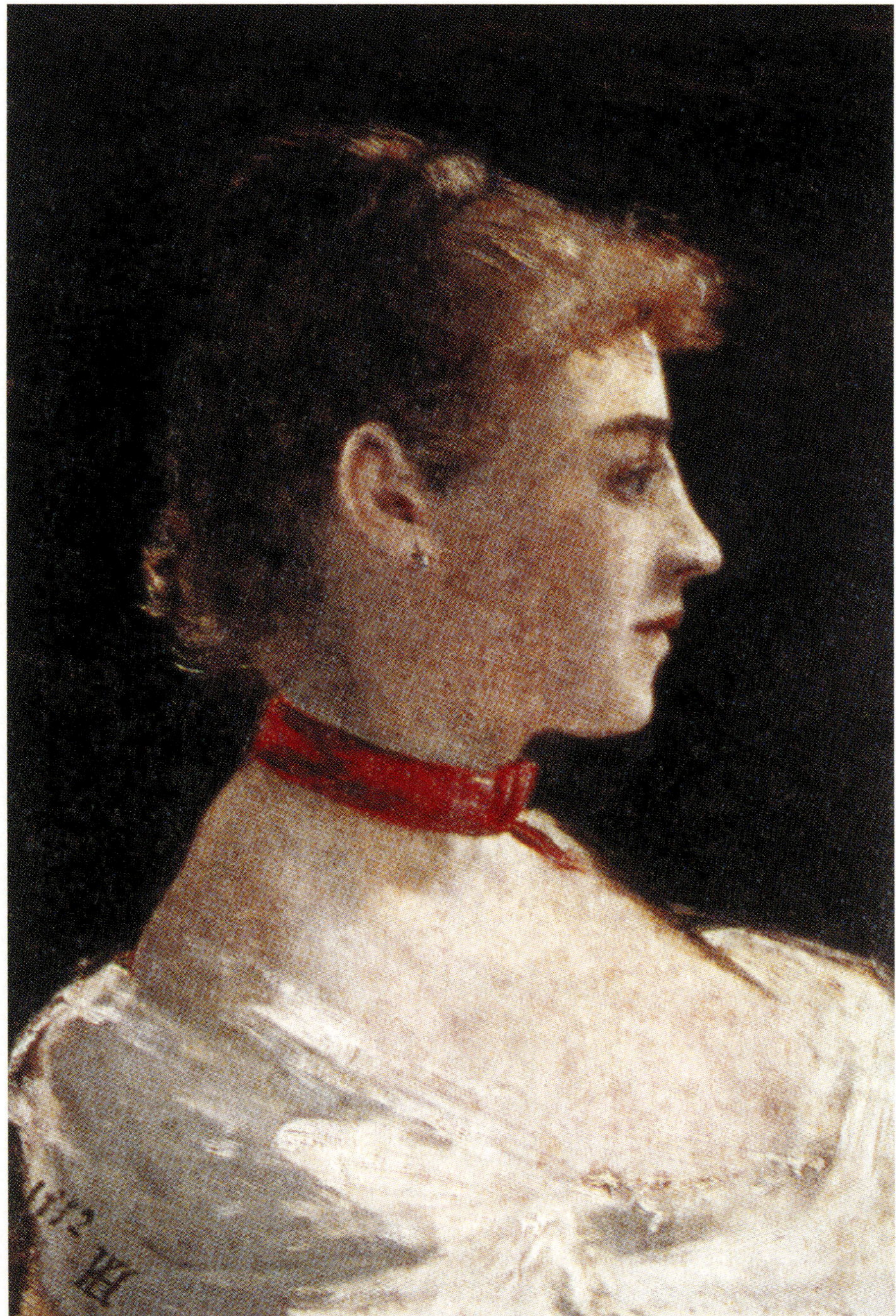

**PLATE 4.** Yamamoto Hōsui, *Portrait of a European Lady*, 1882. Oil on canvas. Tokyo University of Fine Arts and Music.

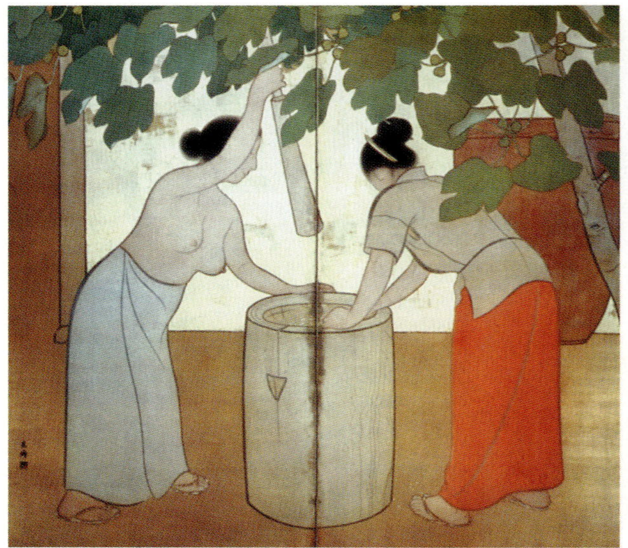

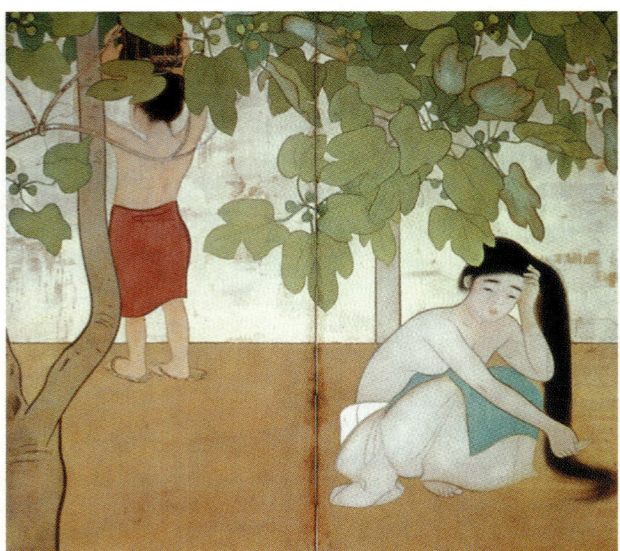

**PLATE 5.** Tsuchida Bakusen, *Island Women*, 1912. Pair of two-fold screens, 166.2 × 185 cm each, color on silk. Collection of The National Museum of Modern Art, Tokyo.

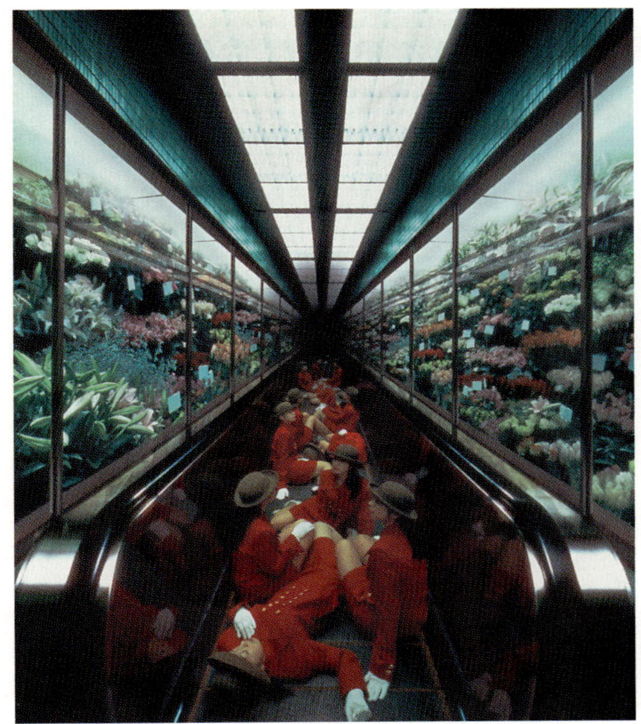

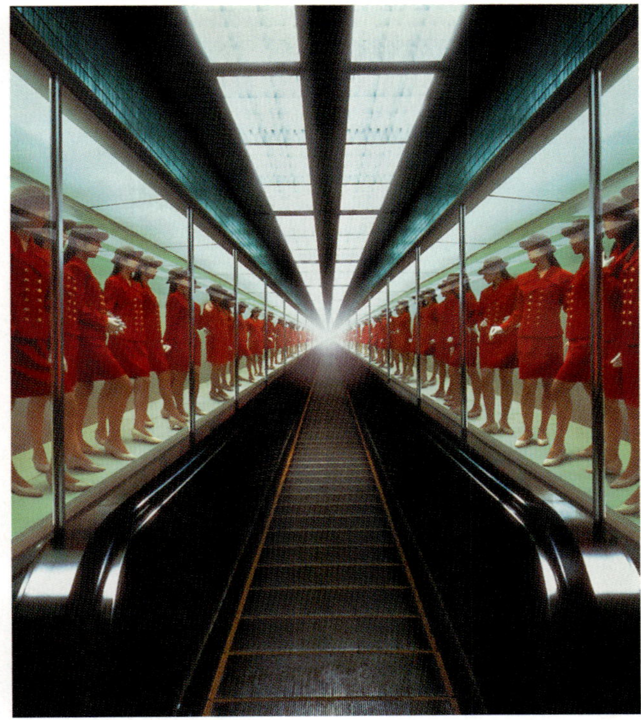

**PLATE 6.** Yanagi Miwa, *Annaijō no heya 1F (Elevator Girl House 1F)*, 1997. 240 × 220 cm, Directprint.

**PLATE 7.** Shirō Masamune, cover art for *Kōkaku kidōtai* (Ghost in the shell), vol. 1 (Tokyo: Kōdansha, 1991).

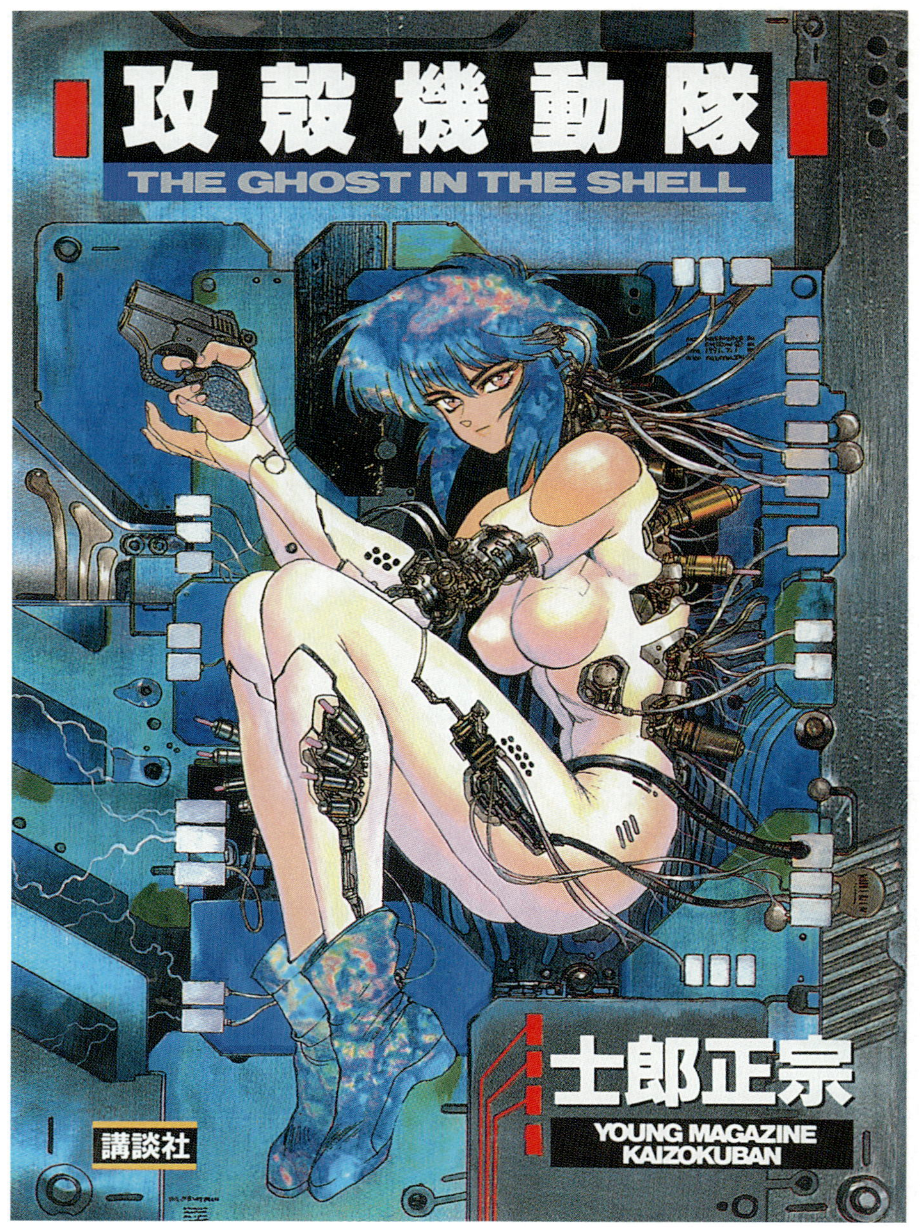

CHAPTER ELEVEN

SHARALYN ORBAUGH

# Busty Battlin' Babes: The Evolution of the *Shōjo* in 1990s Visual Culture

Every day millions of men and boys around the world suit up for battle. Each laces up heavy rubber-soled leather boots, then straps on his gunbelt, a backpack with water and extra ammunition, and a pair of enormous . . . breasts. Then he enters the Tomb Raider™ videogame world in the persona of Lara Croft, the "female Indiana Jones," one of the most popular game characters ever created.[1] As Lara these male gamers seek treasure, battling rival treasure hunters, robots, wild animals, corrupt governments, mummies, and anyone else who gets in the way of a successful mission. They run, climb, jump, swim, roll, shoot, and use both courage and technological savvy to capture the treasure.

According to the official statistics Lara Croft is 5 feet 9 inches tall, weighs 130 pounds, and has measurements of 34D-24-35 (although women commentators have estimated her actual measurements at 36DD-17-34). She wears shorts rolled up to her crotch and tight-fitting shirts or a fitted bomber jacket, emphasizing her long legs, tiny waist, and large bust. Her favorite sports are rock climbing, extreme skiing, and marksmanship (Figure 11.1).[2]

Lara Croft is a prime example of a new breed of fictional character in global visual culture, one whose hybrid attributes—part Barbie doll, part GI Joe—make it possible for male heterosexual viewers to identify with her (without, evidently, experiencing the shame that normally accompanies male identification with female characters) and consume her as a sexualized visual object at the same time.[3] Female gamers may experience this same doubled pleasure of identification and desire when they enter the Tomb Raider universe, but there is far less evidence regarding female opinions about the game.[4]

This chapter will examine gendered identification with fictional characters in one segment of the visual landscape of 1990s popular culture. As in the example of Lara Croft, the cases I examine demonstrate a sort of "hybrid" visual econ-

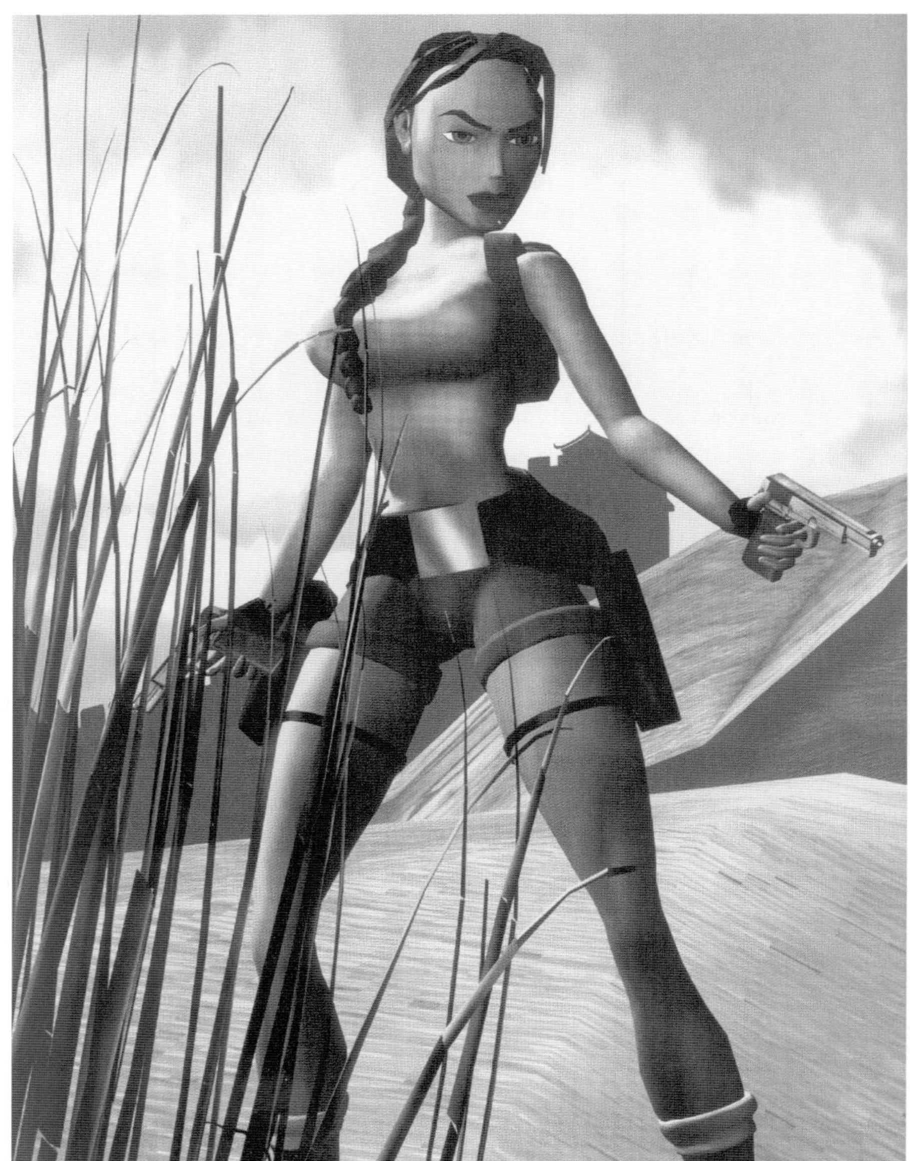

**FIGURE 11.1.** "Lara Croft." From Douglas Copeland and Kip Ward, *Lara's Book: Lara Croft and the Tomb Raider™ Phenomenon* (Rocklin, Calif.: Prima Publishing, 1998), 116.

omy where gender is concerned. In addition, there are other elements of hybridity endemic to the popular culture products I will address.

First, like videogames, the products I examine—primarily *anime* (Japanese animation) and *manga* (narrative comics)—combine the visual and the textual in equal proportions. They are generically hybrid. Moreover, these already hybrid forms are producing increasing numbers of crossovers, such as computer games based on a popular *anime* character (and vice versa) or a comic book serialization of the adventures of a videogame character.[5]

Second, I make little distinction in my discussion of contemporary popular culture between examples or audiences of North American or Japanese origin. This is because it is virtually impossible to disentangle the culturally "pure" or "authentic" elements in pop culture products of the 1990s; those products circulated and continue to circulate widely across national, cultural, and linguistic boundaries.[6] They are culturally hybrid. (For the purposes of this study, however, I will focus primarily on examples from Japan as I sketch the genealogy of one aspect of gendered identification with fictional characters from the 1920s to the present.)

And finally, I am going to argue that the construction or conceptualization of the intended audience for a particular stream of 1990s pop culture is also hybrid in a way: many of the most popular *manga, anime,* and videogames appropriate visual and narrative elements previously identified exclusively with products for girls or products for boys, and combine them to produce a new intended audience.[7] One of the most striking aspects of this hybridity, however, is the fact that it is boys (*shōnen* in Japanese) who are imaginatively entering bodies or universes marked as "for girls" *(shōjo),* rather than the reverse.[8] I will begin, therefore, with a discussion of the significance of this influential cultural image: the *shōjo.*

In 1988, Horikiri Naoto wrote:

> I wonder if we men shouldn't now think of ourselves as "shōjo," given our compulsory and excessive consumerism, a consumerism that in recent years afflicts us like sleepwalking. We are no longer the shabby and middle-aged teacher Humbert Humbert who chased Lolita's rear-end in his dreams. We all have become the forever-young Lolita herself. We are driven night and day to be relentless consumers. . . . The "shōjo," that new human species born of modern commodification, has today commodified everything and everyone.[9]

In 1990 Yamane Kazuma, too, linked the idea of the "girl" with the state of the Japanese national character: "What can we conclude about this complete infantilization of Japan? The answer is straightforward. The girl has jumped up. The girl is boisterous."[10]

In 1991 anthropologist and cultural critic Ōtsuka Eiji wrote:

> The Japanese are no longer producers. Our existence consists solely of the distribution and consumption of "things" brought from elsewhere, "things" with which we play. Nor are these "things" actually tangible, but are instead only signs without any direct utility in life. None of what we typically purchase would, were we deprived of it, be a matter of life or death. These "things" are continually converted into signs without substance, signs such as information, stocks or land. What name are we to give to this life of ours today?
>
> The name is "shōjo."[11]

In the view of these influential male critics, the word *"shōjo"* in the 1980s signified a state of passivity, consumerism, commodification, narcissism, consumption without production, moral and ethical emptiness, and self-referentiality. To the extent that the Japanese national character had in the 1970s and particularly the 1980s taken on this *"shōjo"* nature, it could be described as selfish, irresponsible, weak, and infantile, in the view of these critics.[12]

Others have defined 1980s *shōjo* culture more ambiguously as it functions as a model of the Japanese nation: that is, their attitudes toward the *shōjo* image are more ambiguous, and they also highlight the ambiguity or obscurity of that image. Seo Fumiaki characterized the *shōjo* image as "uncertain, mercurial, elastic" and emphasized, again, its emptiness.[13] Matsui Midori remarks on the "ambiguous subjectivity" of the *shōjo* and the ornamentality, passivity, and whimsicality that is said to characterize her.[14]

The words that appear most often in the titles of the essays in the 1988 collection *Shōjo ron* (Studies of the *shōjo*) as well as the titles of many other books on *shōjo* from this period are revealing of this ambivalent summation: words such as *"meikyū"* (mystery or labyrinth), *"fuyū suru"* (to float or wander), *"musō suru"* (to dream), *"kagami"* (mirror), and "Narushissa" (Narcissus). The plaintive question featured in the title of a book by Fujimoto Yukari seems to sum up this floating, dreaming, wandering state: *Watakushi no idokoro wa doko ni aru no*? (Where is the place for me?) The overall picture of *shōjo*-ness that emerges from such views is of a slightly confused, dreamy, yet seductive vulnerability—that doe-eyed, "please don't hurt me" look that singer Matsuda Seiko used to do so well.

The sexualized aspect of this version of the *shōjo* is repeated in the cover art of *Shōjo ron*: on the front a black-and-white photograph of a naked young girl, perhaps twelve years old, standing sideways with her head turned to look at the camera, budding breasts fully visible; on the back the photograph of an even younger

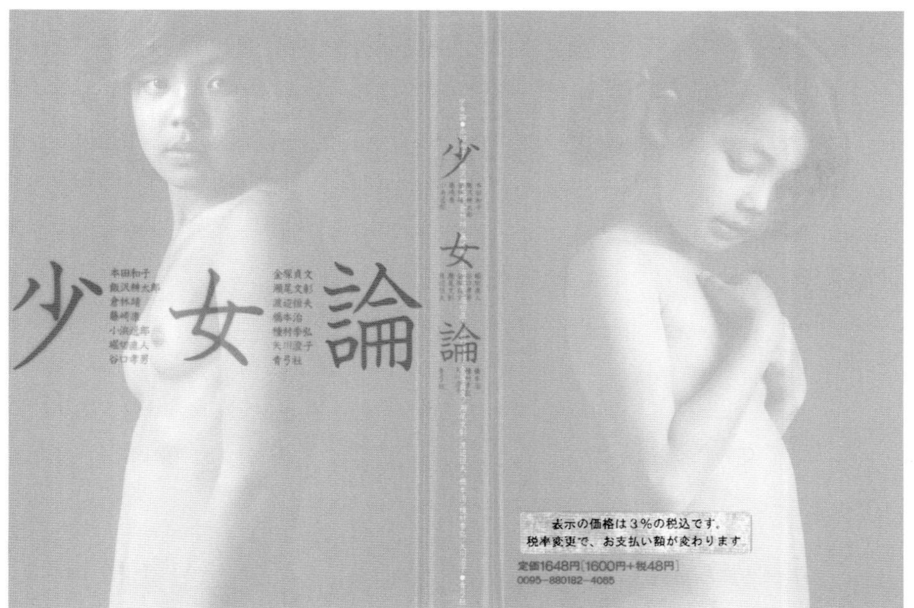


FIGURE 11.2. Front and back cover, Honda Masuko et al., eds., *Shōjo ron* (Tokyo: Aoyumisha, 1988). Photo by Suzuki Sadahiro; design by Suzuki Takashi.

female child, hair in pigtails, coyly covering her flat chest (Figure 11.2). The semitransparent paper cover renders the photographs misty but visible—an effect all too reminiscent of Vaseline on a pornographic camera lens. The eroticized prepubescent girl appears between the covers as well, in essays on the *"shōjo"* paintings of Balthus and Lewis Carroll's photographs of little girls.

Still others have envisioned the *shōjo* more positively as representing the "freest, most unhampered elements of society."[15] Female commentator Honda Masuko's definition of the *shōjo* suggests that it is "neither adult woman nor girl child, neither man nor woman."[16] John Treat for one agrees, arguing that "shōjo constitute their own gender, neither male nor female but rather something importantly detached from the productive economy of heterosexual reproduction."[17] He and others suggest that the nonproductive space represented by *shōjo*-ness might be regarded as a potential site of resistance to the insular nuclear family and to industrial capitalism. In this view the *shōjo* is framed as liminal, outside both the productive and reproductive economies of the adult world, ungendered and innocent but with sexual potential. (Jennifer Robertson has provocatively characterized *shōjo* sexuality as one of "homosexual experience and heterosexual inexperience.")[18] If Japan as a nation is described as inhabiting a *shōjo*-like space according to this view of *shōjo*-ness, then it would be most accurate to call that space/state liminal, transformative, liberatory, and potentially resistant.

In other words, by the early 1990s the discourse of the *shōjo* as sign of the nation was both rich and highly contradictory. Rather than adjudicating among these rival interpretations, I want to emphasize that the cultural critics cited above are all using the image of the *shōjo* to reflect on Japan as a nation and its relationship to (post-) modernity in a global context. They are taking unto themselves the image of the *shōjo,* identifying with her, in order (variously) to criticize or celebrate contemporary Japanese society. Like Horikiri, who likened himself to Lolita rather than the gender-appropriate Humbert Humbert, these critics are practicing what I call "cognitive transvestism"—a cross-gender identification or disguise for the purpose of exemplifying or thinking through a social conundrum.

This is hardly the first time that the culturally defined image of a type of woman or girl was organized and used as a screen for the projection of (largely male) social theories, anxieties, and hopes. While men or boys are occasionally also turned into a particular social image—type-cast in a role that sums up social anxieties—for whatever reason such a role is usually played by images of (young) women.[19] One factor is that many of these roles or type-castings incorporate implications and fears about female adolescent sexuality: flappers and teeny boppers have made their appearance at crucial moments of North American history; and in Japan *moga*, *burikko*, and *kogyaru* (among others) have been identified and used as vehicles for debating social problems in different eras. In high-culture artistic production "the girl" has often functioned as a telegraphic image site for society's or the (male) artist's struggle with important issues of modernity.[20] In the 1980s and 1990s in Japan, the image of the *shōjo* played this role, so in the remainder of this chapter I will examine the image of the *shōjo* as it is marketed to different demographic sectors or taken up by different sectors for their own purposes.

Starting in the Taishō period (1912–1925) and continuing up to the present, the image of "*shōjo*-ness" was marketed to girls themselves in Japan—first in *shōjo zasshi* (girls' magazines), later in *shōjo manga* (girls' comic books), and, even later, in *anime* (many of which had direct connections with *manga*). In marketing *shōjo*-ness to girls, encouraging girls to consume images of themselves as commodities, *shōjo* writers necessarily stressed the positive aspects of girldom: fluid boundaries, transformativity, intimacy, and a "narcissistic" appreciation of the female self.

The writer Yoshiya Nobuko (1896–1973) was the earliest and most famous writer of *shōjo* fiction. She herself was a publicly declared lesbian, and the *shōjo* aesthetic she created emphasized relationships among young women, which were explicitly homosocial and implicitly homosexual. Her first publication, *Hana monogatari* (Flower tales), was a series of short works published in one of the earliest *shōjo zasshi, Shōjo gahō* (Girls' illustrated), between 1917 and 1924.[21] In each of these stories the protagonist was likened to a flower and described in romantic, aesthetically beautiful terms. Although critics have characterized her depictions of female characters as "narcissistic," in fact most were based on a narrative economy of desire and romantic/erotic appreciation. These depictions set the tone for later images of the *shōjo* in *manga* and *anime* explicitly marketed to young girls. (One can also see influences of these early depictions in the 1980s critics' remarks about narcissism and self-absorption.)

During the same period, when "adolescence" as a specific stage in human development was first recognized and exploited, there were many new magazines featuring fiction and essays meant to appeal to boys and young men as well *(shōnen* and *seinen zasshi).*[22] However, unlike girls, boys and young men were expected to be preparing for their eventual leadership roles in society. The narratives in *shōnen manga* therefore featured heroism, practicality, and adventure rather than the dreamy, nonteleological narratives of *shōjo* fiction. In addition, journals for young males, like comics later on, were divided into those for *shōnen* (boys) and those for *seinen* (young men), suggesting a staged developmental path of increasing maturity and social significance: boyhood, young manhood, and finally manhood.[23] Such a path does not exist for females, who are *shōjo* until they "enter society" by marrying and starting a family.[24]

Beginning in the postwar period, comic books featuring serial narratives, which had been introduced in the 1930s, became increasingly popular and increasingly demographically segmented. The image of the *shōjo* marketed to girls took on some new characteristics in this era following the postwar enfranchisement of women. In the 1950s, Tezuka Osamu, Japan's most famous animator, produced a serial comic book narrative titled *Ribon no kishi* (literally, "Ribbon Knight," usually translated as "Princess Knight"), featuring a protagonist who has the body of a female but the "heart" of both a boy and a girl.[25] (It may be no coincidence that Tezuka's hometown is Takarazuka, home of the famous theater troupe in which all the parts are played by women so that some actors are women who specialize in cross-dressing to play male characters.)[26] Sapphire is the only child of a royal family; in the absence of a male heir, she is raised as a boy, learning to fight and defend her kingdom. But Sapphire has many feminine characteristics, too, and in the end learns to accept her feminine gender in a heterosexual romance. The extreme popularity of *Ribbon Knight* suggests that girls appreciated the expansion of narrative possibility—sword fighting and adventure—while still remaining safely within a normatively gendered universe (Figure 11.3).

In the 1960s a new aspect was added to the *shōjo* image in several *manga* based on the Japanese women's Olympic volleyball team, which won the gold medal in the 1964 Tokyo Olympics. In *Attack Number One* and *Sain wa V* (The sign is V[ictory]), the various protagonists had to struggle to overcome personal and physical limitations to achieve success on the volleyball court (Figure 11.4). Self-discipline, female psychological strength, and the satisfaction of teamwork were

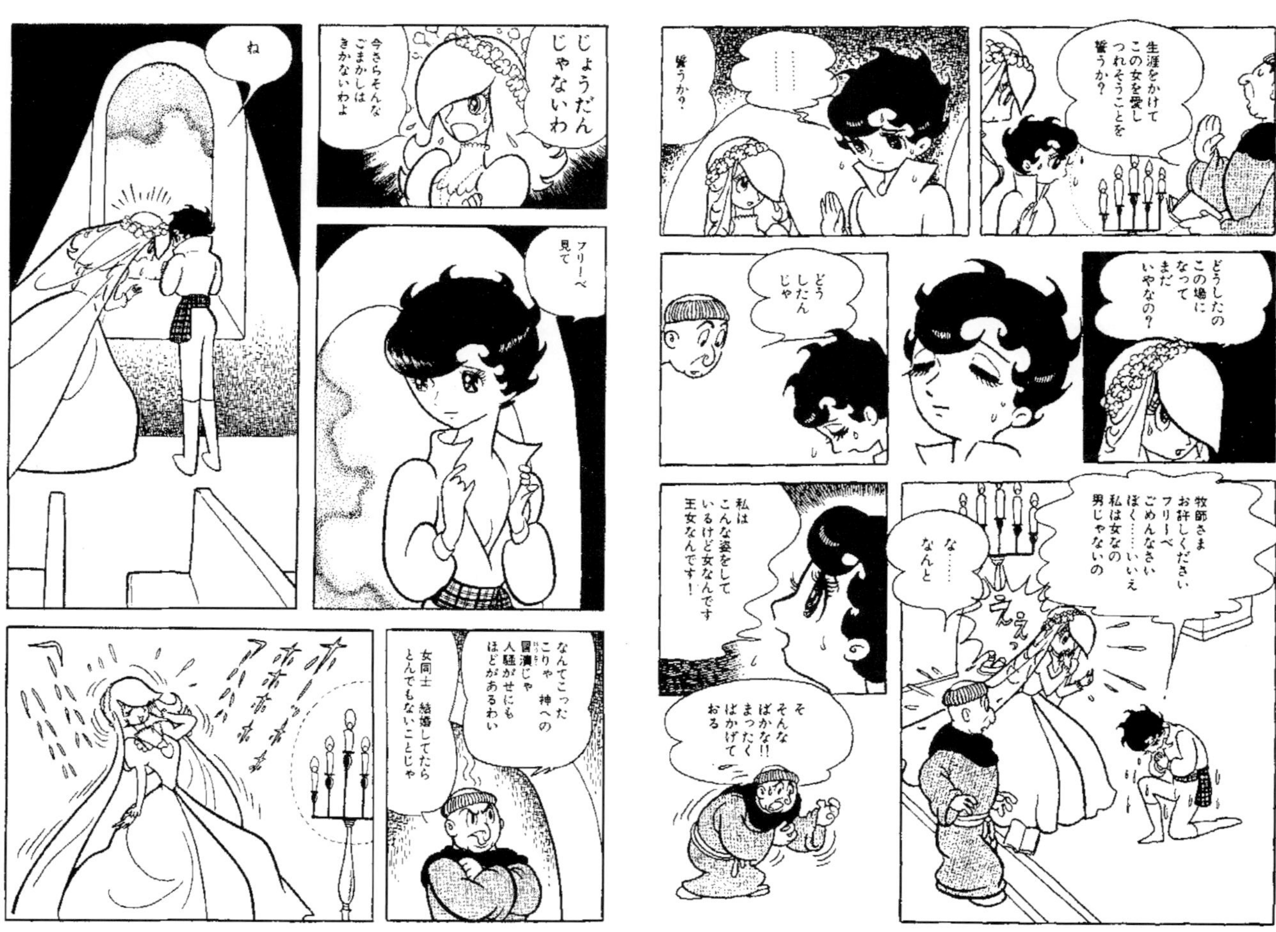


**FIGURE 11.3.** Tezuka Osamu, *Ribon no kishi* (Ribbon Knight). From *Tezuka Osamu manga zenshū,* vol. 6 (Tokyo: Kōdansha, 1977), 222–223. © Tezuka Productions.

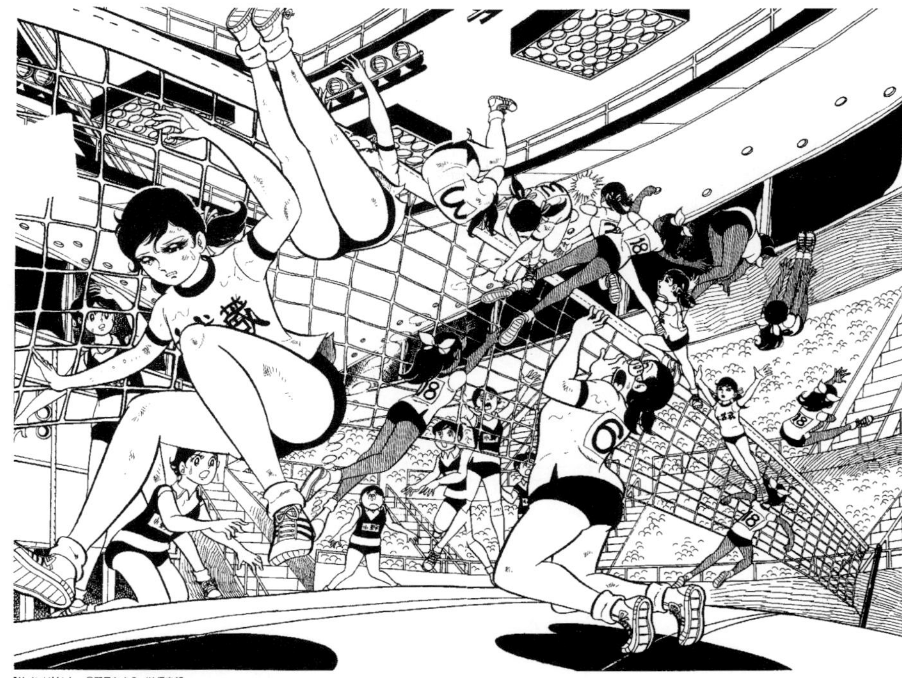



**FIGURE 11.4.** Mochizuki Akira and Jinbo Shirō, *Sain wa V* (The sign is V). From Yaguchi Kunio et al., eds., *Manga no jidai / The Manga Age* (Tokyo: Museum of Contemporary Art and Hiroshima: Hiroshima City Museum of Contemporary Art, 1998), 96–97.

features emphasized in these narratives, written by men for *shōjo manga.* In the "economic high-growth period" of the 1960s, these attributes were useful in indoctrinating women to a future of supporting the hardworking husband and taking care of the education of the children in the isolation of the nuclear family. Women were part of the national economic team as they took care of the home so completely that men were freed to devote themselves solely to work. These narratives and the others like them carried forward the image of the *shōjo* as strong and capable but kept the image firmly locked within the structures of capitalist heteronormativity.

It was in the 1970s that *shōjo manga* came into their own, as women artists began drawing comic book narratives with increasing frequency. The most famous text to emerge from this golden age of *shōjo manga* is *Berusaiyu no bara* (The rose of Versailles), by Ikeda Riyoko. *Berubara,* as it is affectionately known, began in 1972, was a long-running series in *Shūkan Margaretto* (Weekly Margaret), a *shōjo* comic journal, and was eventually published in book form in five volumes.[27] In addition, it was turned into a very popular play by the all-female Takarazuka drama troupe as well as a TV live-action feature and animated series. *The Rose of*

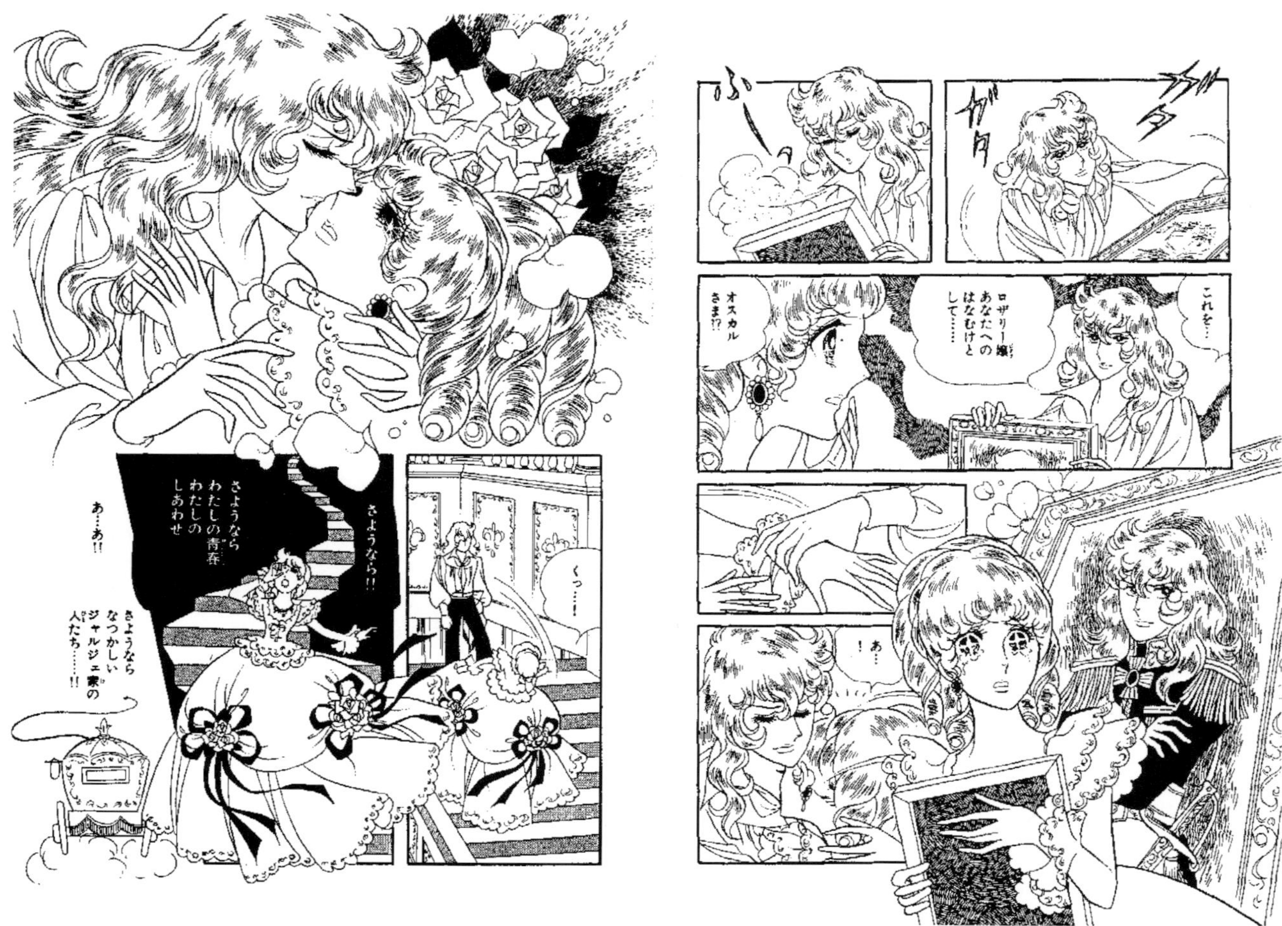


FIGURE 11.5. Ikeda Riyoko, *Berusaiyu no bara* (The rose of Versailles). Vol. 2, 272–273. Tokyo: Shū'eisha, 1994.

*Versailles* was extremely influential because of both its narrative elements and its visual style: it defined what most people envision when they think of *shōjo manga*.

The protagonist, Oscar, like *Ribbon Knight*'s Sapphire, is a girl raised as a boy. In Oscar's case she must be male in order to take on the hereditary position of guard in the royal household in the court of Marie Antoinette. Unlike the heteronormative universe of *Ribbon Knight*, however, the sex/gender arrangements in *The Rose of Versailles* are more complicated, both visually and in terms of plot. All the principal characters in *The Rose* are tall, svelte, and swooningly beautiful, whether male or female. All have long, flowing hair, although the women characters coded as more traditionally feminine usually have their hair carefully coiffed, while the men characters (including Oscar) generally wear theirs loose. All the characters wear elaborate and beautiful costumes; the *manga* pictures delight in

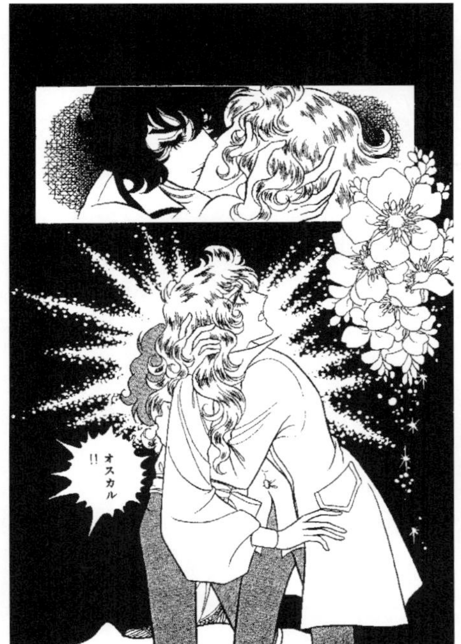


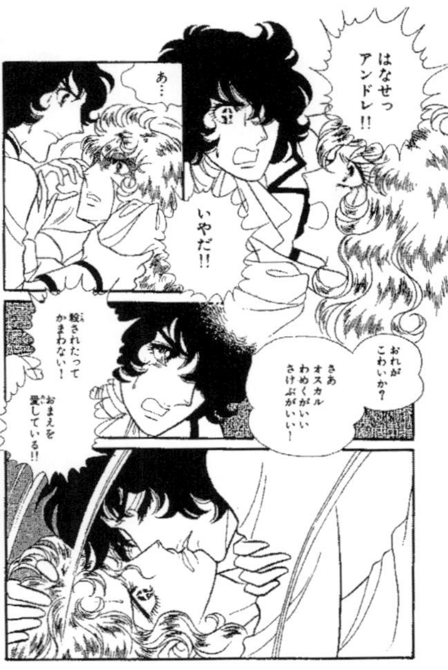


**FIGURE 11.6.** Ikeda Riyoko, *Berusaiyu no bara:* Oscar's romantic life. Vol. 3, 98–99.

depicting the rich details (Figure 11.5). As compared with the visual tone of *Ribbon Knight,* which emphasizes the cute and playful (see Figure 11.3), *The Rose* is gorgeous and adult.

Oscar's dominant sexual and romantic orientation follows the heteronormative expectations associated with his/her biological sex (female) rather than his/her gender (masculine). The final love of his/her life is André, a man. Oscar even "cross-dresses" as a woman at one point to dance with the intriguing Count von Feltzen, lover of Marie Antoinette but object of Oscar's desire as well. Except for this one instance, however, Oscar is never depicted in female attire, and because he/she is as tall and powerful as any of the male characters, it is often unclear whether his/her romantic counterparts are aware that they are in love with a woman; they seem to be desiring Oscar the man. Many female visitors to the court are similarly deceived and fall in love with Oscar, believing him/her to be a man. Before Oscar finally consummates his/her long-term romantic affair with André in volume 5, André goes blind, enhancing the suggestion that at least in visual terms he never confronts the fact that Oscar is a woman (Figure 11.6).

The gender bending (or, more accurately, gender blending) aspects of *The Rose of Versailles* obviously hit an important nerve for its female readers, because this became a virtually omnipresent feature of one important stream of subsequent *shōjo manga* produced by women.[28] Takemiya Keiko's *Kaze to ki no uta* (The song of the wind and the tree) in 1976 featured homosexual relationships, both romantic and sexual, among boys in a European boarding school. With other female *manga* artists of her generation, Takemiya launched a boom in male homoerotic stories aimed specifically at girl readers, featuring protagonists who, while clearly male, are depicted in gorgeous, semi-androgynous visual terms. This boom continues today in the so-called *yaoi* genre of comics.[29] It is possible to get a small sense of the scope of this continuing trend by considering that the Tokyo Comic Market, the largest outlet for amateur and independent professional comics in Japan, had 420,000 *manga* artists selling their work in 1997, and 60 to 70 percent of that work was in the *yaoi* genre.[30]

While this is not the place for a complex examination of the *yaoi* phenomenon, there are a few aspects of this phenomenon I would like to emphasize. First, girl readers of *shōjo* comics in the 1970s and thereafter were invited to identify with characters whose gender and/or sexuality was not that of a straightforwardly heterosexual (or female homosexual) girl. Often they were identifying with characters who were Other to them in terms of sex (male), gender (masculine), national or cultural origin (European), and sexuality (male homosexual). The earlier *shōjo* elements of romance and visual beauty were maintained but in a narrative context very far from the "everyday life" Japanese girls would be assumed to inhabit.

And, second, one reason women *manga* artists may have turned to the depiction of boys is because the franker depictions of the body and sexuality called for in the 1970s produced a problem for artists writing women characters: for women, active sexuality has physical consequences, such as pregnancy. Focusing on young males allowed artists to explore romantic and sexual relationships without having to engage the realities of Japanese female experience, such as the fact that women cease being *shōjo* when they have "entered society" by becoming pregnant.[31] *Manga* author/artist Takemiya Keiko—whose *The Song of the Wind and the Tree* inaugurated the *yaoi* boom—has a more practical explanation. Censorship of *manga* became prevalent in the mid-1970s, in reaction to the increasingly violent and sexually explicit male-authored *manga* that had captured an adult reading audience since the late 1960s. There was a loophole, however: since Japanese obscenity laws recognized only the penis and the vagina as sexual organs, only heterosexual sex was liable to censorship. Fairly graphic depictions of naked boys frolicking with each other were permitted. In order, therefore, to create a fantasy space for the female reader that could include serious sexuality, the action was transposed onto the bodies of semi-androgynous male characters.[32]

Not all *shōjo manga* in the 1970s and thereafter have been in the *yaoi* genre. There have as well been many popular works that depict heterosexual romance taking place in a Japanese setting. But whatever the genre, "classic" *shōjo manga* tended to share a set of conceptual and visual characteristics thought to reflect the nature of the *shōjo* herself: the "fluid boundaries" of female subjectivity were mirrored by the breaking of the hard-edged *manga* frame and a tolerance for—or, rather, encouragement of—narrative flow all over the page (see, for example, Figure 11.5). The frequent use of montage added a temporal element to this spatial notion of fluidity (see Figure 11.4). The ambiguity and transformativity associated with girldom was made manifest in *manga* plots involving magical girls, girls who crossed sex/gender boundaries, or plots in which girl readers were expected to identify with protagonists who were radically Other.[33] A special kind of *shōjo* intimacy was expressed through narratorial comments directed extradiegetically to the reader and later through the visual code of the *hentai shōjo moji*, or "deviant girls' script," used in lettering *manga,* as well as the ubiquitous stars and flowers in the margins of the frame (see Figures 11.5 and 11.6 for examples).[34] Narcissistic enjoyment of self as image could be seen in frequent "pin-up" style poses assumed by both male and female characters (Figure 11.7). Finally, the emphasis on beauty over realism was demonstrated in the way the characters were depicted: all of them, male or female, are beautiful and all in the same style, with slim figures, large, expressive eyes, small mouths, and fine-grained, "feminine" features (Figure 11.8).

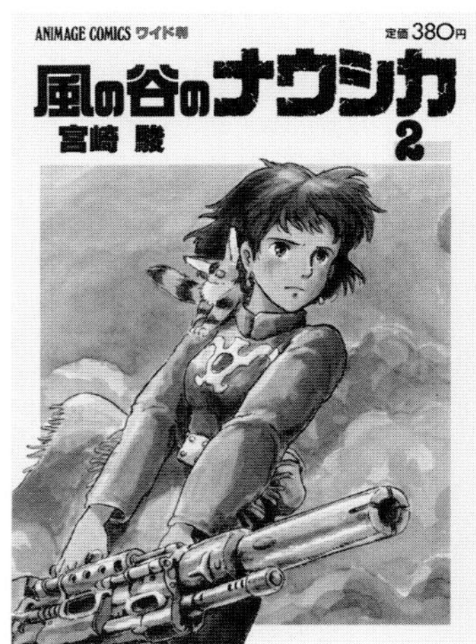


**FIGURE 11.7.** Miyazaki Hayao, cover art for *Kaze no Tani no Naushika* (Nausicaa of the Valley of the Wind), vol. 2. Tokyo: Tokuma Shoten, 2000.

In contrast, *shōnen manga* from the same period generally tended to feature more hard-edged and inflexible framing, no gender-bending story lines, strong visual sexual dimorphism, no special attempts to establish intimacy, and no pin-ups (Figure 11.9). *Shōnen manga* tended to feature male protagonists (often exclusively) and were driven by plot. The occasional appearance of a female character was often for the sake of humor (at her expense), voyeuristic titillation, or to provide sexual/competitive tension between male characters. (One significant exception is found in the genre of live-action or animated television series known as *"sentai-mono"* (group fighting shows), popular from the 1970s and later. Such shows featured a team of (usually) five warriors, who combined their individual skills and machinery to fight evil. Each color-coded group invariably included one female member, dressed in either red or pink, whose powers, while usually coded as "feminine," were nonetheless crucial to the team's success.)[35]

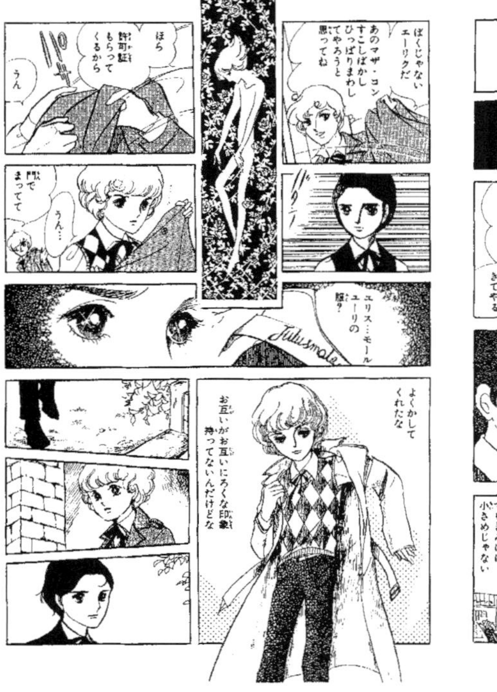

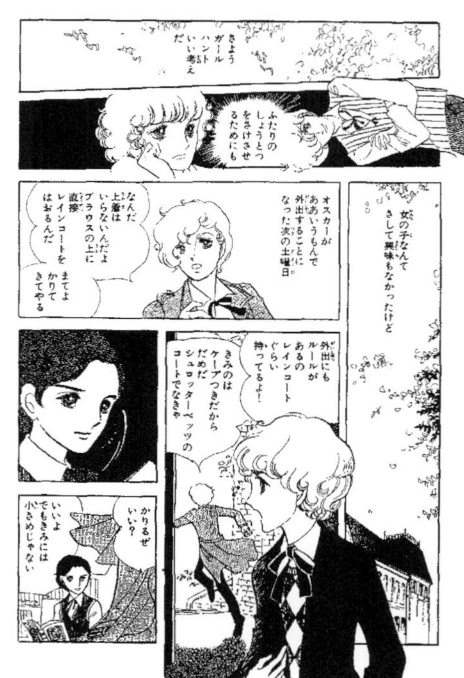


FIGURE 11.8. Hagio Moto, *Tōma no shinzō* (The heart of Thomas), 148–149. Tokyo: Shōgakukan, 1995.

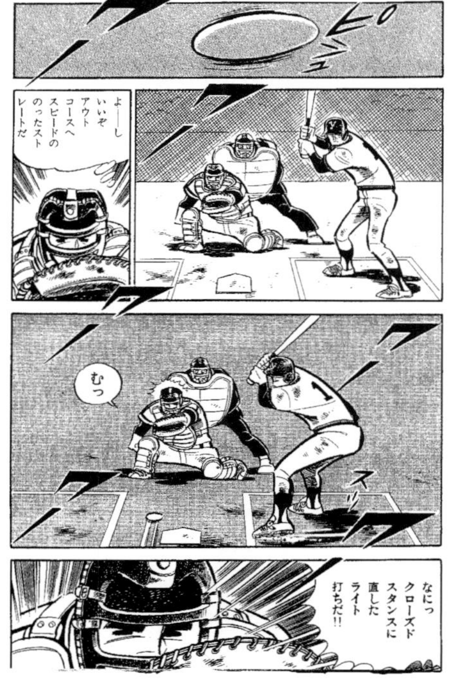

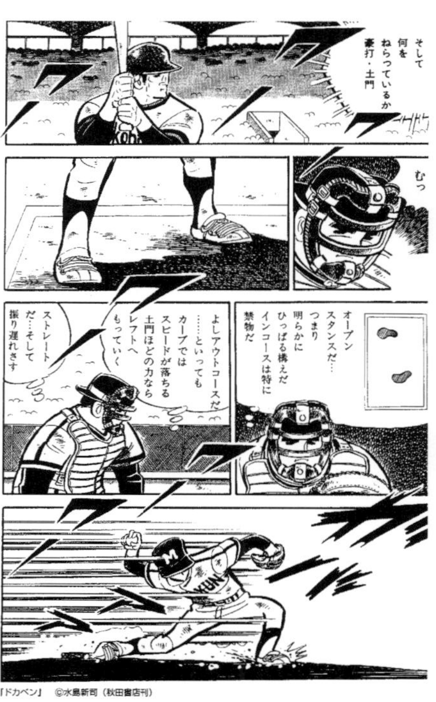


FIGURE 11.9. Mizushima Shinji, *Dokaben*. From Yaguchi Kunio et al., eds., *Manga no Jidai / The Manga Age* (Tokyo: Museum of Contemporary Art and Hiroshima: Hiroshima City Museum of Contemporary Art, 1998), 150–151.

One element shared by *shōnen* and *shōjo manga,* however, was transformativity. From the 1950s through the 1980s, *shōnen manga* featured narratives of combat using robots that could fight separately or combine to form new huge robot weapons; high-tech body armor that allowed the otherwise normal hero to transform into a *"mecha"* (literally, "mechanical") warrior; as well as other kinds of "scientific" paraphernalia of enhancement, entailing a lot of physical violence against human, alien, or demonic enemies. (It is a noteworthy difference, however, that stories for girls featured transformations that originated internally and were ontological in nature; stories for boys featured transformations that were external, mechanical, and emphatically temporary.)

Besides these *"mecha"* narratives, martial arts and sports were popular genres for boys. In narrative terms sexual explicitness was not a problem in stories for boys, since they could depict male sexuality without necessarily having to engage the social consequences. (So long as the visual depiction of direct penis-vagina contact was avoided, they were also not liable to censorship.) Nonetheless, the sex in *shōnen manga* tended toward the raunchy and silly as opposed to the complex sexual narratives of *yaoi* comics.

An argument can be made that, as early as the late 1980s, some of the features that had formerly distinguished *manga* for girls from *manga* for boys began to be used together, to form a hybrid genre, appealing to readers of both sexes/genders. Dvorak has traced this trend up through early- to mid-1990s products such as *Sailor Moon,* which combined the female protagonist, slim-cute body style, interest in romance, and transformativity characteristic of *shōjo* comics with the plot-driven combat stories of *shōnen* narratives.[36] This *shōjo-shōnen* hybridity is even carried through in the form of transformativity featured in *Sailor Moon*: the sailors transform by donning special fighting outfits (as in *shōnen mecha* stories) but do so through some seemingly innate mystical power (as in *shōjo manga*). In addition, *Sailor Moon* retains elements that parallel the voyeuristic and eroticized gaze of many male comics, since there are frequent if brief panty shots as well as the brief and underplayed nudity of the transformation sequences. (These have been toned down or eliminated in the versions of these shows distributed for North American television.) However, these same scenes could be interpreted as echoing the "narcissistic" pleasure of consuming the female image characteristic of earlier *shōjo manga.*[37]

I would argue that the process of hybridity or amalgamation continued and even intensified in the 1990s, but it also changed somewhat from the first examples in the late 1980s. The late 1990s culmination of this trend has brought a range of cultural products that feature female protagonists in narratives that include male-associated elements such as battle, adventure, and high technology. It is clear that many of these narrative products are consumed by both males and females (if not always equally); some continue to debut in venues associated with one gender or the other but then move on to more generalized venues, such as a serial narrative that originally appeared in a *shōjo manga* journal being transformed into an *anime* movie for a general audience.[38] It is also notable that these narratives are not divided by the gender of the artist/writer: both men and women *manga* and *anime* artists have produced stories featuring the "battlin' babes" of my title.[39]

I am thinking here of *manga/anime* such as *Nausicaa* (*manga* artist and *anime* movie director: Miyazaki Hayao) and *The Princess Mononoke* (*anime* movie director: Miyazaki Hayao), the most recent update of *Cutey Honey* (*manga* artist: Nagai Gō; *anime* director: Nagaoka Yasuchika), *Ranma ½* (*manga* artist: Takahashi Rumiko; TV *anime* directors: Sawai Kōji and Toda Hiroshi), *Urusei Yatsura* (*manga* artist: Takahashi Rumiko; *anime* directors: Oshii Mamoru et al.), *Ghost in the Shell* (*manga* artist: Shirō Masamune; *anime* movie director: Oshii Mamoru), *Appleseed* (*manga* artist: Shirō Masamune; *anime* director: Katayama Kazuyoshi), *Sukeban deka* (*manga* artist: Wada Shinji; TV *anime* director: Hirota Takeshi), *Blue Seed* (*manga* artist: Takada Yūzō; *anime* directors: Kamiya Jun et al.), *Cat Girl Nuku Nuku* (*manga* artist: Takada Yūzō; *anime* directors: Moriyama Yūji and Shigematsu Hidetoshi), *Bubblegum Crisis* (*manga* artist: Suzuki Toshimichi; *anime* directors: Akiyama Katsuhito and Hayashi Hiroki), *Bubblegum Crash* (*manga* artist: Suzuki Toshimichi; *anime* directors: Fukushima Hiroyuki and Ishiodori Hiroshi), *Burn Up* (*anime* director: Ide Yasunori), *Burn Up W* (*anime* director: Negichi Hiroshi), *Battle Angel/GUNNM* (*manga* artist: Kishiro Yukito; OAV *anime* director: Fukutomi Hiroshi), *Gunbuster* (*anime* director: Anno Hideki), *Genocyber* (*anime* director: Ohata Kōichi), *Dirty Pair* (*manga* artist: Takachiho Haruka; *anime* directors: Yatabe Katsuyoshi et al.), *Demon Hunter Yōko* (*manga* artist: Mutsuki Jūzō; *anime* director: Yamada Katsuhisa), *RG Veda* (*manga* artists: CLAMP; *anime* directors: Ebata Hiroyuki and Ikegami Takamasa), and the numerous others of this type. These *manga/anime* originated in variously gender-identified venues (*shōjo* or *shōnen manga* journals, for example) and, regardless of the gendered space of their first appearance, are eagerly consumed by both girls and boys (and men and women); were created by both men (such as Miyazaki and Shirō) and women (such as Takahashi and the members of CLAMP), and feature female protagonists in a range of sexualized depictions: from the explicitly objectified and eroticized pin-up style depiction of *Cutey Honey* (Figure 11.10), through the tough busty beauty of Shirō's protagonists (Plate 7) and the cute teenaged femininity of Cat Girl Nuku Nuku or *Ranma 1/2*'s Akane, to the slim and boyish androgyny of Miyazaki Hayao's female characters (see Figure 11.7).[40]

Which elements are appropriated from which gender stream in the production of this hybrid? *Shōjo*-identified elements such as female protagonists, attention to character development and romance, the breaking of visual frames, and transformations that are innate and/or ontological are combined with *shōnen*-identified elements such as action and violence, an emphasis on responsibility toward society, and a tendency toward the eroticized objectification of the female body.

In the beginning of the 1996 *anime* OAV *Burn Up W*, for example, two female SWAT team officers prepare to storm an office building that has been taken over by terrorists. The terrorists threaten violence unless one of the two women will bungee jump naked past their window. She does so, and the terrorists are virtually unmanned with amazement and lust, but at the next moment she bursts through the window and captures them—and it turns out that her apparent nakedness (to the eye of the audience as well as the terrorists) was in fact a flesh-colored bodysuit. In this brief example the female protagonist (*shōjo* element) is combined with action and social responsibility (*shōnen* element), combined with the visual exploitation of the protagonist's sexuality *(shōnen),* combined with a final emphasis on female transformativity and strength *(shōjo),* and, overall, a successful deployment of the masquerade (hybrid).

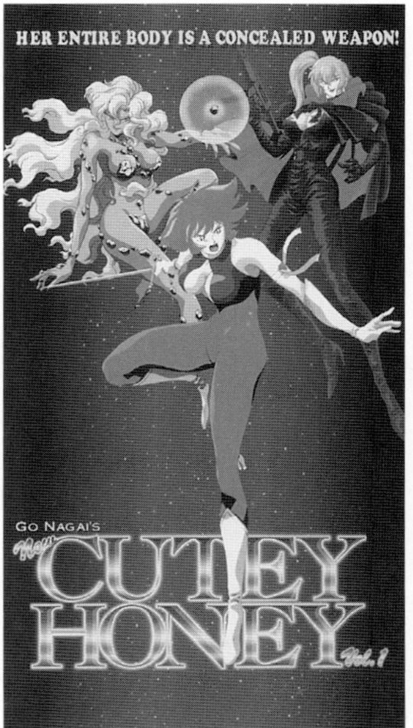


FIGURE 11.10. Nagai Go, *Cutey Honey*. Vol. 1, VHS cover (English edition). Copyright 1994 Go Nagai / Dynamic Planning, Inc. / Toei Video Co., Ltd.

In this hybrid form of narrative, therefore, images of the *shōjo* in many 1990s pop culture narratives absolutely repudiate many of the earlier negative associations—far from being framed as signs of irresponsibility, weakness, and passivity, these new *shōjo* are powerful and active as they lead the fight against the forces of evil.[41] (How much more socially responsible can you get?) They are rarely dreamy and indolent, nor are they figured as passive consumers. And yet, being (unmarried) females, these protagonists retain the *shōjo*-identified characteristics of liminality, relative freedom from socially prescribed roles, and an unmarked gender ("neither male nor female").

Let me return for a moment to the cognitive transvestism practiced by the male critics cited earlier who found that *shōjo* in the 1980s represented them and their national character in some way. These critics identified themselves with the *shōjo,* and young men in Japan today avidly consume and presumably identify with the female characters in these 1990s hybrid narratives. So if one assumes for the moment that the *"shōjo"* still represents the Japanese national character and the (male) Japanese subject, what sorts of cultural projections would these new *shōjo* be accommodating? What is it about the contemporary *shōjo* image that draws that identification, and why is this cognitive cross-dressing so much more positive an experience for young male consumers than for the earlier critics? What does this stream of *shōjo* images provide for the boys (and girls) who are meant to consume them?

These are enormous questions and can only be addressed partially here. I will focus on two aspects of the hybrid *shōjo* or battlin' babe: her variously sexualized depictions and her "true" nature as a cyborg or alien.

Carol Clover has written extensively on the cross-gender identification of boys who watch the slasher subgenre of horror films in the United States. (She focuses on the "classic" years of such films, in the 1970s and 1980s.) This genre is one of the few examples, she notes, of a narrative genre that is patronized almost exclusively by males, in which the main character—the one with whom the audience is not only encouraged but required to identify—is always female: the so-called final girl who is left alive at the end of the film, having vanquished or escaped from the serial killer. As Clover explains, it is always easy to spot the character who will turn out to be the "final girl": she is the only one of all her female friends who is not sexually active, she often has a masculine-sounding name, and she is "intelligent, watchful and levelheaded."[42] She also tends to be taller and/or more svelte than the other female characters and dressed more conservatively. She is, in other words, gendered male, despite her female body. At the end of the film, argues Clover, she "mans" herself and simultaneously "unmans" the killer as she destroys him. She becomes, through the act of destroying the (ambiguously gendered) killer, an adult subject: that is, a man.[43]

Given this argument, it is easy to understand why adolescent male viewers might find the formulaic gender and narrative structure of the classic slasher film appealing and why they would find it easy and ultimately satisfying to identify with the "female" protagonist. But then the question arises: why not simply have the protagonist be a boy from the beginning? Why is it necessary to witness this transformative experience undergone by someone inhabiting a female body? Here Clover argues that the experiences of "abject terror" and victimhood are coded "female," so they are best represented through a female body. In slasher films both male and female characters are killed, sometimes in equal numbers, but it is the girls who scream uncontrollably and whose killing is sometimes drawn out and sexualized.[44] Even the masculine final girl is inevitably dragged through several incidents of terror and torture before she manages to prevail. In order for male viewers to enjoy both the masochistic pleasure of abject terror and the cathartic victory, a masculine-gendered female body is necessary.

Some of these same patterns may lie behind the popularity among boys of 1990s *shōjo* images in pop culture narrative forms. For example, the young female protagonists in Miyazaki Hayao's *Nausicaa* and *The Princess Mononoke* resemble Clover's "final girls": they are slim, short-haired, have gender-neutral names, and exhibit power and confidence; they are gendered male (see Figure 11.7). In Miyazaki's smash hit *The Princess Mononoke,* San is not (apparently) sexually active, unlike many of the other female characters who come across as sexually competent and aggressive adults. (Many of them are former prostitutes.) In *The Princess Mononoke*, however, there is a young male protagonist as well, who is San's counterpart in many ways. He, too, is slim, not (yet) sexually active, and highly competent. There is no need, therefore, for male viewers to identify with San rather than with him. Nor is San alone in undergoing a transformation at the end of the film; all of the main characters do. So again, there is no particular reason why male viewers would be especially encouraged to identify with the masculinized San (nor any evidence that they do). In contrast, in Miyazaki's earlier work *Nausicaa*, the female protagonist is alone in drawing the audience's sympathy, and she alone undergoes a transformation at the end. It is likely that she is relatively easy for boys to identify with, like Clover's "final girl."

I would argue, however, that Japanese *manga/anime* demonstrate a much wider range of depictions of the female protagonist than do slasher films. In many cases the heroine is not a conveniently masculinized or gender-neutral young female; often she is extravagantly feminine in figure and in style (see Figure 11.10). The protagonist of the animated version of *Ghost in the Shell* (directed by Oshii Mamoru) begins the film by making a comment about her menstrual period and then removing her clothing to reveal her Barbie-doll-perfect naked body (like Barbie, without pubic hair) before jumping into action and revealing her more "masculine" traits. The voluptuous eponymous protagonist of *Cutey Honey* is naked through part of the show's theme song, coquettishly begging that we not look at her. When she is dressed it is in a constantly changing parade of revealing and stereotypically titillating costumes: as a nurse, a cowgirl, or a miniskirted traffic cop. (Recall, too, the opening of *Burn Up W*, with its naked bungee jump.)

Nonetheless, it could be argued that even these depictions share some elements with Clover's "final girl." For one thing, despite the bodies represented as adult in some ways, these characters are never depicted as (voluntarily) having (hetero-) sex.[45] Nor are they often depicted as libidinally active in a (narcissistic) masturbatory or homoerotic sense.[46] Moreover, although characters like Cutey Honey have bodies that are undeniably "adult," they are depicted without pubic hair. Breasts, buttocks, and body outlines may be distinctly depicted in all their voluptuous curves, but the vulva is always smooth, hairless, and seemingly imperforate, and the breasts are sometimes without obvious nipples.

This oddly constructed body is brought insistently to the viewers'attention in a scene ubiquitous to the hybrid *anime* genre: the midair twirling transformation, as the heroine changes from "normal girl" into her fighting persona. The midair twirling transformation, including a transitional period of total nudity, was invented by Nagai Gō many years earlier but now has become standard in *shōjo*-hybrid animation.[47] The feminine but imperforate body featured in these scenes underscores an important point: the power of the battlin' babes *derives from* the tension between their sexual potential and their refusal to activate it. The absolute omnipresence of the naked twirling transformation sequence for *shōjo* heroes (never for *shōnen* heroes) may be because they must entirely reveal their liminal bodies—sexually mature, as seen from the full breasts, but "pure" and somehow still childish, underscored by the lack of pubic hair and imperforate genitalia—in order to *take on* their power.[48] Again this tension between sexual potential and innocence is an old, old trope of girldom (as seen in the photographs of naked children both inside and on the cover of *Shōjo ron*) but is activated here in a narrative mode that presupposes male identification as well as male consumption.

To put it slightly differently, the power of the sexually mature but virginal battlin' babe is dependent on her maintaining the sexual purity associated with the *shōjo.* This point is made explicit in the *anime Demon Hunter Yōko.* In this narrative Yōko's mother, who gave in to her carnal desires too early, became unable to claim the demon-hunting power that is the birthright of the females of her family line. Now she is pushing sexual experience on Yōko, whose crush on a male schoolmate makes it hard for her to resist. The grandmother opposes her daughter strenuously, trying to protect Yōko's virginity long enough for her to claim her power. There is clearly a struggle here between one kind of power/pleasure and another; they are figured as absolutely mutually exclusive. This opposition is reminiscent of the slasher film's "final girl," whose power to resist the killer is implicitly linked to her refusal to indulge in sex, unlike her friends. But it is likely also connected with the needs of the male audience, for whom the sight of a libidinally active adult female would almost certainly preclude ready identification.

This liminal (but not masculinized) gendering of the female characters is present in many of these battlin' babe *anime.* The theme song of *Cutey Honey*, for example, appears on first hearing to enact a straightforwardly traditional gendering of the visual economy. This song is all about the gaze and the consumption of the female body as sexualized/commodified spectacle ("she's a fashionable girl," "she has a small butt," "she has big, soft breasts," and so forth). These lyrics can most readily be seen as either a typical heterosexual male framing of the female body or as an image organized for narcissistic or homoerotic consumption by female viewers. But on closer consideration they seem to be a complicated and indeterminate conflation of both—as well as other possibilities. This theme song, which at first seems so perfectly to exemplify the "typical" deployment of the power politics of the (male) gaze, turns out to both exemplify and confound that problematic. (The complete text of the song appears at the end of the essay.)

In reading the power politics of the gaze here, much depends on determining who is the speaker/singer of such lines as "Please don't hurt me," "You make my heart pound when you come near," "No, no, no, don't look at me," "Please don't come near," "You make me excited," and so on. There would seem to be a dialogue here, with some of the lines spoken by the (male?) observer of Honey and some spoken by Honey herself. The observer makes comments on Honey's appearance ("She's got a small butt") and issues commands ("Look this way, Honey"). And since this song plays over scenes of Honey becoming suddenly naked and twirling in the air to transform into her warrior persona, the "Please don't look at me" lines (rendered in female-coded speech) would seem to be hers. But it is difficult to separate the two definitively: both sides appear to express positions of power, as when the observer commands, "Look this way, Honey," or in Honey's announcement at the end, "I'm going to change!" Similarly, both sides express vulnerability; it seems to be the observer saying, "Please, please, don't hurt me; you make my heart pound" and "Please, please, don't come closer; you make me sniffle," while it is Honey begging not to be looked at. This expression of vulnerability on the part of the viewer is quite unusual given the typical power structure of the gaze.

Moreover, examples of lines from both sides of the "dialogue" are in a definitively female-coded speech register, including "You make me sniffle," which seems to refer to the *manga*-coded action of liquid released from the nose signifying sexual excitement. Are both the speakers in this dialogue female as the speech registers (and singer's voice) imply, making this an example of the power politics of the *shōjo*/narcissistic gaze, here explicitly (homo-) sexualized? Or is this an odd "dialogue" conducted solely by Honey in a strange autoerotic visual politics? The narrative consistently features men ogling and desiring Honey, but she is also sexually molested by a powerful female enemy in one episode. As this popular opening song suggests, the gender/sexuality of Honey and that of her intended audience both seem to be ambiguous.

There are as well battlin' babe narratives that feature strong female protagonists who are not constantly victimized by the gaze. The protagonists of Shirō Masamune's *Ghost in the Shell* and *Appleseed* are tough, even violent cyborg police officers, and although they may not exhibit active sexual desire, they are fully active and competent in other adult ways, equal partners with their male colleagues (Figure 11.11).[49] Kishiro Yukito's *Battle Angel* highlights a young female whose tiny body is sexually immature and never revealed but is capable of defeating the largest and most horrific cyborg fighting machines (Figure 11.12). However, even in these less sexualized examples, the protagonists do not undergo the final transformative experience that would "man" them, in Clover's terms. On the contrary, they are always recuperated into a traditional feminine position by the time the narrative ends. Major Kusanagi of the animated *Ghost in the Shell*, one of the most powerful, self-aware, and rational of all recent *anime* protagonists, male or female, ends the film by allowing herself to be "impregnated" by a masculine being known as the Puppet Master, and she "gives birth" to a new life form. In other words, she is manipulated like a puppet into the only role open to a person with a female body who is no longer a *shōjo:* that of "mother." By entering the state of motherhood, Kusanagi is definitively gendered as female for the first time. *Battle Angel*'s Gally loses the young man with whom she had hoped to have a traditional heterosexual romance, leaving her in the permanent position of "widow" (defined by her relationship to a man) rather than the autonomous "phallic virgin" role with which battlin' babe *anime* usually begin.[50]

These 1990s story lines take us right back to the gender politics of Tezuka's *Ribbon Knight* from the 1950s, in which the temporarily masculinized Sapphire returns in the end to her "true" nature, as determined by her sex (female). This return to "natural" sex/gender roles might be taken as reassuring by the male readers/viewers of battlin' babe *manga* and *anime*. However much one might revel in the masochistic pleasures of abjection (explaining the frequency with which the protagonists are raped in some segments of this genre of *anime*), no "normal" boy is going to want to identify with the long-term and undramatic abjection of the adult woman in Japanese family/social structures.[51] The cross-gender identification boys enjoy in the beginning and middle of these narratives must be surrendered, presumably, at the moment when the phallus returns to the male (when Sapphire gives up her sword and agrees to be a woman/wife), and the "normal"

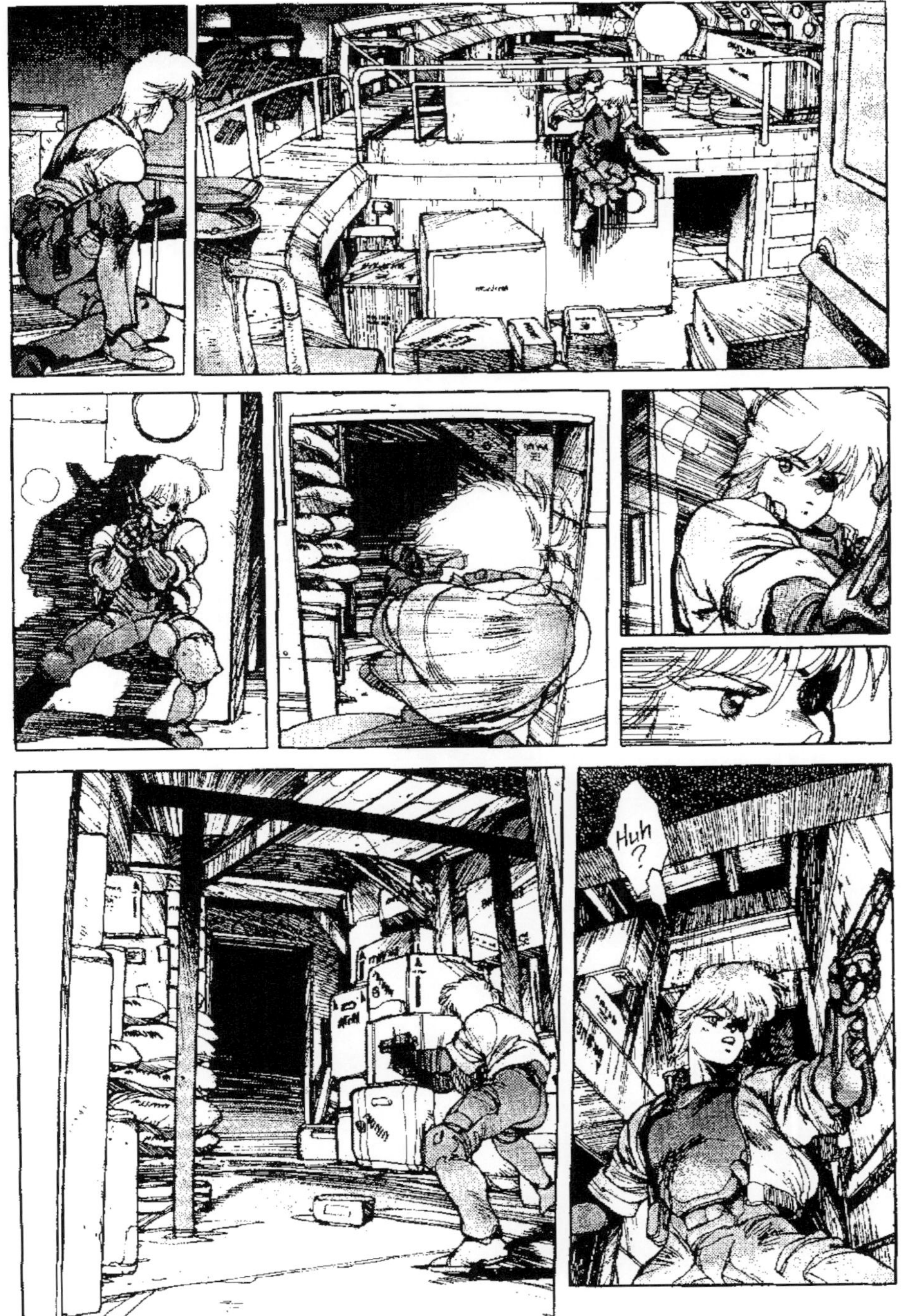


**FIGURE 11.11.** Masamune Shirow, *Appleseed.* Book 4. (Milwaukee: Dark Horse Comics, 1995.)

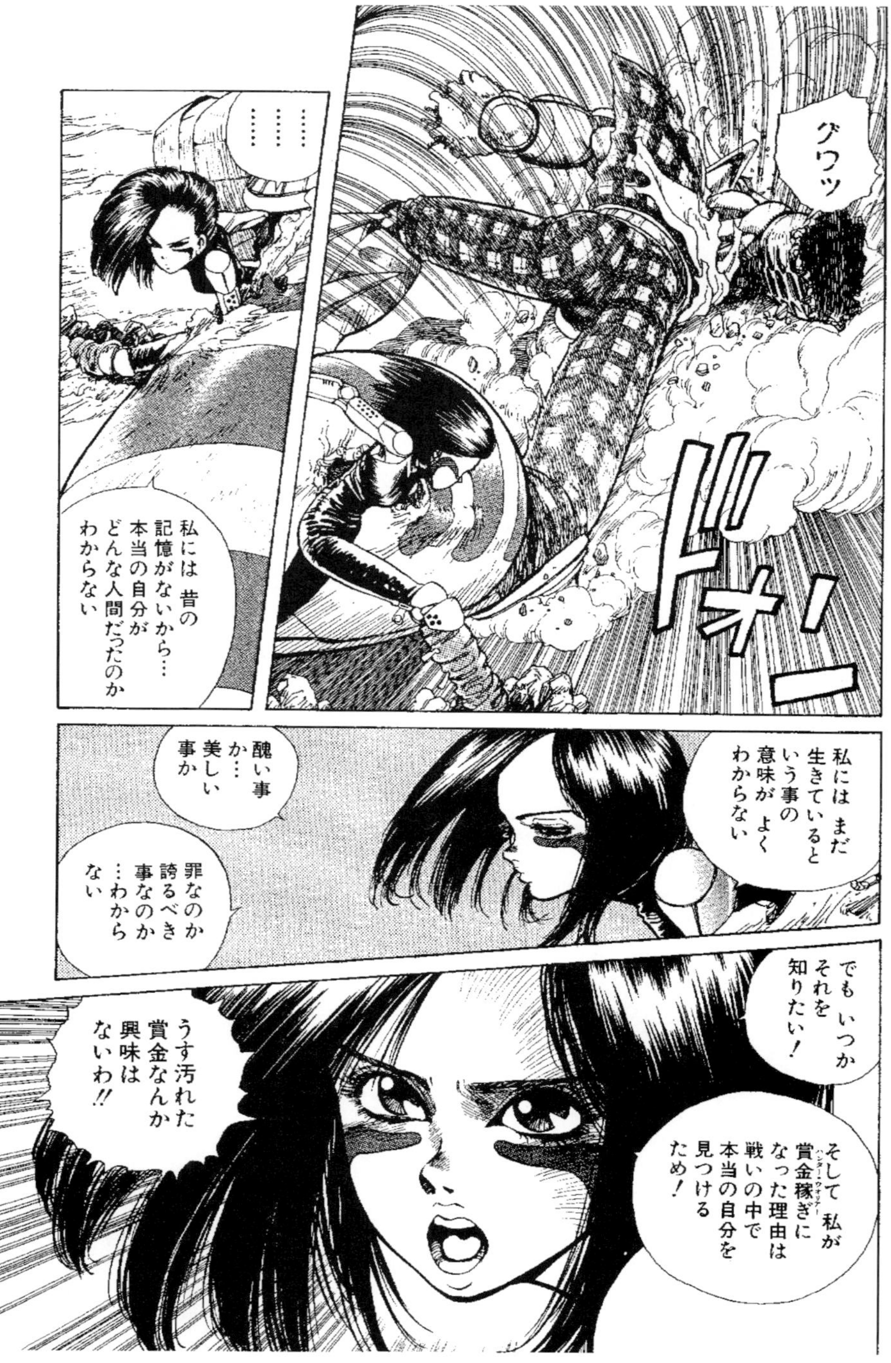


**FIGURE 11.12.** Kishiro Yukito, *GUNNM* (Battle Angel). Vol. 1 (Tokyo: Shū'eisha, 1998), 229. © Yukito Kishiro/Shueisha Inc.

symbolic order is restored. At that point male readers/viewers, too, can go back to their accustomed positions in that order.

Clover's explanation of male identification with the "final girl" in slasher films demonstrates some parallels with battlin' babe narratives. But I would suggest that there are other attractions for the male viewer here as well. For one, the image of the *shōjo* has long been and remains associated with liminality, transformativity, and irresponsibility. These characteristics must have considerable appeal for a young man whose future role in society seems fast-approaching and inescapable. The *shōjo* is not yet anything definite; her role is not fixed and that fixing can be indefinitely deferred. Unlike a *shōnen* she doesn't have an automatic developmental "next stage": the *shōnen* will inevitably over time become a *seinen* and then an *otoko* (adult man), but she can remain a *shōjo.* And so long as she is in the *shōjo* state, she has the innate power to transform into other ontological possibilities, unaided by any outside force. (This possibility is best exemplified in a subgenre of *manga/anime* known by some as "magical girl" narratives. *Sailor Moon* is perhaps the best known example of this subgenre.) Finally, a *shōjo* can exemplify both male and female characteristics without being fixed in a single gender role. Any or all of these factors may appear appealing to someone who is "trapped" in a fixed position of social responsibility.

I would suggest, however, that the attraction goes even further than that. Young men who have become aware of the repressiveness of a rigidly hierarchical social structure may recognize implicitly the value of feminine "masquerade": the active assumption of an ostensibly subservient or inferior role in order to derive the benefits that accrue to one who acquiesces to the demands of the hegemony. Cutey Honey's constant joyful transformation into yet another erotic stereotype is an example of successful masquerade, which wins her the slobbering devotion of all the men around her. Fearing their own displacement in a shrunken and ever more competitive economy, young men may seek out this survival strategy long used by the disempowered. This celebration of the masquerade may partly explain the increasingly sexualized depiction of *shōjo* in the 1990s (as exemplified by Lara Croft or Cutey Honey) as opposed to the slimmer, more androgynous visual paradigm of the "final girl" or *yaoi manga.*

Before concluding I would like to consider briefly the question of what these 1990s phallic virgin narratives offer to young women viewers. It seems clear that there has been a gradual progression in popular culture narratives for girls in terms of the power wielded by the protagonists—from Sapphire in *Ribbon Knight* to the volleyball players in *Attack Number One*, from Oscar to Major Kusanagi, there has been steady progress in strength and autonomy. Moreover, in the 1990s the female protagonists were depicted as actually female in both sex and gender, unlike Sapphire and Oscar, and unlike all the male protagonists of 1970s and 1980s *yaoi* narratives. This would seem to be a positive advance for girls' self-image.

However, there are two problems with this picture. The first is one I mentioned earlier: in these narratives *shōjo* are presented with a choice between libidinal activity or power and autonomy. There is no scenario by which a woman can have both: she can have adult heterosexuality only within the strictures of wife-and-motherhood (though a certain amount of homosexuality or autoeroticism may be permitted), and she can have power only while in the not yet socially grounded state of the phallic virgin *shōjo.*

The second problem may be less apparent to anyone unfamiliar with the battlin' babes narratives listed. In fact, the majority of these "female" protagonists are actually cyborgs, androids, or aliens; they are not human females (cyborgs/androids in *Cutey Honey*, *Ghost in the Shell*, *Appleseed*, *Gunbuster*, *Cat Girl Nuku Nuku*, *Bubblegum Crisis/Crash*, *Genocyber*, *Battle Angel;* aliens or possessors of supernatural powers in *Urusei yatsura*, *Sukeban deka*, *Blue Seed*, and *Demon Hunter Yōko*). In other words, many of these admirable battlin' babes are *man*-made; their strong and talented bodies are not for maximizing their own pleasure or satisfaction but for serving the purposes of the state or their (always male) creator, or both.[52] Unlike earlier *manga/anime* characters, there is no possibility that a real-world girl could realistically aspire to emulate characters who are android or alien. If society's rules could be bent by long-term cross-dressing, then a girl could perhaps be gendered male, as in the cases of Sapphire and Oscar; if one had the discipline and determination, she could become a member of the Olympic volleyball team, like the protagonists of *The Sign Is V* and *Attack Number One*. But there is no effort of social engineering or willpower sufficient to make a girl as powerful as a robot or alien. In that sense these narratives provide a crueler identificatory paradigm for girls than even the *yaoi* comics featuring homosexual European males—there one was clearly in a fantasy mode and free to allow the imagination to roam without the temptation to believe in the possibility of achieving such a life. But in the 1990s battlin' babes narratives, the protagonists appear to be normal females, if sometimes a little too perfect in body shape, inviting but then ultimately rejecting female identification.

Roland Barthes has argued that "pictures . . . are more imperative than writing, they impose meaning at one stroke, without analysing or diluting it,"[53] suggesting that the visual conflation of a *shōjo* body with power is more potent than the knowledge viewers have of the *shōjo*'s true nature as a cyborg or alien. Nevertheless, a feminist reading of these battlin' babe narratives might well argue that in them females may inhabit images that demonstrate power, but that power is still enabled by and circumscribed within ultimate patriarchal hegemony. The cognitive transvestism that is supported by these narratives, allowing boys to become *shōjo,* at least temporarily, may represent a new and relatively rare paradigm in male audience identification. But these narratives ultimately reinscribe hegemonic and heterocentric sex/gender/sexuality ideologies, obviating much of the promise of resistance or social transformation.

### "Cutey Honey" Theme Song

| JAPANESE: | ENGLISH (MY TRANSLATION): |
|---|---|
| *Konogoro hayari no onna no ko* | A girl of today's fashion |
| *O-shiri no chiisana onna no ko* | A girl with a small butt |
| *Kotchi o muite yo, Honey* | Look this way, Honey |
| *Datte nandaka datte datte nanda mon* | It's just that somehow, but, but, I mean . . . |
| *Onegai, onegai, kizutsukenaide* | Please, please don't hurt me |
| *Watashi no haato wa chiku chiku shichau no* | My heart will start pounding |
| *Iya yo, iya yo, iya yo, mitsumecha iya* | No! No! No! Don't look at me! |
| *Honey furasshu!* | Honey Flash! |
| | |
| *Imadoki ninki no onna no ko* | The popular girl these days |
| *Fukutto boin no onna no ko* | A girl with big soft breasts |
| *Kotchi o muite yo, Honey* | Look this way, Honey |
| *Datte nandaka datte datte nanda mon* | It's just that somehow, but, but, I mean . . . |
| *Onegai, onegai, chikayoranaide* | Please, please, don't come close |
| *Watashi no o-hana ga hiku hiku shichau no* | I'll start sniffling |
| *Iya yo, iya yo, iya yo, mitsumecha iya* | No! No! No! Don't look at me! |
| *Honey furasshu!* | Honey Flash! |
| | |
| (Honey's voice, speaking: *Kawaru wa yo.*) | (Honey's voice: I'm about to change.) |

# NOTES

## 1. Introduction

1. Linda Nochlin, "Why Have There Been No Great Women Artists?" *Art News* 69, no. 9 (January 1971): 22–39, 67–71.

2. Norma Broude and Mary D. Garrard, eds., *Feminism and Art History: Questioning the Litany* (New York: Harper and Row, 1982), back-cover blurb.

3. Norma Broude and Mary D. Garrard, eds., *The Expanding Discourse: Feminism and Art History* (New York: Harper and Row, 1992), ix.

4. Broude and Garrard, *Expanding,* ix.

5. Craig Clunas, "Review Essay, Modernity Global and Local: Consumption and the Rise of the West," *American Historical Review* 104, no. 5 (December 1999): 1504–1505.

6. Broude and Garrard, *Questioning,* 1.

7. In Marsha Weidner, ed., *Flowering in the Shadows: Women in the History of Chinese and Japanese Painting* (Honolulu: University of Hawai'i Press, 1990), vii–viii.

8. Weidner, *Flowering in the Shadows,* 5.

9. Tanaka Ichimatsu, "Otoko-e to onna-e" [Man-pictures and woman-pictures], *Hōun,* no. 6 (1933): 75–94.

10. Shirahata Yoshi, "Onna-e kō" [A treatise on woman-pictures], *Bijutsu kenkyū* [Journal of art studies], no. 132 (1943): 201–210; "Onna-e hokō" [Further thoughts on woman-pictures], *Bukkyō geijutsu* [Ars Buddhica], no. 35 (July 1958): 24–28.

11. Wakakuwa Midori, *Josei gaka retsuden* [Lives of female painters] (Tokyo: Iwanami Shisho, 1985).

12. Hagiwara Hiroko, *Kono mune no arashi: Eikoku burakku josei āchisuto wa kataru* [The tempest in this breast: English black women artists speak] (Tokyo: Gendai Kikaku-shitsu, 1990).

13. Ogino Miho, trans., *Jendā to rekishigaku* (Tokyo: Heibonsha, 1992).

14. Hagiwara Hiroko, trans., *Onna / āto / ideorogī: feminisuto ga yomi-naosu geijutsu hyōgen no rekishi* (Tokyo: Shinsuisha, 1992).

15. Suzuki Tokiko, "Feminisuto to bijutsushi" [Feminist art history], *Geijutsugaku kenkyū* [Art studies research] 2 (Meiji Gakuin Ronsō 50, 1992).

16. Chino Kaori, "Nihon bijutsu o kangae-naosu tame ni" [Toward rethinking Japanese art], *Bijutsu techō* [Art notes], October 1992.

17. The only record of this event in the official proceedings of the conference is a one-page synopsis of the project. *Kyoto Conference on Japanese Studies, 1994* (International Research Center for Japanese Studies and The Japan Foundation), vol. 1, 293–294.

18. Again, the only published record in English of this project to date is Sumie Jones, ed., *Imaging Reading Eros: Proceedings for the Conference, Sexuality and Edo Culture, 1750–1850 (Indiana University, Bloomington, August 17–20, 1995)* (Bloomington: The East Asian Studies Center, 1996).

19. On the Edo Boom, see Carol Gluck, "The Invention of Edo," in *Mirror of Modernity: Invented Traditions of Modern Japan,* ed. Stephen Vlastos (Berkeley: University of California Press, 1998), 262–284.

20. According to Philbert Ono, a photo showing pubic hair by Araki Nobuyoshi was published in *Geijutsu shinchō* magazine in May 1991. Shinoyama Kishin's book of the same year, *water fruit,* "essentially becomes Japan's first 'hair nude' photo book." Ono places the start of the boom proper in the following year, with the publication of Miyazawa Rie's *Santa Fe,* and the peak in 1994, when over three hundred "hair nude" publications were issued in one year. Philbert Ono, *PhotoHistory,* from *PhotoGuide Japan* (http://photojpn.org/HIST/1990.html; downloaded March 3, 2001).

21. Curiously, Kawade Shobō's successes did not transfer over to museum catalogs. For the major Utamaro retrospective organized by Asano Shūgō and Timothy Clark in 1995 at both the British Museum and the Chiba City Museum, the English catalog and show included Utamaro's pornographic works, while the Japanese show and catalog did not—although both catalogs were actually printed in Japan. Shūgō Asano and Timothy Clark, *The Passionate Art of Kitagawa Utamaro* (London: British Museum Press, 1995); Asano Shūgō and Timothy Clark, *Kitagawa Utamaro-ten* (Tokyo: Asahi Shinbun-sha, 1995).

22. Andrew Gerstle, "Response to the Panel: 'The Place of Love,' " in Jones, ed., *Imaging Reading Eros,* 104. Haga, not coincidently, is one of the directors of the right-wing Japanese Society for History Textbook Reform. The best information in English on this organization and the political views it embodies can be found in Aaron Gerow, "Consuming Asia, Consuming Japan: The New Neonationalistic Revisionism in Japan," in Laura Hein and Mark Selden, eds., *Censoring History: Citizenship and Memory in Japan, Germany, and the United States* (Armonk, N.Y.: M. E. Sharpe Books, 2000), 74–95.

23. Timon Screech, *Sex and the Floating World: Erotic Images in Japan, 1700–1820* (Honolulu: University of Hawai'i Press, 1999); and in Japanese, Takayama Hiroshi, trans., *Shunga: kata-te de yomu Edo no e* [*Shunga:* Edo pictures read with one hand] (Tokyo: Kōdansha, 1998).

24. For an explicit rebuttal of Screech's thesis, see Shirakura Yoshihiko, "Shunga o dō yomu ka" [How to read *shunga*], in *Ukiyo-e shunga o yomu* [Reading *ukiyo-e shunga*], ed. Shirakura Yoshihiko et al. (Tokyo: Chūōkōronsha, 2000), vol. 1, 5–86.

25. See, for instance, Gary P. Leupp, *Male Colors: The Construction of Homosexuality in Tokugawa Japan* (Berkeley: University of California Press, 1995), and Stephen D. Miller, ed., *Partings at Dawn: An Anthology of Japanese Gay Literature* (San Francisco: Gay Sunshine Press, 1996).

26. In *Geijutsugaku ga wakaru* [Understanding the study of art], Asahi Shimbun Extra Report and Analysis, Special Number 9 (1995).

27. Shuichi Kato, *A History of Japanese Literature,* trans. David Chibbett, 3 vols. (Tokyo: Kodansha International, 1979).

28. See the essays by Suzuki Tomi and Joshua Mostow in Haruo Shirane and Suzuki Tomi, eds., *Inventing the Classics: Modernity, National Identity, and Japanese Literature* (Stanford: Stanford University Press, 2000); and in Japanese, *Sōzō sareta koten: kanon keisei, kokumin kokka, Nihon bungaku* [Invented classics: canon formation, the nation-state, and Japanese literature] (Tokyo: Shin'yōsha, 1999).

29. Fujisawa Shū, "Uji" [Maggot], *Shōsetsu shinchō* 52, no. 5 (1995): 62–70. For a translation, see Alexander Gordon Woodburn, "Translating Modern Japanese Literary Prose: A Theoretical Approach" (M.A. thesis, Asian Studies, University of British Columbia, 2000).

## 2. Gender in Japanese Art

This essay was translated by Martha J. McClintock, Ikumi Kaminishi, and Judith Stubbs; however, the editors must accept final responsibility for any errors or infelicities. Thanks are also due to Christopher Reed for commenting on an earlier draft.

1. The author uses English words both in romanization *(romāji)* and transcribed into the *katakana* syllabary. In the translation, the former are given parenthetically in quotation marks, for example, ("power"), while the latter are given in italic transliteration, for example, *(jendā)* [Ed.].

2. The Chinese character read "Tang" in Chinese and "Tō" in its Sino-Japanese pronunciation is also read "Kara," especially in reference to Chinese art objects in a Japanese context. "Kara" was originally the Japanese name for one of the countries in the southern half of the Korean Peninsula. The use of the term gradually expanded to indicate the entire Korean Peninsula and then foreign countries in general. With the opening of relations between Japan and the Sui and Tang dynasties, the term came to refer specifically to China. As a prefix, it meant something "continental" or "imported." Thus, "Kara" can refer both to "Tang" China specifically and to the "foreign" in general, and the author takes advantage of this semantic slippage in her own use of the term [Ed.].

3. Again, the term "Yamato" originally referred to a specific kingdom within the Japanese archipelago and later came to be used as one of several terms for the unified country as a whole. The term "Nihon," etymologically derived from the same Chinese word as the English "Japan," was first used by the Japanese to refer to themselves in some of the earliest official communications between the Japanese and Chinese courts. Again, the author uses the term "the Japanese" to refer to this historically changing political entity and not some ahistorical "people" or "ethnicity" [Ed.].

4. The screen known as *Konmei-chi* depicted a landscape, including a pond named Konmei-chi (Kunming-chi in Chinese) on the south-facing side. Kunming-chi was a famous pond built by Emperor Wudi (156–78 B.C.) of the Han dynasty in the capital city of

Chang'an. The reverse of the screen, the side facing north, depicted hawking in the Sagano region of Kyoto. The other panel, known as *Ara-umi,* or "Wild Sea," showed strange human figures with fantastically elongated arms and legs, who roamed the seaside. These strange creatures were understood as "foreign" and "non-Japanese." The reverse side of this screen showed the wickerworks of the Uji River, southeast of Kyoto [Trans.].

### 3. The Image of Women in Battle Scenes

Original translation by Martha McClintock.

1. Many studies have been published in the fields of history and sociology using the concept of "gender" or adding analyses from the viewpoint of "gender." Here I would like to offer the definition from Ueno Chizuko's "Sa-i no seijigaku" [The political science of difference], in *Iwanami kōza gendai shakaigaku II: jendā no shakaigaku* [Iwanami lectures in contemporary sociology 2: the sociology of gender] ed. Ueno et al. (Tokyo: Iwanami Shoten, 1995). Ueno reviews the history of the concept of "gender" as it has been interrogated by feminism and introduces the most recent concept of "gender" as a "culturally constucted device" that produces discourse related to the body.

2. Three scrolls are extant. In addition to the *Night Attack at the Sanjō Palace* discussed here, the Seikadō Bunko Bijutsukan houses the *Shinzei* scroll, and the Tokyo National Museum houses the *Imperial Progress to Rokuhara* scroll. These three scrolls and about ten fragments are believed to have been one continuous work, and it has been suggested that they originally formed a massive handscroll depicting the entire *Tales of the Heiji Era.* For information regarding the provenance of these three scrolls and the existence of copies, see Matsubara Shigemi, "Heiji monogatari e-kotoba no denrai to seiritsu" [The provenance and formation of the *Tales of the Heiji Era* picture-text], in *Nihon emaki-mono taisei* [Compendium of Japanese picture scrolls] (Tokyo: Chūōkōronsha, 1977).

3. Regarding the night attack on Sanjō Palace, contemporary documents do not record the names of those who lost their lives, whether on the rebel or the retired emperor's side. In fiction, that is, in the Yōmei Bunko-bon text, it is recorded that the heads of two warriors from the emperor's side—Emon no Jō Ōe no Ienaka and Saemon no Jō Taira no Yasutada—were carried off on halberds, and such an image is also depicted in the illustrated scroll. (On this basis it might be possible to argue that they are two of the lower-level figures depicted in the interior of Sanjō Palace. However, there is no mention of their names in the accompanying text). Even though the Yōmei Bunko-bon text gives the names of these low-ranking warriors who were killed, it is by repeatedly narrating how they were among victims who were high aristocrats that it is emphasized how awful the attack was and what a significant event it was. Whether in literature or in painting, the content represented is not something that simply fulfills the function of transmitting facts; rather it shows the understanding of and feelings toward the event held by the commissioner or audience directly connected to the production of this illustrated scroll.

4. See Kusaka Chikara et al., eds., *Hōgen monogatari, Heiji monogatari, Jōkyūki,* Shin Nihon Koten Bungaku Taikei, vol. 43 (Tokyo: Iwanami Shoten, 1992).

5. The contents of the main text of the Kotohira lineage version of the *Heiji monogatari,* whose composition may date back to the thirteenth century, cannot be ignored in any consideration of the scenes in the handscrolls. In the Kotohira version, focus is turned toward the women of the court as those fleeing the battle in confusion. It is possible that, aside from the painting, a written text was created that emphasized the women as victims. According to Kusaka's research on the composition of the main text and its lineage, the work went through the following stages: the Yōmei Bunko-bon lineage → the illustrated picture scroll → the Kotohira version (though Kotohira-version elements can be recognized in the text of the illustrated scrolls). This sequence might indicate that the depiction of the majority of the victims as women in the handscroll may have influenced the Kotohira version.

6. It is appropriate to compare this scene with Eugene Delacroix's 1827 *Death of Sardanapalus,* a painting that visualizes a similar sort of sexual fantasy. The American art historian Linda Nochlin has analyzed from a feminist perspective the artist's sexual fantasy that depicts the tyranny of the oriental despot Sardanapalus, who had his female slaves destoyed on the occasion of his own downfall. In "The Imaginary Orient," Nochlin notes the importance of the fact that this cruelty is created in the painting as something that provokes the sexual fantasy of the cruel oriental king. However, according to Nochlin, it cannot be said that Delacroix succeeded through his expressive means in creating a sufficient distance between Sardanapalus and the viewer, and viewers at the time of the work's creation were apparently threatened by the erotic bodies of the women. It is essential that the means of expression and the scene be devised so as to maintain a distance between the viewer and the cruelty in the picture in order for the viewer to "enjoy" the violence that has been visually portrayed. See Linda Nochlin, "The Imaginary Orient," in Nochlin, *The Politics of Vision: Essays in Nineteenth-Century Art and Society* (New York: Harper and Row, 1989).

7. "Shōjū Raigōji-bon rokudō-e 'nindō fujōsō-zu' kō" [A study of the Shōjū Raigōji Temple version of the realm of human existence six realms of rebirth painting], *Tezukayama Gakuin Daigaku kenkyū ronshū* [Collected research essays from Tezukayama Gakuin University], no. 29 (February 1995). As Kasuya indicates, this kind of sexually explicit imagery was not painted simply for aesthetic appreciation. Rather, Kasuya's analysis indicates that it had the opposite meaning, as a part of the Buddhist denial of women (in turn part of the doctrine of the extinction of—men's—carnal desire).

8. Hitomi Tonomura, "Black Hair and Red Trousers: Gendering the Flesh in Medieval Japan," *American Historical Review* 99, no. 1 (February 1994): 129–154.

9. Although a limited number of high-ranking aristocrats and young upper-class warriors are not depicted by means of the "slit-eye, hook-nose" technique, they still show evidence of the *tsukuri-e* method, and compared with the women, the color of their skin is white, though not thickly painted. Here again, whiteness is being used as a symbol of high-class status.

10. The sole exception to this lack of gender distinction is the depiction of women's heads from the rear, which become pointed and triangular, a convention that is not applied to men.

11. "Jendā no shiten kara miru ōchō monogatari-e" [Court illustrated romances as seen from the viewpoint of gender], in *Bijutsu to jendā: hi-taishō no shisen* [Art and gender: the asymmetrical record], ed. Suzuki Tokiko et al. (Tokyo: Brücke, 1997).

12. "*Heiji monogatari emaki* ni miru risō no bushi-zō" [The image of the ideal warrior as seen in the *Illustrated Scrolls of the Tales of Heiji*], *Bijutsushi* [Art history], no. 138 (May 1995).

### 4. The Gender of *Wakashu* and the Grammar of Desire

This essay was originally delivered at the 1996 Association for Asian Studies annual meeting held in Honolulu. I was able to present an expanded version at the International Research Center for Japanese Studies (Nichibunken) and at Columbia University in 1998, where I benefited from the comments of many people. Much of the *Wakashu kyara-makura asobi* has been subsequently reproduced by Hayakawa Monta in his *Ukiyo-e to shunga: nanshoku* (Tokyo: Kawade Shobō, 1998).

1. Typically, this is suggested by positioning a liberated Edo-period libidinal economy against a "Western"-derived puritanism started in the Meiji period. For instance, Haga Tōru: "In the thrill and ecstacy of their ["Edoites"] precarious love, the lovers experienced the fullness and joy of life haunted by a premonition of death, which had no hope of achieving any kind of expression in western-influenced, hence ambitiously puritanical, Meiji Japan" ("Precariousness of Love, Places of Love," in Sumie Jones, *Imaging Reading Eros,* 98); or Ueno Chizuko, on the back blurb of a recently published series of *shunga* books: "One cannot help being delighted to learn that the barbarian age, when the 'private parts' of richly expressive *shunga* were blacked out, is at long last over" *(hyōjō yutakana shunga no "hibu" o, kuroku nuri-tsubushita yaban na jidai ga yōyaku owari o tsuketa koto o, yorokobazu ni ha iraremasen).* Hayashi Yoshikazu and Richard Lane, eds., *Kitagawa Utamaro "Ehon Komachi-biki."* Teihon Ukiuo-e shunga Meihin Shūsei [The complete *Ukiyo-e shunga*], vol. 2 (Tokyo: Kawade Shobō Shinsha, 1996). Like its Chinese and Greek counterparts, "barbarian" *(yaban)* suggests foreigners, not benighted indigenes.

2. Stephen D. Miller, "Editor's Preface," in *Partings at Dawn: An Anthology of Japanese Gay Literature,* ed. Stephen D. Miller (San Francisco: Gay Sunshine Press, 1996), 7.

3. Eve Kosofsky Sedgwick, "Tales of the Avunculate: *The Importance of Being Earnest,*" in her *Tendencies* (Durham: Duke University Press, 1993), 52–72.

4. See, for example, the review by Keith Vincent in *Journal of the Association of Teachers of Japanese* 31, no. 2 (October 1997): 109–116.

5. Paul Gordon Schalow in the *Journal of Japanese Studies* 23, no. 1 (Winter 1997): 196–201; and Joshua S. Mostow's review in the *Journal of the History of Sexuality* 7, no. 4 (April 1997): 608–610.

6. *The American Heritage Dictionary,* second college edition (Boston: Houghton Mifflin Company, 1982), s.v. "gender."

7. *Shōgakukan Random House English-Japanese Dictionary* (Tokyo: Shōgakukan, 1973–1974), s.v. "gender."

8. Gayle Rubin, "The Traffic in Women: Notes on the Political Economy of Sex," in *Toward an Anthropology of Women,* ed. Rayna R. Reiter (New York: Monthly Review Press, 1975), 157–200. See also her "Thinking Sex: Notes for a Radical Theory of the Politics of Sexuality," in *Pleasure and Danger,* ed. Carole S. Vance (Boston: Routledge and Kegan Paul, 1984), 267–319, which attempts a similar kind of "mainstream" definition as my Creed above.

9. *Body Guards* (Routledge, 1989), p. 3; quoted in Rosalind Morris, "Three Sexes and Four Sexualities: Redressing the Discourse on Gender and Sexuality in Contemporary Thailand," *positions: east asian cultures critique* 2, no. 1 (Spring 1994): 25.

10. Hayashi Yoshikazu, in his *Enpon kenkyū: Moronobu* [Research on erotic books: Moronobu] (Tokyo: Yūkō Shobō, 1968), gives the date of publication as Enpō 6 (1678) as a two-volume large-format book *(ōhon)* with no publisher listed (p. 63). This information seems based on an entry in Ryūtei Tanehiko's *Kōshoku-bon mokuroku* [Catalog of erotic books] and the *Hishikawa Moronobu gafu* [Hishikawa Moronobu picture books] (p. 101). Nonetheless, the colophon of the edition on which I am basing my discussion is quite clear. The discrepancy suggests the possibility that the work was reprinted at least once, in 1678, in a slightly different format. Clearly it was known and in some kind of circulation as late as Tanehiko's day (d. 1842).

11. Translated by Paul Gordon Schalow as "Wild Azaleas" and contained in Miller, *Partings at Dawn,* 97–124; and in Schalow's more scholarly version as "The Invention of the Literary Tradition of Male Love: Kitamura Kigin's *Iwatsutsuji,*" *Monumenta Nipponica* 48, no. 1 (Spring 1993): 1–31.

12. For a partial English translation of one part of this work, see Lawrence Rogers, "She Loves Me, She Loves Me Not: *Shinjū* and *Shikidō Ōkagami,*" *Monumenta Nipponica* 49, no. 1 (Spring 1994): 31–60.

13. Paul Gordon Schalow, trans., *The Great Mirror of Male Love* (Stanford: Stanford University Press, 1990).

14. In fact, an expression similar to "Kōya 60, Nachi 80" had a long history, perhaps originally unconnected to anything having to do with sex. See Gregory M. Pflugfelder, *Cartographies of Desire: Male-Male Sexuality in Japanese Discourse, 1600–1950* (Berkeley: University of California Press, 1999), 34. In the *Seven Casual Talks on Manners and Customs (Fūzoku shichi yūdan)* of 1756, the numbers are made to refer not to the age of the practitioners but to the number of techniques taught at each respective place. See Timon Screech, *Shunga: kata-te de yomu Edo no e* [*Shunga:* Edo pictures read with one hand], (Tokyo: Kodansha, 1998), 209, or in English, by the same author, *Sex and the Floating World: Erotic Images in Japan, 1700–1820* (Honolulu: University of Hawai'i Press, 1999), 230.

15. The first twenty stories in Saikaku's work concern exemplary *wakashu* among the samurai class, while the second twenty stories move the focus to the theater and kabuki actors.

16. These "ladies" are the high-class concubines or maids of socially elevated men. The same sort of image is identified as a concubine *(mekake)* in scene 8 and as a "masterless lady" *(rōnin jōrō)* in scene 17.

17. Scene 13 also employs honorific language toward the *wakashu,* implying that his social status is superior to the narrator/reader/protagonist.

18. See Hayakawa Monta, "Shunga and Mitate: Suzuki Harunobu's *Eight Modern Views of the Interior* (*Fūryū zashiki hakkei*), in Jones, *Imaging Reading Eros,* 122.

19. My discussion differs substantially from Ueno Chizuko's: "Edo literature is known for the line it draws between *yujo,* or courtesans, and *jionna,* or ordinary women. . . . *Jionna* is the label for those destined to keep house and bear children, while *yujo* designates a category of women who are suitable for sexual activity and pleasure. . . . A *jionna* is assigned to motherhood, simultaneously sanctified and cursed, whereas a *yujo* is denied motherhood. According to this logic, motherhood is considered incompatible with sexuality. . . . However, since no one is born a *yujo,* every woman begins in the category of *jionna.*" Ueno Chizuko, "Lusty Pregnant Women and Erotic Mothers: Representations of Female Sexuality in Erotic Art in Edo," in Jones, *Imaging Reading Eros,* 110.

Here I am attempting to include *wakashu,* class, and age in my description. While motherhood does seem incompatible with male desire in *Wakashu-asobi,* I feel it is misleading to suggest that every female starts as a *ji-onna*: every female starts as a child (though with significant class distinctions) and proceeds to the condition of either wife or prostitute (based in no small measure on those very class distinctions).

20. Schalow, *Great Mirror,* 4.

21. The artist Mary Kelly explores whether " 'being a woman' [is] only a brief part" of a woman's life. See the catalog *Mary Kelley: Interim,* essays by Marcia Tucker, Norman Bryson, and Griselda Pollock; interview by Hal Forster (New York: New Museum of Contemporary Art, 1990), 39 and 56.

22. Robert Darnton, *The Forbidden Best-Sellers of Pre-Revolutionary France* (New York: W. W. Norton and Co., 1995), 85.

23. "Josei no 'Nanshoku ron,' " [Women's "discourse on male-male love"], *Bungaku* [Literature], 6, no. 1 (Winter 1995): 71.

24. I do not wish to deny the possibility of a female reader/viewer using this text, but such use would be an appropriation of a work that clearly addresses itself to an adult male audience. It might also be suggested that an adult male viewer, having himself been a *wakashu,* could enjoy the image nostalgically, longing for his own past when he was able to take the role of the "bottom." Given class differences and the popularity of homosexual prostitution, however, it is unclear whether the supposed transition from *wakashu* to *nenja* was in fact the norm for the townsman *(chōnin)* class to which the text seems to be addressed.

25. This image was also included in a work titled *Nannyo tamatebako* (Treasure chest of men and women) (Pulverer collection), though with a different text. Yet in this text as well, it is clear that the wife is interfering with her husband's pleasure, and there is no reference to what the *wakashu* might be feeling. On the topic of regarding another's pleasure as an intrusion, Pflugfelder notes, "Yoshida Hanbei writes that actor-prostitutes might experience an erection when they sensed their partner approaching orgasm (lit., 'when the breathing behind them gets rough' [*ushiro no hanaiki no arai toki*]), but describes this

phenomenon as 'annoying' (*urusashi*) for the insertee rather than pleasurable. According to the early-eighteenth-century *Yarō kinuburui,* it was unseemly for male prostitutes engaging in sexual intercourse with a male client to display an erection." *Cartographies,* 43, note 52.

26. Pflugfelder, *Cartographies,* 41–42. Similar thinking is apparent in early modern Chinese texts, such as "A Male Mencius's Mother" by Li Yu, where a boy castrates himself to maintain his erotic relationship with his older partner when it is threatened by the boy's increasing sexual arousal, which was believed to be the result of puberty and would render him no longer suitable as an anal insertee. See Sophie Volpp, "The Discourse on Male Marriage: Li Yu's 'A Male Mencius's Mother,'" *positions: east asia cultures critique* 1, no. 4 (Spring 1994).

27. John R. Clarke, *Looking at Lovemaking: Constructions of Sexuality in Roman Art, 100 B.C.–A.D. 250* (Berkeley: University of California Press, 1998), 84. Cf. Plugfelder: "*Shudō* texts configured the *wakashu* primarily from the viewpoint of his senior male admirers. . . . How the *wakashu* might go about fulfilling his own desires, however, and what the nature of these desires might be, were questions that *shudō* texts seldom addressed"; *Cartographies,* 54–55.

28. Hitomi Tonomura, "Black Hair and Red Trousers," 148. On the systematic blindness to lesbianism, see Judith C. Brown, *Immodest Acts: The Life of a Lesbian Nun in Renaissance Italy* (New York: Oxford University Press, 1986).

29. The "bedroom display-piece" is a *harigata,* or dildo. On this text see Tanaka Yūko, *Harigata: Edo wonna no sei* [Dildoes: Edo women's sexuality] (Tokyo: Kawade Shobō Shinsha, 1999), 21–45.

30. On the status of masturbation in the Edo period, see Screech, *Sex and the Floating World,* 33.

31. See Majorie Garber, *Vice Versa: Bisexuality and the Eroticism of Everyday Life* (New York: Simon and Schuster, 1995).

32. Personal communication. Man-woman-*wakashu* combinations appear in the works of Sugimura Jihei, Torii Kiyonobu, Okumura Masanobu, Kitao Shigemasa, and Katsukawa Shunshō.

## 5. Marketing Desire

1. Part of Hōkoku's inscription for this *nikuhitsu-e* titled *Kume sennin zu* [Saint Kume], painted jointly by Kanō Terunobu (1717–1763) and Nishikawa Sukenobu (1671–1750, making 1750 the last date by which the painting could have been done). The citation is from the "Liyun" section of the *Li ji* [Classic of rites]. Nakano Mitsutoshi, *Nihon no kinsei* [Early modern Japan], vol. 12: *Bungaku to bijutsu no seijuku* [The maturity of literature and art] (Tokyo: Chūōkōronsha, 1993), 351 and color plate 1. The story appears in *Konjaku monogatari* [Tales of times now past], 11:24 as "Kume no sennin hajimete Kume dera wo tsukuru koto" [Saint Kume first builds the Kume temple]. The theme is also the subject of parody in Suzuki Harunobu's *Mitate Kume sennin* [Parody of Saint Kume]; see

Nakamura Shin'ichirō et al., *Harunobu: bijinga to ehon* [Harunobu: women and illustrated books] (Tokyo: Shinchōsha, 1992), 56. Nakano interprets this painting as representing the cultural fall from the elite, courtly, Chinese-dominated values of *ga,* or "elegance," to those of *zoku,* or "vulgarity." In fact, however, these complementary terms always existed together in tension.

2. It is no less true of the cultural milieu of Japan today. The prevalence of this phenomenon as early as the seventeenth century provides a context for a "postmodern" novel such as Tanaka Yasuo's *Nantonaku kurisutaru* [Somehow, crystal], a work that, according to Norma Field, reads more like a shopping catalog and list of material cultural icons than like fiction (Norma Field, "*Somehow, Crystal:* The Postmodern as Atmosphere," in *Postmodernism and Japan,* ed. Masao Miyoshi and H. D. Harootunian, [Durham: Duke University Press, 1989], 169–188). The matter-of-fact use of such practices as product placement in films, the explosion of museum-shop reproductions, the production of "three-opera-tenor" TV extravaganzas exploited for public TV subscription drives, and the J. Peterman clothing catalog's novel use of brief fictional episodes in place of the usual product descriptions are examples of similar practices employed in the United States, Europe, and Japan today to blur the line between the arts and advertising, entertainment, and sales.

3. While the novelist Anthony Trollope is well known for taking an active interest in the details of commercial life, writes Richard Mullen, "he viewed the whole subject of advertising with disdain and came to regard it as a mark of decreasing honesty in English society. His worst novel, an absurd attempt at comedy, *The Struggles of Brown, Jones, and Robinson,* was an attack upon advertising." Richard Mullen, *Anthony Trollope: A Victorian in his World* (Savannah: Fredric C. Beil, 1990), 171.

4. Waseda Daigaku Toshokan, ed., *Bakumatsu Meiji no media ten: shinbun, nishikie, hikifuda* [Exhibition of late Tokugawa and Meiji media: newspapers, color prints, advertising leaflets] (Tokyo: Waseda University Press, 1988), 61.

5. Nishiyama Matsunosuke, *Kinsei bunka no kenkyū* [Studies of early modern culture] (Tokyo: Yoshikawa kōbunkan, 1983), 406, citing Santō Kyōzan's *Amei hisho* [A secret treatise on sweets], (1818).

6. Nishiyama, *bunka,* 160, quoting *Shikitei zakki* [Miscellaneous notes on Shikitei Sanba] for Bunka 8, 5/9. Examples of eighty *gesaku* advertising leaflets (*hikifuda*) composed by some fourteen writers are collected in *Gibun kikan* [Compendium of gesaku writing] (1883).

7. Takeuchi Makoto, *Bunka no taishūka* [The creation of mass culture], Nihon no Kinsei, vol. 14 (Tokyo: Chūōkōronsha, 1993), 27. Entries range from the simplest indication of shop name, address, and proprietor to elaborate advertising brochures extolling the lineage and virtues of the goods sold. The work is reproduced in its entirety in Matsuyama Shōnosuke, ed., *Edo chōnin no kenkyū* [Studies in Edo urban culture], vol. 3 (Tokyo: Yoshikawa Kōbunkan, 1976), 429–550.

8. *Hiraga Gennai zenshū* [Complete works of Hiraga Gennai], ed. Irihi Seizō (Tokyo: Kyōrinsha, 1932), vol. 6, 444–446.

9. One thinks of the tendency of Japanese ads in recent years to center on artful puns. A decade ago, one ad for a super glue featured a man dressed up as a Greek philosopher just so that he could hold up a broken pane of glass and announce, "*Pitā garasu no shūri*" (repairs broken glass), a pun on "Pythagoras' theorem" (*Pitagorasu no shiori* [theory]).

10. See Tani Minezō, *Edo no kopīraitā* [Edo ad copywriters] (Tokyo: Iwosaki bijutsusha, 1986), 79. The titles of three *gesaku* works published in 1795 under the name Honzentei Tsubohira (the sort of art name typical of a restaurateur, Tani hypothesizes) are recorded. The title of this work is taken from the adage *suterugami areba* hirougami *ari,* "there are gods of discarding, and there are gods of collecting," punning on the homonymous *hirougami,* "collection of [discarded] papers," and alluding no doubt to the heaps of ad leaflets littering the city. Several of these ads take the form of prefaces beginning with the clichéd phrases "*habakarinagara*" and "*osorenagara*" (If I might have a moment of your time), a more literary equivalent of the Edo street huckster's ubiquitous cry "*gorōjiro gorōjiro*" (Check it out!). *Kokusho sōmokuroku* [General catalog of Japanese books] lists the work as coauthored by Tsubohira and Kyōden, and the date as Tenmei 2, that is, 1782.

11. Plate no. 44, *Nihonbashi Tōri Itchōme ryakuzu* [An overview of Nihonbashi Tōri Itchōme]. Other famous depictions of shops are no. 7, *Odenmachō momen-dana* [Cotton-goods dealers at Odenmachō], showing Tabataya, Masuya, and Shimaya; no. 8, *Suruga-chō,* depicting the huge Mitsui Echigoya stretching an entire block; no. 74, *Odenmachō gofuku-dana* [Dry-goods dealers at Odenmachō], showing Shimamura Onimaruya; and no. 114, *Bikuni-hashi Settchū,* [The nun's bridge in Settchū], showing a boar-meat *(yamakujira)* shop and a roast-sweet-potato shop with its punning sign *"jūsanri,"* a famous rebus that deciphers as "more delicious than chestnuts" *(ku-ri yo-ri umai).*

12. Santō Kyōden's *Shoshiki kaichō nomikonda meihō enki* [The Origins of the Swallowed Sacred Treasure: A Varicolored Ledger, 1802] contains one such ad, complete with the information that the literacy pills could be purchased at Kyōden's shop; see Kokusho Kankōkai, ed., *Kindai Nihon bungaku taikei* [Compendium of modern Japanese literature], vol. 12: *Kibyōshishū* (Kokumin Tosho Kabushiki-gaisha, 1926), 204. See also Uchida Yasuhiro, "Yomihon sakka no seikatsu to shiya" [The life and horizons of *Yomihon* writers], in *Nihon no koten* [Japanese classics], ed. Mizuno Minoru, vol. 19: *Kyokutei Bakin* (Tokyo: Shūeisha, 1980), 158–164, Figure 328. Uchida compares the price of the literacy pills, advertised as "one *momne* five *bu,*" to the value of a day's rice paid to a skilled carpenter, which was one *momne* two *bu.*

13. Tani Minezō, *Nihon okugai kōkokushi* [A history of Japanese outdoor advertising], 157 and Figure 119. Similar plugs appear in Kyōden's *Nenashigusa fude no wakabae: Kinkin sensei zōka no yume* [Young sprouts from a brush of rootless weeds: Master Glitter's dream of transformation] and *Chūshingura zensei no makunashi* [The early lives of the loyal Rōnin in one act].

14. Ibid., Figure 327. Ads for Bakin's medicines can often be found at the ends of his chapters and in the margins of illustrations. In the story *Itozakura shunchō kien* [The marvelous affinity of thread cherries and spring butterflies, 1812], for example, a man and a woman take a moment from eloping to discuss the efficacy of his medicine. Ads for "Shin-

nyotō," a medicine handed down in the Takizawa family, also appears in his *Minō furuginu Hachijō kidan* [The marvelous tale of old Hachijō robes from Minō, 1813].

15. Ibid., Figures 329–330. The front of Sanba's shop is shown papered with ads for Enjūtan and Edo no Mizu; the former was a cough medicine made by Tanaka Sōetsu and sold throughout the Kantō region through agents *(toritsugisho),* while the latter was a cosmetic made by Sanba and sold exclusively at his own store. For *Ukiyoburo,* see Honda Yasuo, *Shikitei Sanba no bungei* [The literary art of Shikitei Sanba] (Tokyo: Kasama Shoin, 1973), 198 and 279. Sanba also sold "Tennyogan" (Heavenly Maiden Pills), "effective for menstrual irregularity and for terminating pregnancy." Obushi Hajime, *Nihon kessaku kōkoku* [Masterworks of Japanese advertising] (Tokyo: Seiabō, 1991), 46–47.

16. Hayashi Yoshikazu, ed., *Kane no waraji* [Sandals of steel] (Tokyo: Kawade Shobō Shinsha, 1984), see esp. pp. 64–65. The section on Kanda Myōjin shrine (p. 121) also contains an inserted ad for a tobacco shop, owned by Matsuzakaya Kōzemon of Kameichō, in which Ikku apparently had an interest.

17. Nishiyama Matsunosuke and Sekioka Senryō, eds., *Senjafuda* (Tokyo: Kōdansha, 1983). The practice of pasting these on temples and shrines is still so common that the warning "post no *senjafuda*" is often seen today displayed prominently on tempting targets.

18. See Nakada Setsuko, *Kōkoku no naka no Nippon* [Japan in advertising] (Tokyo: Daiyamondosha, 1993), 9–13; Yamamoto Taketoshi and Tsuganesawa Toshihiro, *Nihon no kōkoku: hito, jidai, hyōgen* [Japanese advertising: people, periods, terminology] (Tokyo: Sekai Shisōsha, 1992), 2–22; Tani Minezō, *Edo no kopīraitā,* 1–125; Matsumiya Saburō, *Edo kabuki to kōkoku* [Edo kabuki theater and advertising] (Tokyo: Tōhō Shobō, 1973), 117–146.

19. *Kisho fukuseikai kankōsho* [Association for the promotion and reproduction of rare books], ser. 5, vol. 21 (Tokyo: Beisandō, 1927). Well-known kabuki actors like Ichikawa Danjūrō made fortunes in product endorsements; see, for example, the ad for Danjūrō Toothpaste, sold at the Hyōtan-ya, in Ota Nanpo's *Edo kaimono hitori annai* [A personal guide to Edo shopping] (Matsuyama, *Edo chōnin no kenkyū,* 444).

20. Tani Minezō, who lists some twenty such promotional works of fiction (*Edo no kopīraitā,* 234–235), calls this the first literary work to be given away as a promotional item (*keibutsu*) (p. 231; Ejima Kiseki had published a work of the same title seventy years earlier in 1722). Kyōden opened his tobacco shop less than a year after the unprecedentedly harsh punishments meted out to Kyōden and his publisher Tsutaya Jūsaburō by the authorities in 1791 for his authorship of three works of fiction, and his advertising activities increased markedly from this time.

21. "When you place the Heating Stone in the bosom of your kimono and press down, its medicinal power quickly circulates through the five organs." Quoted in Honda Yasuo, *Shikitei Sanba no bungei,* 43. In 1810, Sanba succeeded to his family's business and opened the "Divine Remedy Long-Life-Pill" Medicine Shop, selling a popular nostrum "Enjūtan" concocted by Tanaka Sōetsu of Kyoto. Obtaining exclusive Kantō distribution rights to the product, Sanba opened his new shop in Honchō-nichōme. Sanba, the adopted son-in-law of Rankōdō Yorozuya Tajiemon, a bookseller by trade who also dealt in med-

icines (*Wata onjaku* 1:1 and 2:2), calls himself "writer and tradesman-twice-over" in his story *Pinto jōmae kokoro no aikagi* [The pass-key that unlocks every heart] (ibid., 197).

22. See Koike Masatame, ed., *Edo no ehon* [Edo illustrated books] (Tokyo: Kokusho kankōkai, 1987), vol. 2, 249–263. This *otogibanashi*-like account of Mitsui stands in contrast to Ihara Saikaku's more mundanely factual account recorded in *Nippon eitaigura* [The eternal storehouse of Japan, 1688], 1:4. Echigoya was in fact enagaged in a trade war with Ebisuya and Kameya during this period. When these latter two expanded their Owarichō stores in 1754, they distributed leaflets announcing an "absolute and total sale" *(munen musō ōyasuuri)* in response to which Echigoya in 1757 came up with its innovative and soon almost universally copied novel merchandizing technique of offering "no added charges when you pay cash" *(genkin yasuuri kakene nashi)*. Number 74 of Hiroshige's *Meisho Edo hyakkei* series, for example, shows this slogan written on the sign of Daimaruya (1858), which began in Kyoto in 1717 and opened its Odenmachō store in Edo in 1743; it can also be found written on the shop curtain in Utagawa Toyokuni's depiction of Santō Kyōden's shop. *Tōkyō Kokuritsu Hakubutsukan shozō: Matsukata konekushan ukiyo-e hin ten* [Holdings of the Tokyo National Museum: exhibition of *ukiyo-e* art from the Matsukata collection] (Tokyo: Tokyo National Museum, 1991), Figure 137.

23. "Edo fūryū hakkeishiki: Asakusa seiran" [Eight styles of Edo: A clear view of Asakusa]. See Obushi Hajime, *Nihon kessaku kōkoku,* 106–107.

24. Nakamura Shin'ichirō et al., *Harunobu: bijinga to ehon* (Tokyo: Shinchōsha, 1992), 29.

25. See, for example, Kitagawa Utamarō's portrait of Takashima no Ohisa, a "signboard girl" from the Takashimaya teahouse at Ryōgokubashi.

26. Nakada, *Kōkoku,* frontispiece (the word "toothpastes" is in large, bold writing in the original).

27. Matsumiya, *Edo kabuki,* 121–159.

28. Uirō is still sold today in Honchō, Odawara. Other potions featured in kabuki plays include "Long Life Pills" *(Shitenno yagura no ishizue),* "Female Pleasure Pills" *(Soga kyōdai omoi no hariyumi),* "Marvelous Ointment for Opening the Eyes of the Blind" *(Asagao nikki),* and the disfiguring poisons in *Yotsuya kaidan,* which might have been countered by the "Potion for Making All Bodily Wounds Disappear" *(Kirare yosa)*. See Nakayama Mikio, *Ukiyo-e kabuki shirīzu,* vol. 1: *Kabuki jūhachiban* (Tokyo: Gakugei Shorin, 1988), 24–27. The story *Kōyakuuri miyako no hanabusa* [The ointment seller, flower of Kyoto, 1763] features a stammerer *(domori)* whose stammer disappears only when he's chanting his sales pitch. Such stories about itinerant hucksters usually concern revenge, since it was traditional in fiction and drama to conceal oneself in the guise of an itinerant ointment seller for the purpose of effecting vengeance. This story was apparently stimulated by a vendetta carried out in 1763. See Koike Masatame, *Edo no ehon,* vol. 3, 325–341.

29. Tani Minezō, *Nihon okugai kōkokushi,* 151–152.

30. In the early Tenpō period (1830–1843), the popular *onnagata* Segawa Kikunojō III took Senjo (or Sennyo, "Fairy Maiden") as a stage name, and this is thought to have given rise to the name of the product. Sakamotoya, of Inari-chikamichi in Minami Denmachō, created posters titled *"Senja-mairi"* featuring actors using Senjokō.

31. Takahashi Hakushin, ed., *Ukiyo-e zanmai: Kunisada to Eisen* [Enthralled by the float-

ing world: Kunisada and Eisen] (Tokyo: Arita Shobō, 1980), Plate 83, p. 181. The fan-poem is inscribed "from the *Inari-shū*," no doubt a poetry collection produced by one of the literary groups of the day. More Senjokō ads by Eisen and Kunisada can be seen in Figures 39, 48, 87, 88, 100, 102, and 103.

32. For other examples of Senjokō and Kumonoue cosmetics in *ukiyo-e* prints, see Ozaki Hisaya, "Ukiyo-e no kōkoku ishō" [*Ukiyo-e* advertising designs] in *Edo no asobi* [Edo amusements], *Chōnin Bunka Hyakka Ronshū* [An encyclopedia of townsman culture], vol. 1, ed. Haga Noboru (Tokyo: Kashiwa Shobō, 1981), 123–127.

33. See, for example, Kunisada's *Daimaru gofuku-dana mae no bijin* [Beauties in front of the Daimaru Dry Goods Shop], showing three geisha dressed in Daimaru's latest fashions, in Takahashi Katsuhiko, *Edo no nyū media: ukiyo-e, jōhō, kōkoku to asobi* [Edo's new media: *Ukiyo-e,* information, advertising, and amusements] (Tokyo: Kadokawa, 1992), 73. Takahashi refers to this sort of advertising as "sponsored art."

34. Ozaki Hisaya, "Ukiyo-e no kōkoku ishō," 123–127.

35. Matsumiya, *Edo kabuki,* 232.

## 6. Westernizing Bodies

1. Quoted in Donald H. Shively, "The Japanization of the Middle Meiji," in *Tradition and Modernization in Japanese Culture,* ed. Donald H. Shively (Princeton: Princeton University Press, 1971), 91. Inoue's speech is discussed in Julia Meech-Pekarik, *The World of the Meiji Print: Impressions of a New Civilization* (New York: John Weatherhill, 1986), 144–145. I am indebted to Meech-Pekarik for many points and insights concerning visual art and culture during the Rokumeikan period.

2. *Japan Weekly Mail,* November 7, 1885.

3. Ibid.

4. Quoted in Masao Miyoshi, *As We Saw Them: The First Japanese Embassy to the United States (1860)* (Berkeley and Los Angeles: University of California Press, 1979), 71.

5. Quoted in Miyoshi, *As We Saw Them,* 73.

6. Quoted by Miyoshi, ibid.

7. Quoted by Miyoshi, ibid.

8. On the reception of Western clothing for women in Meiji, see Meech-Pekarik, *World of the Meiji Print,* 138.

9. The empress' proclamation was published in *Chōya shinbun,* January 19, 1887.

10. *"Arimasen"* literally means "does not exist"—perhaps a polite way for Loti to avoid the indiscretion of mentioning the lady's actual name (an equivalent, then, to "Madame X")—though the dismissiveness involved matches Loti's general contempt for this world of "astonishing parvenues."

11. Pierre Loti, "Un bal à Yeddo," from *Japoneries d'automne* (Paris: Calmann-Lévy, 1889), 84–87. Loti's account of the Rokumeikan is discussed by Julia Meech-Pekarik in *World of the Meiji Print,* 148–151.

12. *Japan Weekly Mail,* November 7, 1885.

13. Sugiura Jūgō, in *Kyōiku jiron,* 57, quoted in Donald Shively, "The Japanization of the Middle Meiji," in *Tradition and Modernization in Japanese Culture,* 106.

14. *Japan Weekly Mail,* April 30, 1887.

15. Okakura Tenshin, "Modern Art from a Japanese Point of View," *Quarterly Review* 11, no. 2 (July 1905).

16. For an excellent discussion of the portrait of Tōgai, see John Rosenfield, "Western-Style Painting in the Early Meiji and Its Critics," in Shively, *Tradition and Modernization in Japanese Culture,* 186.

17. Minoru Harada, *Meiji Western Painting,* trans. Akiko Murakata, Arts of Japan 6 (New York and Tokyo: Weatherhill/Shibundo, 1974), 39.

18. On Gérôme's career as a sculptor, see Gerald M. Ackerman, *Jean-Léon Gérôme (1824–1904)* (exhibition catalog, Dayton Art Institute, 1972), 12–13; and Ackerman, *The Life and Work of Jean-Léon Gérôme* (London and New York: Sotheby's, 1986), 175–179, 308–333.

19. One reason for the strangeness of the colors in *Reading* is that the changes in tonality (on the scale from dark to light) are not accompanied by changes in hue. Each of the major colors (red, blue) stands principally in relation to white, rather than to adjacent hues or complementaries.

20. I am not necessarily referring to actual conditions but those implied by the picture's internal space. Yamashita Shintarō could, of course, have painted the portrait from memory.

21. That the Japanese artists knew their bohemian script as well as any is suggested by Blondelle Malone's remarks concerning a visit made to an unidentified art school in Japan, perhaps the Tokyo School of Fine Arts. "We met the director, who spoke English. I asked if there were artists who had studied in Paris and he went for one, the instructor in oil painting. This fellow came in with Paris stamped all over him. . . . We visited the life classes next and the work was very good . . . we met four students . . . with the studio stamped all over them—baggy clothes, Vandyke and Rembrandt beards, and everything that goes to make an artist." Louise Jones Dubose, *Enigma: The Career of Blondelle Mason in Art and Society* (Columbia, S.C.: University of South Carolina Press, 1963), 30–31; cited in Gerald D. Bolas, "American Responses to Western-Style Japanese Painting," in *Paris in Japan: The Encounter with European Painting,* ed. Shuji Takashina, J. Thomas Rimer, and Gerald D. Bolas (exhibition catalog, The Japan Foundation, Tokyo, and the Gallery of Art at Washington University in St. Louis, 1987), 14–15.

22. On Rodin's use of the model, see Ruth Butler, *Rodin: The Shape of Genius* (New Haven and London: Yale University Press, 1993), 436–454.

23. On the structure of sexual difference in European modernism, see Carol Duncan, "The Aesthetics of Power in Modern Erotic Art," in *Feminist Art Criticism: An Anthology* (Ann Arbor: UMI Press, 1988), 59–69.

24. See Luce Irigaray, "Women on the Market," in *This Sex Which Is Not One,* trans. Catherine Porter (Ithaca, N.Y.: Cornell University Press, 1985), 177. An essential bibliography on the concept of "the traffic in women" would include Claude Lévi-Strauss, *The*

*Elementary Structures of Kinship* (Boston: Beacon, 1969); René Girard, *Deceit, Desire, and the Novel: Self and Other in Literary Structure,* trans. Yvonne Freccero (Baltimore: Johns Hopkins University Press, 1972); Gayle Rubin, "The Traffic in Women: Notes Toward a Political Economy of Sex," in *Toward an Anthropology of Women,* ed. Rayna Reiter (New York: Monthly Review Press, 1975), 157–210; and Eve Kosofsky Sedgwick, *Between Men: English Literature and Homosocial Desire* (New York: Columbia University Press, 1985). Eve Sedgwick provides an especially useful critical reading of this literature; see her chapter "Gender Asymmetry and Erotic Triangles," in *Between Men,* 21–27.

## 7. Icons of Femininity

1. *Tsuchida Bakusen ten* [Tsuchida Bakusen: a retrospective] (Tokyo: National Museum of Modern Art, 1997); Kyōto Kokuritsu Kindai Bijutsukan, ed., *Kokuga Sōsaku Kyōkai Kaikoten* [Kokuga Sosaku Kyōkai retrospective] (Kyoto, 1993), 10–23; Ellen P. Conant, ed., *Nihonga: Transcending the Past—Japanese Style Painting, 1868–1968* (St. Louis: Saint Louis Art Museum, 1995), 106–107.

2. On Tanaka Kisaku see Araki Hiroshi, "Meiji-matsu Taishō-ki no nihonga to seiyō bijutsu—Kokuga Sōsaku kyōkai ka'in no sōsaku ni ukagawareru seiyō bijutsu no eikyō ni kansuru shiron" [*Nihonga* and European art from the end of Meiji to the Taishō period—an essay on the influence of European art on the members of the Kokuga Sōsaku Kyōkai] *Tōkyō Zōkei Daigaku zasshi* 5 (March 1989): 41–131, esp. 77.

3. For *Hair,* Bakusen's eventual spouse, a geisha of Gion, posed as model. See Tanaka Hisao, ed., "Tsuchida Bakusen no Nomura Kazuyuki ate shokan" [Tsuchida Bakusen's letters to Nomura Kazuyuki] in *Bigaku bijutsushi ronshū* [Collected essays on aesthetics and art history], 4 (Seijō Daigaku Daigakuin Bungaku Kenkyūka, 1984), 103, letter dated November 6, 1916.

4. *Kokuga Sosaku Kyokai Retrospective*, 171.

5. Ikeda Shinobu, *Nihon kaiga no joseizō: jendā bijutsushi no shiten kara* [The image of woman in Japanese painting: from the point of view of gender-conscious art history] (Tokyo: Chikuma Shobō, 1998), 176–181.

6. See Wolfgang Schamoni, "Die Shirakaba-Gruppe und die Entdeckung der nachimpressioinistischen Malerei in Japan," *Nachrichten der Gesellschaft für Natur-und Völkerkunde Ostasiens,* nos. 127–128 (1980), 57–84.

7. Ikeda, *Nihon kaiga no joseizō,* 176–181.

8. Miyeko Murase, *Jewel Rivers: Japanese Art from The Burke Collection.* (Richmond: Virginia Museum of Fine Arts, 1994), cat. no. 39.

9. Scroll painting in the Pulverer collection, Cologne. Height 8.30 cm. See also Shibata Chiaki, ed., *Seigo jiten* [Dictionary of sexual terms] (Tokyo: Kawade Shobō, 1999), s.v. *"kine"* and *"usu o tsuku."*

10. *Tsuchida Bakusen ten,* 171–172 (letters to Nomura, dated June 23 and October 25); Tanaka Hisao, ed., "Tsuchida Bakusen no Nomura Kazuyuki ate shokan," 36.

11. For Bakusen's life drawing of models, see *Tsuchida Bakusen ten,* 172 (letter of July 6, 1914, to Nomura).

12. *Tsuchida Bakusen ten,* 172 (critique in *Bijutsu shinpō,* November 1913). The same critic hailed Bakusen for having created a new type of Japanese wall painting, reminiscent of the Buddhist fresco paintings in Hōryūji temple.

13. In April 1913 the monthly journal *Shirakaba* reproduced *Les baigneuses,* a seascape by Maurice Denis (1870–1943) (*Shirakaba* 4, no. 6 [1913]).

14. See Joshua S. Mostow, "Picturing Love among the One Hundred Poets," in *Love in Asian Art and Culture,* ed. Arthur M. Sackler Gallery (Smithsonian Institution) (Seattle: University of Washington Press, 1998), 31–47, 45.

15. *Tsuchida Bakusen ten,* 172 (quotation from *Bijutsu shinpō,* November 1913).

16. Neither painting appears in Bunten lists given by Tsuruta Migiwa. The Bunten *nihonga* section was originally divided in the three stylistically different subsections of *nanga, Tosa-ha,* and *bijinga.* In 1915 *bijinga* became confined to a special room *(bijin-shitsu),* including the subcategory of *joseiga.* Tsuruta Migiwa, "Bunten to bijinga," in *Bijinga no tanjō.* [The birth of *bijinga*], ed. Yamatane Bijutsukan (Tokyo: Yamatane Museum, 1997), 164–167, Figures 3, 5, and 6.

17. See Ikeda, *Nihon kaiga no joseizō,* 186–190. On display at the eighth Bunten exhibition in 1914 was Bakusen's *Heavenly Maidens,* a triptych showing two half-naked *apsara* surrounded by bodhisattvas (*Tsuchida Bakusen ten,* 172, cat. no. 9).

18. *Tsuchida Bakusen ten,* cat. no. 9, p. 173.

19. *Tsuchida Bakusen ten,* cat. no. D-5, p. 174.

20. Utamaro, *San bijin zu,* in *Utamaro, Ukiyo-e taikei,* vol. 5 (Tokyo: Shūeisha, 1973), Plate 62.

21. Tsuruta, "Bunten to bijinga," 166; *Tsuchida Bakusen ten,* 174 (letter dated July 7, 1916); critique in *Bijutsu no Nippon,* November issue, 1916.

22. *Tsuchida Bakusen ten,* cat. nos. 13, 14, YD-6 to D-14; pp. 173–174, 175.

23. *Tsuchida Bakusen ten,* 71.

24. Araki, "Meiji-matsu Taishō-ki no nihonga," 46. In a letter from Paris (dated March 23, 1921) Bakusen referred to his admiration of Goya's *Maya.* Tanaka Hisao, "Tsuchida Bakusen no Yoroppa kara shokan" [Tsuchida Bakusen's letters from Europe], in Seijō Daigaku Daigakuin Bungaku Kenkyūka, ed., *Bigaku bijutsushi ronshū* [Collected essays on aesthetics and art history] 6 (July 1987), 106.

25. *Tsuchida Bakusen ten,* 173 (letter to Nomura Kazuyuki, dated April 2, 1916).

26. *Kokuga Sosaku Kyokai Retrospective,* cat. no. 4.

27. The Kokuga Sōsaku Kyōkai was supported by Kyoto merchants dealing in textiles and imported paint. (*Kokuga Sosaku Kyokai Retrospective,* 160).

28. Ibid., 160 and 161. The manifesto was presented to the press on January 16, 1918.

29. Ibid., 160.

30. Doris Croissant, "Fenollosas 'Wahre Theorie der Kunst' und ihre Wirkung in der Meiji Zeit (1868–1912)," in *Saeculum* 38, no. 1 (1987): 52–75, 70.

31. *Tsuchida Bakusen ten,* cat. no. 14.

32. Chiba-shi Bijutsukan, ed., *Kainoshō Tadaoto to Taishō-ki no gaka-tachi* [Kainoshō Tadaoto and Taishō-period painters] (Tokyo: Nihon Keizai Shinbunsha, 1999), 82.

33. See Claire Freches-Thory and Ursula Perucchi-Petri, eds., *Die Nabis, Propheten der Moderne* (Munich: Prestel, 1993), Plates 33, 41, 186; Linda Nochlin, "Morisot's *Wet Nurse:*

The Construction of Work and Leisure in Impressionist Painting," in *Kunst um 1800 und die Folgen: Werner Hofmann zu Ehren,* ed. Christian Beutler, Peter-Klaus Schuster, and Martin Warnke (Munich: Prestel-Verlag, 1988), 263–273; Toby Clark, *Art and Propaganda in the Twentieth Century* (New York: Harry N. Abrams, 1997), 54–61.

34. *Tsuchida Bakusen ten,* 177–178.

35. Araki, "Meiji-matsu Taishō-ki no nihonga," 43–45.

36. *Tsuchida Bakusen ten,* 179–180.

37. *Kokuga Sosaku Kyokai Retrospective,* 20–21, 173.

38. Chiba-shi Bijutsukan, ed., *Kainoshō Tadaoto,* 16, 103 (ill.).

39. *Tsuchida Bakusen ten,* 181. In 1927 the French government bought a version of *Maiko Girl in a Garden* after having Bakusen awarded the rank of a Chevalier de Légion d'Honneur.

40. In 1920 Urakami Kagaku created a "nude painting" of an Indian woman. In 1941 he maintained that he had intended to pictorialize "the eternal woman" *(kyūen no josei).* See Kumamoto Kenjirō, *Kindai Nihon bijutsu no kenkyū* [Research on modern Japanese art] (Tokyo: Tōkyō Kokuritsu Bunkazai Kenkyūjo, 1964), 520.

41. Letter to Nomura Kazuyuki, written on February 23, 1913 (*Tsuchida Bakusen ten,* 171).

42. Shimada Yasuhiro quotes another letter written by Bakusen in 1914: "I have this desire to grasp an essence of the life of nature that would appeal to eternal humankind." *Tsuchida Bakusen ten,* 35.

43. Ihara Saikaku, *Kōshoku ichidai otoko* [Life of an amorous man], in *Ihara Saikaku shū 1,* Nihon Koten Bungaku Zenshū 38 (Tokyo: Shōgakukan, 1991), 255–303.

44. Evelyn Schulz has pointed to a literary *mitate* in Nagai Kafū's (1879–1959*) Diary of a Man Coming Home (Kichōsha no nikki),* published in 1909, where Nagai traced the archaeology of old Edo by comparing Tokyo to Paris. See Evelyn Schulz, *Nagai Kafū: "Tagebuch eines Heimgekehrten": Der Entwurf ästhetischer Gegenwelten als Kritik an der Modernisierung Japans* (Hamburg: Ostasien-Pazifik Trierer Studien zu Politik, Wirtschaft, Gesellschaft, Kultur, 1997), 130–227, 182.

45. Nakai Sōtarō, *Kindai geijutsu gairon* [Survey of modern art] (Tokyo: Nishōdō, 1922), 152–268.

46. See Nagai Takanori, "An Aspect of Cezanne's Reception in Japan: The Formation and Development of the 'Personalist' Interpretation of Cezanne in the 1920s," *Aesthetics* (Tokyo), no. 8 (March 1998): 79–91.

47. Nakai, *Kindai geijutsu gairon,* 267–268

48. Nagai, "An Aspect of Cézanne's Reception," 82. On the impact of German idealism on Japanese aesthetics, see Nakamura Giichi, *Kindai bijutsu ronsō shi* [A history of modern art debates] (Tokyo: Kyuryudo Library, 1981), 82–83.

49. Steve Odin, "An Explanation of Beauty: Nishida Kitarō's *Bi no Setsumei,*" *Monumenta Nipponica* 42, no. 2 (1987): 211–217. Nishida no doubt sided with Okakura Kakuzō's New Nihonga Movement. Interestingly, in 1897 Yokoyama Taikan painted a work titled *Muga* (No-self), showing a little Japanese peasant boy.

50. Nishida Kitarō, *Geijutsu to dōtoku* (1923), trans. David A. Dilworth and Valda H. Vilgielmo, *Art and Morality* (Honolulu: University of Hawai'i Press, 1973).

51. Kuki Shūzō, *Reflections on Japanese Taste: The Structure of Iki,* trans. John Clark (Sydney: Power Publications, 1997). See also Leslie Pincus, *Authenticating Culture in Imperial Japan: Kuki Shūzō and the Rise of National Aesthetics* (Berkeley: University of California Press, 1996).

52. Pincus, *Authenticating Culture,* 98, 115.

53. Quotation from Kuki's talk "L'expression de l'infini dans l'art japonais" given in Pontigny in 1928. Printed in Shūzō Kuki, *Propos sur le Temps: Deux communications faites à Pontigny pendant la décade 8–18 août 1928* (Paris: Philippe Renouard, 1928), 39. In the footnotes added to the publication, Kuki refers to Maurice Denis, Claude Monet, and van Gogh in comparing the postimpressionist preference for line and ornamentation to the Japanese artists Sesshū, Eitoku, and Hokusai (p. 34, note 1).

54. Pincus, *Authenticating Culture,* 46–49, 200. See also Schulz, *Nagai Kafū,* 235, note 39, on Nagai Kafū's *ukiyo-e* collection.

55. Pincus, *Authenticating Culture,* 115. See Nagai, "An Aspect of Cézanne's Reception," 84, on Abe's concept of life force in 1922.

56. Tanaka Hisao, ed., "Tsuchida Bakusen no Yoroppa kara shokan," 66.

57. In a letter dated January 13, 1923, Bakusen comments on his intention of creating "sweet pictures" of beautiful women. Ibid., 253.

58. Tomi Suzuki, "Gender and Genre: Modern Literary Histories and Women's Diary Literature," in *Inventing the Classics: Modernity, National Identity, and Japanese Literature,* ed. Haruo Shirane and Tomi Suzuki (Stanford: Stanford University Press, 2000), 71–95.

59. See Kevin M. Doak, "Ethnic Nationalism and Romanticism in Early-Twentieth-Century Japan," *Journal of Japanese Studies* 22, no. 1 (Winter 1996): 77–103, 99.

60. See Norman Bryson's chapter in this volume.

61. See Ulrike Wöhr, *Frauen zwischen Rollenerwartung und Selbstdeutung: Ehe, Mutterschaft und Liebe im Spiegel der japanischen Frauenzeitschrift* Shin Shin fujin *von 1913 bis 1916* (Wiesbaden: Harrassowitz Verlag, 1997).

62. See Yamaguchi Kenritsu Bijutsukan, ed., *Meiji Nihonga no shin jōkei* [Meiji *nihonga*'s new scenes] (Yamaguchi: Yamaguchi Kenritsu Bijutsukan, 1996). Also Naitō Masato, "Kiyokata and Shunshō: The Influence of the Edo Period Ukiyo-e on Modern Paintings of Beautiful Women," *Orientations,* April 2000, 58–63.

63. Tsuruta, "Bunten to bijinga," 166. See Hisatomi Mitsugu, "Kindai nihonga ni okeru rafu" [*Nihonga* nude painting], *Sansai* 2 (1988): 43–45; Kokuatsu Reiko, "Taishō no nihonga: mizu no onna, mizu no fūkei" [Taishō *nihonga:* women of water, landscapes of water], in *Taishō no atarashiki nami: nihonga 1910–1920 nendai* [Taishō's new wave: *nihonga* 1910–1920], ed. Tochigi Kenritsu Kindai Bijutsukan (Tochigi: Tochigi Kenritsu Kindai Bijutsukan, 1991), 11–15.

64. Murakami Kagaku, *Tsuchida Bakusen,* Gendai Nihon Bijutsu Zenshū 4 (Tokyo: Shūeisha 1972), 132.

65. Carol Gluck, *Japan's Modern Myths: Ideology in the Late Meiji Period* (Princeton: Prince-

ton University Press, 1985), 178, note 364. See also H. D. Harootunian, "Figuring the Folk: History, Poetics, and Representation," in *Mirror of Modernity: Invented Traditions in Modern Japan,* ed. Stephen Vlastos (Berkeley: University of California Press, 1998), 144–159; and Carol Gluck, "The Invention of Edo," 262–284, 279.

66. *Tsuchida Bakusen ten,* 181. Interestingly, paintings of beautiful women lost their appeal after 1939, when artists were called on to revitalize war painting for the glorification of the "Holy War." See Bert Winther-Tamaki, "Embodiment/Disembodiment: Japanese Painting during the Fifteen-Year War," *Monumenta Nipponica* 52 (Summer 1997): 145–180.

## 8. Images of Women in National Art Exhibitions during the Korean Colonial Period

Translation by Alwyn Spies.

1. When Japanese and Korean sources are cited, there are always difficulties translating the words used to denote what is only known in English as "Korea." As there are no formal rules governing the usage of the terms "Han'guk" or "Kankoku" (Korea) and "Chosŏn" or "Chōsen" (Colonial Korea) as well as "Han'gugin" or "Kankokujin" (literally, "person from Korea") and "Chosŏnin" or "Chōsenjin" (person from Colonial Korea), and the usage varies according to the era or the objective or the terms are used interchangeably; in the Japanese version of this essay, as a basic rule, the author uses the terms "Kankoku" and "Kankokujin" (translated as "Korea" and "Korean") as opposed to "Chōsen" and "Chōsenjin" (translated as "Chosŏn" and "Korean subjects") unless directly quoting a historical source or historical name or using the term in a comparable context [Trans.].

2. "Han'guk misul ŭi ilche singmin chanjae rŭl ch'ŏngsanhanŭn kil" [The path to clearing away the remains of Japanese colonialism from Korean art], *Quarterly Art Magazine,* Spring 1983. See also Kim Yunsu, "Han'guk kŭndae misul: kŭ pip'anjŏk sŏsŏl" [Korean modern art: A critical introduction], in *The History of Korean Contemporary Art* (Seoul: Han'guk Ilbosa, 1975), for a discussion of the management of Sŏnjŏn exhibits and the judging methods.

3. Wakakuwa Midori, *Kakusareta shisen* [The hidden view], Iwanami Modern Japanese Art, vol. 2 (Tokyo: Iwanami Shoten, 1996), 1.

4. Norman Bryson, "New Art History," in Takayama Hiroshi, *EYES Maruzen shinkan yōsho annai: bijutsu, shikaku geijutsu* [EYES Maruzen guide to new Western publications: Fine art, visual arts], 7 (1995): 5.

5. Kang Man'gil, "Munhwa chŏngch'i ŭi silsang" [The reality of Cultural Rule], in *Han'gukhyŏndaesa* [Contemporary Korean history] (Seoul: Ch'angja kwa Pip'yŏngsa, 1984), 17–38. See also Kang Tongjin, *Nihon no Chōsen shihai seisaku shi kenkyū* [Historical research on Japan's control policies for Korea] (Tokyo: Tokyo University Press, 1979), and Komagome Takeshi, *Shokuminchi teikoku Nippon no bunka tōgō* [The cultural synthesis of colonial and imperial Japan] (Tokyo: Iwanami Shoten, 1996), 192–234.

6. "Yanghwa ch'ogi 9," *Chungang ilbo,* August 31, 1971.

7. *Tonga ilbo,* August 29, 1929, and October 29, 1929.

8. Chi Myŏng-gwan, "Nihon chishikijin no Kankoku-kan" [Japanese intellectuals' perception of Korea] *Bungaku shisō* [Literary thought] (August 1981): 76. See also "T'ŭkchip-singminji, sagwan, pip'an" [Special edition: critique of the historical perception of colonialism], in *Han'guksa sjimin kangwa* [Citizen's forum on Korean history] (Seoul: Ilchogak, 1987).

9. Kang Sangjung, "Shōwa no shūen to gendai Nippon no 'shinzōchiri = rekishi': kyōkasho no naka no Chōsen wo chūshin toshite" [The last days of Shōwa and contemporary Japan's "mental image geography = history"—focusing on colonial Korea in textbooks], *Shisō* [Thought], October 1989, 36.

10. Hara Takeshi, "Chōsen tōchi shikan" [Personal thoughts on ruling colonial Korea], in *Saitō Makoto bunsho* 9 (Koryo Shorin ei'in-bon, 1990), 61–93.

11. Kang Sangjung, "Nippon no shokuminchi seisaku to orientarizumu" [Japanese colonial policy and orientalism], in *Orientarizumu no kanata e* [Beyond orientalism] (Tokyo: Iwanami Shoten, 1996), 97.

12. Kang, "Shōwa no shūen," 35.

13. Edward Said, *Orientarizumu* (*Orientalism,* Japanese language edition), ed. Itagaki Takezō and Sugita Hideaki, trans. Imazawa Kazuko (Tokyo: Heibonsha, 1986).

14. Chino Kaori, "Gender in Japanese Art," in the present volume.

15. Okada Saburōsuke, "Nyūsengo no shisō" [Impressions after entering Korea], *Chōsen* 88 (July 1922), cited in Nakamura Giichi, "Daiten, Senten, to Teiten" [The Taiwan, Korean, and Imperial exhibitions] *Kyōto Kyōiku Daigaku kiyō,* series A, no. 75 (1989): 265.

16. I think more research needs to be done on the subject of colonial period art and the nature of nativism, but there are two recent pieces of Korean research that deal with this issue: Kim Yŏngna, "1930 nyŏndae ŭi han'guk kŭndae hoehwa" [Modern Korean art in the 1930s], *Misulsa yŏn'gu* 7 (1993): 37–38; and Pak Kyeri, "Ilche sidae 'Chosŏn hyang-t'osaek' " [The nature of "Chōsen nativism" in the Japanese imperial period], *Han'guk kŭndae misulsahak,* vol. 4 (1996).

17. Ueno Chizuko, "Kokumin-kokka to jendā" [The nation-state and gender], *Gendai shisō* [Modern thought], 10 (1996): 21.

18. Yanagi Sōetsu, "Chōsen no tomo ni okuru fumi" [A letter sent to a Korean friend] and "Chōsen no bijutsu" [Korean art], in *Yanagi Sōetsu zenshū,* vol. 6 (Tokyo: Chikuma Shobō, 1981), 35–51 and 89–109.

19. From this time on, because Koreans Japanized their names and the characters for their names, it became impossible to differentiate between Koreans and Japanese solely on the basis of their names.

20. Sim Hyŏnggu, "Siguk kwa misul" [The political situation and art], *Sinsidae* 10 (1941); and Yi T'aeho, "1940 nyŏndae ch'oban ch'inil misul ŭi kun'gukchuŭijŏk kyŏng-hyangsŏng" [Militaristic tendencies in the pro-Japanese art of the early 1940s], in *Kŭndai Han'guk misal nonch'ong* [Modern Korean art theory], ed. Ch'ong Yi Kuyŏl Sŏnsaeng Hoe-gap Kinyŏm Nonmunjip Wiwŏnhoe (Seoul: Hakkojae, 1992).

21. Yi Kyuil, "Yŏksa sok ŭi misurin" [Artists in history], in *Twijibŏ pon Han'guk misul* [Korean art turned inside-out] (Seoul: Sigongsa, 1993), 182.

22. *Ch'inilpa 99 in 3* [The 99 pro-Japanese 3] (Tolbegae, 1993), 59.

23. Wakakuwa Midori, *Sensō ga tsukuru joseizō* [Images of women made by war] (Tokyo: Chikuma Shobō, 1995).

24. Ōe Shinobu, "Higashi ajia shinkyūteikoku no kōtai" [The shift from old to new empire in East Asia], in *Kindai Nippon to shokuminchi I: shokuminchi teikoku Nippon* [Modern Japan and its colonies I: Colonial and imperial Japan] (Tokyo: Iwanami Shoten, 1992), 29.

25. Kang, "Shōwa no shūen," 29.

26. See Norman Bryson's chapter in the present volume.

## 9. The Otherness of Women in the Avant-Garde Film *Woman in the Dunes*

1. According to the preface of the English translation of the screenplay *Woman in the Dunes* (New York: Phaedra Publishers, 1964), in the United States the film's "fame spread by word of mouth," and it was an "underground box office best seller" for at least two years following its release in 1964.

2. Sawa Kōzō, "Hadaka ni sareta sutā no kimochi" [Feelings of a star made naked], *Fujin kōron,* September 1994, 226.

3. Ibid.

4. The question of "visual pleasure" became a hotly debated issue after the 1975 publication of Laura Mulvey's article "Visual Pleasure and Narrative Cinema," and in recent years film analysis has begun to focus on historical and social content under the influence of cultural studies. Mulvey's article has been republished in Sue Thornham, ed., *Feminist Film Theory: A Reader* (New York: New York University Press, 1999).

5. This quotation is from Arthur Knight's review (first appeared in *Sunday Review,* October 31, 1964), which is included as the preface in the above-mentioned English translation of the screenplay *Woman in the Dunes.*

6. Satō Tadao, *Nihon eiga hyakusen* [One hundred selected Japanese films] (Tokyo: Akita shoten, 1976), 200.

7. Although Abe Kōbō wrote the original screenplay, the English translation credits its authorship to Teshigawara Hiroshi. See *Woman in the Dunes* (New York: Phaedra Publishers, 1964).

8. Janet Bergstrom, "Enunciation and Sexual Difference," in *Feminism and Film Studies,* ed. Constance Penley (New York: Routledge, 1988), 161.

9. Roland Barthes, *S/Z,* trans. Richard Miller (New York: Hill and Wang, 1974), 12.

10. John Erickson, "Metoikoi and Magical Realism in the Maghrebian Narratives of Taharben Jelloun and Abedelkbir Khatibi," in *Magical Realism,* ed. Lois Parkinson Zamora and Wendy B. Faris (Durham: Duke University Press, 1995), 427.

11. Susan J. Napier, "The Magic of Identity: Magical Realism in Modern Japanese Fiction," in *Magical Realism,* ed. Zamora and Faris, 466.

12. Kobo Abé, *The Woman in the Dunes,* trans. E. Dale Saunders (New York: Alfred A. Knopf, 1964), 4.

13. Freud's work was first introduced to Japan in the 1910s, and many translations of

his works followed. Soon artists and writers began applying Freud's ideology to their works. (See Sone Hiroyoshi's "*Furoido-ha to geijutsu* kaisetsu," an introduction written for the new edition of Tsushima Kanji's *Furoido-ha to geijutsu,* which was originally published in 1920 by Tenjinsha and was reprinted by Yumani Shobō in 1991, 13–25.) Abe, whose training was in clinical psychology, must have been well acquainted with Freud's work as well as aware of Japanese modernists' interest in Freud. In 1947 together with several other artists and critics including Teshigawara, he founded the avant-garde group Seiki no Kai, and when he joined the avant-garde group Yoru no Kai, he began to study Surrealism under the guidance of Hanada Kiyoteru. See Okaniwa Noboru, *Hanada Kiyoteru to Abe Kōbō* (Tokyo: Daisan Bunmeisha, 1980), 10–14.

14. Tanaka Hiroyuki's article "*Suna no onna* ron," *Nihon bungaku* 35 (December 1986), reveals great insight into Abe's work but ignores Niki's second quest to regain virility, which becomes the main theme in the film. Other critics seem to find the novel's plot difficult to understand. *Kokubungaku kaishaku to kyozai no kenkyū* 42, no. 9, (August 1993), which is a special issue on Abe Kōbō, provides information on current scholarship on Abe's works including *Suna no onna.*

15. See Arthur Knight's review included in the translation of the screenplay.

16. Abé, *Dunes,* 134.

17. Sigmund Freud, "The 'Uncanny,'" in *The Standard Edition of the Complete Psychological Works of Sigmund Freud: An Infantile Neurosis and Other Works,* vol. 17, trans. James Strachery (London: B. Hogan, 1963), 217–252.

18. Many books have been published on Japanese worship of Great Mother/Earth Mother, but a good introduction is Yoshida Atsuhiko's *Nihonjin no megami shinkō* [The Japanese belief in female gods] (Tokyo: Seidōsha, 1995).

19. Beauvoir's work was translated by Ikushima Ryoichi under the title *Dai ni no sei* and published by Shinchōsha in five separate volumes in 1959. The edition remained popular until a new translation was published in 1999.

20. Simone de Beauvoir, *The Second Sex,* trans. and ed. H. M. Parshley (Harmondworth: Penguin Books, 1975), 179.

21. Ibid.

22. Mircea Eliade, *Rites and Symbols of Initiation* (New York: Harper and Row, 1958), xiv.

23. Clare Johnston, "Women's Cinema as Counter-Cinema," in *Sexual Stratagems: The World of Women in Film,* ed. Patricia Erens (New York: Horizon Press, 1979), 136.

24. In E. Dale Saunders' translation of Abe's novel, the expression, *"hontō no onna"* is translated as "a real woman," but the "realness" of this woman is in question. I therefore have used the expression "a true woman." All other quotations from the novel are from Saunders' translation.

25. Abé, *Dunes,* 44 (emphasis added).

26. *Woman in the Dunes* (the screenplay), 23.

27. Abé, *Dunes,* 134.

28. Ibid., 36.

29. Ibid., 38.

30. Ibid., 140.

31. William Currie, "Abe Kobo's Nightmare World of Sand," in *Approaches to the Modern Japanese Novel,* ed. Tsuruta Kinya and Thomas E. Swann (Tokyo: Sophia University Press, 1976), 17.

32. Linda Williams, "Film Bodies: Gender, Genre and Excess," in Thornham, *Feminist Film Theory,* 270.

33. Judging from women's magazines in Japan, the sexual revolution, especially for women (whose sexuality was tightly controlled by the extremely patriarchal family system until the end of the Second World War), seems to have started in the late 1950s, and even *Fujin kōron,* which was directed at well-educated female readers, carried many articles on the importance of freedom of sexual expression for women. Thornham's *Feminist Film Theory* includes many influential essays on this issue with respect to female spectators.

34. Kuroda Toshio, *Rōdōryoku jinkō no chiiki jinkōgakuteki bunseki* [Demographic analysis of labor populations by region] (Tokyo: Kōseishō Jinkō Mondai Kenkyūsho, 1964), vol. 1, 12–13.

35. Akiyama Shun, "Nichijō-teki genjitsu to bungaku no tenkai: 1961–1977" [The development of daily reality and literature: 1961–1977], in *Gendai no bungaku* [Contemporary literature], special issue: *Sengo Nihonbunakushi nenpyō* [Timeline of postwar Japanese literary history] (Tokyo: Kōdansha, 1978), 324.

36. Abé, *Dunes,* 10 (emphasis added).

37. Ibid., 236.

38. In the late 1950s and early 1960s many agrarian communities lost young people to cities. For example, in Iwate Prefecture, the rate of loss of the young labor force aged nineteen to twenty-four was 20 percent. See Kuroda, *Rōdōryoku jinkō,* 15, 22, and 23.

39. Abé, *Dunes,* 224.

40. Ibid.

41. The original Japanese expression is *"aigō seishin,"* which is translated as "Love Your Home" in the Saunders version and "Love of One's Native Place Spirit" in the screenplay, but "Love Your Village" seems most appropriate here.

42. Fredric Jameson, *Postmodernism* (Durham, N.C.: Duke University Press, 1991), 337.

43. Abe was expelled from the Communist Party together with fourteen other writers for publicly criticizing the party's attempts to intervene and control the activities of the writers' wing of the party.

44. East European critics on the whole regarded the village as a distopia, pointing out its similarities with the authoritarian communist regimes of their own countries, and the Japanese critic Takeda Katsuhiko reported that in a discussion group he attended at an American university, a Chinese student who was a refugee from Communist China said that the lack of freedom in the village reminded him of his own country, while American students argued that it was similar to their own tightly controlled society. See Takeda Katuhiko, "*Suna no onna* no hyōka" [Criticism on *Woman in the Dunes*], in *Abe Kōbō zenshū* (Tokyo: Shinchōsha, 1972), vol. 6, "supplement," 10.

45. Abé, *Dunes,* 201.

46. Ibid., 204, emphasis added.

47. Ibid., 230.

48. See the photo of the Onta Matsuri of Asukani-Imasu Shrine in Tsurumi Shunsuke, *Ame no Uzume den* [The Legend of Ame no Uzume] (Tokyo: Heibonsha, 1991), 220.

49. Abé, *Dunes,* 232.

50. Ibid.

51. Ibid., 236.

52. Ibid., 235.

53. Ibid., 238.

54. Keiko I. McDonald, "Man, Sand and Symbols: Teshigawara's *The Woman in the Dunes,*" *Japan Interpreter* 12 (1979): 424.

55. Ibid., 425.

56. *The Second Sex,* 179.

57. These photos are included in Mary Ann Caws, Rudolf Kuenzli, and Gwen Reaberg, eds., *Surrealism and Women* (Cambridge, Mass.: MIT Press, 1995).

58. Amaryll Chanady, "The Territorialization of the Imaginary in Latin America: Self-Affirmation and Resistance to Metropolitan Paradigms," in *Magical Realism,* ed. Zamora and Faris, 138.

59. Whitney Chadwick, *Women Artists and the Surrealist Movement* (Boston: Little, Brown and Company, 1985), 15.

60. Anthony Penrose, *The Legendary Lee Miller* (East Sussex: The Lee Miller Archives, 1998), 11.

61. Ibid.

62. Tanaka Sumiko, " 'Ie' seido kaitai o meguru kōbōsen" [The struggle over the dissolution of the *ie* system], in *Josei kaihō no shisō to kōdō: Sengo hen* [The women's liberation movement and thought: postwar], ed. Tanaka Sumiko (Tokyo: Jijitsushin-sha, 1975), 20–40.

63. Suzuki Tsutomu, ed., *Nihonjin no hyakunen* [A hundred years of the Japanese] (Tokyo: Sekai Bunkasha, 1973), vol. 17, 183.

64. This view, known as "Joshidaisei Bōkoku-ron" (decline of the nation due to increased female students in universities), was said to have been expressed first by a professor at Waseda University in 1959, but female graduate students at Waseda University expressed strong criticism against it, saying even five years later that it was discrimination against women. See Maruyama Kunio, "Shijō sōkeisen: joshi sotsugyōsei no jittai," *Fujin kōron,* April 1964, 66–74.

65. Komano Yōko, "Kawariyuku josei no shokuba" [Women's changing places of work], in *Josei kaihō no shisō to kōdō,* ed. Tanaka Sumiko, 108.

66. Miyake Tsuyako wrote a novel titled *Dansei shiiku hō* [How to train men] in 1958, probably as a criticism against the male writer Kojima Nobuo's provocative article "Josei shiiku-hō no teishō" [Advice on how to train women], published in *Fujin kōron,* September 1958, 74–77. According to "Dansei shiiku udekurabe" (*Fujin kōron,* May 1959), this phrase became so popular among women that in 1959 Miyake's novel was made into a film.

67. Enchi Fumiko published a novel about women who invest in the stock market and buy highly profitable shares under the title *Otoko no meigara* (first serialized in the magazine *Shūkan bunshun* from August 1960 to February 1961), and "Otoko no meigara" became a popular phrase among women when evaluating men. (See Enchi Fumiko, "Watashi no *Otoko no meigara*," in *Fujin kōron,* August 1961.)

68. *Sei seikatsu no chie* [Wisdom in sexual life] was a manual on sex written by Sha Kokken (Tokyo: Ikeda Shoten, 1960) that became a bestseller and was translated into English, French, Swedish, Chinese, and other languages; many articles were published inspired by this book. See Inoue Hisashi, "Sha Kokken *Sei seikatsu no chie*: Pinokio ningyō ga oshieta beddo no ue no danjo byōdō" [Sha Kokken's *Wisdom in sexual life:* sexual equality in bed as taught by Pinocchio], *Bungei shunjū,* September 1988, 482–485.

69. When the reinstatement of the *ie* system became an impossible dream in 1960, some male writers began to articulate men's uneasiness at the loss of their power as head of the family, and in the sphere of critical writing, some also voiced the need for men to become strong husbands and fathers so that they could regain power within the family. Abe's contemporary Etō Jun, in his 1961 introduction to Enchi Fumiko's novel *The Waiting Years,* stated that the *ie* system "must be maintained at all cost." See Etō Jun, "Kaisetsu," in Enchi Fumiko, *Onnazaka* (Tokyo: Shinchōsha, 1961), 215–216.

70. *Otoko girai* [The men haters] was broadcast by Nihon Terebi from April 16, 1963, to April 7, 1964, and the four actors who played the antimale sisters, including Kishida Kyōko, attracted a great deal of media attention. See "*Otoko girai* to iu keredo" [It's called *The men haters* but . . . ], in *Fujin kōron,* August 1963, 9–11.

## 10. Gender in Contemporary Japanese Art

1. Some of the better-known artists from the postwar period in relation to whom the question of nationality is blurred are Yoko Ono, Arakawa Shūsaku, On Kawara, and Sugimoto Hiroshi, all of whom moved to New York and merged into the international art scene there; Isamu Noguchi, who was a U.S. citizen but was closely connected to Japanese art circles during the 1950s; and Korean-born Lee U-Fan, who is considered one of the founders of the Japanese Mono-ha movement in the early 1970s. The lack of consistent order of first and family names in the above-mentioned cases is a part of the issue, since artists who are identified as "non-Japanese" are known by their "Westernized" order of names and often have their names written in *katakana* rather than *kanji* when referred to in Japanese.

2. During the 1990s, for example, there was an increase in the cultural and artistic exchange between Japan and other Asian countries, as seen in Japan's participation in the first international version of the Taipei Biennial in 1998 as well as the opening in March 1999 of Fukuoka Ajia Bijutsukan (Fukuoka Asian Art Museum), whose collection contains modern and contemporary art from various Asian countries. "1998 Taihoku biennāru ripōto" [1998 Taipei Biennial report], *Bijutsu techō* [Art notes], 50, no. 761 (September 1998): 101–108; Maggie Pai, "Challenge to Change," *Asian Art News* 8, no. 4 (July/

August 1998): 36–47; *Ajia no bijutsu: Fukuoka Ajia Bijutsukan no korekushon to sono katsudō* [Asian art: The collection and activities of Fukuoka Asian Art Museum] (Tokyo: Bijutsu Shuppansha, 1999).

3. On postwar trends in female employment in Japan, see also the chapter by Chigusa Kimura-Steven in the present volume.

4. Wakakuwa Midori published twelve essays about females artists in a historical perspective in the magazine *Sōbun* in 1983 and 1984, which were later published and reprinted in one volume; Wakakuwa Midori, *Josei gaka retsuden* [Biographies of female artists] (Tokyo: Iwanami Shinsho, 1985). Ueno Chizuko included aspects of "cunt art" in *Onna asobi* [Women playing] (Tokyo: Gakuyō Shobō, 1988). Linda Nochlin's "Why Have There Been No Great Women Artists?" from 1971 was published in Japanese in *Bijutsu techō* in 1976. See also the bibliography of the present volume for Japanese translations of feminist works.

5. *Tokushū: Women Artists* [Special issue: women artists], *Bijutsu techō* 35, no. 515 (September 1983); "Ganbattemasu 'joryū'" ["Ladies" doing their best], *Gekkan bijutsu* [Monthly art], no. 127 (April 1986); and "90 nendai feminin weebu" [The feminine wave of the 1990s], *Hanga geijutsu* [Print art], no. 74 (1991).

6. *Bijutsu no chōshōjotachi* [The super girls of art], special issue, *Bijutsu techō* 38, no. 566 (August 1986): 19–80.

7. Enomoto Ryōichi and Matsuoka Kazuko, "Ima kakeru onna" [Women on the march], *Bijutsu techō* 38, no. 566 (August 1986): 46–59.

8. Ibid., 50.

9. Ibid., 51.

10. In 1989 art critic Sawaragi Noi made direct reference to the "Super Girls of Art" issue and argued that the frequent use of the "Super Girl" concept had diverted the focus from the qualities that female artists themselves represent and instead placed female artists in the categories of "men" or "children" before they would receive attention. Sawaragi Noi, "Enshin to shite no sei" [The centrifugal sex], *Bijutsu techō* 41, no. 613 (August 1989): 82. Other Japanese art critics too have made specific reference to the concept of "Super Girls."

11. For example, *Bijutsu techō* of July 1984 (vol. 36, no. 528) featured a special edition on *Nyū imeeji no teian* [Propositions on new images]. A special edition on *Gendai kaiga no bōken* [The adventure of contemporary painting] was published in November 1985 (vol. 37, no. 552) focusing on "new painting" in Japan. A similar feature of *Bijutsu techō* in June 1986 (vol. 38, no. 563) introduced the "new wave" of sculpture with a special edition titled *Gendai chōkoku no hatsugen: nyū ueebu to machi no chōkoku* [Speaking of contemporary sculpture: New Wave and sculpture in the streets].

12. *Gendai chōkoku no hatsugen: nyū ueebu to machi no chōkoku.*

13. Yoshiaki Tōno, "Imagineering," *Art Forum,* January 1986, 72–75. Tōno was the curator for the Japanese section of the international exhibition of contemporary art at Toyama Museum for Modern Art in 1984 and focused—the only one among the four curators—on gender issues in his selection and in his part of the catalog text. Tōno

Yoshiaki, "Toyama nau '84: Nihon sekushon" [Toyama now '84: Japanese section], *Toyama Now '84: dai ni kai Toyama kokusai gendai bijutsu-ten* [The Second International Exhibition of Contemporary Art in Toyama] (Toyama: Toyama Kenritsu Kindai Bijutsukan, 1984).

14. Janet Koplos, "Some Kind of Revolution?" *Art in America,* May 1992, 10, 153.

15. Enomoto and Matsuoka, "Ima kakeru," 59.

16. Yuri Mitsuda, "Flowers for Wounds," in *Asian Women Artists,* ed. Dinah Dysart and Hannah Fink (Roseville East, Australia: Craftsman House, 1996), 67.

17. Nancy Shalala, "Quest for the Female Grail," *Japan Times,* May 23, 1993.

18. Lisa Milne, "The Nuances of Naito's Nothing," *Daily Yomiuri,* March 11, 1994.

19. Fumio Nanjo, "Rei Naito: Japanese Pavilion" (URL address http://www.dialnsa.edu/iat97/Venice/Japan/install2.html; last modified October 16, 1997, downloaded July 5, 1999).

20. "Yanobe Kenji," *Ōkina nikki, chiisana monogatari* [Big diary, little tale] / *Mito Annual '92, Private Diary: 10 Japanese Young Artists* (Mito: Mito Geijutsukan Gendai Bijutsu Gyararī, 1992), 66.

21. Interview by Mark Sanders and Fumiya Sawa, photocopy given by Yanobe Kenji to the author during an interview in Kyoto, May 29, 1998.

22. Yanobe Kenji, "'Chōkokufuku' o kita 'ichishimin'" ["One citizen" dressed in "sculptural clothes"], *Bijutsu techō* 43, no. 638 (June 1991): 132.

23. Kusumi Kiyoshi, "Gojira to mobiru suutsu hatsumei gijutsu: mucha no tankyū" [Godzilla and the art of mobile suit invention: in quest of the absurd], in *Kenji Yanobe 1990–1994* (Tokyo: Röntgen Kunst Institute, 1994), 5.

24. Barbara London, "Sculpted Animations for Public Places," in *Kenji Yanobe 1990–1994,* 32.

25. Tone O. Nielsen, "Kenji Yanobe," *Louisiana Revy* 35, no. 3 (June 1995): 56.

26. The term *"otaku"* was coined in 1984 and described certain groups of youth, mostly young men, in Japan. *"Otaku"* is an honorific word literally meaning "your home," but it referred in this case to the formal way in which the young men were addressed by those with whom they were not familiar, such as distant peer group members. *Otaku* were presented in media and other places as "nerds" who would focus all their attention, time, and money on a specific thing at which they aspired to become amateur experts, often something that was exercised on an individual basis such as reading *manga* (comics), watching *anime* (animation film), or playing computer games. For the *otaku* concept in art and culture, see Dana Friis-Hansen, "Portrait of The Young Japanese Artist as a Fanatic," *Louisiana Revy* 35, no. 3, English Supplement (June 1995), 13–15; and Sharon Kinsella, "Japanese Subculture in the 1990s: *Otaku* and the Amateur *Manga* Movement," *Journal of Japanese Studies* 24, no. 2 (1998): 289–316. Kinsella notes that the word *"otaku"* can also be used for women and in the 1990s came to represent a whole generation perceived to be "so intensely individualistic they had become dysfunctional" (p. 313).

27. An argument noted in Sharon Kinsella, "Cuties in Japan," in *Women, Media, and Consumption in Japan,* ed. Lise Skov and Brian Moeran (Honolulu: University of Hawai'i Press, 1995), 220–254.

28. Azby Brown, "The Great Tokyo Art Hoax," *Tokyo Journal,* no. 9 (1993): 31.

29. The concept of *otaku* became the subject of great anxiety in Japan after the "Miyazaki murder case" in 1989, where a young man, Miyazaki Tsutomu, who fit all the descriptions of an *otaku,* was charged with the mutilation and murder of young girls. John Whittier Treat connects *otaku* and *shōjo* with the fiction of Yoshimoto Banana in John Whittier Treat, "Yoshimoto Banana Writes Home: *Shōjo* Culture and the Nostalgic Subject," *Journal of Japanese Studies* 19, no. 2 (1993): 353–387.

30. According to historian Charles Yuji Horioka, the consumption expenditures of single women under the age of thirty increased 15.8 percent between the years 1984 and 1989, while the increase for single men under the age of thirty increased only 2.0 percent in the same period. At the same time single women have almost twice as much savings as single men. Charles Yuji Horioka, "Consuming and Saving," in *Postwar Japan as History,* ed. Andrew Gordon (Berkeley: University of California Press, 1993), 288.

31. Millie R. Creighton, "Marriage, Motherhood, and Career Management in a Japanese 'Counter Culture.'" in *Re-Imaging Japanese Women,* ed. Anne E. Imamura (Berkeley: University of California Press, 1996), 192–220.

32. "Yanagi Miwa," *Artist Interview,* vol. 3 (1998), 1.

33. "Yanagi Miwa: aidentiti o nakushita kōkotsukan" [Yanagi Miwa: ecstatic feelings deprived of identity], *Bijutsu techō* 51, no. 779 (November 1999): 27.

34. Ibid.

35. Author's interview with Yanagi Miwa in Kyoto, May 30, 1998.

36. In 1998 two works by Yanagi Miwa, featuring young women wearing coats from the clothes company Max Mara, were displayed in the Max Mara shop in Minami Aoyama in Tokyo, making it difficult to see whether the photos were actual advertisements for the product or artworks. The same works were later exhibited at an art museum, at which the association with "art" was more clear.

37. In one scene where a male figure is present, namely, Humphrey Bogart together with Ingrid Bergman in a scene from *Casablanca,* Morimura enacts the part of "Bergman," while "Bogart" is a mannequin made to resemble Morimura's features.

38. Laura Mulvey, "Visual Pleasure and Narrative Cinema," in *Art After Modernism: Rethinking Representation,* ed. Brian Wallis (New York: The New Museum of Contemporary Art, 1995), 361–373.

39. Ibid., 363.

40. Ibid., 366.

41. He did this by engaging a large number of crew members to manage the technical aspect, hiring professional makeup experts and dressers, spending extensive time and money to find locations for the photo takes, and learning all aspects of photo recording in detail. Yamaguchi Yumi, "Joyū na otoko: Morimura Yasumasa no joyūryoku" [The actress man: the actress power of Morimura Yasumasa], interview with Morimura Yasumasa, *Freak Out* 12 (1996): 23. When the series was first exhibited in 1996 at Yokohama Art Museum, the museum entrance was made to resemble the entrance to a cinema, and some of the works were exhibited as billboards on frames extended from the wall with

rows of spotlights placed above. Kishimoto Yasushi, director, *Go on the Stage Morimura,* VHS video film, 48 min. (Kyoto: Ufer! Art Documentary, 1996).

42. It can even be argued, as does art historian and critic Chino Kaori, that Morimura's male body can reveal the mechanisms of castration anxiety more radically than a female body, because a female body, whatever message is intended, will always encounter the risk of becoming the object of the heterosexual male spectator's desire. Chino Kaori, "Onna o josōu otoko: Morimura Yasumasa 'Joyū' ron" [A man simulating woman: comments on Morimura Yasumasa's *Actresses*], in *Morimura Yasumasa: bi ni itaru yamai—joyū ni natta watashi / Morimura Yasumasa: The Sickness unto Beauty—Self-Portrait as Actress* (Yokohama: Yokohama Bijutsukan, 1996), 131–135 (English translation, 157–162).

43. Maitland McDonagh, *The 50 Most Erotic Films of All Time: From* Pandora's Box *to* Basic Instinct (New York: Citadel Press, 1996), 62.

44. *Gendai yōgo no kiso chishiki* [Encyclopedia of contemporary words] (Tokyo: Jiyū Kokuminsha, 2000), 1058.

45. Gérard Lenne, *Sex on the Screen: Eroticism in Film* (New York: St. Martin's Press, 1978), 172.

46. According to Okura Yayoi, a member of the Research and Study Group of the Japanese Official Development Assistance, the most popular destinations in the 1970s were South Korea, Taiwan, the Philippines, and Thailand. Okura Yayoi, "Promoting Prostitution," *AMPO Japan-Asia Quarterly Review* 25, no. 4–26, no. 1 (1995): 60–62.

47. In 1996 a total of 693,657 Japanese tourists visited Thailand, an increase of 115 percent compared to 1995. Nihon Jōhō Kyōiku Kenkyūkai, ed., *Heisei 11 nen: Nihon no hakusho* [Whitebook of Japan, 1999] (Tokyo: Seibunsha, 1999), 34. Official statistics do not include the exact purpose of such recreational travel, so it is impossible to say how many trips were organized sex tours. However, in September 1994 a book titled *Tai baishun tokuhon* [Thailand prostitution handbook] was published in Japan and sold 15,000 copies within five months. In January 1995 the foreign minister of Thailand issued a protest against the publication, a degrading guidebook to various types of prostitution in Thailand. The protest indicates that Japanese sex tourism in Thailand was considered a serious topic. Okura, "Promoting Prostitution," 60.

## 11. Busty Battlin' Babes

1. By summer 2001, 21 million Tomb Raider games had been sold worldwide (*Vancouver Sun,* June 15, 2001).

2. The official statistics for Lara come from Douglas Copeland and Kip Ward, *Lara's Book: Lara Croft and the Tomb Raider™ Phenomenon* (Rocklin, Calif.: Prima Publishing, 1998), 29–30. For one example of women suggesting an even more radical set of measurements, see "Measuring Up to Lara Croft" (*Vancouver Sun,* June 18, 2001, B8). Note that the (infamous) body measurements of the Barbie doll are very similar at 5 feet 9 inches, 36-18-33.

3. In Tomb Raider the players manipulate a character whom they can see; thus, al-

though they presumably identify with her as she enacts the moves that will allow the player to win the game, they can also consume her image fully. The game Shadow Warrior, evidently designed to encourage identification across (possible) racial boundaries, uses an unusual visual gimmick: the player manipulates the main character, Lo Wang, from a first-person perspective, seeing only what the character would see of his own body as it moves through the 3D space of the game, such as an arm thrust forward holding a gun. Jeffrey Ow argues that this gimmick is merely a means of disguising the racist, misogynist, and neocolonialist aspects of Shadow Warrior, allowing the gamer to don "yellowface" as he or she enacts the (terrible) script. See Ow, "Revenge of the Yellow-faced Cyborg: The Rape of Digital Geishas and the Colonization of Cyber-Coolies in 3D Realms' *Shadow Warrior*," in *Race in Cyberspace*, ed. Beth E. Kolko et al. (London: Routledge, 2000). Although the same strategy might enhance male gamers' ability to "lose themselves" inside the persona of Lara Croft, this would preclude the visual pleasure of watching her.

4. In following Tomb Raider and Lara Croft links on the Web, I came across numerous Web pages identified with male names that incorporated artwork from the game or commentary on it. I have yet to come across one such site identified with a female-sounding name. But in fact, it is impossible to know the "true" sex of the people who created the sites.

5. As of summer 2000 fans have been able to enjoy Lara Croft's new adventures in comic book form, and in June 2001 the first Tomb Raider movie was released, debuting at the number one spot in the United States, the best ever debut for a film inspired by a videogame. This is just one example of hybridity among these already hybrid media. Many *manga, anime,* and videogames also have tie-ins with other products, such as action figures and "fancy goods," as well as live action movies and television series.

6. The ubiquitous image of the "Italian American" Mario Brothers in the popular videogame Donkey Kong was created in Japan by Nintendo, and Nintendo's Pokemon and Digimon have infiltrated all corners of North American society; William Gibson's *Neuromancer* (the first "cyberpunk" novel), like many of his subsequent novels, was set in Japan and was influenced by his exposure to Japanese fiction and animation in Vancouver and elsewhere; the film *Blade Runner,* which incorporates many "Asian" aesthetic elements, has been influential on many important Japanese *anime;* the *Star Trek: The Next Generation* TV series included several in-group references to popular Japanese *anime* such as *Dirty Pair*; the ever-popular *Power Rangers*™ television series (seven separate series so far) are joint productions that splice together scenes from earlier Japanese productions with new ones shot in California; the recent animated TV series *Cyber Six* is a joint production between Japan and Canada (based on a *manga* from Argentina!), and so on. Examples of the cross-pollination of popular culture elements between Japan and North America are endless and increasingly difficult to disentangle, invisible as they may be to many North Americans.

7. In 1997 I supervised an M.A. thesis at the University of California, Berkeley, by Julianne (Phred) Dvorak, in which she argued that the formerly separate streams of *shōjo* (for girls) and *shōnen* (for boys) *manga* began in the 1980s to come together to form a hy-

brid genre, appealing to readers of both sexes. Dvorak traced this trend to its culmination in such early- to mid-1990s products as *Sailor Moon.* In this essay I will retrace some of the steps Dvorak made in her thesis and then will take the discussion forward to the rest of the 1990s. Although my argument differs from hers in some respects, I am deeply indebted to Dvorak for drawing my attention to this phenomenon and for introducing me to the fascinating topic of *manga/anime* history. Julianne Komori Dvorak, "Sailor Moon and the Shōjo-ization of Male Imagery" (M.A. thesis, Group in Asian Studies, University of California, Berkeley, 1997).

8. Sharon Kinsella has made this argument about various cultural products in the 1980s in "Cuties in Japan," in *Women, Media and Consumption in Japan,* ed. Lise Skov and Brian Moeran (Honolulu: University of Hawai'i Press, 1995), 243–244. In a later article Kinsella extends her argument into the early 1990s: "Japanese Subculture in the 1990s: *Otaku* and the Amateur *Manga* Movement," in *Journal of Japanese Studies* 24, no. 2 (1998): 289–316.

9. Horikiri Naoto, "Onna wa dokyō, shōjo wa aikyō" [For women it's bravery, for girls it's charm], in *Shōjo ron,* ed. Honda Masuko et al. (Tokyo: Aoyumisha, 1988), 40–41. Quoted in John Treat, "Yoshimoto Banana Writes Home: The Shōjo in Japanese Popular Culture," in Treat, ed., *Contemporary Japan and Popular Culture* (Honolulu: University of Hawai'i Press, 1996), 281; Treat's translation.

10. Yamane Kazuma, *Gyaru no kōzō* [Structure of the girl] (Tokyo: Seikaibunkasha, 1990), 11. Quoted in Kinsella "Cuties," 248; Kinsella's translation.

11. Ōtsuka Eiji, *Shōjo minzokugaku* [*Shōjo* ethnology] (Tokyo: Kōbunsha 1991), 18, quoted in Treat, "Yoshimoto Banana Writes Home," 301; Treat's translation.

12. It is doubtless no coincidence that these statements were made at the same time that essays appeared in one branch of North American scholarship making the same point about Japan's "infantile" status with regard to consumerism and empty intellectualism: See Asada Akira, "Infantile Capitalism and Japan's Postmodernisms: A Fairy Tale," as well as the introduction in Masao Miyoshi and H. D. Harootunian, eds., *Postmodernism and Japan* (Durham: Duke University Press, 1989); and Miyoshi and Harootunian, "Japan in the World," in *Japan in the World,* ed. Miyoshi and Harootunian (Durham: Duke University Press, 1993—originally published as a special edition of *Boundary 2,* in 1991). Although these scholars do not explicitly invoke the figure of the *shōjo,* their insistent characterization of Japan as "feminine" (dependent Other to the United States) and infantile suggests the analogy.

13. Seo Fumiaki, "Toshi o fuyū suru shōjotachi" [Girls who wander the city], in Honda Masuko et al., *Shōjo ron,* 159. Quoted in Treat, "Yoshimoto Banana Writes Home," 301; Treat's translation.

14. Midori Matsui, "Little Girls Were Little Boys: Displaced Femininity in the Representation of Homosexuality in Japanese Girls' Comics," in Sneja Gunew and Anna Yeatman, eds., *Feminism and the Politics of Difference* (Halifax: Fernwood, 1993), 177.

15. Kinsella, "Cuties," 244.

16. Honda Masuko, "Shōjogatari: kotoba no meikyū o meguru" [Touring the labyrinth

of words: *shōjo* language], in Honda Masuko et al., *Shōjo ron,* 10. This and all translations are mine unless otherwise noted.

17. Treat, "Yoshimoto Banana Writes Home," 282–283.

18. Jennifer Robertson, *Takarazuka: Sexual Politics and Popular Culture in Modern Japan* (Berkeley: University of California Press, 1998), 65.

19. Note, for example, that the *"atarashii onna"* (new woman) image that was significant in the beginning of the Taishō period had no corresponding *"atarashii otoko"* (new man). At the beginning of the Shōwa period, the newly identified *"moga"* (modern girl) did have her *"mobo"* (modern boy) counterpart, but he never received the attention that she did; the *mobo* never became such an important and ubiquitous cultural icon as the *moga.* One notable exception is the *"otaku"* (usually imagined/identified as male), which became an important social icon in the 1990s. See Kinsella "Japanese Subculture in the 1990s," 308.

20. For a discussion of the historical significance of the artistic depiction of women and girls in various periods in Japan, see Ikeda Shinobu, *Nihon kaiga no joseizō: jendā bijutsushi no shiten kara* [The image of women in Japanese painting: from the point of view of gender-conscious art history] (Tokyo: Chikuma shobō, 1998).

21. For more on Yoshiya, see Hirano Yoshinobu, "Yoshiya Nobuko: Joseisei no manazashi," in *Kokubungaku: kaishaku to kyōzai no kenkyū* 4, no. 11 (1992); and Yoshitake Teruko, *Nyonin: Yoshiya Nobuko* [The woman: Yoshiya Nobuko] (Tokyo: Bungei Shunju, 1982). My thanks to Kazue Harada for bringing these sources to my attention. See also Jennifer Robertson, *Takarazuka,* 71–72. Robertson elucidates the connection between Yoshiya and the all-female Takarazuka theater, the audience of which provides one of the earliest and still most interesting examples of ambiguous gender identification and desire in modern Japan.

22. About the discovery of adolescence, see Rika Sakuma Sato, "What Are Little Girls Made Of? Exploring the Symbolic Boundaries of Femininity in Two Cultures," in *Millennium Girls: Today's Girls around the World,* ed. Sherrie A. Innes (Lanham, Md.: Rowman and Littlefield, 1998), 17–20; and Horikiri Naoto 1988:108–109, quoted in Treat, "Yoshimoto Banana Writes Home," 281.

23. The term for an adult man is *"otoko,"* and there are, of course, many *manga* aimed at an adult male audience. At the same time, males of all ages may continue to enjoy *shōnen* and *seinen manga.*

24. See Jennifer Robertson, "Gender Bending in Paradise: Doing 'Female' and 'Male' in Japan," in *Genders* 5 (1989): 50–69, 56. Also quoted in Sato, "Little Girls," 17. At some point the unmarried woman transmutes into an *"orudo misu,"* an "old maid," a definition completely devoid of the complex possibilities of the *shōjo.* As long as she continues to look young, however, an unmarried woman with no children remains a *shōjo.* There is a genre of sexually explicit *manga* aimed at the post-*shōjo* adult woman, known as the "lady's comic." (Please note that I am referring to dominant social discourse regarding the recognized life stages for males and females. This discourse makes no accommodation for lesbians or for heterosexual women who choose to remain single and/or childless, but that does not mean that such women do not exist in Japan.)

25. In the first episode of *Ribbon Knight,* this gender ambiguity is explained as follows: In "heaven" sexually undifferentiated children waiting to be born are given a liquid to ingest that makes them either male or female. Before administering the drink, an adjudicator looks at each of them and decides whether the child should become strong and brave (a boy) or gentle and nurturing (a girl). The still-undifferentiated Sapphire is forced to drink the boys' liquid by another child, and then the adjudicator, unknowing, gives her the girls' drink. She therefore has all the mental and emotional attributes of both boy and girl but a girl's body because the adjudicator has designated her a girl.

26. Sharon Kinsella, *Adult Manga: Culture and Power in Contemporary Japanese Society* (Honolulu: University of Hawai'i Press, 2000), 95.

27. The enduring popularity of the series is demonstrated by the fact that the five-volume set remains in print everywhere. Since I bought my copy in 1998 I have lent it by request to four Japanese female graduate students who wanted to reread it or who, having heard about it all their lives or having seen it in other media, wanted to experience the original. All were born well after this *manga* narrative was created.

28. Ikeda Riyoko followed up *The Rose of Versailles* with another extremely popular *manga* series, *Orufeusu no mado* (Orpheus' window), which was serialized in 1975 in the *shōjo* comic journal *Weekly Margaret.* Once again Ikeda featured a female-to-male transgendered protagonist, this time setting the narrative against the historical backdrop of the Russian Revolution.

29. The word *"yaoi"* is an acronym for *"yama nashi, ochi nashi, imi nashi"* (no highs, no lows, no meaning) and refers to a subgenre of *shōjo* comics that focus on romantic and sexual relationships, usually between boys. The journal *June* specializes in this genre, but it is nearly the only regularly published commercial journal to do so. Many *yaoi* narratives are produced by amateurs and distributed through "irregular" channels, at comic markets. Because of space limitations I cannot here go into detail about many of the important elements of Japanese popular culture: the history of *yaoi* comics, the various comic markets in Japan, the unusual distribution methods of Japanese comic book artists, and the interactive relationship between artists and fans. For more on these phenomena, see Kinsella, *Adult Manga,* 104–124, and Kinsella, "Japanese Subculture in the 1990s."

30. Kazuko Suzuki, "Pornography or Therapy? Japanese Girls Creating the Yaoi Phenomenon," in Innes, ed., *Millennium Girls,* 244.

31. See Fujimoto Yukari, *Watashi no idokoro,* 134–135.

32. Takemiya Keiko, "Manga gakka de kyōdan debyū, sandome no waga tenki" [My debut at the podium in a *manga* studies department, my third turning point], *Fujin kōron,* no. 1058 (April 22, 2000): 41.

33. See Susan Napier, "Vampires, Psychic Girls, Flying Women and Sailor Scouts: Four Faces of the Young Female in Japanese Popular Culture," for examples of some of these "Other" protagonists in 1980s *manga* with whom girls were expected to identify. In *The Worlds of Japanese Popular Culture: Gender, Shifting Boundaries and Global Cultures,* ed. D. P. Martinez (Cambridge, U.K.: Cambridge University Press, 1998).

34. See Yamane Kazuma, *Hentai shōjo moji no kenkyū* [The study of deviant girls' script]

(Tokyo: Kōdansha, 1986), for an analysis of what the use of this script and related cultural phenomena reveal about the nature of the *shōjo.*

35. For more on this genre, see Saitō Minako, *Kōitten: anime, tokusatsu, denki no hiroinzō* [One touch of crimson: the image of the heroine in *anime,* special effects, and biography] (Tokyo: Birejji Sentaa Shuppankyoku, 1998). The several *Power Rangers* series, broadcast throughout North America, constitute one example of this very popular genre.

36. Dvorak, "Sailor Moon."

37. In addition, *Sailor Moon*'s Sailor Scouts include a lesbian couple, male allies who transform into women in their fighting personae, and other sex- or gender-bending aspects familiar from *shōjo manga.*

38. *Anime* movies are sometimes released to theaters, but many of the most popular are released in a direct-to-video format known as OAV.

39. The majority of the artists listed here are men, although in several cases their relevant work appeared first in *shōjo manga* journals. This reflects as much as anything else the continued domination of the field by men after a promising flowering of female artists in the 1970s. With the unusual exceptions of Takahashi Rumiko and CLAMP, the majority of female *manga* artists are still featured primarily in amateur or independent journals and *anime* productions. (It should be recalled, however, that in Japan amateur and independent products circulate very widely and frequently influence more commercial products.)

Also, a number of these narratives were released in *manga* form many years before being turned into *anime. Sukeban deka,* for example, began serialization as a *manga* in 1976 but was not released as *anime* until the 1990s. Others were updated time after time and rereleased, such as Nagai Gō's *Cutey Honey* or Takachiho Haruka's *Dirty Pair.* In such cases, one often finds that the visual style has changed from "purely" *shōjo-* or *shōnen-*oriented to something closer to a hybrid look.

40. The spectrum of body types and levels of sexualization here may generally parallel the range one finds in North American pop culture products such as *Buffy, the Vampire Slayer* and *Xena, Warrior Princess.* Buffy's cute, slim, perky depiction is a far cry from Xena's well-rounded, busty figure; moreover Buffy aims its sexual appeal at a heterosexual audience, while the more campy Xena has a large lesbian following. Nonetheless I believe the spectrum of "battlin' babes" is currently much broader and richer in Japanese pop culture, including examples that North American audiences would find uncomfortably "masculine" and violent, and other examples that might be considered too explicitly sexualized and "demeaning to women."

41. As I will discuss below, although many of the protagonists of these narratives have bodies that are clearly sexually mature, as indicated by their large breasts and adult stature, they are still classified as *shōjo* in that they are not (hetero-) sexually active, and they are not wives or mothers. There is no word to indicate a transitional period between girlhood and full adult womanhood in Japanese (unlike the case for males); a female who has not yet taken her place in the reproductive economy is still a *shōjo.*

42. Carol Clover, *Men, Women, and Chain Saws: Gender in the Modern Horror Film* (Prince-

ton, N.J.: Princeton University Press, 1992), 44. It is significant that Clover traces the rise of this genre to a post-1970s period of gender retrenchment.

43. Ibid., 49–50.

44. Ibid., 50–52, 59.

45. In some subgenres of *anime* for adults, the *shōjo* protagonist is raped, sometimes graphically and repeatedly; she remains, however, the innocent victim of such adult sexuality, never its agent. See Susan J. Napier, *Anime from* Akira *to* Princess Mononoke: *Experiencing Contemporary Japanese Animation* (New York: Palgrave, 2001), 63–83, on rape in *anime.*

46. In the Shirō Masamune *manga* version of *Ghost in the Shell,* the protagonist, Kusanagi Motoko, is shown engaging in explicitly sexual play with other female cyborgs. Because they are all female, however, this active sexuality does not disqualify them from being considered *shōjo.* In the animated film *Ghost in the Shell,* this element of Kusanagi's character is entirely absent.

47. Nagai's original *manga* of *Cutey Honey* appeared in 1973–1974. The *anime* version I am using is an updated series, from 1994–1995. Nagai became famous in the 1970s for distinctly *shōnen*-oriented stories of the *mecha,* or "giant robot" type, but he is best known for the sexually outrageous narrative elements that he includes even in these otherwise typical *mecha anime.* The naked twirling fall enacted by Kusanagi as she goes into her fighter/assassin persona at the beginning of the more serious *Ghost in the Shell* might be considered an ironic homage to this "naked twirling transformation sequence" tradition.

48. Until recently the lack of pubic hair in depictions of naked women (and men) was the result of Japanese obscenity laws forbidding its depiction. That law has always been ambiguous at best, however, and since the early 1990s has been successfully challenged and overturned in several media. In any case, no matter what the reasons behind the absence of pubic hair, I would argue that the visual contrast between an otherwise voluptuous female body and a bare pubis connotes an intense conflation of the sexually mature and the prepubescent.

49. In the *manga* version of *Ghost in the Shell,* the female protagonist does, in fact, exhibit active desire toward both women and men, although the only explicit sex shown is with women. But in the very popular animated feature film, Kusanagi exhibits no sexual desire whatsoever.

50. The popular OAV version ends with Gally's "widowhood." The much longer *manga,* however, explores the implications for her of going through life without the boy, for whom she continues to grieve.

51. Since I am exploring male identification with female characters here, this is not the place to discuss the very interesting phenomenon of girls' and women's identification with abject characters in the *yaoi* narratives; nonetheless this phenomenon deserves much more scholarly attention than it has yet received. The best thing I have seen on this subject so far is Midori Matsui's "When Little Girls Were Little Boys." Many *shōjo manga* deal explicitly with the discomfort adolescent girls feel at the roles they see waiting for them in the post-*shōjo* sexual economy.

52. This is made explicit in the *anime* film *Genocyber*, where the adoptive father (and creator) of two cyborg girls sexually tortures them.

53. Roland Barthes, *Mythologies,* trans. Annette Lavers, 5th edition (London: Granada Publishing, 1981), 110. Quoted in Isolde Standish, *Myth and Masculinity in the Japanese Cinema* (Richmond, Surrey, U.K.: Curzon Press, 2000), 202.

# BIBLIOGRAPHY

"Abe Kōbō." *Kokubungaku kaishaku to kyōzai no kenkyū* [Studies in the materials and interpretation of Japanese literature], 42, no. 9 (August 1993).

Abé, Kobo [Abe Kōbō]. *The Woman in the Dunes*. Trans. E. Dale Saunders. New York: Alfred A. Knopf, 1964.

Ackerman, Gerald M. *Jean-Léon Gérôme (1824–1904)*. Exhibition catalog. Dayton Art Institute, 1972.

———. *The Life and Work of Jean-Léon Gérôme*. London and New York: Sotheby's, 1986.

*Ajia no bijutsu: Fukuoka Ajia Bijutsukan no korekushon to sono katsudō* [Asian art: the collection and activities of Fukuoka Asian Art Museum]. Tokyo: Bijutsu Shuppansha, 1999.

Akiyama Shun. "Nichijō-teki genjitsu to bungaku no tenkai: 1961–1977" [The development of daily reality and literature: 1961–1977]. In *Gendai no bungaku* [Contemporary literature] special publication: *Sengo Nihon bungakushi nenpyō* [Timeline of postwar Japanese literature history]. Tokyo: Kōdansha, 1978.

Akiyama Terukazu. "Heian jidai no 'Kara-e' to 'Yamato-e,' jō." *Bijutsu kenkyū* 120 (1941): 377–389.

———. "Heian jidai no 'Kara-e' to 'Yamato-e,' ge." *Bijutsu kenkyū* 121 (1942): 8–24.

———. *Heian jidai sezoku-ga no kenkyū*. Tokyo: Yoshikawa Kōbundō, 1964.

Alpers, Svetlana. *The Art of Describing: Dutch Art in the Seventeenth Century*. Chicago: University of Chicago Press, 1983. Trans. by Kōfuku Akira, *Byōsha no geijutsu—17 seiki no Oranda kaiga*. Tokyo: Arina Shobō, 1993.

*The American Heritage Dictionary*. Second college edition. Boston: Houghton Mifflin Company, 1982.

Araki Hiroshi. "Meiji-matsu Taishō-ki no nihonga to seiyō bijutsu—kokuga sōsaku kyōkai ka'in no sōsaku ni ukagawareru seiyō bijutsu no eikyō ni kansuru shiron" [*Nihonga* and European art from the end of the Meiji to the Taishō period—an essay on the influence of European art on the members of the Kokuga Sōsaku Kyōkai]. *Tokyo Zōkei Daigaku zasshi* 5 (March 1989): 41–131.

Asada Akira. "Infantile Capitalism and Japan's Postmodernisms: A Fairy Tale." In *Postmodernism and Japan,* ed. Masao Miyoshi and H. D. Harootunian. Durham: Duke University Press, 1989.

Asano Shūgō and Timothy Clark. *Kitagawa Utamaro–ten*. Tokyo: Asahi Shinbunsha, 1995.

———. *The Passionate Art of Kitagawa Utamaro*. London: British Museum Press, 1995.

Barthes, Roland. *Mythologies*. Trans. Annette Lavers. 5th edition. London: Granada Publishing, 1981.

———. *S/Z*. Trans. Richard Miller. New York: Hill and Wang, 1974.

Beauvoir, Simone de. *The Second Sex*. Trans. and ed. H. M. Parshley. Harmondworth: Penguin Books, 1975. Trans. by Ikushima Ryoichi, *Dai ni no sei*. Tokyo: Shinchōsha, 1959.

Bergstrom, Janet. "Enunciation and Sexual Difference." In *Feminism and Film Studies,* ed. Constance Penley. New York: Routledge, 1988.

*Bijutsu no chōshōjotachi* [The super girls of art]. Special issue. *Bijutsu techō* 38, no. 566 (August 1986): 19–80.

Bolas, Gerald D. "American Responses to Western-Style Japanese Painting." In Takashina et al., eds., *Paris in Japan*.

Broude, Norma, and Mary D. Garrard, eds. *The Expanding Discourse: Feminism and Art History*. New York: Harper and Row, 1992.

———. *Feminism and Art History: Questioning the Litany*. New York: Harper and Row, 1982. Trans. by Sakagami Keiko, *Bijustsu to feminizumu—hanpaku sareta josei imēji*. Tokyo: Parco Shuppankyoku, 1987.

Brown, Azby. "The Great Tokyo Art Hoax." *Tokyo Journal,* no. 9 (1993).

Brown, Judith C. *Immodest Acts: The Life of a Lesbian Nun in Renaissance Italy*. New York: Oxford University Press, 1986.

Bryson, Norman. "New Art History." In Takayama Hiroshi, *EYES Maruzen shinkan yōsho annai: bijutsu shikaku geijutsu* [EYES Maruzen guide to new Western publications: fine arts, visual arts], 7 (1995): 5.

———. " 'Orientarizumu' igo" [After "orientalism"]. Trans. Tan'o Yasunori. *Kindai gasetsu* 2 (1993).

———. "Yōga to bunka kōryū ni okeru seiteki wakugumi" [*Yōga* and the sexual structure of cultural exchange]. In *Higashi Ajia bijustsu ni okeru "hito no katachi"* [The human figure in the visual arts of East Asia], International Symposium on the Preservation of Cultural Property. Tokyo: Tokyo National Research Institute of Cultural Properties, 1994.

Butler, Judith. *Gender Trouble: Feminism and the Subversion of Identity*. New York: Routledge, 1990. Partial Japanese translation by Hagino Mie, "Sekkusu/jendā/yokubō no shutai," *Shisō,* no. 846 (December 1994) and no. 847 (January 1995).

Butler, Ruth. *Rodin: The Shape of Genius*. New Haven and London: Yale University Press, 1993.

Caws, Mary Ann, Rudolf Kuenzli, and Gwen Reaberg, eds. *Surrealism and Women*. Cambridge, Mass.: MIT Press, 1995.

Chadwick, Whitney. *Women Artists and the Surrealist Movement*. Boston: Little, Brown and Company, 1985.

Chanady, Amaryll. "The Territorialization of the Imaginary in Latin America: Self-Affirmation and Resistance to Metropolitan Paradigms." In Zamora and Faris, eds., *Magical Realism*.

Chi Myŏng-kwan. "Nihon chishikijin no Kankoku-kan" [Japanese intellectuals' perception of Korea]. *Bungaku shisō* [Literary thought], August 1981.
———. "Tuikjip—shikminjisakwanbipan" [Special edition: critique of the historical perception of colonialism]. In *Han'guksa shiminkangzwa* [Korean history citizen lectures]. Seoul: Il Cho Gak, 1987.
Chiba-shi Bijutsukan, ed. *Kainoshō Tadaoto to Taishō-ki no gaka-tachi* [Kainoshō Tadaoto and Taishō-period painters]. Tokyo: Nihon Keizai Shinbunsha, 1999.
Chino Kaori. *10–13 seki no bijutsu* [Art of the tenth to thirteenth centuries]. Iwanami Nihon Bijutsu no Nagare, vol. 3. Tokyo: Iwanami Shoten, 1993.
———. "Nanbokuchō-Muromachi jidai no emaki-mono: atarashii hikari no naka de" [The painted handscrolls of the Nanbokuchō and Muromachi periods in a new light]. In *Nihon bijustsu zenshū,* vol. 12. Tokyo: Kōdansha, 1992.
———. "Nihon bijutsu o kangae-naosu tame ni" [Toward rethinking Japanese art." *Bijutsu techō* [Art notes], October 1992.
———. "Nihon bijutsushi to feminizumu" [Japanese art history and feminism]. *Geijutsugaku ga wakaru* [Understanding the study of art]. Asahi Shimbun Extra Report and Analysis, Special Number 9. 1995.
———. "Onna o josou otoko: Morimura Yasumasa 'Joyū' ron" [A man simulating woman: comments on Morimura Yasumasa's *Actresses*). In *Morimura Yasumasa: bi ni itaru yamai—joyū ni natta watashi / Morimura Yasumasa: The Sickness unto Beauty—Self-Portrait as Actress.* Yokohama: Yokohama Bijutsukan, 1996.
Chino Kaori and Nishi Kazuo. *Fikushon toshite no kaiga.* Tokyo: Pelican-sha, 1991.
Clark, Toby. *Art and Propaganda in the Twentieth Century.* New York: Harry N. Abrams, 1997.
Clarke, John R. *Looking at Lovemaking: Constructions of Sexuality in Roman Art, 100 B.C.–A.D. 250.* Berkeley: University of California Press, 1998.
Clover, Carol. *Men, Women, and Chain Saws: Gender in the Modern Horror Film.* Princeton, N.J.: Princeton University Press, 1992.
Clunas, Craig. "Review Essay, Modernity Global and Local: Consumption and the Rise of the West." *American Historical Review* 104, no. 5 (December 1999).
Conant, Ellen P., ed. *Nihonga: Transcending the Past—Japanese Style Painting, 1868–1968.* St. Louis: Saint Louis Art Museum, 1995.
Copeland, Douglas, and Kip Ward. *Lara's Book: Lara Croft and the Tomb Raider™ Phenomenon.* Rocklin, Calif.: Prima Publishing, 1998.
Creighton, Millie R. "Marriage, Motherhood, and Career Management in a Japanese 'Counter Culture.'" in *Re-Imaging Japanese Women,* ed. Anne E. Imamura. Berkeley: University of California Press, 1996.
Croissant, Doris. "Fenollosas 'Wahre Theorie der Kunst' und ihre Wirkung in der Meiji Zeit (1868–1912)." *Saeculum* 38, no. 1 (1987): 52–75.
Currie, William. "Abe Kobo's Nightmare World of Sand." In *Approaches to the Modern Japanese Novel,* ed. Tsuruta Kinya and Thomas E. Swann. Tokyo: Sophia University Press, 1976.
Darnton, Robert. *The Forbidden Best-Sellers of Pre-Revolutionary France.* New York: W. W. Norton and Co., 1995.

Doak, Kevin M. "Ethnic Nationalism and Romanticism in Early-Twentieth-Century Japan." *Journal of Japanese Studies* 22, no.1 (Winter 1996): 77–103.

Dubose, Louise Jones. *Enigma: The Career of Blondelle Mason in Art and Society*. Columbia, S.C.: University of South Carolina Press, 1963.

Duncan, Carol. "The Aesthetics of Power in Modern Erotic Art." In *Feminist Art Criticism: An Anthology*. Ann Arbor: UMI Press, 1988.

Dvorak, Julianne Komori. "Sailor Moon and the Shōjo-ization of Male Imagery." M.A. thesis, Group in Asian Studies, University of California, Berkeley, 1997.

Edwards, Walter. "Buried Discourse: The Toro Archaeological Site and Japanese National Identity in the Early Postwar Period." *Journal of Japanese Studies* 17 (1991): 1–23.

Eliade, Mircea. *Rites and Symbols of Initiation*. New York: Harper and Row, 1958.

Enchi Fumiko. *Otoko no meigara* [How to choose a man]. Tokyo: Dai'ei Tōkyō Satsu'eijo, 1961.

———. "Watashi no *Otoko no meigara*" [My *How to Choose a Man*]. *Fujin kōron,* August 1961.

———. *Onnazaka* [The waiting years]. Tokyo: Shinchōsha, 1961.

Enomoto Ryōichi and Matsuoka Kazuko. "Ima kakeru onna" [Women on the march]. *Bijutsu techō* 38, no. 566 (August 1986): 46–59.

Epstein, Julia, and Kristina Straub. *Body Guards*. London: Routledge, 1989.

Erickson, John. "Metoikoi and Magical Realism in the Maghrebian Narratives of Taharben Jelloun and Abedelkbir Khatibi." In Zamora and Faris, eds., *Magical Realism*.

Etō Jun. "Kaisetsu." In Enchi Fumiko, *Onnazaka*.

Field, Norma. "*Somehow Crystal:* The Postmodern as Atmosphere." In *Postmodernism and Japan,* ed. Masao Miyoshi and H. D. Harootunian. Durham: Duke University Press, 1989.

Freches-Thory, Claire, and Ursula Perucchi-Petri, eds. *Die Nabis, Propheten der Moderne*. Munich: Prestel, 1993.

Freud, Sigmund. "The 'Uncanny.'" In *The Standard Edition of the Complete Psychological Works of Sigmund Freud: An Infantile Neurosis and Other Works,* vol. 17, trans. James Strachey. London: B. Hogan, 1963.

Friis-Hansen, Dana. "Portrait of the Young Japanese Artist as a Fanatic." *Louisiana Revy* 35, no. 3, English Supplement (June 1995), 13–15.

Fujimoto Yukari. *Watashi no idokoro wa doko ni aru no* [Where is the place for me?].

Fujisawa Shū. "Uji" [Maggot]. *Shōsetsu shinchō* 52, no. 5 (1995): 62–70.

"Ganbattemasu 'joryū'" ["Ladies" doing their best]. *Gekkan bijutsu* [Monthly art], no. 127 (April 1986).

Garber, Majorie. *Vice Versa: Bisexuality and the Eroticism of Everyday Life*. New York: Simon and Schuster, 1995.

*Gendai chōkoku no hatsugen: nyū ueebu to machi no chōkoku* [Speaking of contemporary sculpture: New Wave and sculpture in the streets]. Special issue. *Bijutsu techō* 38, no. 563 (June 1986).

*Gendai kaiga no bōken* [The adventure of contemporary painting]. Special issue. *Bijutsu techō* 37, no. 552 (November 1985).

*Gendai yōgo no kiso chishiki* [Encyclopedia of contemporary words]. Tokyo: Jiyū Kokuminsha, 2000.

Gerow, Aaron. "Consuming Asia, Consuming Japan: The New Neonationalistic Revisionism in Japan." In *Censoring History: Citizenship and Memory in Japan, Germany, and the United States,* ed. Laura Hein and Mark Selden. Armonk, N.Y.: M. E. Sharpe Books, 2000.

Gerstle, Andrew. "Response to the Panel: 'The Place of Love.'" In Jones, ed., *Imaging Reading Eros.*

Girard, René. *Deceit, Desire, and the Novel: Self and Other in Literary Structure.* Trans. Yvonne Freccero. Baltimore: Johns Hopkins University Press, 1972.

Gluck, Carol. "The Invention of Edo." In Vlastos, ed., *Mirror of Modernity.*

———. *Japan's Modern Myths: Ideology in the Late Meiji Period.* Princeton: Princeton University Press, 1985.

Hagiwara Hiroko. *Kono mune no arashi: Eikoku burakku josei ātisuto wa kataru* [The tempest in this breast: English black women artists speak]. Tokyo: Gendai Kikakushitsu, 1990.

"Han'guk misul ŭi ilche singmin chanjae rŭl ch'ōngsanhanŭn kil" [The path to clearing away the remains of Japanese colonialism from Korean art]. *Quarterly Art Magazine* (Korea), Spring 1983.

Hara Takeshi. "Chōsen tōchi shikan" [Personal thoughts on ruling colonial Korea]. In *Saitō Makoto bunsho* 9. Kōryō Shorin Ei'in-bon, 1990.

Harada, Minoru. *Meiji Western Painting.* Trans. Akiko Murakata. Arts of Japan 6. New York and Tokyo: Weatherhill/Shibundo, 1974.

Harootunian, H. D. "Figuring the Folk: History, Poetics, and Representation." In Vlastos, ed., *Mirror of Modernity.*

Hayakawa, Monta. "Shunga and Mitate: Suzuki Harunobu's *Eight Modern Views of the Interior* (*Fūryū Zashiki Hakkei*). In Jones, ed., *Imaging Reading Eros.*

———. *Ukiyo-e to shunga: nanshoku.* Tokyo: Kawade Shobō, 1998.

Hayashi Yoshikazu. *Enpon kenkyū: Moronobu* [Research on erotic books: Moronobu]. Tokyo: Yūkō Shobō, 1968.

Hayashi Yoshikazu and Richard Lane, eds. *Kitagawa Utamaro "Ehon Komachi-biki."* Teihon Ukiyo-e Shunga Meihin Shūsei [The complete *ukiyo-e shunga*], vol. 2. Tokyo: Shōbō Shinsha, 1996.

*Hiraga Gennai zenshū* [Complete works of Hiraga Gennai]. Ed. Irihi Seizō. Tokyo: Kyōrinsha, 1932.

Hirano Yoshinobu. "Yoshiya Nobuko: joseisei no manazashi." In *Kokubungaku: kaishaku to kyōzai no kenkyū* 4, no. 11 (1992).

Hisatomi Mitsugu. "Kindai nihonga ni okeru rafu" [*Nihonga* nude painting]. *Sansai* 2 (1988).

Honda Masuko. "Shōjogatari: kotoba no meikyū o meguru" [Touring the labyrinth of words: *shōjo* language]. In Honda et al., eds., *Shōjo ron.*

Honda Masuko et al., eds. *Shōjo ron.* Tokyo: Aoyumisha, 1988.

Honda Yasuo. *Shikitei Sanba no bungei* [The literary art of Shikitei Sanba]. Tokyo: Kasama Shoin, 1973.

Horikiri Naoto. "Onna wa dokyō, shōjo wa aikyō" [For women it's bravery, for girls it's charm]. In Honda et al., eds., *Shōjo ron.*

Horioka, Charles Yuji. "Consuming and Saving." In *Postwar Japan as History,* ed. Andrew Gordon. Berkeley: University of California Press, 1993.

Ihara Saikaku. *Kōshoku ichidai otoko* [Life of an amorous man]. In *Ihara Saikaku shū 1.* Nihon Koten Bungaku Zenshū 38. Tokyo: Shōgakukan, 1991.

Ikeda Shinobu. "*Heiji monogatari emaki* ni miru risō no bushi-zō" [The image of the ideal warrior as seen in the *Illustrated Scrolls of the Tales of the Heiji Era*]. *Bijutsushi* [Art history], no. 138 (May 1995).

———. "Jendā no shiten kara miru ōchō monogatari-e" [Court illustrated romances as seen from the viewpoint of gender]. In *Bijutsu to jendā: hi-taishō no shisen* [Art and gender: the asymmetrical regard], ed. Suzuki Tokiko et al. Tokyo: Brücke, 1997.

———. *Nihon kaiga no joseizō: jendā bijutsushi no shiten kara* [The image of women in Japanese painting: from the point of view of gender-conscious art history]. Tokyo: Chikuma Shobō, 1998.

Inoue Hisashi. "Sha Kokken *Sei seikatsu no chie:* Pinokio ningyō ga oshieta beddo no ue no danjo byōdō" [Sha Kokken's *Wisdom in Sexual Life:* sexual equality in bed as taught by Pinocchio]. *Bungei shunju,* September 1988, 482–485.

Irigaray, Luce. *This Sex Which Is Not One.* Trans. Catherine Porter. Ithaca, N.Y.: Cornell University Press, 1985.

Jameson, Fredric. *Postmodernism.* Durham, N.C.: Duke University Press, 1991.

Johnson, Barbara. *A World of Difference.* Baltimore: Johns Hopkins University Press, 1987. Trans. by Ōhashi Yōichi, *Sa'i no sekai.* Tokyo: Kinokuniya Shoten, 1990.

Johnstone, Clare. "Women's Cinema as Counter-Cinema." In *Sexual Stratagems: The World of Women in Film,* ed. Patricia Erens. New York: Horizon Press, 1979.

Jones, Sumie, ed. *Imaging Reading Eros: Proceedings for the Conference, Sexuality and Edo Culture, 1750–1850 (Indiana University, Bloomington, August 17–20, 1995).* Bloomington: East Asian Studies Center, 1996.

Kang Man'gil. "Munhwa chŏngch'i ŭi silsang" [The reality of Cultural Rule]. In *Han'guk hyŏndaesa.* Seoul: Ch'angja kwa Pip'yŏngsa, 1984.

Kang Sangjung [Kan Sanjun]. "Nippon no shokuminchi seisaku to orientarizumu" [Japanese colonial policy and orientalism]. In *Orientarizumu no kanata e* [Beyond orientalism]. Tokyo: Iwanami Shoten, 1996.

———. "Shōwa no shūen to gendai Nippon no 'shinzōchiri = rekishi': kyōkasho no naka no Chōsen wo chūshin toshite" [The last days of Shōwa and contemporary Japan's "mental image geography = history"—focusing on colonial Korea in textbooks]. *Shisō* [Thought], October 1989.

Kang Tongjin. *Nihon no Chōsen shihai seisaku shi kenkyū* [Historical research on Japan's colonial policies for Korea]. Tokyo: Tokyo University Press, 1979.

Kaplan, E. Ann, ed. *Women in Film Noir.* Rev. ed. London: British Film Institute, 1980. Trans. by Mizuta Noriko, *Firumu nowāru no onna-tachi.* Tokyo: Tahata Shoten, 1988.

Kasuya Makoto. "Shōjū raigō-ji-bon rokudō-e 'nindō fujōsō-zu' kō" [A study of the

Shōjū Raigōji temple version of the "Picture of the Realm of Human Existence" Six Realms of Rebirth painting]. *Tezukayama Gakuin Daigaku kenkyū ronshū* [Collected essays from Tezukayama Gakuin University], no. 29 (February 1995).

Kato, Shuichi. *A History of Japanese Literature.* Trans. David Chibbett. 3 vols. Tokyo: Kodansha International, 1979.

Katō Tetsuhiro. "Bijutsushigaku no 'Kiki' to sono kokufuku." In *Geijustugaku no kiseki* (Geijutsugaku Fōramu 1). Tokyo: Keisō Shobō, 1992.

Keller, Evelyn F. *Reflections on Gender and Science.* New Haven: Yale University Press, 1985. Japanese trans. by Kijima Yukiko and Kawashima Keiko. Tokyo: Kosakusha, 1993.

*Kenji Yanobe 1990–1994.* Tokyo: Röntgen Kunst Institute, 1994.

Kim Yŏngna. "1930 nyŏndae ŭi han'guk kŭndae hoehwa" [Modern Korean art in the 1930s]. *Misulsa yŏn'gu* 7 (1993): 37–38

Kim Yunsu. "Han'guk kŭndae misul: kŭ pip'anjōk sŏsŏl" [Korean modern art: a critical introduction]. In *The History of Korean Contemporary Art.* Seoul: Han'guk Ilbosa, 1975.

Kinoshita Naoyuki. *Bijutsu to iu mise-mono: abura-e-jaya no jidai.* Tokyo: Heibonsha, 1993.

Kinsella, Sharon. *Adult Manga: Culture and Power in Contemporary Japanese Society.* Honolulu: University of Hawai'i Press, 2000.

———. "Cuties in Japan." In *Women, Media and Consumption in Japan,* ed. Lise Skov and Brian Moeran. Honolulu: University of Hawai'i Press, 1995.

———. "Japanese Subculture in the 1990s: *Otaku* and the Amateur *Manga* Movement." *Journal of Japanese Studies* 24, no. 2 (1998): 289–316.

Kishimoto Yasushi, director. *Go on the Stage Morimura.* VHS video film, 48 min. Kyoto: Ufer! Art Documentary, 1996.

*Kisho fukuseikai kankōsho.* Ser. 5, vol. 21. Tokyo: Beisando, 1927.

Kitazawa Noriaki. *Me no shinden: "bijutsu" juyō-shi nōto.* Tokyo: Bijutsu Shuppansha, 1989.

Koike Masatame, ed. *Edo no ehon* [Edo illustrated books]. 4 vols. Tokyo: Kokusho Kankōkai, 1987.

Kojima Nobuo. "Josei shiiku-hō no teishō" [Advice on how to train women]. *Fujin kōron,* September 1958, 74–77.

Kokuatsu Reiko. "Taishō no nihonga: mizu no onna, mizu no fūkei" [Taishō *nihonga:* women of water, landscapes of water]. In *Taishō no atarashiki nami: nihonga 1910–1920 nendai* [Taishō's new wave: *nihonga,* 1910–1920], ed. Tochigi Kenritsu Kindai Bijutsukan. Tochigi: Tochigi Kenritsu Kindai Bijutsukan, 1991.

Kokusho Kankōkai, ed. *Kindai Nihon bungaku taikei* [Compendium of modern Japanese Literature], vol. 12: *Kibyōshi.* Tokyo: Kokumin Tosho Kabushiki-gaisha, 1926.

Komagome Takeshi. *Shokuminchi teikoku Nippon no bunka tōgō* [The cultural synthesis of colonial and imperial Japan]. Tokyo: Iwanami Shoten, 1996.

Komano Yōko. "Kawariyuku josei no shokuba" [Women's changing places of work]. In Tanaka Sumiko, ed., *Josei kaihō no shisō to kōdō.*

Koplos, Janet. "Some Kind of Revolution?" *Art in America,* May 1992, 10, 153.

Kuhn, Thomas. *The Structure of Scientific Revolutions.* Chicago: University of Chicago Press, 1962. Trans. by Nakayama Shigeru, *Kagaku kakumei no kōzō.* Tokyo: Misuzu Shobō, 1971.

Kuki, Shūzō. *Propos sur le temps: Deux communications faites à Pontigny pendant la décade 8–18 août 1928*. Paris: Philippe Renouard, 1928.

———. *Reflections on Japanese Taste: The Structure of Iki*. Trans. John Clark. Sydney: Power Publications, 1997.

Kumamoto Kenjirō. *Kindai Nihon bijutsu no kenkyū* [Research on modern Japanese art]. Tokyo: Tokyo Kokuritsu Bunkazai Kenkyūjo, 1964.

Kuroda Toshio. *Rōdōryoku jinkō no chiiki jinkōgakuteki bunseki* [Demographic analysis of labor population by region]. Tokyo: Kōseishō Jinkō Mondai Kenkyūsho, 1964.

Kusaka Chikara et al., eds. *Hōgen monogatari, Heiji monogatari, Jōkyūki*. Shin Nihon Koten Bungaku Taikei, vol. 43. Tokyo: Iwanami Shoten, 1992.

Kusumi Kiyoshi. "Gojira to mobiru sūtsu hatsumei gijutsu: mucha no tankyū" [Godzilla and the art of mobile suit invention: in quest of the absurd]. In *Kenji Yanobe 1990–1994*. Tokyo: Röntgen Kunst Institute, 1994.

*Kyoto Conference on Japanese Studies, 1994*. Vol. 1. International Research Center for Japanese Studies and The Japan Foundation.

Kyōto Kokuritsu Kindai Bijutsukan, ed. *Kokuga Sōsaku Kyōkai kaikoten* [Kokuga Sōsaku Kyōkai retrospective]. Kyoto, 1993.

"90-nendai feminin weebu" [The feminine wave of the 90s]. *Hanga geijutsu* [Print art], no. 74 (1991).

Lenne, Gérard. *Sex on the Screen: Eroticism in Film*. New York: St. Martin's Press, 1978.

Leupp, Gary P. *Male Colors: The Construction of Homosexuality in Tokugawa Japan*. Berkeley: University of California Press, 1995.

Lévi-Strauss, Claude. *The Elementary Structures of Kinship*. Boston: Beacon, 1969.

London, Barbara. "Sculpted Animations for Public Places." In *Kenji Yanobe 1990–1994*.

Loti, Pierre. *Japoneries d'automne*. Paris: Calmann-Lévy, 1889.

Maruyama Kunio. "Shijō sōkeisen: joshi sotsugyōsei no jittai." *Fujin kōron,* April 1964, 66–74.

*Mary Kelley: Interim*. Essays by Marcia Tucker, Norman Bryson, and Griselda Pollock; interview by Hal Forster. New York: New Museum of Contemporary Art, 1990.

Matsubara Shigemi. "Heiji monogatari e-kotoba no denrai to seiritsu" [The provenance and formation of the *Tales of the Heiji Era* picture-text]. In *Nihon emaki-mono taisei* [Compendium of Japanese picture scrolls]. Tokyo: Chūōkōronsha, 1977.

Matsui, Midori. "Little Girls Were Little Boys: Displaced Femininity in the Representation of Homosexuality in Japanese Girls' Comics." In *Feminism and the Politics of Difference,* ed. Sneja Gunew and Anna Yeatman. Halifax: Fernwood, 1993.

Matsumiya Saburō. *Edo kabuki to kōkoku* [Edo kabuki theater and advertising]. Tokyo: Tōhō Shobō, 1973.

Matsumiya Shōnosuke, ed. *Edo chōnin no kenkyū* [Studies in Edo urban culture]. Tokyo: Yoshikawa Kōbunkan, 1976.

McDonagh, Maitland. *The 50 Most Erotic Films of All Time: From* Pandora's Box *to* Basic Instinct. New York: Citadel Press, 1996.

McDonald, Keiko I. "Man, Sand and Symbols: Teshigawara's *The Woman in the Dunes*." *Japan Interpreter* 12 (1979).

"Measuring up to Lara Croft." *Vancouver Sun,* June 18, 2001, B8.
Meech-Pekarik, Julia. *The World of the Meiji Print: Impressions of a New Civilization.* New York: John Weatherhill, 1986.
Miller, Stephen D., ed. *Partings at Dawn: An Anthology of Japanese Gay Literature.* San Francisco: Gay Sunshine Press, 1996.
Milne, Lisa. "The Nuances of Naito's Nothing." *Daily Yomiuri,* March 11, 1994.
Mitsuda, Yuri. "Flowers for Wounds." In *Asian Women Artists,* ed. Dinah Dysart and Hannah Fink. Roseville East, Australia: Craftsman House, 1996.
Miyake Tsuyako. *Dansei shiiku hō* [How to train men]. Tokyo: Chūō Kōronsha 1958.
Miyoshi, Masao. *As We Saw Them: The First Japanese Embassy to the United States (1860).* Berkeley and Los Angeles: University of California Press, 1979.
Miyoshi, Masao, and H. D. Harootunian eds. *Japan in the World.* Durham: Duke University Press, 1993.
Morris, Rosalind. "Three Sexes and Four Sexualities: Redressing the Discourse on Gender and Sexuality in Contemporary Thailand." *positions: east asian cultures critique* 2, no. 1 (Spring 1994).
Mostow, Joshua S. "Picturing Love among the One Hundred Poets." In *Love in Asian Art and Culture,* ed. Arthur M. Sackler Gallery (Smithsonian Institution). Seattle: University of Washington Press, 1998.
———. Review of Gary P. Leupp, *Male Colors: The Construction of Homosexuality in Tokugawa Japan. Journal of the History of Sexuality* 7, no. 4 (April 1997): 608–610.
Muller, Richard. *Anthony Trollope: A Victorian in His World.* Savannah: Fredric C. Beil, 1990.
Mulvey, Laura. "Visual Pleasure and Narrative Cinema." In *Visual and Other Pleasures.* Bloomington: Indiana University Press, 1989. Also in *Art after Modernism: Rethinking Representation,* ed. Brian Wallis. New York: The New Museum of Contemporary Art, 1995. Trans. by Saitō Ayako, "Shikaku-teki kairaku to monogatari eiga." *Imāgo,* November 1992.
Murakami Kagaku. *Tsuchida Bakusen.* Gendai Nihon Bijutsu Zenshū 4. Tokyo: Shūeisha, 1972.
Murase, Miyeko. *Jewel Rivers: Japanese Art from the Burke Collection.* Richmond: Virginia Museum of Fine Arts, 1994.
Nagai Takanori. "An Aspect of Cezanne's Reception in Japan: The Formation and Development of the 'Personalist' Interpretation of Cezanne in the 1920s." *Aesthetics* (Tokyo), no. 8 (March 1998): 79–91.
Naitō Masato. "Kiyokata and Shunshō: The Influence of the Edo Period Ukiyo-e on Modern Paintings of Beautiful Women." *Orientations,* April 2000, 58–63.
Nakada Setsuko. *Kōkoku no naka no Nippon* [Japan in advertising]. Tokyo: Daiyamondosha, 1993.
Nakai Sōtarō. *Kindai geijutsu gairon* [Survey of modern art]. Tokyo: Nishōdō, 1922.
Nakamura Giichi. "Daiten, Senten, to Teiten" [The Taiwan, Korean, and Imperial exhibitions]. *Kyōto Kyōiku Daigaku kiyō,* series A, no. 75 (1989).
———. *Kindai bijutsu ronsō shi* [A history of modern art debates]. Tokyo: Kyūryūdō Library, 1981.

Nakamura Mikio. *Ukiyo-e kabuki shirizu,* vol. 1: *Kabuki jūhachiban.* Tokyo: Gakugei Shorin, 1988.

Nakamura Shin'ichirō et al. *Harunobu: bijinga to ehon* [Harunobu: women and illustrated books]. Tokyo: Shinchōsha, 1992.

Nakano Mitsutoshi. *Nihon no kinsei* [Early modern Japan], vol. 12: *Bungaku to bijutsu no seigaku* [The maturation of literature and art]. Tokyo: Chūōkōronsha, 1993.

Nanjo, Fumio. "Rei Naito: Japanese Pavilion." URL address http://www.dialnsa.edu/iat97/Venice/Japan/install2.html; last modified October 16, 1997, downloaded July 5, 1999.

Napier, Susan J. *Anime from* Akira *to* Princess Mononoke: *Experiencing Contemporary Japanese Animation.* New York: Palgrave, 2001.

———. "The Magic of Identity: Magical Realism in Modern Japanese Fiction." In Zamora and Faris, eds. *Magical Realism.*

———. "Vampires, Psychic Girls, Flying Women and Sailor Scouts: Four Faces of the Young Female in Japanese Popular Culture." In *The Worlds of Japanese Popular Culture: Gender, Shifting Boundaries and Global Cultures,* ed. D. P. Martinez. Cambridge, U.K.: Cambridge University Press, 1998.

Nielsen, Tone O. "Kenji Yanobe." *Louisiana Revy* 35, no. 3 (June 1995).

Nihon Jōhō Kyōiku Kenkyūkai, ed. *Heisei 11 nen: Nihon no hakusho* [Whitebook of Japan, 1999]. Tokyo: Seibunsha, 1999.

"1998 Taihoku biennaaru ripooto" [1998 Taipei Biennial report]. *Bijutsu techō* 50, no. 761 (September 1998): 101–108.

Nishida Kitarō. *Geijutsu to dōtoku.* 1923. Trans. by David A. Dilworth and Valda H. Vilgielmo, *Art and Morality.* Honolulu: University of Hawai'i Press, 1973.

Nishiyama Matsunosuke. *Kinsei bunka no kenkyū* [Studies of early modern culture]. Tokyo: Yoshikawa Kōbunkan, 1983.

Nishiyama Matsunosuke and Sekioka Senryō, eds. *Senjafuda.* Tokyo: Kōdansha, 1983.

Nochlin, Linda. "The Imaginary Orient." *Art in America* 1983. Reprinted in Nochlin, *The Politics of Vision: Essays on Nineteenth-Century Art and Society.* New York: Harper and Row, 1989.

———. "Morisot's *Wet Nurse:* The Construction of Work and Leisure in Impressionist Painting." In *Kunst um 1800 und die Folgen: Werner Hofmann zu Ehren,* ed. Christian Beutler, Peter-Klaus Schuster, and Martin Warnke. Munich: Prestel-Verlag, 1988.

———. "Why Have There Been No Great Women Artists?" *Art News* 69, no. 9 (January 1971). Reprinted in *Women, Art, and Power and Other Essays.* New York: Harper and Row, 1988. Trans. by Matsuoka Kazuko, "Naze josei no dai-geijutsuka wa arawarenai no ka." *Bijutsu techō,* May 1976.

*Nyū imeeji no teian* [Propositions on new images]. Special issue. *Bijutsu techō* 36, no. 528 (July 1984).

Obushi Hajime. *Nihon kessaku kokoku* [Masterworks of Japanese advertising]. Tokyo: Seiabō, 1991.

Odin, Steve. "An Explanation of Beauty: Nishida Kitarō's *Bi no Setsumei.*" *Monumenta Nipponica* 42, no. 2 (1987).

Ōe Shinobu. "Higashi Ajia shinkyūteikoku no kōtai" [The shift from old to new empire in East Asia]. In *Kindai Nippon to shokuminchi I: shokuminchi teikoku Nippon* [Modern Japan and its colonies I: Colonial and imperial Japan]. Tokyo: Iwanami Shoten, 1992.

Okakura Tenshin. "Modern Art from a Japanese Point of View." *Quarterly Review* 11, no. 2 (July 1905).

Okaniwa Noboru. *Hanada Kiyoteru to Abe Kōbō.* Tokyo: Daisan Bunmeisha, 1980.

*Ōkina nikki, chiisana monogatari* [Big diary, little tale] / *Mito Annual '92, Private Diary. 10 Japanese Young Artists.* Mito: Mito Geijutsukan Gendai Bijutsu Gyararii, 1992.

Okura Yayoi. "Promoting Prostitution." *AMPO Japan-Asia Quarterly Review* 25 no. 4–26, no. 1 (1995): 60–62.

Ono, Philbert. *PhotoHistory.* In *PhotoGuide Japan* URL http://photojpn.org/HIST/1990.html; downloaded March 3, 2001.

" 'Otoko girai' to iu keredo" [It's called "The Men Haters" but . . . ]. *Fujin kōron,* August 1963, 9–11.

Ōtsuka Eiji. *Shōjo minzokugaku* [*Shōjo* ethnology]. Tokyo: Kōbunsha, 1991.

Ow, Jeffrey. "Revenge of the Yellowfaced Cyborg: The Rape of Digital Geishas and the Colonization of Cyber-Coolies in 3D Realms' *Shadow Warrior.*" In *Race in Cyberspace,* ed. Beth E. Kolko et al. London: Routledge, 2000.

Ozaki Hisaya. "Ukiyo-e no kōkoku ishō" [*Ukiyo-e* advertising designs]. In *Edo no asobi* [Edo amusements]. *Chōnin bunka hyakka ronshū* [An encyclopedia of townsman culture], vol. 1. Tokyo: Kashiwa Shobō, 1981.

Pai, Maggie. "Challenge to Change." *Asian Art News* 8, no. 4 (July/August 1998): 36–47.

Pak Kyeri. "Ilche sidae 'Chosŏn hyangt'osaek' " [The nature of "Chōsen nativism" in the Japanese imperial period]. *Han'guk kŭndae misulsahak,* vol. 4 (1996).

Parker, Rozsika, and Griselda Pollock. *Old Mistresses: Women, Art, and Ideology.* New York: Pantheon Books, 1981. Trans. by Hagiwara Hiroko, *Onna / āto / ideorogī: feminisuto ga yomi-naosu geijutsu hyōgen no rekishi.* Tokyo: Shinsuisha, 1992.

Penrose, Anthony. *The Legendary Lee Miller.* East Sussex: The Lee Miller Archives, 1998.

Pflugfelder, Gregory M. *Cartographies of Desire: Male-Male Sexuality in Japanese Discourse, 1600–1950.* Berkeley: University of California Press, 1999.

Pincus, Leslie. *Authenticating Culture in Imperial Japan: Kuki Shūzō and the Rise of National Aesthetics.* Berkeley: University of California Press, 1996.

Robertson, Jennifer. "Gender Bending in Paradise: Doing 'Female' and 'Male' in Japan." *Genders* 5 (1989): 50–69.

———. "Japanese Females as Western Men: Cross-Dressing and 'Cross-Ethnic-ing' in the Takarazuka Review." *Association for Asian Studies: Abstracts of the 1993 Annual Meeting.* Ann Arbor: Association for Asian Studies, 1993.

———. *Takarazuka: Sexual Politics and Popular Culture in Modern Japan.* Berkeley: University of California Press, 1998.

Rogers, Lawrence. "She Loves Me, She Loves Me Not: *Shinjū* and *Shikidō Ōkagami.*" *Monumenta Nipponica* 49, no. 1 (Spring 1994): 31–60.

Rothschild, Joan, ed. *Machina ex Dea: Feminist Perspectives on Technology.* New York: Pergamon Press, 1983. Trans. by Watanuki Reiko et al., *Josei vs tekunorojī.* Tokyo: Shinhyōron, 1989.

Rubin, Gayle. "Thinking Sex: Notes for a Radical Theory of the Politics of Sexuality." In *Pleasure and Danger,* ed. Carole S. Vance. Boston: Routledge and Kegan Paul, 1984.

———. "The Traffic in Women: Notes on the Political Economy of Sex." In *Toward an Anthropology of Women,* ed. Rayna R. Reiter. New York: Monthly Review Press, 1975.

Said, Edward. *Orientalism.* New York: Random House, 1978.

———. *Orientarizumu* [*Orientalism,* Japanese language edition]. Ed. Itagaki Takezō and Sugita Hideaki, trans. Imazawa Kazuko. Tokyo: Heibonsha, 1986.

Saitō Minako. *Kōitten: anime, tokusatsu, denki no hiroinzō* [One touch of crimson: the image of the heroine in *anime,* special effects, and biography]. Tokyo: Birejji Sentā Shuppankyoku, 1998.

Sakai, Naoki. "Modernity and Its Critique: The Problem of Universalism and Particularism." In *Postmodernism and Japan,* ed. Masao Miyoshi and H. D. Harootunian. Durham: Duke University Press, 1989. Japanese version: "Kindai no hihan: Chūzetsu shita tōki (Postomodan no shomondai)." *Gendai shisō* 15 (December 1987): 184–207.

Sato, Rika Sakuma. "What Are Little Girls Made Of? Exploring the Symbolic Boundaries of Femininity in Two Cultures." In *Millennium Girls: Today's Girls around the World,* ed. Sherrie A. Innes. Lanham, Md.: Rowman and Littlefield, 1998.

Satō Tadao. *Nihon eiga hyakusen* [One hundred selected Japanese films]. Tokyo: Akita Shoten, 1976.

Sawa Kōzō. "Hadaka ni sareta sutā no kimochi" [Feelings of a star made naked]. *Fujin kōron,* September 1994.

Sawaragi Noi. "Enshin to shite no sei" [The centrifugal sex]. *Bijutsu techō* 41, no. 613 (August 1989).

Schalow, Paul Gordon. "The Invention of the Literary Tradition of Male Love: Kitamura Kigin's *Iwatsutsuji.*" *Monumenta Nipponica* 48, no. 1 (Spring 1993): 1–31.

———. "Josei no 'nanshoku ron'" [Women's discourse on male-male love]. *Bungaku* [Literature], 6, no. 1 (Winter 1995).

———. Review of Gary P. Leupp, *Male Colors: The Construction of Homosexuality in Tokugawa Japan. Journal of Japanese Studies* 23, no. 1 (Winter 1997): 196–201.

———, trans. *The Great Mirror of Male Love.* Stanford: Stanford University Press, 1990.

Schamoni, Wolfgang. "Die Shirakaba-Gruppe und die Entdeckung der nachimpressioinistischen Malerei in Japan." *Nachrichten der Gesellschaft für Natur-und Völkerkunde Ostasiens,* nos. 127–128 (1980), 57–84.

Schor, Naomi. *Reading in Detail Aesthetics and the Feminine.* New York: Methuen, 1987.

Schulz, Evelyn. *Nagai Kafū: "Tagebuch eines Heimgekehrten": Der Entwurf ästhetischer Gegenwelten als Kritik an der Modernisierung Japans.* Hamburg: Ostasien-Pazifik Trierer Studien zu Politik, Wirtschaft, Gesellschaft, Kultur, 1997.

Scott, Joan W. *Gender and the Politics of History.* New York: Columbia University Press, 1988. Trans. by Ogino Miho, *Jendā to rekishigaku.* Tokyo: Heibonsha, 1992.

Screech, Timon. *Sex and the Floating World: Erotic Images in Japan, 1700–1820.* Honolulu: University of Hawai'i Press, 1999. Trans. by Takayama Hiroshi, *Shunga: kata-te de yomu Edo no e* [*Shunga:* Edo pictures read with one hand]. Tokyo: Kōdansha, 1998.

Sedgwick, Eve Kosofsky. *Between Men: English Literature and Homosocial Desire*. New York: Columbia University Press, 1985.

———. *Tendencies*. Durham: Duke University Press, 1993.

Seo Fumiaki. "Toshi o fuyū suru shōjotachi" [Girls who wander the city]. In Honda Masuko et al., eds., *Shōjo ron*.

Sha Kokken. *Sei seikatsu no chie* [Wisdom in sexual life]. Tokyo: Ikeda Shoten, 1960.

Shalala, Nancy. "Quest for the Female Grail." *Japan Times,* May 23, 1993.

Shibata Chiaki, ed. *Seigo jiten* [Dictionary of sexual terms]. Tokyo: Kawade Shobō, 1999.

Shirahata Yoshi. "Onna-e hokō" [Further thoughts of woman-pictures]. *Bukkyō geijutsu,* no. 35 (July 1958): 24–28.

———. "Onna-e kō" [A treatise on women-pictures]. *Bijutsu kenkyū* [Ars Buddhica], no. 132 (1943): 201–210.

Shirakura Yoshihiko. "Shunga wo dō yomu ka" [How to read *shunga*]. In *Ukiyo-e shunga wo yomu* [Reading *ukiyo-e shunga*], ed. Shirakura Yoshihiko et al., vol. 1. Tokyo: Chūōkōronsha, 2000

Shirane, Haruo, and Suzuki Tomi, eds. *Inventing the Classics: Modernity, National Identity, and Japanese Literature*. Stanford: Stanford University Press, 2000.

———. *Sōzō sareta koten: kanon keisei, kokumin kokka, Nihon bungaku* [Invented classics: canon formation, the nation-state, and Japanese literature]. Tokyo: Shin'yōsha, 1999.

Shively, Donald H., ed. *Tradition and Modernization in Japanese Culture*. Princeton, N.J.: Princeton University Press, 1971.

*Shōgakukan Random House English-Japanese Dictionary*. Tokyo: Shōgakukan, 1973–1974.

Sim Hyŏnggu. "Siguk kwa misul" [The political situation and art]. *Sinsidae* 10 (1941).

Spivak, Gayatri Chakravorty. *In Other Worlds: Essays in Cultural Politics*. New York: Methuen, 1987. Trans. by Suzuki Satoshi, et al., *Bunka toshite no tasha*. Tokyo: Kinokuniya Shoten, 1990.

Standish, Isolde. *Myth and Masculinity in the Japanese Cinema*. Richmond, Surrey, U.K.: Curzon Press, 2000.

Suzuki, Kazuko. "Pornography or Therapy? Japanese Girls Creating the Yaoi Phenomenon." In Innes, ed., *Millennium Girls*.

Suzuki Tokiko. "Feminisuto no bijutsushi" [Feminist art history]. *Geijutsugaku kenkyū* [Art studies research], 2. Meiji Gakuin Ronsō 50. 1992.

Suzuki Tokiko and Chino Kaori, eds. "Nōman Buraison Kyōju to 'atarashii bijutsushigaku' no mosaku." *Gekkan hyakka,* February 1994.

Suzuki, Tomi. "Gender and Genre: Modern Literary Histories and Women's Diary Literature." In Shirane and Suzuki, eds., *Inventing the Classics*.

Suzuki Tsutomu, ed. *Nihonjin no hyakunen* [A hundred years of the Japanese]. Tokyo: Sekai Bunkasha, 1973.

Takahashi Hakushin, ed. *Ukiyo-e zanmai: Kunisada to Eisen* [Absorbed in pictures of the floating world: Kunisada and Eisen]. Obihira: Arita Shobō, 1980.

Takahashi Hiroko. " 'Atarashii bijutsushigaku' no shigeki-teki na jitsurei." *Sofia* 163 (1992).

———. "Bijutsushigaku no atarashii dōkō." *Bijutsu techō,* October 1993.

Takahashi Katsuhiko. *Edo no nyū media: ukiyo-e, jōhō, kōkoku to asobi* [Edo's new media: *ukiyo-e,* information, advertising, and amusements]. Tokyo: Kadokawa, 1992.

Takashina, Shūji, J. Thomas Rimer, and Gerald D. Bolas, eds. *Paris in Japan: The Encounter with European Painting.* Exhibition catalog. Tokyo: The Japan Foundation, and St. Louis: Gallery of Art at Washington University, 1987.

Takeda Katushiko. "*Suna no onna* no hyōka" [Criticism on *Woman in the Dunes*]. In *Abe Kōbō zenshū,* vol. 6. Tokyo: Shinchōsha, 1972.

Takemiya Keiko. "Manga gakka de kyōdan debyū, sandome no waga tenki" [My debut at the podium in a *manga* studies department, my third turning point]. *Fujin kōron,* no. 1058 (April 22, 2000).

Takeuchi Makoto. *Bunka no taishūka* [The creation of mass culture]. Nihon no Kinsei, vol. 14. Tokyo: Chūōkōronsha, 1993.

Taki Kōji. *Tennō no shōzō.* Tokyo: Iwanami Shinsho, 1988.

Tanaka Hiroyuki. "*Suna no onna* ron." *Nihon bungaku* 35 (December 1986).

Tanaka Hisao, ed. "Tsuchida Bakusen no Nomura Kazuyuki ate shokan" [Tsuchida Bakusen's letters to Nomura Kazuyuki]. *Bigaku bijutsushi ronshū* [Collected essays on aesthetics and art history], 4. Tokyo: Seijō Daigaku Daigakuin Bungaku Kenkyūka, 1984.

———. "Tsuchida Bakusen no Yoroppa kara shokan" [Tsuchida Bakusen's letters from Europe]. *Bigaku bijutsushi ronshū* [Collected essays on aesthetics and art history], 6. Tokyo: Seijō Daigaku Daigakuin Bungaku Kenkyūka, 1987.

Tanaka Ichimatsu. "Otoko-e to onna-e" [Man-pictures and woman-pictures]. *Hōun,* no. 6 (1933): 75–94.

Tanaka Sumiko, ed. *Josei kaihō no shisō to kōdō: sengo hen* [The Women's Liberation Movement and thought: postwar]. Tokyo: Jijitsushinsha, 1975.

Tanaka Yūko. *Harigata: Edo onna no sei* [Dildoes: Edo women's sexuality]. Tokyo: Kawade Shobō Shinsha, 1999.

Tani Minezō. *Edo no kopīraitā* [Edo ad copywriters]. Tokyo: Iawasaki Bijutsusha, 1986.

———. *Nihon okugai kōkokushi* [A history of Japanese outdoor advertising]. Tokyo: Iwasaki Bijutsusha, 1989.

Tan'o Yasunori, ed. *Sensō bijutsu no yōtai.* Tokyo: Waseda University, Tan'o Kenkyūshitsu, 1993.

———. "Sensō o meguru fūshi no gyakusetsu." In *Nippon no fūshi.* Saitama: Saitama-ken Kindai Bijutsukan, 1993.

Thornham, Sue, ed. *Feminist Film Theory: A Reader.* New York: New York University Press, 1999.

*Tokushū: Women Artists* [Special issue: Women artists]. *Bijutsu techō* 35, no. 515 (September 1983).

*Tōkyō Kokuritsu Hakubutsukan shozō: Matsukata korekushon ukiyo-e hin ten* [Holdings of the Tokyo National Museum: exhibition of *ukiyo-e* art from the Matsukata Collection]. Tokyo: Tokyo National Museum, 1991.

Tōno Yoshiaki. "Imagineering." *Art Forum,* January 1986, 72–75.

———. "Toyama nau '84: Nihon sekushon" [*Toyama now '84:* Japanese section]. *Toyama Now '84: dai ni kai Toyama kokusai gendai bijutsu-ten* [The Second International Exhibition of Contemporary Art in Toyama]. Toyama: Toyama Kenritsu Kindai Bijutsukan, 1984.

Tonomura, Hitomi. "Black Hair and Red Trousers: Gendering the Flesh in Medieval Japan." *American Historical Review* 99, no. 1 (February 1994): 129–154.
Treat, John Whittier. "Yoshimoto Banana Writes Home: *Shōjo* Culture and the Nostalgic Subject." *Journal of Japanese Studies* 19, no. 2 (1993): 353–387.
*Tsuchida Bakusen ten* [Tsuchida Bakusen: a retrospective]. Tokyo: National Museum of Modern Art, 1997.
Tsurumi Shunsuke. *Ame no Uzume den* [The legend of Ame no Uzume]. Tokyo: Heibonsha, 1991.
Tsuruta Migiwa. "Bunten to bijinga." In *Bijinga no tanjō* [The birth of *bijinga*], ed. Yamatane Bijutsukan. Tokyo: Yamatane Museum, 1997.
Tsushima Kanji. *Furoido-ha to geijutsu*. 1920. Rpt. Tokyo: Yumani Shobō, 1991.
Uchida Yasuhiro. "Yomihon sakka no seikatsu to shiga" [The life and horizons of *yomihon* writers]. In *Nihon no koten* [Japanese classics], ed. Mizuno Minoru, vol. 19: *Kyokutei Bakin*. Tokyo: Shūeisha, 1990.
Ueno Chizuko. "Kokumin-kokka to jendā." *Gendai shisō* 10 (1996).
———. "Lusty Pregnant Women and Erotic Mothers: Representations of Female Sexuality in Erotic Art in Edo." In Jones, ed., *Imaging Reading Eros*.
———. *Onna asobi* [Women playing]. Tokyo: Gakuyō Shobō, 1988.
———. "Sa-i no seijigaku" [The political science of difference]. In *Iwanami kōza gendai shakaigaku II: jendā no shakaigaku* [Iwanami lectures in contemporary sociology 2: the sociology of gender], ed. Ueno et al. Tokyo: Iwanami Shoten, 1995.
*Utamaro. Ukiyo-e taikei,* vol. 5. Tokyo: Shūeisha, 1973.
Vincent, Keith. Review of Stephen D. Miller, ed., *Partings at Dawn: An Anthology of Japanese Gay Literature*. *Journal of the Association of Teachers of Japanese* 31, no. 2 (October, 1997): 109–116.
Vlastos, Stephen, ed. *Mirror of Modernity: Invented Traditions of Modern Japan*. Berkeley: University of California Press, 1998.
Volpp, Sophie. "The Discourse on Male Marriage: Li Yu's 'A Male Mencius's Mother.'" *positions: east asia cultures critique* 1, no. 4 (Spring 1994).
Wakakuwa Midori. *Josei gaka retsuden* [Lives of female painters]. Tokyo: Iwanami Shinsho, 1985.
———. *Kakusareta shisen* [The hidden view]. Iwanami Modern Japanese Art, vol. 2. Tokyo: Iwanami Shoten, 1996.
———. *Sensō ga tsukuru joseizō* [Images of women made by war]. Tokyo: Chikuma Shobō, 1995.
Wakakuwa Midori and Hagiwara Hiroko. *Mō hitotsu no kaiga-ron: feminizumu to geijutsu*. Tokyo: Shōkōdō, 1991.
Wallis, Brian, ed. *Art after Modernism: Rethinking Representation*. New York: New Museum of Contemporary Art, 1995.
Waseda Daigaku Toshokan, ed. *Bakumatsu Meiji no media ten: shinbun, nishikie, hikifuda* [Exhibits of late-Tokugawa and Meiji media: newspapers, color prints, advertising leaflets]. Tokyo: Waseda University Press, 1988.
Weidner, Marsha, ed. *Flowering in the Shadows: Women in the History of Chinese and Japanese Painting*. Honolulu: University of Hawai'i Press, 1990.

Williams, Linda. "Film Bodies: Gender, Genre and Excess." In Thornham, ed., *Feminist Film Theory*.

Winther-Tamaki, Bert. "Embodiment/Disembodiment: Japanese Painting during the Fifteen-Year War." *Monumenta Nipponica* 52 (Summer 1997): 145–180.

Wöhr, Ulrike. *Frauen zwischen Rollenerwartung und Selbstdeutung. Ehe, Mutterschaft und Liebe im Spiegel der japanischen Frauenzeitschrift* Shin Shin fujin *von 1913 bis 1916*. Wiesbaden: Harrassowitz Verlag, 1997.

*Woman in the Dunes*. Screenplay credited to Teshigawara Hiroshi. New York: Phaedra Publishers, 1964.

Woodburn, Alexander Gordon. "Translating Modern Japanese Literary Prose: A Theoretical Approach." M.A. thesis, Asian Studies, University of British Columbia, 2000.

Yamaguchi Kenritsu Bijutsukan, ed. *Meiji Nihonga no shin jōkei* [Meiji *nihonga*'s new scenes]. Yamaguchi: Yamaguchi Kenritsu Bijutsukan, 1996.

Yamaguchi Yumi. "Joyū na otoko: Morimura Yasumasa no joyūryoku" [The actress man: the actress power of Morimura Yasumasa]. *Freak Out* 12 (1996).

Yamamoto Taketoshi and Tsuganesawa Toshihiro. *Nihon no kōkoku: hito, jidai, hyōgen* [Japanese advertising: people, periods, terminology]. Tokyo: Sekai Shisōsha, 1992.

Yamane Kazuma. *Gyaru no kōzō* [Structure of the girl]. Tokyo: Seikaibunkasha, 1990.

———. *Hentai shōjo moji no kenkyū* [The study of deviant girls' script]. Tokyo: Kōdansha, 1986.

"Yanagi Miwa." *Artist Interview*, vol. 3 (1998).

"Yanagi Miwa: Aidentiti o nakushita kōkotsukan" [Yanagi Miwa: ecstatic feelings deprived of identity]. *Bijutsu techō* 51, no. 779 (November 1999).

Yanagi Sōetsu. "Chōsen no tomo ni okuru fumi" [A letter sent to a Korean friend] and "Chōsen no bijutsu" [Korean art]. In *Yanagi Sōetsu zenshū*, vol. 6. Tokyo: Chikuma Shobō, 1981.

Yanobe Kenji. "'Chōkokufuku' o kita 'ichishimin'" ["One citizen" dressed in "sculptural clothes"]. *Bijutsu techō* 43, no. 638 (June 1991).

"Yanobe Kenji." In *Ōkina nikki, chiisana monogatari* [Big diary, little tale] / *Mito Annual '92, Private Diary: 10 Japanese Young Artists*. Mito: Mito Geijutsukan Gendai Bijutsu Gyararī, 1992.

Yi Kyuil. "Yŏksa sok ŭi misurin" [Artists in history]. In *Twijibŏ pon Han'guk misul* [Korean art turned inside-out]. Seoul: Sigongsa, 1993.

Yi T'aeho. "1940 nyŏndae ch'oban ch'inil misul ŭi kun'gukchuŭijŏk kyŏnghyangsŏng" [Militaristic tendencies in the pro-Japanese art of the early 1940s]. In *Kŭndae Han'guk misul nonch'ong* [Modern Korean art theory], ed. Ch'ong Yi Kuyŏl Sŏnsaeng Hoegap Kinyŏm Nonmunjip Wiwŏnhoe. Seoul: Hakkonjae, 1992.

Yoshida Atsuhiko. *Nihonjin no megami shinkō* [The Japanese belief in female gods]. Tokyo: Seidōsha, 1995.

Yoshitake Teruko. *Nyonin: Yoshiya Nobuko* [The woman: Yoshiya Nobuko]. Tokyo: Bungei Shunju, 1982.

Zamora, Lois Parkinson, and Wendy B. Faris, eds. *Magical Realism*. Durham, N.C.: Duke University Press, 1995.

# INDEX

HAWAI'I Production Note for Mostow / Gender and Power in the Japanese Visual Field

Cover and interior design by April Leidig-Higgins.
Text in Monotype Garamond.
Composition by Copperline Book Services, Inc.

Printing and binding by Thomson-Shore, Inc.
Printed on 70 lb. Fortune Matte.